SOME MODERN CULTS, SECTS, MOVEMENTS AND WORLD RELIGIONS

BEING THE SIXTH ANNUAL SPIRITUAL SWORD LECTURESHIP OF THE GETWELL CHURCH OF CHRIST MEMPHIS, TENNESSEE

Garland Elkins and Thomas B. Warren, Editors

NATIONAL CHRISTIAN PRESS, INC.
P.O. Box 1001 Jonesboro, Ark., 72401

SOME MODERN CULTS, SECTS, MOVEMENTS AND WORLD RELIGIONS

ISBN 0-934916-46-2

Printed by Sun Belt Press, Inc., Birmingham, Ala.

THE SPIRITUAL SWORD LECTURESHIP, OCTOBER, 1981

THEME: SOME MODERN CULTS, SECTS, MOVEMENTS, AND WORLD RELIGIONS

PART X SOME "WORLD" RELIGIONS

CHAPTER 1
THE BIBLE IS OUR GUIDE . . . OUR ONLY GUIDE

Ira North

We readily see the necessity of authority in most every sphere of life. The matter of a correct standard of authority in religion is of supreme importance. There are standards accepted which are fallible, unsafe, and unsound. Jeremiah said, "It is not in man that walketh to direct his steps" (Jeremiah 10:23). And the wise man declared, "There is a way which seemeth right unto a man, but the end thereof are the ways of death" (Proverbs 14:12).

The Bible Is Sufficient

The Bible declares itself to be an all-sufficient rule of faith and practice. Peter declared that "his divine power hath given unto us all things that pertain unto life and godliness, through the knowledge of him that hath called us to glory and virtue" (II Peter 1:3). And the apostle Paul said, "All scripture is given by inspiration of God, and is profitable for doctrine, for reproof, for correction, for instruction in righteousness: That the man of God may be perfect, throughly furnished unto all good works" (II Timothy 3:16, 17).

The Word of God will save, guide, and comfort. "Receive with meekness the engrafted word, which is able to save your souls" (James 1:21). David declared, "Thy word is a lamp unto my feet, and a light unto my path" (Psalms 119:105). And Paul speaking to a group of Christians stated, "Wherefore comfort one another with these words" (I Thessalonians 4:18). Since the Bible furnishes us unto "every good work," a human creed is not needed. If it contains less than the Bible, it contains too little, if it adds to the Bible, it contains too much, if it is different than the Bible, it is dangerous, and if it contains exactly the same, it is unnecessary. (See Revelation 22:18, 19.)

Better Safe Than Sorry

The journey of life is so important that it necessitates a guide that is infallible. Man travels this way but once and he is eternity bound with his immortal soul at stake. Suppose you were in charge of a store and it was your responsibility to measure cloth. Suppose further that you had a correct yard stick, one that met the standard of authority for weights and measures set up by our government. Would you keep an additional yard stick which was a little longer or shorter than the correct one? We have an infallible guide from God, the Bible and should we take a chance with a fallible guide that is a little shorter or longer than the standard?

Human Creeds Divide

We could not logically ask others to give up one human creed to accept another one of the same origin. Human creeds breed division, party names, and sects.

The following tribute to the Bible written by an unknown author could never apply to a creed written by man. "This Book contains the mind of God, the state of man, the way of salvation, the doom of sinners and the happiness of believers. Its histories are true, its doctrines are holy, its precepts are binding, and its decisions are immutable. Read it to be wise, believe it to be safe, and practice it to be holy. It contains light to direct you, food to support you, and comfort to cheer you. It is the traveler's map, the pilgrim's staff, the sailor's compass, the soldier's sword, and the Christian's charter. Here paradise is restored, heaven is opened and the gates of hell are disclosed. Christ is its subject, our good its design, and the glory of God its end. It should fill the memory, rule the heart, and guide the feet. Read it slowly, frequently, prayerfully. It is a mine of wealth, a paradise of glory and a river of pleasure. It is given you in life, will be open at the judgment and will be remembered forever. It involves the highest responsibility, rewards the greatest labor and condemns all who trifle with its holy contents."

Let us all go back to the Bible and accept it as our guide — our ONLY guide.

CHAPTER 2
THE SIN OF UNAUTHORIZED RELIGIONS

Perry B. Cotham

There are many religions in the world. In fact, history affords no example of a people without some form of religion. However, Christianity is the only Biblical and God-ordained religion in the world today.

Christ the Founder of Christianity

God speaks to us through his divine Son, Jesus Christ (Heb. 1:1, 2), and we must hear Christ "in all things" (Acts 3:22, 23). At the Transfiguration God the Father declared concerning Christ: "This is my beloved Son, in whom I am well pleased, hear ye him" (Matt. 17:5). Christ affirmed after his resurrection that "all authority" had been given to him (Matt. 28:18).

Christ promised the apostles the power of the Holy Spirit to guide them into all the truth (John 16:13). Following the Lord's ascension, on the day of Pentecost, the Holy Spirit came to the apostles, and they spoke the great truths of Christianity (the faith of the gospel) "as the Spirit gave them utterance" (cf. Luke 24:49; Acts 1:4-8; 2:1-4). Moreover, their inspired teaching was authenticated by divine demonstration. The word "was confirmed...both with signs and wonders, and divers miracles, and gifts of the Holy Ghost..." (Heb. 2:3, 4; cf. Mark 16:20). Some of these miracles of confirmation are recorded in the book of Acts; e.g., healing a lame man (3:1-11), raising the dead (9:36-42; 20:9-12), and being bitten by a viper yet remaining unharmed (28:3-6).

Paul affirmed that the truths of Christianity were "revealed unto his [Christ's] holy apostles and prophets by the Spirit" (Eph. 3:5); that "all scripture is given by inspiration of God . . . that the man of God may be perfect, thoroughly furnished unto all good works" (II Tim. 3:16, 17). With the completion of the New Testament "all things pertaining to life and godliness" had been given (II Pet. 1:3). The Bible is the inerrant, complete, verbally inspired word of God (I Cor. 2:13). There is nothing that can be rightfully added to this complete revelation, and nothing that can be rightfully changed or taken from it (Gal. 1:8, 9; Rev. 22:18, 19). Since these truths have been recorded we can now read and understand what has been divinely given (Eph. 3:3, 4).

Hence, Christianity is the revelation of God through Jesus Christ to man today. Christ is the author of Christianity, the religion contained in the New Testament, and Christians are urged to "earnestly contend for the faith which was once delivered unto the saints" (Jude 3).

There were many systems of religion in the world when Christ established his church (Matt. 16:18; Acts 2), yet he affirmed: "I am the way, the truth, and the life: no man cometh unto the Father, but by me" (John 14:6). This same truth was affirmed by the inspired apostles (Acts 4:12). So Jesus Christ is man's only savior and his teaching is the only Biblical religion in the world.

Departures to Come

The Lord, through Paul, predicted that there would come departures from the faith, "a falling away." "Now the Spirit speaketh expressly, that in the latter times some shall depart from the faith, giving heed to seducing spirits, and doctrines of devils; speaking lies in hypocrisy; having their conscience seared with a hot iron; forbidding to marry, and commanding to abstain from meats..." (I Tim. 4:1-3; cf. II Thess. 2:3). As we look back through the pages of history we can see how and when these departures, following the establishment of the Lord's church, developed.

During the first four centuries there arose great sects, like Montanism, Ebionitism, Gnosticism, and Arianism. Later emerged Mohammedanism (Islam), which today is the second largest religion in the world. Likewise, Catholicism gradually arose and this system continues today as a mixture of Judaism, paganism, and Christianity. Consequently, it is an apostasy from the true faith. From the fifth to the fourteenth century, the period known as the Dark Ages swept over the earth, and the Lord's church was either totally lost or in seclusion. The Reformation Movement began in the early part of the sixteenth century as a reaction against the evils of Catholicism and coercion in religion. Soon after the Protestants had broken away from the ecclesiastical hierarchy (the Church of Rome) they began to divide among themselves, to oppose one another's theologies, to form different standards of authority in religious affairs. Each had his own creed, his discipline, his confession of faith. In their efforts to break away from Rome they found themselves bound by creeds and subscribing to an authority equally human. Today, Protestantism in its various denominational forms is nothing more than Christianity polluted and corrupted by theological speculations. It, too, is of human origin. Moreover, human religions and various cults continue to increase at the present time. However, all religions in the world today — from the Biblically bankrupt and diluted forms of Christianity represented by the many denominations with their human creeds, names, and doctrines, to the most authoritarian cults, such as illustrated by the Jim Jones movement in Guyana, South America, or to the various forms of paganism as practiced in Asia — exist without divine authority.

Serious-minded people ask, "Are all of these religions right, or are they wrong?" The answer, from the teaching of the Bible, is that they are wrong. Christianity has no Biblically-authentic rivals. All other religions, ancient and modern, are frauds.

Sin of Biblically-Unauthorized Religions

With this background study we are now ready to notice in particular the theme of this lecture—namely, **the sin of unauthorized religions.**

First, what is sin? Sin is the transgression of God's law (I John 3:4). Therefore, any system of religion in the world today that attempts to supplement Biblical doctrine or to diminish or reduce Biblical truth, or propagate ideas foreign to Biblical principles, sin in so doing. Any such system of religion that differs from pure Christianity, stands as an organization that is sinful in the sight of God; it exists without divine authority and God's approval.

Time will permit noting only a few of the evils of unauthorized religions. In the first place, the more than 250 various denominations in the realm of "Christianity" ("Christendom" or "Christian Church") cause division among those who claim to follow the Lord. This is definitely contrary to the teaching of the Bible. The word of God teaches that there is just one church (in a general sense) — one body of saved people built by and belonging to Christ, and over which he rules as head (Acts 2:47; I Cor. 12:20; Eph. 1:22,23).

A denomination is a religious body with either more or less or different Biblical positions and characteristics distinguishing it from the religious body revealed in the New Testament. It is utterly impossible for any denomination to exist without believing something, doing something, being something, saying something, or having something that is not in the word of God. What if denominations do teach more or less than is in the Bible? The doctrine they teach that is in the Bible does not make them denominations; but to teach Biblical truth, plus some ideas not found in the Bible, is to propagate religious error.

Christ prayed that his disciples all be one (John 17:20,21). He realized the harm that division would cause. After asking in his prayer on the eve of his crucifixion "that they all may be one," he added, "that the world may believe that thou has sent me." One of the greatest hindrances to the spread of the pure gospel of Christ today in all of the world is the multiplicity of religious denominations, cults, and movements among the professed followers of Christ. One denomination may be as good as another, but this does not prove that any is on an equal plane with Christ's church.

Through Paul the Holy Spirit pleaded for unity among the disciples of Christ and condemned divisions (I Cor. 1:10-13; Gal. 5:19-21; Eph. 4:1-4). In the days of the apostles, Christians were not divided into a number of different denominations, but they were all members of the same church, the spiritual body of Christ. All of the followers of Christ were in the Lord's church (Acts 2:47), but none of them were members of any of our present-day denominations or cults. The church of the Bible is not now nor ever has been a denomination. Men have no divine right to establish other churches or religions and claim that they are the Lord's. Different religious organizations (denominations) are merely human institutions, the decisions of their church councils are purely the opinions of uninspired men, and the state of confusion is wrong in God's sight. People today can be simply Christians without becoming members of any denomination.

In the second place, having many unauthorized religions in the world today is a tremendous waste of money. Think of any modern city in the United States with its numerous houses of worship — church buildings, temples, and cathedrals. There is one on almost every corner downtown, and sometimes two in the same block. What a terrible expense to build and maintain these houses, not to mention the cost of trying to keep a preacher for each particular group. This money could better be used to feed the poor and preach the gospel in foreign lands to those who have never once heard the sweet name of Jesus.

Among most big religious television programs it is obvious that a strong appeal is made for money each week. And they get the money — according to all reports we have read recently in newspapers and magazines. Examples of these, known to almost all of us, are such "televangelists" as Jerry Falwell, receiving about $52 million a year; Oral Roberts, $60 million; and the Armstrongs (before their breakup in 1978), $75 million.[1] Then there are others such as Rex Humbard, Jim Bakker, Pat Robertson, Jimmy Swaggert, and Robert Schuller.[2]

Paul, in writing to the Corinthians, said: "I seek not yours, but you" (II Cor. 12:14). But teachers in all false religions seem to be more interested in getting the **money** than in presenting the pure teaching of Christianity for the salvation of **souls**. (Cf. Acts 16:19; 19:25-41.) Although support for the preacher of the gospel is in harmony with the Scriptures (I Cor. 9:14), the main motive of every true preacher is not to build a personal empire to his glory but to save their souls. The well-chosen words of Matthew Henry on this text regarding the apostle's attitude are appropriate:

> He sought not to enrich himself, but to save their souls: he did not desire to make a property of them to himself, but to gain them over to Christ, whose servant he was.[3]

Remove the financial underpinning and much of the false teaching would be eradicated. Oral Roberts' latest scheme for getting money from his television audience seems to be his claim of having seen a large vision of Jesus — "some 900 feet tall" — and the Lord telling him he is going to get the money for his new building project; that his partners will give it to him. (Sadly, they most likely will.) Hershel Dyer, minister of Tulsa, Oklahoma, in an article in the **Firm Foundation** reports on this, and then comments:

> So, it really comes down to: If you are one of Oral's partners it would be **disobeying Christ** not to send him some money![4]

Every religious delusion the world has ever known in the name of Christianity has been founded upon some so-called "special revelation," or a "vision," or some "direct leading of the Holy Spirit." This is obviously a most effective means of obtaining money for the maintenance of false (unauthorized) religions, even from millions of people who can least afford to give their money away.

In the third place, another sin which is easily observed in unauthorized religions is that they fail to elevate man to a holy and righteous life. Despite claims to the contrary, almost all so-called natural, or pagan, religions, such as Buddhism, Confucianism, and Hinduism, are nothing but systems of human philosophy. Any and all systems of religion which men have devised from their own conceptions are woefully inadequate in that they fail to hold in check the natural appetities and passions of man. In proof of this fact we need but to notice Paul's indictment of paganism and of man's need of the gospel of Christ, God's power to save, from his language recorded in Roman 1:18-32, in which he described the ancient pagan world. The same is true today of these religions. Idolatry has ever been the besetting sin of the pagan world. "Ungodliness and unrighteousness" still is rampant in all pagan religions. Man always becomes like the "god" he worships. Herein lies the weakness of the system. Yet paganism is held by about 65% of the world's population.

When people give God up, and God gives them up, to work all manner of unrighteousness, then such sins as fornication, adultery, wickedness, licentiousness, drunkenness, homosexuality, covetousness, maliciousness, envy, murder, and stealing follow. Idolatry is always a tendency downward, whereas Christianity always elevates man to a higher plane of living (I Cor. 6:9-11). People may go to the pagan temples and bow down to their "gods" and pray (I have seen them do it by the hundreds), but these religions cannot purify the heart from sin and make a different person out of the individual. However, the pure gospel of Christ, when believed and obeyed, purifies the heart and corrects the life.[5]

Even in our own "enlightened America" we see the failure of human religious systems to make a better society. Perhaps there is no country in all the world that has any larger or more expensive church buildings than in the United States. Yet at the present time Americans are confronting the greatest moral decline in the history of this country. We have about one divorce out of every two marriages. Some are referring to this as the "divorce explosion." Drug use is alarming. Crime is on the increase. Policemen, in their line of duty, are being murdered. Our penitentiaries are crowded. Twelve million Americans are alcoholics, and twenty-eight million children live with alcoholic parents. We have our religions, but what America needs — like every other nation — is not more religions of man's device but more genuine Christianity. There is no other hope for this sin-cursed world.

Finally, in the fourth place, unauthorized religons instill in people a false sense of security. Members are told they are saved from sin (when they have not obeyed the gospel, II Thess. 1:7-9; Acts 2:38; Mark 16:16), and that they should "feel good" because all is well with them. These are false teachers giving a false promise. Jesus said, "If the blind lead the blind, both shall fall into the ditch" (Matt. 15:14). Solomon said, "There is a way which seemeth right unto a man, but the end thereof are the ways of death" (Prov. 14:12). The love of God is stressed by these false teachers, but seldom do they proclaim the wrath of God against sin, and for man to genuinely repent (Luke 13:5; Acts 17:30; Rom. 11:22; Heb. 12:29). So people continue to live and die in sin thinking all the time that everything is well with their souls. But sinners shall not go unpunished at the judgment

(Matt. 25:31-46; II Cor. 5:10; Eccl. 12:14). Yet some who have not the "love of the truth" will "believe a lie" and "be damned" (II Thess. 2:10-12). (Cf. Matt. 15:13.)

Many See the Need

Many in the religious world today are beginning to see the utter failure of unauthorized religions and are seeking a solution. The way out of this confusion is simple. One must be willing to go back to the Bible and do Bible things in Bible ways and call Bible things by Bible names. Peter wrote, "If any man speak, let him speak as the oracles of God" (I Pet. 4:11). If one will do this he will find fellowship of believers in Christ who stand only for New Testament Christianity and no unauthorized religions. This has long been the plea of those associated with the Restoration Movement. This movement, begun in this country by Stone, Campbell, and others, has been an effort to destroy all religions of human origin and make a complete return to the pure teaching of Christianity as it existed in the beginning and is set forth in the New Testament.[6] The whole world is invited to come along with us and help restore the Lord's church without all the "extras" of modern-day unauthorized religions.

With this thought in mind our desire is world evangelism. We must not fail the Lord who sends us or the world that needs us. We should not simply be "proclaimers of the faith" behind stained-glass windows in our own expensive church buildings, but go out into all of the world where the masses are and preach and teach the gospel where it is yet to be heard. This is the primary function and the outstanding obligation of the Lord's church (Matt. 28:19; I Tim. 3:15). We must take the gospel to every land. The need has never been greater and the multitudes have never been larger. Untold millions are dying...**untold**. Our mission, therefore, is clear — we are commissioned to help others find the true God by taking the message of Jesus his Son to the lost at home and abroad.

Conclusion

In this lecture we have noted that there is only one true system of religion and that is Christianity as it is revealed in the New Testament; that the Bible is the only inspired book in the world that contains a complete revelation of God's will to man; and that the many religions of the world today which exist without divine authority should not be trusted in matters pertaining to the eternal destiny of one's soul. We have noticed that human religions are sinful because (1) they cause division among the professed followers of Christ and hinder the progress of Christianity; (2) they are a great waste of money; (3) they fail to elevate man to a higher plane of righteous living; and (4) they give to man a false hope of his eternal security.

My purpose in this assignment has necessitated a negative approach. Had I been assigned a topic such as "The Superiority of the Christian Religion," I could have easily discussed how Christianity has done more than any other world religion to enhance the dignity of man, elevate the status of women, underscore the value of children, respect the contractual and legal rights of others, dignify decent labor, eradicate superstition, safeguard property, and propagate the values that eventually maintain democratic national life. Christianity, a religion of hope and liberation, is the only religion founded through the death — the atoning death — of its founder, and can point to an open grave.

Think what sweeping changes would be achieved by a complete restoration of New Testament Christianity throughout all the world! It would destroy Catholicism and Protestantism, and bring about Christian unity, and give to the church a power as in the early days of Christianity. Think what a restoration would do in lands now dominated by pagan religions and cults. The gospel of Christ would sweep over these countries and bring to the people their salvation and cause great rejoicing. An identical reproduction of the church of our Lord would automatically destroy all man-made religions. Then, like a mighty army, the soldiers of the cross would go into lands now under Communist control and win those people over to Jesus who is King of kings and Lord of lords.

May God hasten the day when people all over the world will turn from all forms of human religions and follow the simple truths of New Testament Christianity!

FOOTNOTES

1. **This report was given in the** *Dallas Morning News,* Febturay 19, 1981, page 14A.

2. There are of course many ministers on radio and T.V. who are honestly and legitimately trying to share the "good news" of the kingdom of God with their listeners; but perhaps the worst consequence of the professional T.V. moochers is the fact that many come to think of Christianity as nothing more than a rip-off.

3. Matthew Henry's *Commentary on the Bible,* Vol. VI, page 643

4. Hershel L. Dyer, "Oral Roberts' Alleged Vision of Jesus Christ," *Firm Foundation,* Austin, Texas, Vol. 98, No. 3 (January 20, 1981), page 8

5. Bruce Johnson, missionary in Madras, India, says: "Disease is a great and widespread problem in India. Cattle, goats, and pigs roam the streets eating filth and making filth as they go. The city water is not safe to drink (without purifying). Surely the sins of the Hindu religion and the filth of India are connected. Many Hindu marriages are evil. The greatest evil, now outlawed but still widely practiced, is the dowry system. A family must give large amounts of money and gifts with the bride before she will be accepted by the young man's family. Think of the man who has five or six daughters and no sons! Sometimes a young bride is burned to death because her dowry was too small, or because her parents did not give the promised dowry payments. But then human life is cheap since Hinduism teaches that you will only be reborn again. Suicide is not uncommon. Polygamy is practiced. Dead bodies can be seen at times on the street, bloated and flies swarming over them."(Private letter, February 22, 1981).

Larry Fryer, missionary in Sri Lanka, writes: "Before construction is begun for a new bridge in Sri Lanka it has been the belief of the people, and still is being practiced in secrecy, that a child should be offered as a sacrifice for the safety of the workers and the happy completion of the bridge. I am told that a child is murdered and its body disposed of before the beginning of the work. It is also the practice of some, and I have witnessed it, for people who want purification to have hooks stuck in their back, neck, and legs, and their bodies to be suspended for a period of time by the hooks. I saw this happen to two men who were then taken down the streets for people to see." (Private letter, March 11, 1981).

Many other examples could be given of the evils of pagan religions.

6. "The chief aim of the Restoration Movement in the nineteenth century was to bring about unity in the world of religion on a Biblical basis." (J. M. Powell, "The Restoration Movement and Christian Unity," *Gospel Advocate,* Vol. CXXIII, February 19, 1981, No. 4, page 112).

CHAPTER 3
THE BIBLE WARNS AGAINST FALSE TEACHERS

Foy L. Smith

Under the general theme of this lectureship, SOME MODERN CULTS, MOVEMENTS, AND WORLD RELIGIONS, I have been assigned the topic, THE BIBLE WARNS AGAINST FALSE TEACHERS. We never even approach a realization of the need for strong teaching until we begin making a survey of some of the great world religions and cults. The development of these religious systems, and some could hardly be called that, shows the danger of apostasy. And it all began with an apostasy in the eldership of the Lord's church in the first century. We are called "dooms day prophets" and "proclaimers of only bad news" when we stand up and sound forth warnings against apostasy.

The five largest world religions are Catholicism, Mohammedanism, Hinduism, Shintoism, and Buddhism. Catholicism grew out of an apostasy and all the others with possibly the exception of the philosophies of Buddhism, including the more modern and lesser religions came after Catholicism. There are about six hundred million Catholics in the world today and of that number at least fifty million are here in the United States — one fourth of our entire population. There are approximately three million Muslims in our country, and about seven hundred fifty thousand Black Muslims. World-wide their numbers are staggering. Of course the Moslems (or) Muslims are offshoots of Mohammedanism. There are more than two hundred million Hindus in India, more than all "Protestant Christians." It is hard on our missionaries because it is said that they have "built a wall around their faith so that none would stray from it." The story is always the same in India. They multiply like flies, we feed them, and they boot us out of the country. Millions we sent for food a few years ago were used to develop a hydrogen bomb.

The Japanese Shinto religion dates back to the sixth century A.D. It is an offspring of Buddhism and Chinese culture. Sixty one million practice this false religion which has always included emperor worship. There were at least one hundred thousand Buddhists in our country in 1951. This includes worship of Buddah going back to 556 B.C. It has often been challenged as being a religious faith at all. It teaches deliverance through enlightenment, wisdom, compassion; also teaches reincarnation.

All these and other religions are false and condemned by the Sacred Writings. We must continue to look upon them as false religions and strike out against them with the "sword of the Spirit" (Eph. 6:17). I do not want to preach everybody else's sermon in this lesson, but we do know that in a lectureship like this there is, unavoidably so, a certain amount of overlapping. And this is justified on the ground that each one has his own style and approach which makes his lesson a bit different. These great facts that are being presented need to be pounded into our hearts over and over. With this in mind I wish to mention two other religious groups — one old and powerful, the other not so old, not so large, but they do have enough conviction to fight even in these days for what they believe. The first is:

Judaism

There are five branches of Judaism but I shall mention the most important three; Orthodox Judaism, Reform Judaism, and Conservative Judaism. The first group holds to the old world Jewry, holds to the "Torah," believes in return of Jews to Israel, and looks for a future Messiah. The second group are liberals. These do not believe in a personal Messiah but believe in a return of Jews to Palestine — not on religious ground but as a place for refuge. The third group hold positions between the two already mentioned. The men worship with heads covered and wear prayer shawls. They seek to reconcile old beliefs with current cultures. The fourth and fifth forms of Judaism are the Reconstruction and the Black Jews.

Seventh Day Adventists

I mention these people because I know more about them than I do most of the other religious groups mentioned. I had encounter after encounter with them when just a boy in a small Oklahoma town in which I was born and reared and where I did my first preaching. They will throw Bible in your face all day. In a debate they really labor to establish their positions on Bible ground. They have to be admired at least for this. Many back in those days would sign propositions for debate only if we agreed to stay with the Bible and away from secular and historical works. While they had a reason for this it was refreshing to find someone who wanted to "argue" on the basis of what the Bible teaches. Adventists are traced back to seventh day Baptists of New England and the Old World. A small group began observing the Sabbath near Washington, N.H. in 1844. They think highly of the writings of Ellen White but they don't want this injected into a debate if it can be left out. And truth can whip them without this. They are evangelical basically. They believe in "gifts of prophecy" and are autonomous. They hold rigidly to the ten commandment law and practice adult baptism only. There are about six hundred thousand in the United States.

These religions, though false, do not center around a single person as most cults do. And they existed long before modern cults came along. Since the Bible warns us against false teachers, and since these religions are propagated by teaching, it is necessary that we pay some attention to their cardinal doctrines.

It is a false doctrine of Catholicism that says the Catholic Church is the only true church, and that the Catholic Church gave the world the Bible. It is not the oldest church. The Lord's church is. And the Catholics did everything they could do to destroy the Bible. Martin Luther, who became "the father of the reformation," found it hidden away in a stall of a Roman monestary. He almost gave his life because he maintained it should be an open Book for every person to study. The average Catholic today knows nothing about the Bible. The late brother L. R. Wilson had a discussion once with a couple of priests. They tried to quote some of the simplest scriptures and couldn't. Yet Catholicism says that these guys are the only ones who can interpret the Bible for the masses. Peter denies this by saying that no scripture is to be given a "private interpretation" (II Pet. 1:20). **We must expose this false teaching.**

The "Papacy" fallacy must be exposed. Peter was not the first pope, nor was he a pope at all. I do a fast burn when I hear news commentators refer to the present pope as "the two hundred sixty-fourth pope since Saint Peter who was the first pope and head of the church." They all do it from Cronkite right down to the lowliest newscaster on the most out of the way station. I know they all read what comes off the teletype machine but I still resent it. Peter means "rock" in Greek. "Thou art Peter and upon this rock I will build my church" (Matt. 16:18). Catholics say the rock was Peter. They know better but they know that gullibles will never bother to challenge them. "Petros" and "Petra" in Greek are two words meaning rock, but they are of different gender. Peter (rock) was a small pebble, but the rock on which the church was built was a "large immovable rock." The rock was the truth Peter confessed, not Peter himself (I Cor. 10:4). This is false teaching and the Bible warns against it (II Thess. 2:3, 4). The Catholics have perverted the doctrine of baptism, prayer, the Lord's Supper, music by introducing the instrument, sanctification, etc. **These false teachers — great enemies of the cross, must be opposed!**

The Moslems accept Jesus as a prophet but not as the Son of God, and they teach that their holy book the "Koran" was dictated by the angel Gabriel. They believe their lives and deeds are all formally ordained. They have some good traits, however, such as, they drink no intoxicating beverages, gambling and adultery are shunned, and they remove their shoes when they go into their houses of worship. But they will always have their outbreaks of violence, with particular attention called to Malcolm X and others. They are popular today especially among figures in the sports world. Denying the divinity of Jesus puts them in the category of **false teachers** and the Bible warns against all such.

The Hindus have tried to create a trinity and the result has been divisions and subdivisions with over fifty-seven sects, each with its own gods and ceremonies. Vishnu, "sun god" is one of the most popular. They believe he can incarnate himself into human form and come down and lead the people to reformation when they stray. The modern cult "Krishna" has risen from this. Their god "Shiva" tells them to find happiness through wine, mystical gesticulation, sexual looseness, etc. The practice of "contemplation," "Yoga," and "mysticism" have come from all of this. It is wrong for man to create his own god and this is what Hinduism has done. "Thou shalt have no other gods before me" means very little to them (Ex. 20:3). And a religion that has as one of its main doctrines satisfaction in sexual looseness is going to pay no attention to the commandment that says, **"Thou shalt not commit adultery"** (Ex. 20:17).

We applaud the Japanese in many ways and must condemn them in others. Their religion is idolatrous since they have many deities — birds, beasts, trees, seas, mountains, persons in authority, thunder, even foxes and wolves. Each home has its own shrine. Maybe we haven't warned against this kind of error enough since we fear some of our own homes have their shrines . . . even special prayer-mats, and sometimes a stump out in the forest somewhere. I heard one preacher say he could get something at his "special" prayer spots he couldn't get anywhere else. Shades of Shintoism! Buddhism in many ways is similar to Shintoism and just as false. **The Bible warns against false gods.** These religions know not the true God, yet are gaining in popularity in our own country.

Before getting to modern cultism let me say a few things about Judaism. I speak of it in the broad sense. It denies our Messiah, calling him a "fraud, pretender, and fake." Jesus says "I am the Way . . . no man cometh to the Father but by me" (John 14:6). A Baptist preacher in Texas got into big trouble some time ago by saying that God will not hear a Jew's prayer. From the text just quoted and from I Tim. 2:5 what do you say? If you doubt the pressure-power of Judaism just stick your neck out a bit and you will learn that it is real. They have a special organization — B'nai-B'rith — to handle their cause when they feel they have been slandered. I know for I personally came face to face with a threat that unless I retracted a statement I had made in a bulletin I would be handled by "B'nai B'rith." I had said the Jews are atheists regarding our Lord, and boy — was the fat in the fire!

We must go on exposing the false teachers of Judaism. When they slander our Christ what else can we do and be true to him? A Jewish author said in a book a few years ago: "Anyone who will call him 'Lord' is guilty of the rankest sort of blasphemy!" Well, dear listener, I will call him Lord! And I will call him Emmanuel! And I will call him Christ! (Rev. 17:14; Acts 2:36). Now go ahead and report me! It is a shame that a people so talented as the Jews stand so lost by their rejection of Christ. Surely they will hear him say one day, "I that speak unto thee am he" (John 4:26). But, alas, it will be too late then and their wailing wall will avail them nothing. Such false teachings must be exposed. Their minds are still "blinded" by the reading of the old Testament (II Cor. 3:14). But, how, oh how, could they have read it and then mistake our Lord when He came?

When I debated a Seventh Day Adventist preacher in my late teens I felt that truth won a victory. However, if I had known brother Foy E. Wallace's argument on Luke twenty-four then, the victory would have been overwhelming. No Sabbatarian — including Garner Ted Armstrong — can stand in view of this inspired argument. Put verses one, thirteen, and twenty-one together. We will learn that they (the women bearing spices) came to the grave on the **"first day of the week."** Then we learn that "two of them went **that same day** to a village called Emmaus." And then, "today is the **third day** since these things happened." What do we have? Here it is: the first day — that same day — and the third day — were the **same day.** The **first day** and the **third day** were the same. Now note verses forty-six that says that Christ **"did rise from the dead the third day."** That's it! The first day and the third day were the same. Christ arose on the third day; therefore, he arose from the dead on the FIRST DAY OF THE WEEK! The Bible warns against false teachers, and Adventists are wrong on their Sabbath-Day contention today. **Sabbath once? Yes! Now? No!**

False Teachings Promote Cultism Today

A cult has been defined as "a group of people polarized around someone's interpretation of the Bible." A more recent definition says: "If you can move it with you it's a cult." Cultism thrives principally on two things: ignorance and uncertainty. Extremists and fanatics swarm around cult leaders. We naturally think of the "People's Temple" — Jim Jones — and the horrors that unfolded in the jungles of Guyana in November of 1978. Nine hundred and thirteen committed suicide with this crazed leader. Jones moved his cult from place to place until he settled in Guyana. He influenced the powerful in many circles, including some in the political world. Rep. Leo Ryan, D-Calif. was murdered as he approached the aircraft that was to take him and others out of Guyana. His daughter was interviewed on TV recently. She — get this — is now a member of a fanatical cult similar to "Rev" Jones' cult. She was asked if she would kill if the leader told her to do so. She replied: "I would give it serious consideration." Then asked if she would take her own life if commanded to, she replied that she probably would! When the Bible warns against false teachers it has in mind all such characters. **They must be exposed for what they are.**

Armstrong's World Church is said to be the fastest growing and most secure American cult, established in 1934 by Herbert W. Armstrong. His more famous son, at odds with his famous father, is called a "master of communications." They have borrowed their doctrines of "soul-sleeping," the Sabbath observance, the millenium, etc., from the Adventists, Russell, and Jehovah's Witnesses. They teach that the Trinity is not three divine persons, but rather all who accept Armstrong's teachings. When The "Old Man" kicked his son out, Garner Ted just packed up and moved to Tyler, and Big Sandy, Texas. He moved his cult to another location!

The Bible condemns the teachings of Christian Science — which is neither Christian nor Science. The main claim of this cult is the claim to heal sickness — that really, there is no such thing as sickness — just mind, no matter. Their "holy book" is by their founder — Mary Baker Glover Patterson Eddy, and is entitled: **"Science And Health With Key To The Scriptures."** This doctrine prohibits the atonement of Christ and denies retribution, both of which are cardinal Bible doctrines. Eddy claimed to have been healed by Dr. Phineas Quimby who used hypnosis and called his method "Christian Science." After his death Eddy denied him, took the title "Christian Science" for her own movement and began "garnering in the lonely dollars." In the NY Sun in 1895 (Dec. 19th) she challenged the world to disprove that she had cured "consumption in last stages, malignant tubercular diptheria, and cancer so bad the flesh was eaten back to expose the jugular vein." A Dr. Charles Reed of Cincinnati, later President of AMA accepted the challenge through the Sun, and issued his own challenge to her saying if she could cure any one of them, "I shall proclaim her omnipotence from the housetops..." Needless to say his was never accepted. **This powerful cult is a powerful hoax and must be exposed.**

Jehovah's Witnesses come under the Divine warning against false teachers. They reject the trinity, deity of Christ, his bodily resurrection and retribution for sin. Their publication WATCHTOWER goes into eighteen million homes, and their membership numbers about two million. Their zeal is commendable, their missionaries, like Mormon elders, look like they represent something and someone when they go out to make contacts. It would be good if some preachers gave more careful attention to the way they dress. We preach by what we do, as well as what we say. This false movement has come by way of "Pastor" Russell and "Judge" Rutherford. They cannot be excused on the ground that they are zealous. This makes them more dangerous. The Bible strikes out against false teachers and these men and their movements are false.

There are even more modern-day cults than these. REX HUMBARD'S CULT is built around one man. Guess who? Rex himself. He can't preach but he can promote! They all have this in common — they are all promoters. They know how to rake in "mucho dinero." Rex has built professionalism around his program like others have, having celebrities appear to give their "testimonies." He knows how to cry when he gets his neck in a financial noose — which is much of the time. But his movement is powerful. Make no mistake about that. Should he leave Akron he would move his cult right along with him.

Jim Bakker has his cult headquartered in Charlotte, N.C. He went into a very expensive building some time ago and has daily TV programs under the caption: "The P T L Club" — (praise the Lord). He also knows how to cry. I saw him cry one morning recently because he had bills he could not pay. He bawled aloud saying, "Lord, I cannot live without souls." Thirty minutes later he was laughing and boasting about his fabulous house and Rolls Royce! His counterpart on the West Coast is at Fontana, Calif., a few miles from Riverside, and I saw the host and his wife raise six hundred thousand dollars some time ago in a three hour beg-a-thon. They own channels on satellites and bounce their perversions all over the world. We still must warn people when we can against these false teachers.

Earnest Angley also of Akron, Ohio, is perhaps the airwaves most popular "healer." He is a master at hypnotizing an audience and even has big stars watching and listening every Sunday. He "heals" all who throng to him and announces how to be saved by looking straight out at the TV audience, saying. "Repeat after me, 'Come in Jesus! Come in Jesus! Come in Jesus'!" Then he assures, "If you meant it, it is done." Only trouble is, we do not find that kind of plan in God's word. **God's word warns against such**

teachers. People just don't seem to ever read Rev. 16:14 that speaks of the "spirits of devils working miracles." Earnest can also turn on the tears when he needs "do-re-mi" — especially the "dough."

Possibly today's biggest cultist is Oral Roberts of Tulsa, Okla. Oral's newest project is "City of Hope." According to reports, he needed money so badly he dreamed up a new sceme last year — had a vision and saw a ninety foot Christ. This figure was holding up the six hundred foot building — tallest of the three in the complex — and saying, "Oral, your prayer partners will not let you down." Now if you want to see a real cry-baby when he needs money you ought to see Oral. The same Oral who owns a million dollar house in Palm Springs, California, plus one worth perhaps half that much in Tulsa. The same one who wears five hundred dollar suits, and drives Mercedes Benz and Cadillac automobiles. But, man, can he ever cry! His whole empire is built around him solely — should he move it would just go with him. He heads a cult.

But now this brings me to something even move serious than anything I have talked about so far. It is . . .

Cultism In The Church Of The Lord

It is embarrassing to have to expose false teachings and movements within the Lord's body, but since such are rampant we must cry out against them. We have always had some false teachers in the church, but we have some today who just a few years ago were considered solid, sound Bible preachers and teachers. Their influence in many circles is still great and for this reason they are all the more dangerous. We live in a world of experts, and it is the so-called "experts" who are giving us so much trouble today. We can't have gospel meetings anymore — they must be called "seminars." We can't carry on a good program of Bible teaching and personal work — these must take on the high-sounding term, OUTREACH. And we have ministers, ministers, ministers running out our ears! Everything is a ministry. Everything has to be different. Preachers who "try out" now a days are not judged by their love of the truth and ability to preach it, but how flashy do they dress, how much hair do they have and does it meet the eyebrows in front; do they have any ears, and most importantly do they know how to "strike oil" in eighteen to twenty minutes? And with most of these "birds" that's about fifteen minutes too long! And as for striking oil they wouldn't strike it if they drilled all day! About all they know to preach (?) is what the Baptists did twenty years ago. But the Baptists aren't doing most of those things now because they didn't work twenty years ago. Many are trying to build up the church by means of old denominational schemes that the denominations had sense enough to discard about as many years ago. "You gotta' be motivated!" I've heard this until I could get on the housetop and scream . . . "motivated to do what? To say what?" I tell you now when we preach the gospel like Paul did we will create the motivation! "Motivate" and "share" and "experience" and "witness" — horrors upon horrors and shades of denominationalism! Are these supposed to be gospel preachers and teachers who are slinging all this garbage around? "Man, ole' Smith's really mad!" You better believe it, friend. I'm good and mad at what a bunch of streamlined, sissified, pretty-boy Willies are trying to do to the church — and saddest of all, succeeding to a great degree! **Yep! I'm good and mad!**

It is a sad day that has come upon us, a day in which talent, dedication, and love for truth mean so little. **The Bible warns against false teachers.** And this means "in the church" as well as out of it.

How can a "church of Christ" preacher establish a cult? He does it by gaining complete control. Control over the elders, deacons, and the membership. I am not opposed to large congregations if they are kept scripturally sound. I am not a "little building only" preacher. I am not opposed to buildings large enough and fine enough to do what must be done. I am opposed to many of the competitive cathedral-like buildings we are building across the brotherhood today. Big buildings are often used to build big names! Oral Roberts can't be fired. He will fire anyone who opposes him. Rex Humbard can't be fired. He will run his entire "board" off and elect a new one if the board gets in his way. I have known of instances where fine elders had to get out because they opposed the scheming, get-ahead-any-way-you-can-preacher. Some of the big schemes we have going in the brotherhood today are kept alive only because the preacher is the big boss. What he says goes. Every one is dominated by him and those who oppose his antics can get out. This is an identifying mark of a cult. Should the preacher finally have to leave he will just take most of the congregation with him across town and continue right on. He just moves his cult right along with him.

The cult leader is on an ego trip. Jim Jones of the Guyana episode said, "One day the whole world will be talking about Jim Jones." This is exactly what Hinckley, would-be assassin of President Reagan, said in his letters to Jodie Foster. The cultist sets up a dictatorship keeping his followers in darkness, always emphasizing a strong belief in God. This is the clincher and to his followers he becomes a god. Jim Jones had his own buses and his associate, Hugh Fortson, Jr., said they would stop along the way, recruit, and take the recruits along with them.

A certain cultist in our own ranks has been operating not too many hundreds of miles from here for some time now. He arrived in the small city with his two privately owned buses to become youth minister. He bought a big old two story house for his cult. His recruiting began at once with the most receptive and gullible of all — the youths, not only of that congregation but over the entire city and surrounding areas. He advanced the Crossroads philosophy — "total commitment" — everything one does is either worship or it is sinful. It was learned, sadly so, that this cultist could lie with a straight face if it served his purpose. This is a matter of recording and I can furnish the tapes. In fact, I have them with me! He hit town wanting one of the churches to give him forty acres that had been given to them — for the "boot camp" as he called it that he wanted to set up for young people from far and near. If you don't think this smacks close to being a Jim Jones Guyana type cult you better do some thinking again, for that's exactly what this fellow and others like him set up — communes. This cultist has probably already destroyed some of the finest young people in that city and will, if not stopped, destroy more. He, like most false teachers who succeed with their cults, has ability and persuasiveness. This makes his endeavors far more destructive. We come now to our last division, which should be a proper conclusion to everything that has been said. Let it be the same as the main heading of this lesson. I do not know of a better way to sum it all up:

The Bible Warns Against False Teachers

Even in olden days the Lord God said, "Thy teachers have transgressed against me" (Isa. 43:27). This was the spirit of Paul's admonition to "Preach the word" in II Tim. 4:3. He said the time would come when men would not endure "sound doctrine; but after their own lusts shall heap to themselves teachers, having itching ears" (V. 3). Well, time is with us now. We have many, many itching ears and we have the preachers and teachers who are in the scratching business ready to accommodate them. Peter also spoke of times including ours: "And there shall be false teachers among you" (II Pet. 2:1). John speaks the end of all who would teach contrary to the doctrine of our Lord: "A false witness shall perish" (Rev. 21:28). Jehovah God hates false ways; always has and will as long as time lasts. **Listen to Him:** "I hate every false way" (Psm. 119:104); listen again: "A false balance is not good" (Prov. 11:1): **listen again:** "For truly my words shall not be false" (Job 36:4). Evidently cultists and false brethren think some are false; **listen again:** "They prophecy a false vision" (Jer. 14:14). What a description of today's "prophets" and shysters; **listen again:** "Diviners have told false dreams" (Zech. 10:2). The TV channels are flooded with such dreams. **Listen again:** "...in perils among false brethren" (II Cor. 11:26). Today's cultists would not be unfamiliar to Paul. **Listen again:** "The people were astonished at his doctrine" (Matt. 7:28). People are astonished today when they stop long enough to listen to it. They find out that "anything" does not go. **Listen again:** "What new doctrine is this" (Mark 1:27)? They didn't want Jesus' new doctrine then; many today want nothing unless it is new. They don't want the old doctrine — almost two thousand years old, in fact. Our Lord's "new doctrine" then was greatly different from "new doctrine" today! **Listen again:** "They continued in the apostles' doctrine" (Acts 2:42). We do not go wrong on this kind of doctrine. **Listen again:** "The deputy believed, being astonished at the doctrine of the Lord" (Acts 13:12). Our Lord's simple, beautiful, powerful words are still "astonishing!" **Listen again:** "Mark them which cause divisions and offenses contrary to the doctrine which ye have learned; and avoid them" (Rom. 16:17). We are in dire need of some brotherhood marking today! If you think this is being done try to get some of the prominent editors among us to expose some of our liberals and modernists! **Listen again:** "All scripture, is given by inspiration of God, and is profitable for doctrine" (II Tim. 3:16). Listen again: "...that they may adorn the doctrine of God our Savior" (Titus 2:10). **And finally:** "Whosoever transgresseth and abideth not in the doctrine of Christ hath not God" (II Jno. 9). These scriptures and hundreds more in both Testaments condemn false doctrine. They are divine warnings and we must heed them or suffer eternal consequences. In view of these declarations — negative and positive commands teaching the same truth — that we must stand for truth — that we must abhor and fight evil; declarations that show the greatness of God and His word, all I can think to say is . . .

We verily are "kept by the power of God!" (I Pet. 1:5).

CHAPTER 4
WHAT IS A CULT?

Curtis A. Cates

Introduction

An invasion is taking place in America, establishing beachheads throughout our beloved country. The invaders are characterized by heretical ideas, by exotic attitudes and practices, by deception, and by the language of Ashdod.[1] And, the church of Christ has not been exempt from the insidious influence of these invaders.

The age of Aquarius has certainly dawned upon us, as was predicted by the astrologers and was expressed in a popular song thus: "This is the dawning of the age of Aquarius." Even some of our Christian college groups were giving encouragement to rank paganism by singing this song in their programs. When has interest in cultism, mysticism, astrology, and Eastern religion been more popular in America?[2] Thousands and thousands of young people are being duped to leave home and parents to join in groups which falsely promise to bring direction, happiness, and security.[3] Moreover, the freak religions are in such a constant flux until even "fiction cannot keep up with reality."[4]

The 1960's were characterized by rioting and drugs, whereas the 1970's and early 1980's are characterized by young people moving in multitudes to religious cults;[5] there is "a bullish market in this country for holistic religious cults."[6] In this age of messiahs, "each campus has its share of gurus, and young people are flocking to join religious movements that are often cults."[7] These false prophets are influencing the gullible to leave business, husband or wife, children, everything to quest for what becomes "the impossible dream."[8] Truly, not every religion leads to the same God, as sectarianism and denominationalism attempt to establish; there is but one way (John 14:6).[9] It is critical that elders, evangelists, and every Christian be watchmen on the wall, alert to certain deceptive and malicious elements even among ourselves who mimic cultic elements "to draw away disciples after them" (Acts 20:29, 30).[10]

Danger of Cultism

> Conventional American wisdom has never come to terms with the spiritual upheavals and cult phenomena that started growing out of the disarray of American society a decade ago. As a secular society, we've ignored the power of messianic personalities and their persuasive techniques; and we've forgotten the terrible charm of alsolutism — or paranoia — in an age of uncertainty.[11]

"The spiritual vacuum of the twentieth century is the inevitable womb of a durable cultism."[12] Normally, few would ever forsake their religious background or lifestyle for a self-proclaimed messiah or prophet and a weird cultic group. But, many young people are somehow attracted and estranged "by every new promise of peace of mind, of emotional closeness to other human beings, of a future filled with hope and fulfillment."[13] The dangers of cultism have included "the repudiation of individualism," or free will,[14] the destruction of the "ability to feel,"[15] "the desire to save one's self apart from Biblical revelation,"[16] "the devastation of many people who have been caught in the well-spun web of various of these cults,"[17] and the inflicting of "injuries upon every element of society."[18]

Growth of Cultism

The cults have had alarming success in attracting young followers.[19] Sparks stated, "Make no mistake: these cults are growing. Daily they are picking off numbers of people."[20] Cults have very little attraction to people during times of heroic struggle and hardship, as during World War II, but during times of ease as now, when no ordeal is on the horizon which will test individual courage and ideals and when one has neither purpose or direction, the cults flourish and hold much attraction.

> Give a man a fish and you feed him for a day. Teach a man to fish and you feed him for a lifetime. Give a man a life's supply of fish and you destroy him. The hunger that drives men and women toward novel, difficult, self-abnegating paths is seldom born of economic need.[21]

Streiker continued by observing that cults capitalize upon these circumstances by having rigid and difficult ways, harsh standards of discipline, and membership which must be merited by wholehearted devotion.[22]

The threat of cultism is extremely serious; "All new religions vigorously seek new members," especially among "college students and young adults whose combination of idealism and disillusionment make them willing and eager converts."[23] The Lord's people must combat these heresies, these counterfeit religions. Like those of the circumcision in Peter's day, these are "unruly men, vain talkers and deceivers . . . whose mouths must be stopped; men who overthrow whole houses, teaching things they ought not, for filthy lucre's sake" (Titus 1:10, 11).

In investigating the subject under consideration, attention will be given to defining cultism, to examining general characteristics of cultic groups, to observing Biblical precepts appropriate to the study, and to recommending urgent action to be taken by God's people.

Definition Of Cultism

The cultic heresy has been variously defined by the authorities, each definition pointing to departures from holy writ. Walter Martin stated, "A cult might...be defined as a group of people gathered about a specific person or person's interpretation of the Bible," such as the Jehovah's Witnesses, Christian Scientists, and Mormons. He continued,

> From a theological viewpoint, the cults contain not a few major deviations from historic Christianity. Yet, paradoxically, they continue to insist that they are entitled to be classified as Christians.[24]

> "A cult, then, is any religious movement which claims the backing of Christ or the Bible, but distorts the central message by 1) an additional revelation, and 2) by displacing a fundamental tenet of faith with a secondary matter."[25]

Streiker defined the cult thus:

> A cult is a movement of social protest and personal affirmation. It offers a total way of life to those who are alienated from their families and the attitudes by which their families prepare them for successful adulthood. Cults attract the dispossessed, the bored, the lonely. Neither poverty nor youth is a necessary precondition for feeling the lure of a cult.[26]

Though this definition may be sufficient for some to recognize cultic practices and groups when they encounter them, the author feels it appropriate to suggest some additional criteria in determining the legitimacy and scripturalness, or lack of it, when faced with new methods and doctrines, both within and without the church of Christ.

Characteristics Of Cultism

In investigating cultic practices and teachings, one would do well to ask certain questions by which he might "prove the spirits, whether they are of God; because many false prophets are gone out into the world" (I Jno. 4:1).

The Bible

First, what is their attitude toward the Bible? Do they add to or take from its precepts? Virtually all of the cults have supplanted the Scriptures with their own oracles and letters, whether it be the "letters" of Moses David Berg of the Children of God, the letters being the "New Wine,"[27] or the **Divine Principle** of Sun Myung Moon,[28] or whether they simply redefine and change the semantics of Biblical teaching as does the liberal and neo-orthodox theologian, using the terminology in a totally non-Biblical sense in order to deceive the unsuspecting.[29] "Trick terminology is a powerful propaganda weapon."[30] And, the Bible is quoted extensively.[31]

> The average non-Christian cult owes its very existance to the fact that it has utilized the terminology of Christianity, has borrowed liberally from the Bible, almost always out of context,

and sprinkled its format with evangelical cliches and terms wherever possible or advantageous.[32]

Jesus Christ

Second, do they exalt Jesus Christ, or do they exalt some counterfeit "messiah"? Some cults completely discount Christ as the Messiah, affirming that Christ failed in His mission, thus the need for a new "lord," "father," "messiah."[33] Now some man is the teacher of teachers.[34] Jim Jones not only claimed to be the spirit of Christ, Buddha, and Lenin, but he also claimed to be God.[35] In a cultic religion, the allegiance has to be "monopolized by a central authority,"[36] upon whom they are highly dependent and whom they may never have seen.[37] The doctrine is based upon his or her "revelations" or decrees, and the authority of Scripture is little regarded.[38] This authoritarian pronouncement tends to become supernatural.[39] It seems that each age has "to have a living incarnation of God."[40] In this day of idolatrous worship of men,[41] the "power of messianic personalities and their persuasive techniques" **must not** be ignored![42]

Indoctrination

Third, is mind control utilized in their "conversion" procedures? Cults have been universally accused of taking away a person's free will,[43] of brainwashing.[44] They have been accused of using "fear, guilt, hate, self-doubt, and rituals to maintain control of the mind."[45] Ted Patrick, noted authority on deprogramming, stated that the brainwashing begins "with the moment the recruiter 'hooks' his listener," or " 'on-the-spot hypnosis.' " "Once the potential member is hooked, the cult keeps up a steady barrage of indoctrination until conversion is complete."[46] One person is suing the Unification church for ten million dollars, according to the lawsuit, because she

> "lost control of her life, underwent an emotional breakdown, gave up all her family and friends and lived in fear and guilt for approximately five years while constantly begging (fund-raising) for Moon."[47]

Some have been charged with reducing the gullible to "'working slaves.'"[48] Sparks warned,

> These widely divergent religious movements have one awesome and terrifying thing in common. They are mindbenders. They're not just after converts in the conventional sense. They want your mind, and they want absolute control over it. All too often they succeed. The goal of their mind control is behavior modification; many call it just plain brainwashing.[49]

Dr. Richard Martino, director of the Institute of Behavioral Science, Coconut Grove, Florida, charged, " 'They are turning well-adjusted children and young adults into zombies, robots and automatons.' "[50] When young people have been exposed to the effects of the "witnessing machines" of the cults, they show signs of "the glassy stare and the programmed grin."[51] Patrick observed, " 'Thinking to a cult member is just like being stabbed in the heart with a dagger.' " He continued, " 'It's very painful, because they've been told that the mind is Satan and thinking is the machinery of the devil.' "[52] " 'They never give you an opportunity to withdraw and reflect upon what is happening.' "[53]

Rigorous Schedule

Fourth, do they attempt to structure and schedule virtually every moment of a person's life and make him feel guilty when he varies from the schedule? Krause stated that the Guyana cultic thinking "came ready-made: what is right, what is wrong, who shall be saved and who not, how to eat, how to dress, how to live."[54] The daily work is demeaning;[55] it is "very regimented."[56]

> The cults impose harsh standards of discipline. It is not enough for you to choose them; they must also accept you. And you must merit your membership by wholehearted devotion. If you fail, you will be disciplined or expelled. If you remain, you will know that you belong to the chosen, the elite, those set apart from ordinary mortals.[57]

The "rigidly held schedule" assures the cult of maintaining "perfect control, not approximate control." Often this entails being tailed by a "brother" or "sister" sometimes called a "shadow." The schedule is very demanding, the food is often high in starch and low in protein, and little sleep is allowed. The leaders are severe taskmasters.[58]

Isolation

Fifth, does the group attempt to isolate members from the outside world and to alienate them from their families? Stoner and Parke wrote, "To be a member of a cult a person must remove himself from society, cut himself off from job, education, friends, and family."[59]

> "This [the Guyana Massacre] wouldn't have happened if they hadn't been so isolated," says Dr. J. Thomas Ungerleider of the UCLA Neuropsychiatric Institute. "With no feedback from the outside world you can do incredible things with peer pressure. Paranoia becomes a useful tool. It's a binding force. With it, you'll engage in peer-pressure activities even more."[60]

Cult recruits have difficulty returning home, and the outside world fades from view, for "group members who break up all relationships on the outside will be dependent on staying with that group."[61] Many have left possessions, parents, and children behind to follow cult leaders into the "parapsychological wilderness."[62] When parents have attempted to visit their children, some have been beaten up by cult members.[63] J. Isamu Yamamoto charged,

> You are taught that everyone not in the movement is under the influence of Satan and that you should mistrust them. They insist that the devil works strongest through those closest to you to destroy your faith. This naturally offsets the concern of parents and friends, most of whom want you to leave. You are told that their motivation is love, but because love in the world is fallen, they cannot understand that their motivation is evil. If someone talks to you from outside the Family [the cult] no doubt they are trying to take your mind away.[64]

Deception

Sixth, is deception used in the recruiting process? Cults capitalize upon conflict, loneliness, and temporary problems in people's lives when they recruit. And, they use deception.

> It does seem apparent that some religious cults use recruiting practices that in the world of business would be labeled "deceptive marketing practices." An honest contract between religion and convert cannot be made if information about the group, its identity and the degree of commitment necessary for members to belong, is withheld.[65]

Some even term the deceit as "heavenly deception."[66] On many occasions of recruiting — even to the extent of exploitation — the name of the cultic group is not identified. They appeal to that "unique combination of optimism, idealism and narcissism that is present in every personality."[67]

Non-Members

Seventh, what is their attitude toward non-cultists? Those who are not members of the cult are ridiculed. They are termed "the ignorant" and "subhuman"; the non-member "does not deserve to be called a man."[68] Anyone who opposes their teachings is motivated by the "satanic force of blind prejudice and ignorance."[69] Members are superior to others.[70]

Furthermore, "they are conditioned to the 'us against them' outlook that characterizes so much religious and political fanaticism."[71] They are led to believe that outsiders are hostile[72] and should be mistrusted. They develop a persecution complex.[73]

The Bible View Of Cultism

Is cultism "the faith which was once for all delivered unto the saints" (Jude 3)? Or, might it not be that they are "false teachers, who shall privily bring in destructive heresies, denying even the Master that bought them, bringing upon themselves swift destruction" (II Pet. 2:1)?

One, inasmuch as the inspired word of God is perfect, furnishing completely unto every good work (II Tim. 3:16, 17), inasmuch as the gospel is not to be perverted, thereby becoming a spurious gospel (Gal. 1:6-9), and inasmuch as one is to "speak as the oracles of God" (I Pet. 4:11), those who engage in cultic practices teach doctrines of men and thus worship God in vain (Matt. 15:9).

Two, inasmuch as Christ is "the way, the truth, and the life" (Jno. 14:6), inasmuch as Christ "is the propitiation for our sins" (I Jno. 2:2), and inasmuch as only "one is your master, even the Christ" (Matt. 23:10), the cultic "messiahs" are "false Christs and false prophets" who lead disciples astray today just as they did prior to the destruction of Jerusalem (Mark 13:22).

Three, inasmuch as even Christ did not coerce people to follow Him (Lk. 18:18-23) and inasmuch as Christ stands at the door and knocks (Rev. 3:20), not violating man's freedom of will, cultic leaders who use programming, brainwashing, and mindbending techniques fashion "themselves into apostles of Christ," just like their father Satan "fashioneth himself into an angel of light" (II Cor. 11:13-15).

Four, inasmuch as children have responsibilities toward their parents (Mark 7:10-13) and inasmuch as husbands and wives have responsibilities toward their homes (I Tim. 5:8), the cultic practice of "total commitment" involving so much time in "recruiting" that family and job are neglected is man-made tradition (Col. 2:8).

Five, inasmuch as Christians are not to be taken from the world though they are not of the world (Jno. 17:14, 15) and inasmuch as "None of us liveth unto himself, and none dieth unto himself" (Rom. 14:7), the isolation of cultic groups is a perversion designed to open the way to deceit and to ultimate control.

Six, inasmuch as "Christianity is cautious as it advises potential members to convert from sincere inner-conviction and desire and not because of conflict and temporary life problems,"[74] inasmuch as New Testament Christianity did not "deceive its recruits or withhold information from them in the conversion process,"[75] and inasmuch as the early church did not exploit or prey upon the vulnerabilities of youth,[76] the cultic practices of deception are foreign to Biblical principles of evangelism in which God gives the increase (I Cor. 3:6).

Urgent Recommendations For Action

Certain challenges and recommendations for action are very urgent in meeting the crisis of the cults.

First, become very familiar with the principles of restoring simple New Testament Christianity; Christians must learn the truth so well that they would be able to detect any departure from the truth and the counterfeit elements so apparent in the cultic practices and systems. The cults can have considerable truth but be so diluted with human error and heresy as to be more deadly than rank, thorough-going falsehood.

Second, do not water down the saving power of the gospel through compromise or through a desire not to offend. The gospel has always offended those not wanting to conform their lives to its precepts. While it is vital to "speak the truth **in love**" (Eph. 4:15), it is the **truth** that actually makes men free (Jno. 8:32). Though Christians have love and compassion for those in bondage to cultism, they must vigorously oppose the cultic practices.

Third, Paul commands that Christians "mark them that are causing the divisions and occasions of stumbling, contrary to the doctrine which ye learned, and turn away from them" (Rom. 16:17). Some among us have seen fit to disregard such Scriptures and have praised rather than marked the cultic practices which have made inroads into and have split some congregations. Paul also warns, "Who, knowing the ordinance of God, that they that practice such things are worthy of death, not only do the same, but also consent with them that practice them" (Rom. 1:32). Such makes a farce of Christianity and the church.

Fourth, let the church not be drawn into evangelism simply for the purpose of evangelism! The dominant lesson from the pulpit today seems to be just that. Whatever happened to sound, Biblical lessons on the plan of salvation, the oneness of the church, the worship, Christian living, helping the needy, and other great themes of the Scriptures? The author is not opposed to evangelism; in fact, his life has been devoted to encouraging it. However, the church must have something living and vibrant to which to convert people. When the church was distinctive in its plea and preaching and when its members were peculiar in their being different from the world, the church of Christ was the fastest growing religious group in America. As a former professor of the author would state, what proceeds from so many preachers' mouths is "too thin to slosh." If the church preaches the unadulterated gospel of Christ, God will provide the increase. Did not our Lord proclaim, "And I, if I be lifted up from the earth, will draw all men unto myself" (Jno. 12:32)?

Fifth, allow the brilliance of the truth and its promises to shine against the darkness of cultic practices. The death of Christ for man makes man important and proves his dignity and worth. The gimmicks and philosophies of men simply cannot give peace with God and fellowship with the only begotten Son of God.

Conclusion

In this age of Aquarius, of existential philosophy, of secular humanism, and of departure from the Messiah to embrace cultic leaders and practices, many people — and particularly the young — have discontinued the pursuit for ultimate and absolute truth as a hopeless quest. However, the way to God through Christ is open today as it has been for nearly two thousand years. When the dust shall have settled and when the Lord shall have received His own, the winning side will not have been led by some guru or by some slippery-tongued shyster.

> The kingdom of the world is become the kingdom of our Lord, and of his Christ: and he shall reign for ever and ever" (Rev. 11:15).

FOOTNOTES

1. Lowell D. Streiker, *The Cults Are Coming* (Nashville: Abingdon, 1978), p. 7.
2. Edmond G. Gruss, *Cults and the Occult in the Age of Aquarius* (Grand Rapids: Baker Book House, 1974), p. 67.
3. Joseph Rubinstein and Brent D. Slife, eds., *Taking Sides: Clashing Views on Controversial Psychological Issues* (Guilford, Connecticut: The Dushkin Publishing Group, Inc., 1980), p. 44.
4. "Children of Doom," *Time* 103 (February 18, 1974): 90.
5. "Religious Cults: Newest Magnets for Youth," *U. S. News and World Report* 80 (June 14, 1976): 52.
6. George McKenna and Mirella Baroni-Harris, *Taking Sides: Clashing Views on Social Issues* (Guilford, Connecticut: The Dushkin Publishing Group, Inc., 1980), p. 78.
7. Carroll Stoner and Jo Ann Parke, *All God's Children: The Cult Experience — Salvation or Slavery?* (Radnor, Pennsylvania: Chilton Book Company, 1977), p. 3.
8. "Cults: Out of This World," *Time* 106 (October 20, 1975): 25.
9. Fritz Ridenour, ed., *So, What's the Difference?* (Glendale, California: Regal Books Division, G/L Publications, 1969), p. iii.
10. See also this author's article entitled "Cultism — Could It Arise in the Church?" *The Spiritual Sword,* 12 (October, 1980): 14-19.
11. Charles A. Krause, *Guyana Massacre: The Eyewitness Account* (New York: Berkley Publishing Corporation, 1978), p. 113.
12. Roger R. Chambers, *The Plain Truth about Armstrongism* (Grand Rapids: Baker Book House, 1972), p. 5.
13. Streiker, pp. 8, 9.
14. McKenna, pp. 78, 79.
15. Rubinstein, p. 44.
16. Walter R. Martin, *The Kingdom of the Cults: An Analysis of the Major Cult Systems in the Present Era* (Minneapolis: Bethany Fellowship, Inc., Publishers, 1974), p. 12.
17. Jack Sparks, *The Mindbenders: A Look at Current Cults* (Nashville: Thomas Nelson, Inc., Publishers, 1977), p. 15.
18. Eugene H. Methvin, "Scientology: Anatomy of a Frightening Cult," *Readers Digest Reprint* (May, 1980), p. 1.
19. William J. Peterson, *Those Curious New Cults* (New Canaan, Connecticut: Keats Publishing, Inc., 1973), p. 205.
20. Sparks, p. 15.
21. Martin, p. 10.
22. Ibid.
23. Stoner, p. 23.
24. Martin, p. 11.
25. Gruss, p. 3.
26. Streiker, p. 9.
27. "The Children of God: Disciples of Deception," *Christianity Today* 21 (February 18, 1977): 18, 19.
28. J. Isamu Yamamoto, *The Puppet Master* (Downers Grove, Illinois: InterVarsity Press, 1977), p. 73.
29. Martin, pp. 18, 19.
30. Ibid., p. 19.
31. Sparks, p. 13.
32. Martin, p. 20.
33. Yamamoto, pp. 53, 56, 81, 82, 87.
34. Gordon R. Lewis, *What Everyone Should Know about Transcendental Meditation* (Glendale, California: Regal Books Division, G/L Publications, 1975), p. 69.

35. Krause, p. 115.
36. McKenna, p. 82.
37. Streiker, p. 9.
38. Stoner, p. 4.
39. Martin, p. 26.
40. Sparks, p. 18.
41. "Children of God," p. 20; George W. Corneli, "Those 'Guru' Cults — Religion or Exploitation?" *Reader's Digest* 108 (February, 1976): 96, 98.
42. Krause, p. 113.
43. Methvin, p. 3.
44. Krause, p. 117.
45. Rubinstein, p. 45.
46. Ibid., p. 49.
47. "Ex-Moonie Seeks Millions in Lawsuit Against Church," *Oregon Journal,* Portland, Oregon (April 14, 1981): 13.
48. Stoner, p. 13.
49. Sparks, p. 16.
50. Corneli, p. 97.
51. "Children of God," pp. 21, 22.
52. Rubinstein, pp. 49, 50.
53. Yamamoto, p. 61.
54. Krause, p. 118.
55. Stoner, p. 4.
56. "Children of God," p. 19.
57. Streiker, p. 10.
58. Yamamoto, pp. 61, 63, 107.
59. Stoner, p. 4.
60. Krause, p. 115.
61. McKenna, p. 84.
62. James R. Gaines, "Cults: Bo-Peep's Flock," *Newsweek* 86 (October 20, 1978): 32.
63. Corneli, p. 97.
64. Yamamoto, p. 63.
65. Stoner, p. 30.
66. Yamamoto, p. 66.
67. Stoner, pp. 5, 7, 27.
68. David Haddon, *Transcendental Meditation: A Christian View* (Madison, Wisconsin: InterVarsity Press, 1976), p. 12.
69. Martin, p. 25.
70. Stoner, p. 4.
71. Methvin, p. 4.
72. Ibid.
73. Yamamoto, pp. 63, 93.
74. Stoner, p. 24.
75. Ibid., p. 25.
76. Ibid., p. 26.

CHAPTER 5
IS CHRIST A CREATED BEING?

Guy N. Woods

I am sensible of the high honor that has come to me in being invited to this lectureship, and thus privileged to share in the fine fellowship of faithful friends and beloved brethren in the Lord, and to participate in this stimulating and profitable lectureship.

I have long known and appreciated the great Getwell congregation and its work in the proclamation and defense of the truth.

Is Christ A Created Being?

The implications of this question are surely shocking to all faithful Christians. There is in it the suggestion that some people concede the historicity of the Christ of the scriptures, but deny that he is uncreated and eternal, and co-existent with the Father. This view of the nature of Christ is that advocated by those who style themselves *Jehovah's Witnesses.* Since we are to examine it in detail in this lecture, it is well for us to take a brief look into the background of those who subscribe thereto.

The movement had its origin in the efforts of Charles T. Russell, usually referred to as "Pastor Russell," born in the vicinity of Pittsburg, Penna., and raised to believe the principles and precepts of historic Christianity but who, at the age of twenty, repudiated the religion of his parents and became skeptical toward all religion. In this state he remained, until he began to read the writings of Mrs. Ellen G. White, founder of Adventism, from whom he adopted his views of the nature of man, future punishment, and other peculiar positions of that alleged prophetess; and, from this beginning, launched a mighty movement which spread rapidly throughout the world, and from which he acquired great wealth and much eminence. Headquarters of the movement were eventually established in Brooklyn, N.Y., with branches in many lands; and from there its missionaries and literature are sent out to more than one hundred countries, and its tenets are preached in approximately that many languages. Its devotees are most industrious in the propagation of its distinctive doctrines and are a familiar sight on street corners throughout the land as they seek to sell the *Watchtower,* official publication of the sect, and its other periodicals and books. In 1950, the organization, known as "The Watch Tower Bible and Tract Society," issued its "New World Translation of the Christian Greek Scriptures," (to which we shall have occasion frequently to refer in this lecture), alleged to be a translation "the most accurate to date" (page 792), and is now in process of publishing a translation of the Old Testament Scriptures.

Though Mr. Russell had published, sometime prior to 1916, a tract of 128 pages entitled "Millions Now Living Will Never Die," in which he claimed to give "Bible proof that there are millions of people now living who will never enter the grave," one chapter of which bore the caption, *"How to Live Forever,"* (Mr. Russell was not one of these. He became ill on a train through Texas from which he was removed, dying shortly thereafter in Pampa of this state on Oct. 31, 1916).

Following the death of the founder of the movement, "Judge" J. F. Rutherford assumed leadership of the organization, and through unusual ability as an organizer and writer greatly extended its sphere and influence. From his prolific pen flowed an unending stream of material which the society published, and yet circulates with certain significant revisions, deletions and emendations! It was the view of Mr. Rutherford, often expressed, that certain saints were soon to be raised from the dead to live on the earth "and take charge of the visible affairs of the earth," and he regarded it as proper to build a house for their habitation prior to their appearance. Accordingly, he caused to be erected, *at the expense of the society,* of course, an imposing mansion with a dreamy mountain view in lovely San Diego, California, for "the aforementioned princes of the earth," which he, as care-taker, *proposed to occupy* until such time as they appeared. Here, at *Beth Sarim* ("house of the princes") as he chose to call it he lived, and, unfortunately, died, before the realization of his hopes; and, the Watch Tower society, having cooled to such a plan for the princes, allowed the property to pass to private hands. We were privileged to visit Beth Sarim recently and to admire the lovely location which Rutherford chose for himself and the princes!

The movement has been variously known as Russellism, Rutherfordism, Millennial Dawnism, designations which they reject; and it has been styled by its devotees as "International Bible Students," "Jehovah's Witnesses," and members of "the New World Society." Its teaching is an admixture of Adventism, Swedborgianism, Unitarianism; and, on the nature of Christ, *Arianism.*

A tract entitled, "What Do Jehovah's Witnesses Believe," issued by the Watchtower press, warns that reviewers of their doctrines often present a biased and unfriendly picture of their positions, and asks, "We would not expect to obtain from the scribes and Pharisees a correct picture of what Jesus believed, would we?" We think their caution is proper; and we shall, therefore, appeal *only to their official publications,* carefully documenting each statement therefrom, in ascertaining what they really believe. On the same page of the leaflet (p. 2), where the foregoing statement appears are these words, "Jehovah's first creation was his Son." Following this, they cite certain scriptures, which we shall hereafter examine in detail. For the moment our purpose is to determine, from their writings, what Jehovah's Witnesses believe and teach regarding the nature of Christ. Their tract declares, "Jehovah's first creation was his Son." This statement, appearing in a leaflet, the design of which is to acquaint people with the tenets of the movement, is simple, unequivocal and without ambiguity. From it we learn that this religious society believes and teaches that (a) Christ is not eternal, but a creature of Jehovah; and (b) he was the first of all God's creatures to be made. It is proper to deduce from this that having been *created* by Jehovah, he was non-existent until this creative act occurred; and is, therefore not co-existent with the Father nor equal with him.

This view is often stated and affirmed in a variety of ways in their official publications: "He is not the author of the creation of God; but after God had created him as his first-born Son, then God used him as his working Partner in the creating of all the rest of creation" (*Let God Be True,* Page 33, Revised Edition).

"Who was the first son of God created? The very one who is 'the beginning of the creation of God' identifies himself to us. He is the same one that later was born as a man by the miracle of God and was called Jesus Christ" (*The New World,* page 16).

In their book, *Creation,* page 15, under the sub-heading, "Beginning of creation," they insist that "long before the creation of the earth, when there was no sea, when there were no springs and lakes, before there were any mountains or hills, yea, before the sun and the moon and the stars were made, God began his creation; and that beginning was his beloved One, known in the Holy Record as the Logos. The word Logos is one of the names or titles given to the beloved Son of God, and carries with it deep meaning."

"The term Logos is one of the titles applied to the first or beginning of God's creation." (*Deliverance,* page 12).

"Jehovah God had now set out on the purpose of endless creation. He now had beside him a 'master workman' endowed with wisdom. This had received life from God. This made him the Son of God. In begetting this Son or bringing him forth to life Jehovah was the only Producer or Creator, unassisted. His first living creature was therefore the 'only begotten Son of God'." (*The Truth Shall Make You Free,* page 43).

"The question now arises as to the other creatures that were produced after God's firstborn Son, the Word. Were these other creatures each a direct creation of God as his Son the Word was?" (*Ibid.,* page 48).

These quotations might be indefinitely extended, but these will suffice to show the clear and unmistakable position of those who call themselves Jehovah's Witnesses on the nature of Christ. They reveal the view that Christ *received life from God,* is a creature, was created in the beginning of God's creation, is not the author of the creation of God; and is, hence, not eternal.

What was the name of this "creature" which the writers of the Watchtower society seek to identify as Christ before he came to the world? Russell long ago sought to answer this question in these words: "Our Redeemer existed as a spirit being before he was made flesh and dwelt amongst men. At that time, as well as subsequently, he was properly known as 'a god' — a mighty one. As chief of the angels and next to the Father he was known as the Archangel (highest angel messenger), whose name Michael, signifies, 'Who is God,' or God's representative. As he was the highest of all Jehovah's creation, so also he was the first, the direct creation of God..." (Studies in the Scriptures, series 5, page 84). Recent writers for the Watchtower organization have expressed the same views:

"Being the only begotten Son of God and the 'first born of every creature,' the Word would be a prince among other creatures. In this office he bore another name in heaven, which name is 'Michael'" (*The Truth Shall Make You Free,* 1943, page 48).

These quotations, taken verbatim from the official publications of the Watchtower society, reveal with unmistakable clarity that "Jehovah's Witnesses" believe and teach (a) Christ is not eternal; (b) he was *created* by the Father long ages past; (c) he lived in heaven, a spirit being, from the time of his creation until he came to the earth and was endowed with flesh; and (d) during this interval he was *Michael,* the archangel.

We have indicated earlier that these people cite certain passages of scripture in an effort to sustain this shocking and incredible theory. It is our intention to examine *each passage* they offer which bears any remote relation at all to the subject, and scrutinize it minutely. The first scripture they usually offer, in their attempts to justify such a position is Rev. 3:14: "And to the angel of the church in Laodicea write: These things saith the Amen, the faithful and true witness, the beginning of the creation of God." The One identified here as "the Amen," and "the faithful and true witness," is, undoubtedly, Christ himself. This seems conclusively to follow; and we conclude it without hesitation. The One thus identified is declared to be "the beginning of the creation of God." Watchtower writers urge that the significance of this phrase is that Christ was created as the first, or beginning act, of God (*Let God Be True,* revised edition, page 32).

The meaning of this statement turns on the significance of the word *archee* translated *beginning* here and approximately forty times elsewhere in the common version. It cannot be properly interpreted to mean that which is caused to begin, as "Jehovah's Witnesses" allege. On the contrary, it designates him who is the beginning of creation in the sense that he was there and caused creation to begin! As Lange well says: "The Logos was not merely existent, however, in the beginning, but was also the *efficient principle,* the beginning of the beginning . . . and when it is said that the Logos was in this beginning, his eternal existence is already expressed, and his eternal position in the godhead already indicated thereby." (Lange's Commentary on John 1:1). It follows, therefore, that Revelation 3:14 teaches that Christ is "the beginning of the creation of God," in the sense that he was "the efficient principle," the active agent in causing it to start! (Compare John 1:3).

Fortunately, we are not dependent on deductions in determining the significance of this passage with reference to what it teaches regarding the eternity of Christ. All truth is harmonious; and the scriptures never contradict themselves. Melchizedek, "king of Salem, priest of the Most High" is said to have been "without father, without mother, without genealogy, having neither beginning of days nor end of life, *but made like unto the Son of God,* abideth a priest continually" (Heb. 7:1-3). The sense in which this ancient priest was "made like unto the Son of God" was that he had "neither beginning of days nor end of life." If this passage bears any significance at all, it teaches that Christ was *without beginning or end.* It is, therefore, a thorough refutation of the Watchtower theory.

Often cited by these writers in support of this theory is Col. 1:15, which asserts that Christ "is the image of the invisible God, the first-born of all creation." Because he is described as "the firstborn of all creation," it is alleged that Christ was the first creature in the creation. They say, "Thus he is ranked with God's creation, being first among them..." (*Let God Be True,* Rev. ed., page 33). They assume that the word "firstborn" is used literally to indicate that Christ came into existence as the *first* of God's creatures. They err in the assumption that the word is to be assigned a literal significance in this passage. It is obvious that the term has a figurative usage here. A creative act is one thing; a birth is another. It is absurd to affirm that Christ was *born* of God, in the usual sense of the word, if he were *created.* Moreover, the passage itself proves that Christ possessed the same nature as the Father since he is "the image of the invisible God." Being of the same essence and nature as the Father, Christ is as eternal as He; and this passage may not be properly cited to show that our Lord is a created being. On the contrary, he is before all creation, being *author* of creation himself: "For in him were all things created...all things have been created through him, and unto him; and he is before all things, and in him all things consist" (Col. 1:15-17). The translators of the Watchtower Version, well aware of the force of this statement, have deliberately tampered with the text here and inserted without any justification the word "other" to make the foregoing statement read: "By means of him all *other* things were created...all *other* things have been created through him and for him. Also he is before all *other* things by means of him all *other* things were made to exist" (Page 589, *New World Translations*). Theirs is a serious offense against the Word of God with reference to which warnings are often penned in the sacred writings (Cf. Deut. 4:2; Prov. 30:6; Rev. 22:13). Col. 1:15 simply suggests that Christ is prior to all creation so that without him creation would not have occurred. As "the first born of all creation," he is anterior to all creation, and therefore *no part of creation.* The word "firstborn," is from the Greek *prootootokos*, and means born before. Thus Christ is separated from, and declared to be anterior to, *creation.* In being before all creation, he was not himself created. *What is before all creation must be regarded as eternal.* Christ was before all creation; therefore, he is eternal!

Moreover, the passage reveals that not only was Christ (a) before all creation and (b) the author of it, he is the *end* or design of creation, for *all* things were created "for him." He is, therefore, not a created being. It teaches us that *Christ* created all things; and from the Hebrew writer we learn that "he that built all things is God" (Heb. 3:4). It follows, therefore, that Christ is God (theos), i.e., possesses *deity.*

Though decisive against the theory, John 1:1 which they grossly mistranslate, is frequently cited by "Jehovah's Witnesses" in an effort to bolster their view that Christ is merely a creature and not an eternal part of the godhead. "In the beginning was the Word, and the Word was with God, and the Word was God," the passage reads in reliable versions; and these people concede that reference to Christ is made by the phrase, "the Word," or Logos, as it is in the Greek Testament. Regarding this passage they have said: "Hence he may be called 'the Word or Logos.' Being a mighty one and holding this high official capacity as Logos, and being before all other creatures, he was a God, but not the Almighty God, who is Jehovah...Happily, the New World Translation of the Christian Greek Scriptures (published 1950) renders John 1:1.2: 'Originally the Word was, and the Word was with God, and the Word was a god. This one was originally with God' " (*Let God Be True*, Rev. ed., pages 33, 34).

It will be observed that the phrase, "and the Word was God," of the American Standard Version (the King James Translation, and all other reliable ones) is made to read in the Watchtower Bible, "and the Word was a god." Specifically, the indefinite article "a"is inserted, and the word *God* is spelled with a lower case "g," rather than capitalized, as in the usual versions of the Scriptures. From this they deduce the view that Christ is merely "a god," a phrase which they thereupon interpret to mean *a created being*. Moreover, they take great liberty with the first phrase of the text, *en archee een ho logos*, "In the beginning was the Word," by the rendering, "Originally the Word was," to which they attach a foot-note, reading, "Literally, In (At) a beginning," by which they insinuate their doctrine of Christ's *creation* in the indefinite article "a" of the footnote. This is an unwarranted handling of the Greek text in that it disregards the rules requiring the definite article in translation though not in the Greek text. Here, the beginning is sufficiently definite without the article, and is undoubtedly an allusion to the beginning of Gen. 1:1. In this beginning the Word *was, een,* existed, not *egento,* became, or came into being. The meaning is, Before creation, before anything was made, at the very beginning of creation, the Word already *was*. The *beginning* (archee) here, and also that of Gen. 1:1, was evidently the beginning of creation; and inasmuch as the Word (logos), Christ *was there,* he was before all creation, therefore, no part of it. He was indeed the agent of creation, "All things were made by him; and without him was not anything made that was made" (John 1:3). It would not be possible to affirm the eternity of Christ more positively than is done in this great prologue of the gospel of John.

The Word (*logos*), the Christ, was not only *in the beginning* and before creation, "the Word was *with* (pros) God." As Vincent well says, "With (*pros*) does not convey the full meaning," but "there is no single English word which will give it better. The preposition *pros,* which with the accusative case, denotes motion toward, or direction, is also often used in the New Testament in the sense of *with*; and that not merely as being *near* or *beside*, but as a living union and communion; implying the active notion of intercourse...Thus John's statement is that the divine Word not only abode with the Father from all eternity, but was in the living, active relation of communion with him" (Vincent's *Word Studies,* Vol. 2, pages 33, 34). This intimate union of Christ with the Father is described by the Lord himself in John 17:5 and John 1:18.

"And the Word was God!" God, from the Greek *theos* denotes *deity;* and by a common figure of speech (the *synecdoche*), where the whole is put for a part, the name of the divine nature is assigned to the second person of the godhead as, for example it is assigned to the first person in John 1:18 and to the third person — the Holy Spirit — in Acts 5:3,4.

The affectation of scholarship in a lengthy article in the appendix of the so-called New World Translation of the "Jehovah's Witnesses" to justify their rendering of the clause, *kai theos een ho logos,* "and the Word was God," (ASV; KJV, etc.), as "and the Word was a god," does not obscure the fact that these translators have abandoned true scholarship and evolved their own rules in their determined effort to deny to our Lord eternity of being.

The order of the words in this clause is such as to give emphasis; *God* is a predicate noun in the clause, not the subject. It is obvious that the subject is "the Word"; the inspired writer is revealing who the Word is, not who God is! The Watchtower writers make much of the fact that the article *(ho) the,* does not appear before *theos* (God) in the passage, hence their rendering, "and the Word was *a god."* This rendering is untenable for various reasons: (1) It is a recognized principle of Greek grammar that the subject takes the article and the predicate omits it. "Hence arises the general rule, that in the simple sentence the subject takes the article, the predicate omits it. The subject is definitely before the mind, the predicate generally denotes the class to which the subject is referred, or from which it is excluded, *but the notion of the class is itself intermediate" (Handbook of the Grammar of the Greek Testament,* Green, page 193). (2) If the article appeared before the predicate noun here, it would be the equivalent of saying the Word (Christ) is the entire godhead, which would be untrue. He is one of three persons who constitute it. It should be observed that in the second clause of the sentence, *kai ho logos een pros ton theon,* "and the word was with God," the article appears before *theos;* for here God (as the first person) is specified absolutely. In the third affirmation, the article is omitted because it was John's design to denote the character or nature of the Word as *deity,* rather than to specify his person. Thus (a) our Lord *existed* in the beginning before *all creation;* (b) he was *with* the Father in intimate communion before anything was made; (c) he was, himself, the active agent in creation; (d) he was *God* (deity) in the beginning. There are three distinct propositions in this marvelous affirmation of the apostle: (1) In the beginning Christ already *was;* therefore, without beginning himself, and pre-existent. (2) He enjoyed the closest association and fellowship with the Father, being "with (pros) God." (3) Lest it be assumed that all of this might be, and yet the second person be an inferior being, John declares that Christ *is* God — is possessed of the nature of God.

The wondrous being who is anterior to all creation and therefore uncreated, timeless and eternal, is identified at verse 14 of John 1: "And the Word became flesh, and dwelt among us..." This was, of course, the Christ. No more important passage may be found in the scriptures respecting the nature of Christ. It declares (1) his eternity; (2) his close relationship to the

Father; (3) his work in creation; (4) his *distinction* from the Father; and (5) his possession of the *nature* of God. These fundamental propositions inhere in John's great treatise, and cannot be obscured.

Writers for the Watchtower society often cite Prov. 8:22-30, in an effort to sustain their theory of a *created* Christ. In this highly figurative portion of scripture Wisdom is personified by the sacred writer and declared to be before creation: "Jehovah possessed me in the beginning of his way, before his works of old. I was set up from everlasting, from the beginning, before the earth was . . . then I was by him as a master workman..." The word "possessed" has the marginal reading, *"formed."* It is alleged that Christ is alluded to under the figure of Wisdom in this passage and that it was he who Jehovah formed in the beginning. This passage, far from proving that Christ is a created angel, as Jehovah's Witnesses teach, demonstrates his eternity and timelessness! (1) The "Wisdom" of the passage was possessed "in the beginning"; (2) he was before "his works of old"; (3) he was "set up *from everlasting.*" Hebrew writers, by such expressions, often denoted eternity. If *Wisdom,* in this passage, refers to Christ, it affirms his eternity, instead of controverting it. Further, it establishes the deity of Christ: Wisdom is said to have been with the Father as "a master workman" (Verse 30). Christ is uniformly declared to have been the creator of the universe in the scriptures (Col. 1:16; Heb. 1:2, 10; John 1:3, etc.). The creation is often appealed to, in the Bible, to prove that he who accomplished this is the true God rather than the idols (Isa. 40:18-28; Jer. 10:13-16; Prov. 3:19). But, it is impossible that a creature should be endowed with attributes which only deity can possess. Christ possessed all of the attributes of God, *theos,* deity. Therefore, Christ is God, posseses the divine nature, and was, in eternity, equal of the Father!

This, indeed, is affirmed by Paul, in the great declaration of Phil. 2:5-8 which reads: "Have this mind in you, which was also in Christ Jesus: who, existing in the form of God, counted not the being on an equality with God a thing to be grasped, but emptied himself, taking the form of a servant, being made in the likeness of men..." Christ was (1) originally in the *form* of God. The "form" of anything is the manner in which it reveals itself; and this, of course, is determined by the nature which it has. Christ was in the form of God — deity — therefore, he possessed the nature of deity. (2) He was *on an equality with God.* (3) He did not regard this equality with God as a "thing to be grasped," i.e., held on to as an improper assumption — he was entitled to it as the equal of God! (4) He voluntarily surrendered this position and came to the world to be endowed with flesh in order that he might serve as our High Priest. This passage, in the most positive fashion, demonstrates the eternity, deity, and position of Christ before he came to the world. Aware of the force of this passage on their doctrine, the Watchtower society in its "New World Translation" offers this pitiful paraphrase and ridiculous rendering: "Keep this mental attitude in you which was also in Christ Jesus, who, although he was existing in God's form, gave no consideration to a seizure, namely, that he should be equal to God. No, but he emptied himself,..." When men deal thus with the sacred scriptures, they forfeit their right to the respect of their readers, abandon any semblance of scholarship, and demonstrate their departure from the truth.

We have now examined the *principal* passages cited in various publications of the Watchtower society to support this organization's view that Christ is merely a created being, and not co-equal with the Father and eternal in nature, and have found that each of these, where they touch the issues at all, teach his eternity, deity and full equality with God the Father, instead of that which "Jehovah's Witnesses" allege. Though limitations of time preclude further examination of their claims, we oblige ourselves, at any proper time and place, to demonstrate that any other verses which they may offer may be similarly resolved, if they relate to the nature of Christ at all.

The errors of *Jehovah's Witnesses* are not minor and inconsquential; they strike at the foundations of Christianity. They are an admixture of Arianism, Unitarianism, and infidelity; and, believed and relied on until death, will plunge their hapless dupes into endless perdition. Because theirs is a situation as fatal as that to which the apostle alluded, we urge all of this sect who desire salvation to

> "Come ye out from among them, and be ye separate, saith the Lord" (II Cor. 6:17).

—from the book **Jesus Christ, the Son of God.**

CHAPTER 6
MAN (SOUL, ETC.) UNDER JEHOVAH'S WITNESS DOCTRINE

Rex A. Turner

Introduction

The subject scheduled for this hour reads: "Man (Soul, etc.) Under Jehovah's Witness Doctrine." This study will be quite revolting to all god-fearing people. The Jehovah's Witness doctrine is an undeniable system of cultism. It is a system which provides a way for men to lead ungodly lives without the fear of ultimate punishment, especially eternal punishment.

The case is that numerous tenets of the Jehovah's Witness doctrine are wild, outlandish, ridiculous, repugnant, and a downright affront to both God and man; and yet no one tenet of the doctrine is more exciting and more readily received than the tenet which gives a definition of the soul of man, together with the comfort which necessarily ensues on the basis of that specific definition of the word soul.

Pastor Russell, the founder of the movement, affirmed that the soul is the breath of life — simply that and nothing more. In short, he affirmed that man positively does not have an immortal soul and that hell-fire does not exist. This doctrine relative to the soul, the advocates claim, is the "good news of the gospel." The advocates rise to a high point of eloquence when they speak so critically against those preachers who preach "the nightmare of eternal torture."

Pastor Russell, and later "Judge" Rutherford, leaders of the movement, spoke with great irony as they asserted that Mark 9:47, 48, has long been the favorite text of "the hell-fire screechers." They spoke out with strong emphasis against "that notorious pagan doctrine, "the Trinity." One leader in the movement, H. E. Pennock, observed that "there are some clergymen, no doubt, who are really sincere in thinking that Jesus was his own father, and the Almighty is the Son of Himself; and that each of these is a third person who is the same as the other two, and yet different from them."

The Source Of The System

All god-fearing people are bound to ask: "From whence came such a god-defying, god-reviling doctrine? In order to be informed and forewarned, two overviews, at the very outset, are pertinent and necessary; namely, (1) a historical overview of the man who concocted the fallacious godless system; and (2) an overview of some of the major tenets or holdings of the doctrine. In short, a proper perusal of the subject on this occasion necessarily calls for an overview of the man and the doctrine.

The Man And The Doctrine

An Overview of the Man

With respect to an overview of the man, the founder of the Jehovah's Witness movement was Charles Taze Russell, 1852-1916. There seems to be no doubt but that Russell was perturbed about his eternal state and thereby seized upon the doctrine of soul-sleeping and annihilation as had been promulgated by those who gave rise to Adventism. In short, the Russellites — or Jehovah's Witnesses — are first cousins to the Seventh-Day Adventists.

Charles Taze Russell was of Pittsburg, Pennsylvania. There he dealt in gent's furnishings and proved himself to be bold, shrewed, and of considerable business ability. He emerged upon the scene of Theology in the self-asserted role of an exegetical scholar. In actuality, he emerged as an exegetical contortionist. In 1879, he founded "Zion's Watchtower," and in 1881, he founded the "Watchtower Bible and Tract Society." He spread his teaching through the "Watch Tower Publication." In 1909, he moved his headquarters to the Brooklyn Tabernacle, New York City. His writings are contained in a series of six volumes of books, entitled, **Millennial Dawn.** Russell died aboard a transcontinental train on November 9, 1916. "Judge" J. F. Rutherford — who actually was no judge — succeeded him.

As a man of viable indepth character, Charles Taze Russell did not make a good showing. He was involved in several significant scandals, as follows:

1. Russell's wife sued him for divorce on account of his improper relationships with a woman by the name of Rose Ball. He vehemently denied the allegation, but when the embrassing facts of evidence were presented, he admitted that the accusation was true. The court granted his wife the divorce on the basis of his "conceit" and "domination."
2. Russell then planned to defraud his wife of her dower interest by transferring all of his property to certain corporations over which he had full control. He also sought to defraud his wife of her alimony, as fixed by the court, by fleeing from one state to another.
3. Russell dealt in so-called "miracle wheat" which was supposed to grow fifteen times as much per acre as normal wheat. He proposed that the "miracle wheat," priced at sixty dollars per bushel, could be sold only to the faithful.
4. Russell secured enormous funds by persuading ignorant and trusting people that the world was soon to come to an end and that they should turn their property into his hands for his hurried and urgent proclamation of what he termed "the true gospel."

An Overview of the Doctrine

With respect to an overview of the doctrine, an overview of some of the chief tenets of the Jehovah's Witness doctrine should necessarily include at least nine, and with the selection of the nine tenets, numerous other tenets — like the second coming of Christ — are by-passed.

1. Pastor Russell claimed for himself that he was "the faithful and wise servant, whom the Lord hath set over his household, to give them their food in due season" (as per Matt. 24:45); and that therefore, no one understood certain revelations, including the book of Revelation, prior to his coming upon the scene.

2. Pastor Russell denied that Jesus Christ is co-existent and co-eternal with God — thus that there was a time when Jesus Christ was not. In short, he denied that Jesus Christ was ever or will ever be God. While emphasizing his strong faith in the supernatural inspiration of the scriptures and his criticism and denouncement of the higher critics and new-thought theologians, he was, himself, guilty of blasphemy!

3. Pastor Russell affirmed instead that Jesus Christ was a created being, a created angel, like other created angels, and that in fact he was, or is, Michael, the archangel.

4. Pastor Russell further affirmed that when Jesus Christ walked on earth he was a mere man; that he had given up his spirit being; that he had only one nature at that time; and that the one nature was human nature.

5. Pastor Russell still further affirmed that the death of Christ on the cross was only the death of a mere man; and therefore, a mere man made an atonement for man — that is, only humanity was sacrificed for humanity.

6. Pastor Russell, as a corollary to his afirmation that the death of Jesus Christ was only an atonement of a mere man made for man, denied that the work of atonement was completed by the death of Jesus Christ on the cross; and he affirmed, instead, that the work of atonement will be completed at the close of the millennial reign of Christ on earth.

7. Pastor Russell, as a continuing corollary, denied the resurrection of the body of Jesus Christ; instead, he alleged that the body of Jesus was supernaturally removed from the tomb to prevent its being an obstacle to the faith of the disciples; that the body was either dissolved into gases; or that else God has it in possession as a corpse.

8. Pastor Russell affirmed that death always means extinction, the cessation of being, an annihilation, or a period of absolute unconciousness — a period of absolute non-existence and thus all dead have ceased to be.

9. Pastor Russell affirmed that at the time of the millennium Jesus Christ will function as a secondary God, and further that the wicked will be given a second chance.

The tenets of the Russellite doctrine, as set forth herewith, are by no means all of this God-dishonoring system, but these tenets will suffice to provide a background for an understanding of the subject of this particular lecture — that is, the Jehovah's Witness doctrine relative to man.

Man, Or The Soul, Under The Jehovah Witness Doctrine

Pastor Russell's affirmation of how that the term death always means extinction, or cessation of being, was grounded in his definition of the term Soul. The meaning of the term "soul" is "breath," the Pastor affirmed; and his major proof text was from the book of Genesis which reads: "Jehovah God formed man of the dust of the ground, and breathed into his nostrils the breath of life; and man became a living soul" (Gen. 2:7). Man is a soul but does not have a soul, as in the case of all animals and fowls that breathe, Pastor Russell argued; and therefore, death is the absence of life, he concluded. He further concluded that man is so constituted as to be incapable of eternal torment; that eternal torment is not only impossible but also unreasonable to contemplate; that it repugnant to a system of justice; and that it is contrary to the principle of love.

There is no wonder then that "Judge" J. F. Rutherford, the successor to Pastor Russell's godless system, should harp on the subject, "Where Are the Dead?" This he did in both his speaking and writing. "His Honor" would proceed to inform his audiences that "preachers are dumb-dogs that cannot speak for their master."

The subject, "Where Are the Dead?" was calculated to excite certain classes of people. Many found comfort and relief to hear that the dead are as if they had never lived or existed; that they are as if asleep; that they positively are in no throes of punishment; that at the Millennial Dawn they will be brought back to life; and that even if they were wicked in the first life they will be given a second chance. To illustrate, the effect of such a false doctrine, suppose the case of a mother who has lost a wayward son to death — and especially if she is ignorant of the Word, or inclined to regard it lightly — that mother would be inclined to embrace the doctrine. Further, those who have no purpose in life, or commitment to righteousness except to live after the flesh, will be inclined to revel in those false hopes. What a comfort, and how humanly desirable this God-dishonoring doctrine was in the beginning of the movement, and it continues to be so until this day!

The burden at hand at this point is to inquire as to whether or not Pastor Russell was correct in his affirmation that the soul is the breath of life and that this is the full and only meaning of the word soul? The case is that one meaning of the word "soul" is breath of life. True, as Russell affirmed, man is a soul; but untrue is his affirmation that man is a soul but does not have a soul.

When Moses wrote of how that man became a "living soul," or a breathing person, the reference was to the mortal, or animal, or biological life of Adam. The life of the physical body of Adam was under consideration, but the word "soul" in other instances embraces the immortal nature, the non-breathing nature, of both man and God. To illustrate, God is a spirit. He does not "breathe" as man does — he has no animal breath — and yet the scriptures speak of God as possessing a soul. One reading from the Old Testament and one from the New Testament will suffice to establish the fact that God possesses a soul. One selection from the Old Testament reads: "If ye walk in my statutes . . . I will set my tabernacle among you: and **my soul** shall not abhor you . . . But if ye will not harken unto me . . . I will destroy your high places, and cut down your sun images and cast your dead bodies upon the bodies of your idols; and **my soul** shall abhor you" (Lev. 26:3, 11, 14, 30). The selection from the New Testament reads: "Behold my servant whom I have chosen; my beloved in whom **my soul** is well pleased: I will put my Spirit upon him, and he shall declare judgment to the Gentiles" (Matt. 12:18). This very reading explodes Pastor Russell's averment that the word soul is restricted to one meaning only — that of animal life.

While the physical life of a man does die, the spiritual life of a man does not and cannot die. Jesus emphasized this fact when he admonished the apostles: "Be not afraid of them that kill the body, but are not able to kill the soul; but rather fear him who is able to destroy (or cast out from his presence) both soul and body in hell" (Matt. 10:28). The case here is that there were those who could kill the body, but they could not kill the soul. This confirms the fact that man has an immortal soul — a soul that man cannot kill or destroy — as well as a physical soul.

In the book of Revelation, John "saw underneath the altar the souls of them that had been slain for the Word of God and for the testimony which they held; and they cried with a great voice, saying, How Long, O Master, the holy and true, dost thou not judge and avenge our blood on them that dwell on the earth?" (Rev. 6:9, 10). The facts to be emphasized relative to the souls under the altar include the following:

1. Those souls under the altar had been slain.
2. The blood of their physical bodies had been shed.
3. Their physical bodies were dead — that is, their bodies had been made to be lifeless corpses.
4. Those souls were, nonetheless, rational beings.
5. They remembered the violence to which they had been subjected while on earth.
6. They also remembered that the occasion of the violence done to their physical bodies was the result of the testimony which they gave in behalf of Jesus Christ.
7. They were calling upon their Master to avenge their blood which had been shed while they were on earth.

The necessary conclusion imposed by the case of the souls under the altar is that while their earthly bodies, or souls, were dead corpses, their immortal souls were very much alive and active. Those souls were martyred saints. In short, the averments of the late Pastor Russell relative to his restricted meaning of the word "soul" is downright ridiculous.

Conclusion

In conclusion, relative to the Jehovah's Witness Doctrine, there are four pertinent observations which should be stated and underscored.

The first observation is that rank rationalization is fundamental to Pastor Russell's system. He forced the inspired scriptures to square with his human reason.

The second observation is that Pastor Russell developed his system for the chief purpose of giving comfort, including a second chance, for those who had died, or who were dying in sin. The doctrine encourages sinners to continue in their sinful ways.

The third observation is that Pastor Russell's system puts a premium on wickedness. There is no righteousness which can possibly ensue from such a godless system.

The fourth observation is that every man is under a heavy obligation to read out of the word of God that which it actually and accurately sets forth. He is not privileged to read into the word of God his rationalizations, his unholy desires, and his unholy commitments.

CHAPTER 7
SIN AND "SALVATION" ACCORDING TO JEHOVAH'S WITNESS DOCTRINE

Charles Chumley

Our purpose in this study is to investigate the teaching of the Jehovah's Witnesses regarding sin and salvation in the light of the teaching of the Scriptures. We have no ill-will toward any member of this religious group and only admiration for the zeal and industry they manifest in promoting this cause. In keeping with the scriptural injunction, however, to "prove all things; hold fast that which is good..." We want to examine the scriptures, whether these things are so (I Thess. 5:21; Acts 17:11).

Drawing upon representative publications setting forth their teaching, we will allow them to speak for themselves and then look to the word of the Lord for the light it may shed upon these themes.

Man Has No Soul

According to the view of the Bible account found in many publications by Jehovah's Witnesses, God created man in the beginning to live forever on the earth, and He placed Adam and Eve in the garden of Eden. "In this garden they could live forever in ideal happiness with all their sons and daughters, whom they could bring into this earth as perfect human beings."[1] They were not spiritual beings nor did they have souls. "Man's conscious existence as a living human creature is soul. He has no soul apart and distinct from his human body. Like the lower animal creatures, man alive is a living soul."[2] When confronted by the tempter, Eve was induced to violate the law of God, and Adam joined her. "By this lawless act they became guilty of sin, and so they brought upon themselves the penalty of sin."[3] "After Adam had used up the tremendous vitality of his once-perfect body, he died at the age of 930 years. This was within the symbolic 'day' of one thousand years that God had set."[4]

Inherited Sin

What of Adam's descendants? What of those who did not disobey God's law in Eden? The answer is that "all of Adam's offspring were born after his disobedience. Thus his offspring inherited sin and death from him."[5]

Jesus A Substitute For Adam

Jehovah required a perfect man as substitute for Adam. This is the only way that man can get life. "Divine justice demanded the life of the perfect man Adam and took that life. Divine justice could receive nothing as a substitute for Adam except the life of a perfect human being. Adam was put to death because he was a sinner. The one who would redeem Adam must die **as** a sinner, yet without sin. And all this Jesus did."[6]

The "Little Flock" And The "Other Sheep"

Some of those who follow Jesus as they learn perfect obedience will be chosen by God to become spirit beings who will enjoy eternal life in heaven. The great majority, however, will attain to everlasting life here on earth. "Jesus Christ is the Right Shepherd of all those who gain life through him in the righteous new world . . . Those following him who become his spiritual brothers and joint heirs in the Kingdom are comparatively few, just 144,000 in number, and so he calls them a 'little flock...' But not all who eventually gain life through the Right Shepherd enter into the Kingdom sheep-fold . . . These 'other sheep' are all others of human kind who acknowledge him as the one Right Shepherd who surrendered his soul for them to gain everlasting life. So they follow him as Shepherd and thus become members of his flock, though not of the Kingdom fold. They attain to eternal life on earth."[7]

The New Birth

Those who would walk in the way that leads to heavenly life must be born again in keeping with the requirements Jesus set before Nicodemus. It is to be a spiritual birth. "Not only God's spirit or invisible active force performs a part in this birth to heavenly life, but also what Jesus called 'water' plays its part first. Not the water of baptism, although heirs of heaven must copy their Forerunner and be immersed in water; but the water of the truth. Water has cleansing, purifying power, and so does the word of truth..."[8] Those who hear the truth and want to accept it must prove by their deeds that they accept it and that they have faith in God and in his Christ. "To symbolize his becoming dead to his own will, Jesus insisted upon being submerged under the waters of the Jordan river by God's prophet, John the Baptist. As he was thus immersed, he was praying, not confessing any sins, for he had none. His baptism was not for the forgiveness of sins, but was for symbolizing his dedication of himself to do God's will."[9] The one who hears the word of truth must prove his faith in it by becoming a follower of Christ, copying him by making an "unconditional, irrevocable presentation of himself to God to do the divine will." When he does this, he must have full faith in Christ as his ransom and as his sole means of gaining righteousness from God. "Does he then get baptized in water to symbolize this dedication of himself to God's sacred service? Yes, in imitation of Jesus and in obedience to his command, he gets baptized at the earliest opportunity as believers on the day of Pentecost did and as Saul of Tarsus and Cornelius did."[10]

What is it to be born of the spirit? "Just as the water from which a believer is born is not a person, neither is the spirit. But the believer is born from God and by means of his spirit or life-giving active force."[11] When

Jesus came forth from the water, God begot him as his spiritual son. He was also anointed with God's spirit and so became the Messiah or Anointed One.

The baptism in water was only a symbol. It was not Jesus' main baptism. "He must undergo a baptism into death by which he proved his complete integrity, obedience and faithfulness to God to the limit and by which also he laid down his human life as a ransom sacrifice for condemned mankind."[12]

Believers can also be baptized into Christ's death, and they can be resurrected to heavenly life. They must sacrifice their human lives in God's service, and they must relinquish the prospect of living as human creatures perfected in the righteous new world. "However, the 'little flock' who go to heaven are not the only ones who receive salvation. As we have seen, they will have earthly subjects. Jesus referred to these as his 'other sheep,' of whom 'a great crowd' are even now serving God faithfully."[13]

Members of the "little flock" know that God has called them to heavenly life because of the operation of God's spirit, which implants and cultivates in them the hope of heavenly life. The operation of God's spirit effects a change in the entire outlook of such a person so that his thoughts and prayers are centered upon serving God. Those who had believed in the immortality of the human soul and had hoped that their souls would go to heaven now know that according to God's inspired word the human soul dies and goes out of existence. "So those who die must depend on God to resurrect them to whatever place he wills for them."[14]

Baptism

What then, according to J. W. doctrine, does Christian baptism signify? "It is not a washing away of one's sins, because cleansing from sin comes only through faith in Jesus Christ (Ephesians 1:7). Rather it is a public demonstration testifying that one has made a solemn dedication to Jehovah God and is presenting himself to do His will."[15]

The fact that one has accepted the message of salvation, has devoted himself to God through Christ, and has been baptized in water, however, does not mean final salvation. It is only the beginning of obedience to God; it sets him on the way to everlasting life.[16]

The Kingdom

When he was upon the earth the first time, Jesus Christ, perfect in flesh and blood vindicated Jehovah's universal sovereignty by his complete faithfulness to the interests of God's Kingdom and also ransomed mankind. "He did provide the ransom, but God did not then establish the Kingdom with him . . . Christ's return being for him to rule in the Kingdom, then his second coming means his entering actively into the power of the Kingdom. When he ascended to heaven he sat down at God's right hand to wait for that time entering into his authority and ruling like Melchizedek over his enemies as his footstool . . . The evidence already considered proves that A.D. 1914 God's Kingdom was born and his Son was enthroned with authority to rule with an iron rod amid his foes . . . So A.D. 1914 marks the time of Christ's invisible return in spirit."[17]

The Kingdom has already come to power in the heavens and will soon take full charge of affairs on earth. While God's Kingdom by Christ will rule for all eternity, by the close of the first thousand years it will have accomplished a particular purpose toward the earth. "It will have removed every trace of unrighteousness."[18] Those who are resurrected to life on earth will have opportunity of gaining eternal life in paradise. They will have access to instruction from God in "Scrolls" that will be opened. They will be "judged individually according to their deeds"; those deeds will be the ones they do after being resurrected and after learning the contents of the "scrolls." "By responding to the education provided, even those who were once as dangerous as wild animals will change their ways, just as many have already done upon coming into association with the Christian congregation."[19]

"All humankind on earth will stand as perfect creatures before the throne of the Supreme Judge, Jehovah God — in every respect they will be equal to the first perfect humans in Eden." One final test will be given. Satan and his demons will be released from the abyss, and everyone may individually have the privilege of personally answering Satan's challenge to their heavenly Father. Those who remain loyal will be judged worthy of eternal life, and their names will be written in God's 'book of life.' Anyone who turns away in rebellion will be destroyed forever. "Never, no never, will the earth, or any part of God's vast universe, be disturbed again by sin and rebellion. Made into a paradise where righteousness prevails, the earth will serve for all time to come as a jewel of praise to Jehovah's name."[20]

Observations

A brief consideration of the preceding teaching in the light of the word of God, will show at the very outset that there are great contrasts between the teaching of Jehovah's Witnesses and the teaching of the Bible.

Man Has A Soul

Far from being like the lower animal creatures with no soul apart and distinct from his human body, man was created a little lower than the angels (Ps. 8:5); was made in the spiritual image of God (Gen. 1:26) for "God is spirit" (John 4:24); is capable of thinking, reasoning, communicating with his heavenly Father, whose offspring he is (Acts 17:28, 29); possesses a soul that no man can kill (Matt. 10:28), a soul that is conscious after death (Matt. 22:32; 17:3; Rev. 6:9-11).

Inherited Sin

Sin is a violation of God's law as Jehovah's Witnesses teach, but they err in saying that Adam's descendants inherited his sin. The Bible teaches that as a consequence of Adam's sin death passed upon all men because all sinned (Rom. 5:12; 3:23), but it nowhere teaches that all men have inherited Adam's sin. Rather, it teaches that each man is a free moral agent and that he is accountable for the sin he has committed, not inherited (Ezek. 18:19, 20; Matt. 12:36; 16:27; Rom. 14:12; II Cor. 5:10).

Jesus A Substitute For Adam

The idea that God refused to accept anything as a substitute for Adam except the life of a perfect human being (Christ) is a misrepresentation of both God and Christ. If Jesus served as a substitute for the sinner (Adam), it must necessarily follow that if God is just, when Christ paid the penalty for the sinner, God must let the sinner go free. God has no more claims on him or, we might add, on his descendants who, as Jehovah's Witnesses say, inherited his sin.

Our Lord's mission cannot be represented in this way. Jesus' propitiation reaches forward, as well as backward, and is especially for sins yet to be committed, to enable generations yet unborn to escape the penalties of sins they may commit. He died for us, for our sakes — He is the propitiation for our sins to redeem us — He gave his life a ransom for us, but nowhere is it said in our stead, or in Adam's stead, nor is this idea conveyed in a single passage in the New Testament.

> "A substitute must occupy the place of the principal. The place of the principal — the sinner — was spiritual alienation from God. Jesus Christ never was in spiritual alienation from God. The substitute must suffer the penalty to which the principal was doomed. The principal — the sinner — was doomed to eternal spiritual death. Jesus Christ never suffered spiritual death, nor the fires of the unquenchable **gehenna.** The principal is released from all the penalties paid by the substitute. Physical death was the death that was suffered by the Savior for sinners, but no mortal has been released from the pains of physical, temporal death. Therefore Jesus was not in any proper sense a substitute for the sinner.
>
> "He did not die a spiritual death, but He, by giving up a temporal, physical life so opened the way to eternal life that man through humble penitence and turning from his sins to God may escape, not temporal death, but still going down to the grave may gain eternal life through Jesus Christ our Lord."[21]

The "Little Flock" And The "Other Sheep"

The distinction between the "little flock" and the "other sheep" is unsupported by the scriptures. It rests upon a misuse of John 10:16, a passage that was fulfilled when Jesus brought Jew and Gentile together in one body (Eph. 2:11-18).

The New Birth

Jesus told Nicodemus that one must be born anew, or from above, in order to see the kingdom of God. Two verses later our Lord said that one must be born of water and the Spirit in order to enter the kingdom of God (John 3:3, 5). In instance after instance of conversion in the book of Acts, those who heard and believed the message revealed by the Holy Spirit to the apostles and other inspired men — the gospel —repented of their sins and were baptized in the name of Jesus Christ unto the remission of their sins. On the day of Pentecost, for example, the apostle Peter preached, and all that received his word were baptized, and the same day there were added to the church about three thousand souls. These entered the church, which is the kingdom (Acts 2:36-41; Col. 2:12; 1:13). They experienced the new birth.

Baptism

The Scriptures nowhere refer to baptism in water as a symbol of dedication of oneself to God's sacred service. It is rather the response of the obedience of faith to a command of the Lord and is unto the remission of sins. (Mark 16:15, 16; Acts 2:38; 22:16).

While salvation is by faith (Eph. 2:8), the scriptures do not say that it is by faith only. James tells us that we are not justified by faith only (James 2:24). Jesus said, "He that believeth and is baptized shall be saved" (Mark 16:16).

The Kingdom

The kingdom was not established in 1914 but on the Day of Pentecost in the city of Jerusalem, and Jesus Christ reigns on the throne of David over that kingdom now (Acts 2:29-38). Those in the days of the apostle Paul who were members of the church were also in the kingdom. Paul writes to members of the church at Colossae, speaking of God, "who delivered us out of the power of darkness, and translated us into the kingdom of the Son of his love" (Col. 1:13). The premillennial concept of the kingdom is manifestly false.

That those resurrected from the dead will have opportunity to study the "scrolls" and bring their lives into harmony with God's will at that time is an idea that is not found in the scriptures. The Bible offers no hope of a second chance (Luke 16:19-31; Acts 13:44-46; II Thess. 2:10-12; Heb. 10:26, 27).

In every area having to do with sin and salvation that we have considered, the teaching of Jehovah's Witnesses is at odds with the plain import of the Bible message. At no point is this fact clearer than in their treatment of baptism. "It is not a washing away of one's sins, because cleansing from sin comes only through faith in Jesus Christ."[22] This, in the face of Jesus' command, "He that believeth and is baptized shall be saved" (Mark 16:16); the apostle Peter's answer to the Jews on the Day of

Pentecost, "Repent ye, and be baptized every one of you in the name of Jesus Christ unto the remission of your sins..." (Acts 2:38); and Ananias' statement to Saul of Tarsus, "And now why tarriest thou? arise, and be baptized, and wash away thy sins, calling on his name" (Acts 22:16).

By an arbitrary and often capricious definition and use of scriptural terms, by the use of passage after passage without regard for proper context, and with unbounded imaginative speculation they pursue their unusually singular interpretation from the first book of the Bible to the last. It is especially important in this day of cults and cultism that the simplicity and purity of New Testament Christianity be held up in sharp contrast to every form of error.

FOOTNOTES

1. *The Truth That Leads To Eternal Life* (New York: Watchtower Bible and Tract Society, 1968), p. 31.
2. *This Means Everlasting Life* (Brooklyn: Watchtower Bible and Tract Society, 1950), p. 30.
3. *The Truth That Leads To Eternal Life,* p. 30.
4. Ibid, pp. 31, 32.
5. Ibid, p. 32.
6. J. F. Rutherford, *The Harp of God* (Brooklyn: International Bible Students Association, 1925), p. 135.
7. *This Means Everlasting Life,* pp. 236-238.
8. Ibid, p. 115.
9. Ibid, p. 117.
10. Ibid, p. 118.
11. Ibid.
12. Ibid, p. 119.
13. *The Truth That Leads To Eternal Life,* p. 75.
14. Ibid, p. 79.
15. *The Truth That Leads To Eternal Life,* pp. 183, 184.
16. *This Means Everlasting Life,* p. 181.
17. *This Means Everlasting Life,* pp. 220, 221.
18. *The Truth That Leads To Eternal Life,* p. 112.
19. Ibid, pp. 110, 111.
20. Ibid, pp. 112, 113.
21. David Lipscomb, "Living Pulpit," *Gospel Advocate,* Vol. X, No. 12 (March 19, 1868), p. 267.
22. *The Truth That Leads To Eternal Life,* p. 183.

Bibliography

Primary Sources:

Rutherford, J. F. *The Harp of God.* Brooklyn: International Bible Students Association, 1921.

Note: The two following books have no indication of authorship.

The Truth That Leads To Eternal Life. New York: Watchtower Bible and Tract Society, 1968.

This Means Everlasting Life. Brooklyn: Watchtower Bible and Tract Society, 1950.

General Works:

Hoekema, Anthony A. *The Four Major Cults.* Grand Rapids: Eerdmans, 1972.

Lambert, O. C. *Russellism Unveiled.* Port Arthur, Texas: Lambert & Son, 1940.

Martin, Walter R. *The Kingdom of the Cults.* Minneapolis: Bethany Fellowship, 1972.

Martin, Walter R. and Klann, Norman H. *Jehovah of the Watch Tower,* Rev. ed. Grand Rapids: Zondervan, 1959.

Tomlinson, L. G. Churches of Today. 10th Edition. Nashville, Tennessee: Gospel Advocate, 1962.

Wilhite, J. Porter. *Modern Churches and the church.* Oklahoma City, Oklahoma: Telegram Book Company, 1956.

Periodical:

Lipscomb, David. "Living Pulpit," *Gospel Advocate,* Vol. X, No. 12. (March 19, 1868), p. 267.

CHAPTER 8
"THE CHURCH, THE KINGDOM, AND THE MILLENNIUM ACCORDING TO JEHOVAH'S WITNESS DOCTRINE"

Darrell Conley

Introduction

The doctrines of the Jehovah's Witnesses (hereinafter referred to as J. W.'s regarding the church, the kingdom, and the millennium are so intertwined it is impossible to treat them separately. Their doctrine on these subjects falls on the ears of students of the Bible like fingernails scraping a chalkboard. It is an edifice built from passages torn from their contexts, fantasy, and exigency. The growth of the J. W.'s testifies to the capacity of human beings to believe almost anything so long as it pleases them; and their cabalistic treatment of the Bible is witness to their ability to see what is not there. The simple story of the gospel becomes in their hands a tortuous tale of a kingdom that both is and is not, of resurrections that are not resurrections, and of punishment that is not punishment. Their hope is of a bloody Armaggedon, a second chance at salvation during a literal millennium, and an eternal earth.

The Church

The church of Christ according to J. W.'s "consists of Jesus Christ the head and the 144,000 members of his body."[1] They have a distinct aversion to the word "church," almost invariably preferring "congregation." It always refers to the 144,000. This same group is variously called the anointed class, the chosen, the elect, the kingdom class, the little flock, the sanctuary class, the sons of Levi, and the new creation. According to Rutherford, "this new creation had its beginning with Jesus Christ at the time of his baptism in Jordan when he was begotten to the divine nature and anointed with the holy spirit without limitation."[2] (Notice the lack of capitals in the pronouns referring to Christ and in "holy spirit." The J. W.'s believe that Christ is a creature and that the Holy Spirit is a mere force.)

Do not confuse "the little flock" with "the other sheep." Only the 144,000, "the little flock," will spend eternity in heaven with Christ. The "other sheep" will, however, survive Armageddon and will spend eternity in a paradise here on earth. Although Russell made a distinction between two classes of spirit-begotten people, modern J. W.'s claim that "the other sheep" are not spirit-begotten. Russell also taught that the door to immortality would be closed in 1918, but since the J. W.'s grew so far past the 144,000 mark, they recognized in 1931 "the other sheep." This group is also called "Jonadabs." This term is taken from II Kings 10:15-28 and Jeremiah 35. Just as Jonadab, who was not an Israelite, dwelt in Israel and assisted them, the Jonadabs today are not of the anointed class but will be rewarded on earth if they follow "the little flock."

Thus the church, according to J. W.'s, consists only of the 144,000 and had its beginning at the baptism of Christ. But it is not exactly the same as the kingdom. "The Church at present, therefore, is not the Kingdom of God set up in power and glory, but in its incipient, embryo condition."[3] So Russell wrote in 1886. The J. W.'s teach that the church apostatized soon after its establishment and was not restored until Russell began his Bible class in the 1870's. The final release from "Babylonish captivity," however, did not occur until 1919.[4] The J. W.'s look on all other churches as being false and servants of Satan.

The Bible knows nothing of two classes of Christians. There is one body, not two (Eph. 4:4). Christ died to make of Jew and Gentile "one new man, so making peace; and might reconcile them both in one body" (Eph. 2:15-16). "For even as we have many members in one body, and all the members have not the same office: so we, who are many are one body in Christ" (Romans 12:4-5). "For in one Spirit were we all baptized into one body" (I Cor. 12:13). The J. W.'s baptize all of their members, but teach that only a few enter the body, the rest, "the other sheep," are left outside the body.

They base their doctrine on a perversion of Revelation 7. They contrast the 144,000 sealed out of the twelve tribes of Israel, which they take to be the church, "the anointed class," with the great multitudes of verse 9, which they claim are "the other sheep," those who will never make it to heaven. They arbitrarily take the obviously ideal number of 144,000 as literal, while considering the Jewishness of those 144,000 as figurative. They claim the great multitude of verse 9 will never get to heaven, but will remain eternally in a paradise here on earth. Yet where does Revelation 7 place this group? Standing before the Lamb (verse 9), in the temple of God (verse 15), where the sun will not strike them (verse 16), and where the Lamb and God are (verse 17). In Revelation 14:3 the 144,000 are said to be before the throne. If that puts them in heaven, why doesn't the same language in Revelation 7:9 do the same for "the great multitude," alias "the other sheep"?

The church, of course, did not begin at the baptism of Jesus. Long after His baptism, Jesus said that the church was yet future (Matt. 16:18). It did begin on Pentecost as recorded in Acts 2:37-47. Later, in Acts 11:15, Peter refers to the events on that day of Pentecost as "the beginning."

Acts 2:36-47 makes it clear that all who gladly received the gospel and were baptized were added by the Lord to the church. Although we do not join the church, we choose either to become part of the body of Christ or not by either choosing to obey the gospel or not, since all who obey are added to the church. "Not so," say the J. W.'s. "Those brought into the congregation are selected or chosen by God through Jesus Christ, the one first chosen. They do not gain entrance to the congregation of their own accord or desire..."[5] Thus, God picks and chooses some to be a part of the church and go to heaven, and the greater number to be part of "the other sheep" to remain eternally on earth. How contrary this is to what Peter taught at the house of Cornelius: "Of a truth I perceive that God is no respecter of persons: but in every nation he that feareth him, and worketh righteousness, is acceptable to him" (Acts 10:34-35).

As far as the work of the church is concerned, the J. W.'s believe that they are to publish abroad what they call "the Kingdom message." But whether or not people accept it or reject it is evidently of little importance, since almost everyone (as we shall see later) will be "resurrected" and given a second chance. In fact, this present age, from the death of Christ until "Armageddon," seems of little consequence. Russell says,

> The conversion of the world in the present age was not expected of the Church, but that her mission has been to preach the gospel in all the world *for a witness* [italics his] and to prepare herself under divine direction for her great future work. God has not yet by any means exhausted his power for the world's conversion. Nay, more: he has not yet *even attempted* [italics his] the world's conversion.[6]

How different from the urgency of the words of Christ: "Say not ye, There are yet four months, and then cometh the harvest? behold, I say unto you, Lift up your eyes, and look on the fields, that they are white already unto harvest" (John 4:35).

The Kingdom

As we have seen, the J. W.'s teach that the same 144,000 make up the church and the kingdom. But the church and the kingdom are not exactly the same. The church had its beginning at the baptism of Christ, whereas the kingdom did not have its beginning until October 1, 1914. Russell wrote in 1886, "Serious has been the error introduced into the nominal Christian Church, which misinterprets this promised kingdom to mean the Church nominal in its present condition..."[7] "The undefeatable purpose of Jehovah God to establish a righteous kingdom in these last days was fulfilled in A.D. 1914."[8]

But since the Bible is too plain in teaching that the church and kingdom are the same institution and that it was established in about A.D. 30, the J. W.'s must give a slight nod in that direction:

> True, there is a sense in which the Church is the Kingdom of God on earth . . . In the parables of our Lord, the Church is frequently called the kingdom; and the Apostle speaks of it as the kingdom over which Christ now reigns, saying that God hath translated us out of the kingdom of darkness into the kingdom of his dear Son...[9]

But having admitted this, Russell then hastens to deny it on the same page:

When the parables of our Lord are carefully examined, it will be found that they clearly teach that the coming or setting up of the kingdom of God in power is future; and as a matter of course, not until the King comes[10]

Russell has not rid himself of his problem; he has only contradicted himself. The kingdom was future at the time Christ spoke His parables, but it was not future after its establishment on Pentecost. Russell said in 1886 that the coming of the kingdom *in power* was yet future. But Jesus said, "There are some here of them that stand by, who shall in no wise taste of death, till they see the kingdom of God come with power" (Mark 9:1). In Luke 24:49 He said, "Tarry ye in the city, until ye be clothed with power from on high." In Acts 1:8 He told His apostles, "But ye shall receive power, when the Holy Spirit is come upon you." The kingdom was to come with power during the lifetime of some in the first century. The power was to come when the Holy Spirit came. The Holy Spirit came on the day of Pentecost. It therefore follows with the force of a demonstration that the kingdom came in power on Pentecost. On that day it came fully and in power. It came with visible and audible signs of power. How absurd to say, "Oh, no. It didn't come then; it came secretly, when Christ came secretly on October 1, 1914"! But what can you expect from the people who brought you the end of the world in 1975.

In 1921 Judge Rutherford had the gall to write:

The chief thing to be restored is the human race to life; and since other Scriptures definitely fix the fact that there will be a resurrection of Abraham, Isaac, Jacob, and other faithful ones of old, and that these will have the first favor, we may expect 1925 to witness the return of these faithful men of Israel from the condition of death, being resurrected and fully restored to perfect humanity and made the visible, legal representatives of the new order of things on earth.[12]

The J. W.'s said, "Yes, in a sense the kingdom did begin in the first century, but not really. Just wait till 1914."

The Times of the Gentiles extend to 1914, and the heavenly kingdom will not have full sway till then.[13] We consider it an established truth that the final end of the kingdom of this world, and the full establishment of the Kingdom of God, will be accomplished at the end of A.D. 1914.[14]

But the end did not come. What did they say then? Russell simply denied what he had been preaching for over 30 years:

Studying God's Word, we have measured the 2,520 years, the seven symbolic times, from that year 606 B.C. and found that it reached down to October 1914, as nearly as we were able to reckon. We did not say positively that this would be the year."[15]

As we have seen Rutherford predicted the end in 1925. When that date failed, did it stop him? Of course not. In 1929 he had a house built to house the Old Testament patriarchs after their resurrection. On December 24, 1929 the property was deeded over to them, but Rutherford lived in it, not Abraham, Isaac, and Jacob and when Rutherford died in 1942, the property was sold. In 1975 we were being told by the J. W.'s that the kingdom was about to break forth. But that year came and went, and they remain unashamed.

What is the nature of this tardy kingdom that the J. W.'s claim is here, but not here? Those in the kingdom (the 144,000) are to rule the world.[16] They claim that the 144,000, beginning in 1918, have been changed into invisible spirit creatures. (Those yet living will be changed at death).[17] They rule and will continue to rule over the world and the "other sheep." But one day (they have believed since 1914 that the time is at hand) God will "forcibly" establish the kingdom in the world."[18]

> The very purpose of the Kingdom is to crush out rebellion and restore righteousness universally. Hence, Satan and his wicked organization will be destroyed beneath the irresistible power of that theocratic government.[19]

Armageddon

This final crushing of the nations of the world will occur in a literal, bloody battle called Armageddon. Valerie Tomsett, a former J. W., says:

> To Jehovah's Witnesses, Armageddon is the beginning and the end of all their religion and beliefs. Their expectation is survival — the hope that they and they alone, will live through the dreaded Battle of Armageddon. Everything, and I cannot emphasize this too strongly, literally everything, hangs on this. It is this belief that keeps them knocking on doors in all weathers, year in and year out.[20]

If this sounds too strong, listen to the J. W.'s themselves describe the greatest benefit of being a J. W.:

> Finally, and above all other benefits, comes the satisfaction of seeing his heavenly Father's name and sovereignty vindicated by the eternal destruction of Satan's wicked world with all its supporters.[21]

Valerie Tomsett tells of one young J. W. who told his playmates that Jesus was soon going to kill them. They ran screaming home.[22] In 1941, Rutherford counselled J. W.'s to wait until after Armageddon to have children.[23] When William Whelan wrote his book *Armageddon Around the Corner* in 1962, he offered to refund the purchase price if Armageddon came before the reader finished the book![24] Needless to say, it was a safe offer.

The Millennium

The close of the battle of Armageddon, which will be won by the J. W.'s against the combined military might of the world, will usher in the millennium.[25] No one but J. W.'s will have survived Armageddon.[26] The earth will become a paradise — peace and plenty for all forever. Death will vanish except for a very few, e.g., those who refuse to obey Jehovah. Children will be born to those who survive Armageddon, but they will be without flaw.

Many of the dead will be "resurrected" during the millennium. Since the J. W.'s teach that the soul dies with the body, what they mean by death is not separation of body and spirit as the Bible teaches (James 2:26), but annihilation; and resurrection is not really resurrection, but recreation. In effect, God has your blueprint on file and will just remake you. The J. W.'s describe it as a "reactivating of the life pattern of the creature."[27]

It seems that the majority of mankind will be reactivated. "The greater mass of humankind will find life here on earth amid paradise conditions."[28] But some will not be "raised": those who died in the battle of Armageddon, those who are too wicked, those who have sinned against the "holy spirit," and various others — Adam and Eve, Cain, the people of Sodom, and Judas.

The righteous dead will be raised to eternal life on earth, and the unrighteous dead raised to be given a second chance, called "the resurrection of judgment." Judgment Day will extend throughout the millennium. It is not a judgment as much as it is a test. If the reactivated pass the test, they will receive eternal life on earth. If not, God will simply pull the plug on them. But most will pass the test and live happily ever after. That is, if they and everyone else can pass the final exam. At the close of the millennium Satan and his demons will be loosed and will attempt to lead everyone astray. Satan and all who follow him will be cast into the lake of fire and there annihilated. It evidently does not disturb J. W.'s that even their "tame Bible" the New World Translation, says, "And the Devil who was misleading them was hurled into the lake of fire and sulphur, where both the wild beast and the false prophet already were; and they will be tormented day and night forever and ever" (Rev. 20:10). How can one who has been annihilated be tormented forever and ever?

The Bible teaches that the soul survives the death of the body. Jesus said, "And fear not them which kill the body, but are not able to kill the soul" (Matt. 10:28). But if the soul dies when the body dies, then anyone who killed the body would also kill the soul. This would make the Lord's statement untrue. The story of the rich man and Lazarus in Luke 16 plainly teaches the survival of the soul after death.

The Bible teaches that some will be punished forever. "And these shall go away into everlasting punishment" (Matt. 25:46). But the Bible knows nothing about a second chance after death. "It is appointed unto men once to die, but after this cometh judgment" (Hebrews 9:27).

Conclusion

If nothing else, the J. W. doctrines of the church, the kingdom, and the millenium vividly demonstrate the absurdity of the idea that there is no danger in speculative eschatology. Such speculation warps the very fabric of the Bible and colors one's approach to every verse and "will eat as doth a gangrene" (II Tim. 2:17).

FOOTNOTES

1. J. F. Rutherford, *The Harp of God* (Watch Tower Bible and Tract Society, Brooklyn, N.Y., 1921), p. 279.
2. Ibid, p. 279.
3. C. T. Russell, *The Plan of the Ages*, Vol. I (Watch Tower Bible and Tract Society, Brooklyn, N.Y., 1886), p. 284.
4. *Qualified To Be Ministers* (Watch Tower Bible and Tract Society, Brooklyn, N.Y., 1955), pp. 292, 296.
5. *Let God Be True* (Watch Tower Bible and Tract Society, Brooklyn, N.Y., 1946), p. 128.
6. *The Plan of the Ages*, Vol. I, p. 95.
7. Ibid, p. 282.
8. *Let God Be True*, p. 143.
9. *The Plan of the Ages*, Vol. I, p. 283.
10. Ibid, p. 283.
11. *The Harp of God*, p. 303.
12. J. F. Rutherford, *Millions Now Living Will Never Die!* (International Bible Students Association, 1920), p. 88.
13. *The Watchtower*, March 1880, p. 2.
14. *The Time Is At Hand*, (Watch Tower Bible and Tract Society, Brooklyn, N.Y., 1886), p. 99.
15. *The Watchtower*, November 1, 1914.
16. *The Plan of the Ages*, Vol. I, p. 275.
17. *Let God Be True*, pp. 138, 139.
18. *The Plan of the Ages*, Vol. I, p. 283.
19. *Let God Be True*, p. 142.
20. Valerie Tomsett, *Watch Tower Chaos*, (Lakeland, 1974), p. 21.
21. *Let God Be True*, p. 233.
22. *Watch Tower Chaos*, p. 26.
23. Ibid, p. 29.
24. Ibid, p. 27.
25. *You May Survive Armageddon* (Watch Tower Bible and Tract Society, Brooklyn, N.Y.), pp. 338, 339.
26. Ibid, p. 347.
27. *Make Sure of All Things* (Watch Tower Bible and Tract Society, Brooklyn, N.Y.), p. 311.
28. *Let God Be True*, p. 279.

CHAPTER 9
"HELL" UNDER JEHOVAH'S WITNESS DOCTRINE

Goebel Music

Introduction

This great lectureship reminds me just a little of the statement of Acts 17:6, in which it is declared of the early Christians: "These that have turned the world upside down are come hither also." I am fully convinced if we do not **get off the defense and on the offense,** we'll never take the world for Christ. Although we have had some measure of success in growth, if you'll investigate the matter candidly you'll soon reach the conclusion that we are not stirring the world as did the church of the first century.

One of the great reasons that the early church turned the world upside down was because of their militancy, their aggressiveness, their appeal to and use of the sword of the Spirit. They refused to accept the view that the gospel was just another religious message, one of many. They were convinced that men were lost and that the gospel and the gospel only was God's power to save (Rom. 1:16; I Cor. 1:18). This is why we find them going into the midst of the Jewish doctors of the law (Acts 2, 3, 9), to the Greek doctors of philosophy (Acts 17), to the Samaritans (Acts 8), to the Gentiles (Acts 10-11) and even preaching to those in wayside places (Acts 8:26ff). They did not sneak in, slip in, slide in, slink in, steal in, slither in, skim or skid in, they very boldly, bravely, brazenly and barefacedly went right into their midst declaring there was but one God, one church, salvation was in Christ, the only begotten Son of God and they preached him as the crucified, buried and resurrected Messiah and dared them to refute it. And, brethren, until we get back to that type of preaching, being completely surrendered to the Master, with faithfulness to Christ above every thing else, we will never, in our lifetime, see the gospel carried to every creature.

Only out of genuine love and deep concern for the souls of men do we exhibit the differences between the doctrines of men and those revealed by the Holy Spirit of God. To those who would accuse us otherwise, let me hasten to point out that the Jehovah's Witnesses do the same thing. In the 1946 edition of *Let God Be True* they publicly state their love to all religious groups, and then declare: "...false principles of all religions are attacked by Jehovah's Witnesses, who expose such harmful theories and traditions of men to the truth of God's Word, the Bible."[1] They then add: "Exposing of religious errors and revealing Bible truths does not disturb the honest person desiring to serve God."[2] Therefore, let me hasten to say that **true love** in the heart of every child of God **demands two things:** (1) **preaching** the gospel to every creature (Mark 16:15-16; I Cor. 1:21), and (2) **defending** that power of God to save when it is attacked by various teachers of error (I John 4:1; I Peter 3:15; Jude 3; I Thess. 5:21; Phil. 1:15). As G. K. Wallace said: "Fighting Christians are loving servants." When the heart is properly motivated, and with the truth of God at stake, there is no need for anyone to get upset at the denunciation, disclosure and divulgence of that which is contrary to the will of the Master.

The subject assigned me in this, the sixth Spiritual Sword Lectureship, is: " 'Hell' Under the Jehovah's Witness' Doctrine." To fully treat this subject in such a short space is an impossibility, however, there are a few items in their maneuverings to get rid of the Biblical doctrine of hell that we must point out. I believe these listings are a must to help us understand their view of "hell," and also a must to make its progression of thought logical for our comprehension.

No Man Has Or Possesses A Soul

J. F. Rutherford in his book entitled *Riches,* says "it is a lie" to say that when the body dies his soul lives on forever. In fact, he says this is "Satan's lie."[3] He then says, on the next page, that "one lie needs support by another lie." Do you want to know what the other lie is? It is that man has an immortal soul. "God says that every man is a soul. No man has or possesses a soul."[4] To further substantiate this *The Truth That Leads To Eternal Life,* a book copyrighted in 1968 by the Watch Tower Bible & Tract Society, says: "Since the human soul is man himself, then it cannot be some shadowy thing that merely inhabits the body or that can exist apart from the person . . . Yes, your soul is really you, with all your physical and mental qualities . . . when the person dies, it is the human soul that dies."[5] In their book, *Make Sure Of All Things Hold Fast To What Is Fine,* it is stated again in these words: "Man himself is a soul . . . human soul dies; not immortal."[6] In Series V of *Studies In The Scriptures,* we read: "The body of the dog that had never been animated would not be a dog; it requires first the infusion of the spark of life, the breath of life, then doghood begins . . . according to the Scriptural account every dog is a soul, every horse is a soul, every cow is a soul, every bird and every fish are souls."[7] "...man is a combination of two things, namely, the 'dust of the ground' and 'the breath of life.' The combining of these two things (or elements) produced a living soul or creature called man . . . Thus we see that the claim of religionists that man has an immortal soul, and therefore differs from the beast, is not Scriptural."[8]

A man would be foolish, indeed, to deny that the Hebrew **nephesh** refers to a breathing being (Gen. 1:20, 21, 24, 30). In Genesis 2:7 only the natural, physical body of Adam is mentioned, not the spiritual (I Cor. 15: 44-45). The soul is biological life (cf. Exodus 21: 23; Matt. 2:20) and was mortal (cf. Num. 23:10). When this breath, animating principle, leaves the body of a "living soul" you have a dead soul (cf. Num. 5:2; 6:6). However, to restrict the meaning of the word **nephesh** (Greek **psuche**) is to admit one's ignorance of the scriptures. The meaning is usually determined by the context. Indeed, there is no doubt that the word soul is used to refer to the animating principle of life (Acts 2:41, 43; Rom. 13:1; I Pet. 3:20). But I deny that this is the only way the word is used! **Note the following:**

1) God is said to have a soul (Heb. 10:38; Matt. 12:18; Isaiah 1:14; Lev. 26:11,30). Since God is a spirit (John 4:24) he has no animating principle. Soul and spirit must be the same.
2) Man's soul, physical life, can die (Gen. 37:21; Num. 31:19), but his spiritual, immortal soul cannot die (Matt. 10:28).
3) Man does possess a soul (Gen. 35:18; Psalms 103:1; Rev. 20:4 and I Kings 17:21).
4) Two verses that show beyond a doubt that the soul lives after bodily life ceases are Matthew 10:28 and Revelation 6:9-10.
5) The Bible states there is an "outer" man and there is an "inner" man (II Cor. 4:16).
6) Other verses could be added to this list, such as the thoughts found in I Peter 1:9; Luke 21:19; Matt. 26:41; and a comparison of Heb. 10:39 with I Cor. 5:5. In addition, the various actions, emotions and feelings of the soul could be cited, like Gen. 34:8; Ez. 18:20; Acts 2:43; Psalms 57:1; Job 14:22; II Kings 4:27; Psalms 43:5; 42:6; etc.

Man's Spirit Is Sustained By Breathing

In the 1965 edition of *Make Sure Of All Things Hold Fast To What Is Fine,* I find the following statement: "Active life force in earthly creatures; sustained by breathing."[9] This, then, according to their view, has the spirit of man as that which cannot suffer torment. In this section of the above-mentioned book they list several references to prove their dogma, such as: Gen 7:22; Job 27:3-4; Ecc. 3:19; 12:7; Gen. 6:17; Psalms 104:30; etc.

There is nothing in these verses that would sustain the idea of a life force sustained by breathing, also the word spirit (Greek **pneuma**) has more than one meaning (John 3:8; IIThess. 2:8; Matt. 4:1; etc.). "Spirit" is used of the invisible part of man, that is, it is not inanimate for it "knows" (I Cor. 2:11). It is the part of man that will be saved in the day of the Lord Jesus (I Cor. 5:5). God alone is the source of immortality (I Tim. 6:16). His Spirit is eternal (Heb. 9:14), and so is man's (John 11:25-26). Man was made in the **image** of God (Gen. 1:26), and this must mean spirit for that is what God is (John 4:24), and a spirit does not have flesh and bones (Luke 24:39). Man's spirit was "formed in man by the Lord" (Zech. 12:1). **Note the following:**

1) God is termed the "Father of spirits" (Heb. 12:9).
2) The spirit is to return unto God who gave it (Ecc. 12:7).
3) It is used to designate the inner man (Luke 23:46; Acts 7:59; Heb. 12:22f).
4) God is said to be the God of the living and Jesus had just mentioned Abraham, Isaac and Jacob, therefore, though their bodies had decayed they were yet alive (Matt. 22:23-32).
5) A person can live apart from the body (II Cor. 5:6-8).
6) Their idea would make absurd such verses as Matt. 26:41; Acts 7:59.
7) The corpse of Dorcas was present but she was not present (Acts 9:36ff).

Death Means Unconscious Existence

The Jehovah's Witnesses will disavow any conscious existence of the soul after death. Therefore, I cannot accurately describe their position as psychopannychism, for to them there is no soul to sleep after death. The idea is more one of soul-extinction, as no soul survives after death. When man dies he becomes completely nonexistent.[10] "...death is a period of absolute unconsciousness—more than that, it is a period of absolute non-existence,..."[11] In chapter five of *The Truth That Leads To Eternal Life,* entitled "Where are the Dead?" I find this statement, "Simply stated, death is the opposite of life... Where was Adam before God formed him from the dust and gave him life? Why, he simply did not exist. At his death Adam returned to the same lifeless, unconscious state... The Bible clearly teaches that the dead are unconscious and lifeless in the grave."[12]

Basically, one can be dead yet not annihilated or non-existent. **Note the following:**

1) "...for in the day that thou eatest thereof thou shalt surely die" (Gen. 2:17).
2) "But Jesus said unto him, Follow me; and leave the dead to bury the dead" (Matt. 8:22).
3) "...for this thy brother was dead, and is alive again; and was lost, and is found" (Luke 15:32).
4) "Wherefore, my brethren, ye also were made dead to the law through the body of Christ; that ye should be joined to another, even to him who was raised from the dead,..." (Rom. 7:4).
5) "For I through the law died unto the law, that I might live unto God" (Gal. 2:19).
6) "But she that giveth herself to pleasure is dead while she liveth" (I Tim. 5:6).
7) Samuel did not cease to exist when he died (I Sam. 28). Moses and Elijah, long after their death, came back and spoke to Jesus (Matt. 17:3). Lazarus and the rich man did not cease to exist at death (Luke 16:19-31). This is also true of those slain for the Word of God (Rev. 6:9ff).

Sheol And Hades Mean Grave

Accompanying the teaching of non-existence at death is always the false teaching that hades is mankind's grave. They say the Hebrew word **sheol** and the Greek word **hades** means grave. They go to great lengths to show that these words do not designate eternal torment. Because these words are sometimes translated by the English word "hell" they seek to establish that there is no eternal punishment. They simply say that "grave" is the receptacle of the body, where it returns to dust. This is the meaning given to it in *Make Sure Of All Things Hold Fast To What Is Fine.*[13] "In the Hebrew Scriptures of the Bible the word 'hell' is translated from the word **sheol**...The **King James Version** of the Bible,...translates it 31 times as 'hell,' 31 times as 'grave,' and 3 times as 'pit.' The **Catholic Douay Version** of the Bible translates **sheol** as 'hell' 63 times and 'pit' once and 'death' once. In the Christian Greek Scriptures the word 'hell' is sometimes translated from the Greek word **hades.**"[14]

Concerning **hades,** W. E. Vine says "...it has been unhappily rendered 'hell' (Psalms 16:10) and 'grave' (Gen. 37:35)...it never denotes the grave, nor is it the permanent region of the lost."[15] He goes on to say that it is defined as the unseen state of both the righteous dead and unrighteous dead (Luke 23:43; Acts 2:31; Luke 16:19-31). The best description of hades is found in Luke 16:23-26, a place for the righteous separated by a gulf from the place for the unrighteous. Thayer says it is "the common receptacle of disembodied spirits."[16] **Sheol** is the Old Testament equivalent for **hades. Note the following:**

1) In the preface of the **Revised Version** of 1885 it is stated: "The Hebrew word **Sheol** which signifies the abode of departed spirits, and corresponds to the Greek **Hades**...is variously rendered in the **Authorized Version** by grave, pit and hell...with the marginal note 'Heb. SHEOL' to indicate that it DOES NOT signify the place of burial..."[17]
2) "So these two words, which the *King James* translators translated hell, do not mean the grave. They refer to the unseen region where departed spirits are received. Greek lexicographers who agree with this include the giants of that field: Thayer, Robertson, Vincent, Wuest."[18]
3) To help answer their arguments on verses like Psalms 16:10; Acts 2:27-31; Ecc. 9:10 etc., one need only remember Ecc. 12:7.
4) If hell means only the grave, then only the wicked will be turned into a grave (Psalms 9:17). Where will the righteous be buried?
5) If hell means grave, children who receive correct training will never go to the grave (Pro. 23:13-14).
6) When Christ raised Lazarus from the dead, from where did he come? The answer again is Ecc. 12:7.
7) Many are the verses difficult for them to explain if **sheol** and **hades** mean the grave: Isaiah 14:9; Ez. 32:27; Psalms 6:5; I Sam. 28; Matt. 17:3-4; Rev. 6:9-11; etc.

Their Usage Of Gehenna

Jehovah's Witnesses are quick to point out that the Greek word **Gehenna** is a transliteration of the Hebrew **Ge Hinnom** and means literally "The Valley of Hinnom." When they point out the history of the place they are correct (II Kings 16:3; 1:6; 13:10; II Chr. 28:3; 33:6), but highly incorrect when they say "**Gehenna** alludes to city dump and incinerator outside Jerusalem; symbolizes second death."[19] Since they teach that the grave is the end and since Jesus talks of a hell of fire, they must do something. In their book, *Let God Be True,* they speak of **Gehenna** as everlasting destruction or extinction.[20] Also, they say that **Gehenna** means a condition of death from which there will be no resurrection.[21] "When Jesus said that persons would be thrown into **Gehenna** for their bad deeds, what did he mean? Not that they would be tormented forever. Jesus used that valley of fire and brimstone as a proper symbol of everlasting destruction."[22]

Let the serious student of the Bible examine the passages where the Master used the word **Gehenna** (twelve times so used by the Holy Spirit and eleven were directly from Jesus: Matt. 5:22, 29-30; 10:28; 18:9; 23:15, 33; Mark 9:43-47; Luke 12:5; James 3:6). If a person will just half way study these, he will find that Jesus gave the word a spiritual sense. He certainly did not mean that men would be cast into the literal valley of Hinnom. **Note the following:**

1) Jesus spoke of something other than death (Luke 12:5).
2) Jesus spoke of God's ability to destroy both soul and body in hell (Matt. 10:28).
3) Men can kill and that is all they can do, but God can go beyond that and destroy in hell after death.
4) This makes their teaching incorrect when they say that death is the highest penalty known . . . no punishment could be greater..."[23]
5) **Gehenna** refers to the place of eternal punishment (Matt. 25:46).
6) Question: "If hell is nothing more than death, why fear God more than man?" What is it that God can do that man cannot do?
7) What is the "sorer punishment" of Hebrews 10:29?
8) Since they admit it "symbolizes second death," all we need to prove for the second death is such verses as Rev. 21:8; 20:10; 14:10-11 and these clearly state the second death is fire and brimstone.

Fire Is Symbolical

In reference to the "second death" and the description of it by the words "fire and brimstone," they state it is symbolic torment, "not eternal torment in fire . . . torment with fire is also symbolic."[24] They also say that the lake of fire is a symbol because death and hades are thrown into it (Rev. 20:14; 21:8).

If it does symbolize something, that something is eternal punishment. Note carefully the passage of Rev. 14:11 about the smoke going up for ever and ever and then ask yourself if that comes from their torment. Another thought is that even if the fire is symbolical, the torment is not. Why use the words "for ever and ever" if, as they teach, death means annihilation and that instantaneous? Then, too, even if death and hades are figures it does not necessarily mean that the fire is. The passage clearly says "...if any was not found written in the book of life, he was cast into the lake of fire." Who is the "he"?

Eternal Punishment

Jehovah's Witnesses say the word "eternal" or "everlasting" when used in connection with punishment means that it is eternal in the sense that it is done and over with and will not be repeated. "The doctrine of eternal torment in hell is another one of Satan's vicious lies, which lies are taught to the people only by religionists, and the purpose of this Devil lie is to turn people away from God . . . Hell means the condition of death, not a place of torture. When a man prefers to continue in wickedness, God mercifully puts him to sleep in death, and that man never again awakens."[25] "The simple truth about the matter is that when a person dies, he is dead, unconscious, and knows nothing."[26] "It is absurd to suppose that God would perpetuate Adam's existence forever in torment for any kind of a sin which he could commit, but especially for the comparatively small offense of eating forbidden fruit."[27]

In reference to the idea of "eternal punishment," Rutherford said: "Is it reasonable that God gives that creature an asbestos body so that he can be burned forever?"[28] "If hell is a place of eternal torment, and if the Devil is the chief fireman, who is going to keep up the fire when the Devil is destroyed?"[29] These two quotes are given just to show his deliberate attempts to sway the minds of the untaught.

In Matthew 25:46 Jesus said, "And these shall go away into eternal punishment: but the righteous into eternal life" (**note,** it is the punishment and not the results, as they say, that is eternal). The Greek word for "eternal" is **aionion,** and this is the same word that the Lord used to describe eternal life. The same word that is used to describe the life of the righteous is used to describe the punishment of the wicked. If one holds that punishment is not eternal then he would have to, to be consistent, hold that the life of the righteous is not eternal, for whatever is said of the one is said of the other. This certainly is in harmony with Revelation 14:11 which states that the wicked are punished "for ever and ever." Again, in Revelation 14:10-11 it is said that they have no rest day and night. **Note the following:**

1) It is well that they learn the meaning of the word "destroy," as they seemingly think it can only mean annihilation or extinction. The Greek **apollumi** denotes ruin, loss, not of being but of well-being."[30] It occurs 85 times and means destroy, perish, lose.
2) The word "destruction" in II Thessalonians 1:9 is from **olethros,** and, according to Thayer means "the loss of a life of blessedness after death, future misery."[31]
3) Even though they translate **kolasis** as "cutting off," there is no authoritative translation that I know of or Greek lexicon which will bear this out. Thayer says it means "punishment."[32] Arndt and Gingrich state it means to "undergo punishment, continued torment, injury" and as the number two meaning says it is "divine retribution, punishment."[33] Matthew 25:46 is tough on them!
4) It is from **basanizo** (Revelation 20:10) that we have the word "tormented" and, according to Thayer it means "to vex with grievous pains."[34] Others say that it means "to torment, or vex, to put to torture." Evidently the punishment of Matthew 25:46 means the same as "tormented" in Revelation 20:10 (cf. verses 14-15; 14:9-11).

Conclusion

We need to see the progression of thoughts in the teaching of the Jehovah's Witnesses. It would be easy to believe what they do about man to perhaps ease their consciences. If man does not have a soul within, then the possibility of suffering torment in hell for their disobedience to God is greatly reduced.

It seems to me that much of their trouble comes from the mistranslation of the words, **sheol** and **hades** by the King James translators. In fact, about half of the chapter dealing with "hell" in *Let God Be True,* is built on the mistranslation of these words and their misunderstanding of the true message. It seems that a good way to help clear this problem up would be to use the *American Standard Version.* A correct understanding of the words employed would greatly aid them in their understanding of orthodoxy. I do not just mean the word **sheol** and **hades** either!

Our God is a consuming fire (Hebrews 12:29), an unsparing God. Divine love is limited by the perverse freewill of man. God's love lays upon him the obligation to punish transgression, a fact seen throughout all the word of God. To prove this we can look at those of Noah's day and also those of Sodom.

I know of no other group on earth that teaches such a damnable heresy as do the Jehovah's Witnesses. With all my soul I love their soul, but I detest the teaching that continues to cause such havoc among people. I highly compliment their zeal, but what is zeal without knowledge? (Romans 10:1ff).

If you were taught that you had no soul, that the spirit was just an active life force sustained by breathing, that death is an unconscious existence, that hell is the grave, that Gehenna was nothing but a city dump, fire was symbolical, well, why would you be concerned about eternal punishment — what would be the use for it? Such is the teaching of the Jehovah's Witnesses that relate to eternal punishment.

FOOTNOTES

1. Watch Tower, *"Let God Be True"*(Brooklyn, New York: Watch Tower Bible and Tract Society, Inc., 1946), p. 221.
2. Ibid, p. 222.
3. Rutherford, J. F., *Riches* (Brooklyn, New York: Watch Tower, 1936), p. 179.
4. Ibid, p. 180.
5. Rutherford, J. F., *The Truth that leads to Eternal Life* (Pennsylvania: Watch Tower Bible and Tract Society), Copyright 1968, pp. 36-37.
6. Watch Tower, *"Make Sure of All Things — Hold Fast to What is Fine"*(Pennsylvania: Watch Tower Bible and Tract Society, 1965), p. 403.
7. Watch Tower, *Studies in the Scripture,* Series 5, *The Atonement* (Brooklyn London: International Bible Students Association, 1913), p. 323.
8. *"Let God Be True",* op. cit., pp. 59-60.
9. *"Make Sure of All Things — Hold Fast to What is Fine,"* op. cit., p. 466.
10. Hoekema, Anthony A., *The Four Major Cults* (Minneapolis: Bethany Fellowship, Inc., Publishing Company, 1963.
11. *Studies in the Scripture,* Series 5, op. cit., p. 329.
12. *The Truth that leads to Eternal Life,* op. cit., p. 324.
13. *"Make Sure of All Things — Hold Fast to What is Fine,"* op. cit., pp. 448-449.
14. *The Truth That Leads to Eternal Life,* op. cit., p. 41.

15. Vine, W. E. *Expository Dictionary of New Testament Words,* (Old Tappan, New Jersey: Fleming H. Revell Company, 1966), II, pp. 187-188.

16. Thayer, Joseph Henry. *A Greek-English Lexicon of the New Testament,* (New York - Cincinnati - Chicago: American Book Company, copyright, 1886 by Harper and Brothers), p. 11.

17. Hearn, Roy J., *Handbook on Materialism* (Firm Foundation Publishing House, 1950), p. 9.

18. Moffitt, Jerry, *Thrust* (Vol. 1 Issue I) *Jehovah's Witness* (Austin, Texas: Southwest School of Bible Studies), p. 59.

19. *"Make Sure of All Things — Hold Fast to What is Fine,"* op. cit., p. 230.

20. *"Let God Be True,"* op. cit., p. 77.

21. Rutherford, J. F., *Creation* (Brooklyn: Watch Tower Bible and Tract Society, 1927), p. 286.

22. *The Truth that leads to Eternal Life,* op. cit., p. 44.

23. *Creation,* op. cit., p. 288.

24. *"Make Sure of All Things — Hold Fast to What is Fine,"* op. cit., p. 234.

25. Rutherford, J. F., *Enemies,* (Brooklyn, New York: Watch Tower Bible and Tract Society, 1937), pp. 127-128.

26. Watch Tower, *"This Good News of the Kingdom"* (Watch Tower Bible and Tract Society, Brooklyn, New York, 1954), p. 12.

27. *Studies in the Scriptures* (series I) *The Plan of the Ages,* op. cit., p. 159.

28. Rutherford, J. B., *Where Are the Dead,* (Brooklyn, 1932: Watchtower), p. 15.

29. Ibid, p. 17.

30. *Expository Dictionary of New Testament Words,* op. cit., p. 302 and *A Greek-English Lexicon of the New Testament,* op. cit., p. 64.

31. *A Greek-English Lexicon of the New Testament,* op. cit., p. 443.

32. Ibid, p. 353.

33. Arndt, William F. and Gingrich, F. Wilbur, *A Greek-English Lexicon of the New Testament and Other Early Christian Literature,* (The University of Chicago Press, 1957), p. 441.

34. *A Greek-English Lexicon of the New Testament,* op. cit., p. 96.

CHAPTER 10
ONE CAN BE SAVED BY BELIEVING AND OBEYING THE BIBLE—THE BOOK OF MORMON IS UNNECESSARY AND UNSCRIPTURAL

Thomas B. Warren

Introduction

The Bible is the word of God. As such it has a number of properties or attributes.

1. *It is inerrant.* It does not make errors. Since it is *God's* word, and since God does not lie (Heb. 6:18; Titus 1:2; I Sam. 15:29; John 10:35), then it is clear that there are no errors in the Bible.

2. *It is inspired.* This means that it is "God-breathed" (II Tim. 3:16-17). The men who wrote the Bible were guided by the Holy Spirit in so doing (II Pet. 1:20-21; I Cor. 2:9-13; John 14:26; 16:13). The apostles and prophets, guided by the Holy Spirit, wrote the Bible (Eph. 3:5). Therefore, the Bible is the word of God—not the word of man (I Thess. 2:13).

3. *It is authoritative.* Men must not fail to do what God has told them to do (that is, they must not "take from" the word, Deut. 4:2; Rev. 28:19). Men must not "add to" the word (that is, they must not do what the Bible does not authorize them to do, Lev. 10:1-2; I Chron. 15:1-15; II John 9-11). Men must not pervert (twist, change) that word, trying to make it teach what God never intended (Gal. 1:6-9). Men must not bind on other men what God has not bound in His word (Gal. 2:3-5). Further, men must not forbid what God has allowed (I Tim. 4:1-3). No man can be saved who does not recognize the truth that the Bible is the authoritative word of God and then live in harmony with that truth.

4. *The Bible is complete, all-sufficient.*

(1) *By general statements, the Bible is seen to be all-sufficent.* Paul said, "Every scripture inspired of God is also profitable for teaching, for reproof, for correction, for instruction which is in righteousness: that the man of God may be complete, furnished completely unto every good work" (II Tim. 3:16-17).

Peter said, "Seeing that his divine power hath granted unto us all things that pertain unto life and godliness, through the knowledge of him that called us by his own glory and virtue" (II Peter 1:3).

John said,

"I testify unto every man that heareth the words of the prophecy of this book, if any man shall add unto them, God shall add unto him the plagues which are written in this book: and if any man shall take away from the words of the book of this prophecy, God shall take away his part from the tree of life, and out of the holy city, which are written in this book (Rev. 22:18-19).

Paul said,

"I marvel that ye are so quickly removing from him that called you in the grace of Christ unto a different gospel; which is not another gospel: only there are some that trouble you, and would pervert the gospel of Christ. But though we, or an angel from heaven, should preach unto you any gospel other than that which we preached unto you, let him be anathema. As we have said before, so say I now again, If any man preacheth unto you any gospel other than that which ye received, let him be anathema" (Gal. 1:6-9).

(2) *The Bible is seen to be all-sufficient spiritually.* The Bible is all-sufficient (when understood and properly applied) to meet every basic need of man. For example, the Bible is all-sufficient: (a) *metaphysically* (to explain ultimate reality); (b) *epistemologically* (to tell man what he most needs to know); (c) *psychologically* (to tell him what he needs to gain genuine peace of mind and to meet the times of tribulation and stress during earthly life); (d) *socially* (to show that the home is the basic unit of society, and that society is best improved not by sweeping social reform but by changing the individuals who comprise society by leading them to believe and obey the Gospel of Christ, Prov. 14:34), (e) *morally* (to prove to man the objective [absolute] standard by which to measure his conduct; to corroborate the fact that there is real right and real wrong) and (f) *spiritually* (to give man the information he needs to understand his own lost condition (in sin) and how to be saved from that sin).

The remainder of this article will be concerned basically with point (f) above.

I. *The Bible is all-sufficient to show one what to do to be saved from past (alien) sins.*

1. *The Bible makes clear* that all responsible persons are guilty of sin (Isa. 53:6; Rom. 3:23), causing the sinner thus separated to face everlasting punishment in Hell (Rom. 6:23; Mark 9:43-50; Rev. 20:10-15) provided he does not submit himself to God (in obedience to His will, II Thess. 1:7-9; Matt. 7:13-27).

2. *The Bible makes clear* that if one will believe in the one true God (Heb. 11:6) and in His Son Jesus Christ (John 17:3; 20:30-31; 8:24), will believe the Gospel (Mark 16:15-16), will repent of his sins (Acts 2:38; 17:30-31; II Pet. 3:9-10), will confess with his mouth Jesus Christ as Lord (Rom. 10:9-10; Matt. 10:32-33), and will be baptized (immersed) in water unto the remission of sins, he will be saved (Matt. 28:18-20; Mark 16:15-16; Acts 2:38; 22:16; Rom. 6:3-5; Gal. 3:26-27; John 3:3-5).

Since God has made these promises (noted above) in His word, and since God does not lie (Heb. 6:18), it is *certain* that if *any* man will obey the instructions referred to in the paragraph above, he *will be saved* (by the *blood of Christ,* Heb. 9:22; 10:3-4; 9:11-15; Eph. 1:7; Rom. 5:8-9; Acts 20:28). It is not possible that there will be even one case of failure. Jesus said, "...and him that cometh to me I will in no wise cast out" (John 6:37). Christ will not fail to save anyone who obeys the instructions which He has given to man in the Bible. He is the savior of *all* who obey Him (Heb. 5:8-9).

Thus, it is clear that if a man obeys the New Testament in being baptized (Mark 16:15-16; Acts 2:38; 22:16), he will be saved from past or "alien" sins (that is, the ones he committed *before* he was *baptized* into Christ). Since this is the case, what need does a lost man have for any book other than the Bible? What need does he have for, say, *The Book of Mormon, Doctrine and Convenants, or The Pearl of Great Price?* Absolutely none. In fact, to claim that men need these "extra," so-called inspired books is to deny that the Bible is the word of God for such a claim brands the Bible as a book of falsehoods.

II. *The Bible is all-sufficient to show man how to live the faithful Christian life after being saved from his past (alien) sins.*

1. *The Bible shows man how to live in love,* both for God and man (Matt. 22:34-40; I Cor. 13:1-7), both for his brethren and others (Matt. 5:43-48), both for his friends and for his enemies (Rom. 12:20-21), and for his own family (Eph. 5:22-6:4).

2. *The Bible shows man how to live in purity,* both in body (I Cor. 6:12-20; Gal. 5:19-21) and in mind (Phil. 4:8; Prov. 23:7; Gal. 5:22-23).

3. *The Bible shows man how to live in humility* (Acts 10:34; Jas. 1:9-11; 2:1-6; I Peter 5:6; Rom. 12:3).

4. *The Bible shows man how to live sacrificially;* that is, for the good of others, sincerely wishing their welfare (Phil. 2:5-8; II Cor. 8:9; Matt. 16:21-26; Luke 9:23-24; Matt. 25:31-46; Luke 10:25-37).

5. *The Bible shows man how to live in submission to God's will.* This man must do even if it costs him all of his property, his family, his friends, his freedom, and even his own life (Luke 14:26-33; Acts 21:13; Rev. 2:10; II Tim. 4:6-8).

6. *The Bible shows man that he must ever recognize the authority of God by submitting to God's word.* Man must neither add to nor take away from God's word (Deut. 4:2; Rev. 22:18-19); he must not pervert God's word (Gal. 1:6-9); he must worship God in spirit and in truth, doing only those things which God has authorized in His word (Lev. 10:1-2; I Chron. 15:1-15; II John 9-11; John 4:24); he must not bind on other men what God has not bound (Gal. 2:3-5); he must not do what God has said not to do (Gal. 5:19-21; Rev. 21:8).

Due to lack of space, to avoid the citing of more details, the matter may be summed up by the message which Jesus gave to the church of Christ in Smyrna, "Be thou faithful unto death, and I will give thee the crown of life" (Rev. 2:10). Of the certainty of the reward which will come to each person who lives the faithful Christian life, the apostle Paul said,

> For I am already being offered, and the time of my departure is come. I have fought the good fight, I have finished the course, I have kept the faith: henceforth there is laid up for me the crown of righteousness, which the Lord, the righteous judge, shall give

to me at that day; and not to me only, but also to all them that have loved his appearing (IITim. 4:6-8).

III. *Thus, the Bible makes clear that only the Bible is needed.*

1. *We have seen* that the man who obeys the gospel plan of salvation will be saved from sin thus becoming a *Christian* (Acts 11:26), a child of God (Gal. 3:26-27) — not a "Mormon" or a "Latter Day Saint."

2. *We have seen* that all of those who are baptized into Christ (Rom. 6:3-5) and who live the faithful Christian life will receive the "crown of life" (that is, the crown which is "eternal life," cf. Gal 6:7-9). There will be no exceptions to this. No one who lives a life of "sowing to the Spirit" will fail to reap eternal life!

3. *Thus, from points 1 and 2 above,* we have seen the all-sufficiency of the Bible. Since "Mormons" claim that other books are needed, their claim amounts to a *rejection* of the *Bible.*

While we love their souls — and would do any right things to help them to see the truth of the all-sufficiency of the Bible — we could not be "good soldiers of Christ" (II Tim. 2:3) if we allowed their doctrine to pass unchallenged.

The Gospel — "the whole counsel of God" (Acts 20:27) — was preached in the first century. Any claim to the effect that the complete Gospel of Jesus Christ was not preached until centuries later is false. It is our sincere prayer that not only every "Mormon" but all other men as well will accept (by faith in and obedience to) "the faith once for all delivered unto the saints" (Jude 3).

The Bible is God's *all-sufficient* revelation to man (II Tim. 3:16-17). It sets out (1) all that is necessary for man to *become* a saved person and (2) all that is necessary for one to *live* acceptably to God *as* a saved person. May every man *accept* and follow *the Bible* and *reject* the *Book of Mormon.*

CHAPTER 11
EXTRA BOOKS OF "LATTER DAY SAINTS" CONTRADICT EACH OTHER AND THE BIBLE

Roy H. Lanier, Jr.

Introduction

"The Book of Mormon must either be true or false . . . If false it is one of the most cunning, wicked, bold, deep-laid impositions ever palmed upon the world; calculated to deceive and ruin millions who will sincerely receive it as the word of God, and will suppose themselves securely built upon the rock of truth until they are plunged with their families, into hopeless despair. The nature of the book of Mormon is such that, if true, no one can possibly be saved and reject it; if false, no one can possibly be saved and receive it."[1]

Thus the claims of the *Book of Mormon* are succinctly stated by Orson Pratt. Yet, it is all too easily seen that such a book contradicts itself, other books of claimed inspiration among the Latter Day Saints, and contradicts the Bible.

This is the book with so many errors in grammar that one author said it was "guaranteed to make an English teacher swoon,"[2] Such a mass of errors was published as "3,913 Changes,"[3] while another author, Brodie Crouch, lists two thousand one hundred and twenty five changes in the *Book of Mormon* alone in late editions.[4] Further, the book was given over mainly to the issues of the time in which it was written.[5] Still yet, if this book be true, then the Bible is guilty of gross plagiarism, so rude that New Testament writers did not even give the Mormon writers any credit for quoting them![6]

One of the most famous and embarrassing passages which still plagues the *Book of Mormon* is when Moroni "...went forth among the people waving the rent of his garment in the air, that all might see the writing which he had wrote upon the rent."[7] Since that 1830 Palmyra Edition of the *Book of Mormon,* it is no wonder that so many changes have been made.!

Mormon Books Contradict Themselves

The Latter Day Saints accept several extra books as inspired, just as authentic as the Old and New Testaments. (Though I believe that the extra-Biblical scriptures of Mormonism were all products of the mind of Joseph Smith, the Mormons claim both the *Book of Mormon* and most of the *Pearl of Great Price* to be modern translations of ancient documents, whereas the *Doctrine and Covenants* is the record of recent revelations.) Mormons cherish the *Doctrine and Covenants,* regarding it as an accurate, chronological record of the adding of revelation upon revelation for the formulating and perfecting of the young church.[8]

Most people are more familiar with the *Book of Mormon* than the *Doctrine and Covenants* or the *Pearl of Great Price*. The *Book of Mormon* has fifteen books within it: *I Nephi, II Nephi, Jacob, Enos, Jarom, Omni, Words of Mormon, Mosiah, Alma, Helaman, III Nephi, IV Nephi, Mormon, Ether* and *Moroni.*

The *Doctrine and Covenants* has one hundred and thirty-six "Sections," and the references are given as "Sections and verses." (Thus it might be "Doc. & Cov. 4:5," meaning *"Doctrine and Covenants,* Section 4, verse 5.)

The *Pearl of Great Price* has a *Book of Moses* and a *Book of Abraham,* with chapters and verses. It also has *Writings of Joseph Smith,* with two extracts, and *The Articles of Faith,* with thirteen verses or articles of faith.

The following are contradictions which can be seen by any reader of the books.

1. Joseph Smith as "Author and Proprietor" or just "Translator."

"Author and Proprietor" (*Book of Mormon,* 1830 Edition, Title Page)	"Translator" (*Book of Mormon,* Any subsequent Edition, Title Page)

2. Adam either as the Ancient of Days or as Michael:

Adam-Ondi-Ahman, because said he, it is the place where Adam shall come to visit his people, or the Ancient of Days shall sit, as spoken of by Daniel the prophet. (Doc. & Cov. 116)	And the Lord appeared unto them, and they arose up and blessed Adam, and called him Michael, the prince, the Archangel. (Doc. & Cov. 107:54)

3. Plural marriage or not:

...for they have not forgotten the commandment of the Lord, which was given our fathers — that they should have save it were one wife, and concubines they should have none, and there should not be whoredoms committed among them. (Jacob 3:5)	David also received many concubines, and also Solomon and Moses...in nothing did they sin... David's wives and concubines were given unto him of me... (Doc. & Cov. 132:38-39)

4. Lord's Supper as wine or not:

...only in assembling yourselves together to offer up your sacraments before him. And, behold, this should be wine, yea, pure wine of the grape of the vine, of your own make. (Doc. & Cov. 89:5-6)	it mattereth not what ye shall drink when ye partake of the sacrament. (Doc. & Cov. 27:2)

5. Waters either love or filthiness:

...which led to the fountain of living waters, or to the tree of life; which waters are a representation of the love of God. (I Nephi 11:25)

And they said unto me: What meaneth the river of water which our father saw? And I said unto them that the water which my father saw was filthiness;...(I Nephi 15:27)

6. Decapitated man struggles for breath:

And it came to pass that when Coriantumr had leaned upon his sword, that he rested a little, he smote off the head of Shiz. (Ether 15:30)

And it came to pass after he had smitten off the head of Shiz, that Shiz raised upon his hands and fell; and after that he had struggled for breath, he died. (Ether 15:31)

7. The speaker is either Jesus or the Father: (in the same chapter)

Listen to the voice of Jesus Christ your Redeemer, the Great I am... (Doc. & Cov. 29:1)

But, behold I say unto you that I, the Lord God,...through faith on the name of mine Only Begotten Son. (Doc. & Cov. 29:42)

Behold, I am Jesus Christ, and I come quickly. Even so, Amen. (Doc. & Cov. 49:28)

Thus saith the Lord, for I am God and have sent mine Only Begotten Son into the world... (Doc. & Cov. 49:5)

8. Martin Harris must leave family, but rejoice:

Leave they house and home, except when thou shalt desire to see thy family; (Doc. & Cov. 19:36)

Behold, canst thou read this without rejoicing and lifting up thy heart for gladness? (Doc. & Cov. 19:39)

9. Negroes cursed, yet no difference in black and white:

Pharaoh, being a righteous man... but cursed him as pertaining to the priesthood. (Abraham 1:26, *Pearl Of Great Price*)

...he inviteth them all to come unto him and partake of his goodness; and he denieth none that come unto him, black and white, bond and free, male and female; and he remembereth the heathen; and all are alike unto God, both Jew and Gentile. (II Nephi 26:33)

10. The first to see the pre-mortal Christ:

...the Lord showed himself unto him...(brother of Jared, verse 1)... behold I am Jesus Christ...never have I showed myself unto man whom I have created... (Ether 3:13-15)

Three years previous to the death of Adam, he called Seth, Enos, Cainan...and the Lord appeared unto them...(Doc. & Cov. 107:53-54)

11. One or many gods:

And I, God said: Let there be light; and there was light. (Moses 2:3, *Pearl Of Great Price*)

And they (the Gods) said: Let there be light; and there was light. (Abraham 4:3, *Pearl of Great Price*)

12. Who planted Eden:

And I, the Lord God planted a garden eastward in Eden...(Moses 3:8, *Pearl Of Great Price*)

And the Gods planted a garden eastward in Eden...(Abraham 5:8, *Pearl Of Great Price*)

Mormon Books Contradict The Bible

Of even far more serious nature, the *Book of Mormon, Doctrine and Covenants,* and *Pearl of Great Price* contradict the Bible, the Holy Word of God. There are so many of these instances, it is hard to pick just a few. Please notice some of the more interesting:

1. Jesus born in Jerusalem or Bethlehem:

And bebold, he shall be born of Mary at Jerusalem...(Alma 7:10)

And Joseph also went up from Galilee...unto the city of David which is called Bethlehem...and she brought forth her firstborn son...(Luke 2:4,7)

2. Partake unworthily or be unworthy to partake the Supper:

...not to suffer anyone knowingly to partake of my flesh and blood unworthily... therefore if ye know that a man is unworthy to eat and drink of my flesh and blood ye shall forbid him. (III Nephi 18:28-29)

Wherefore whosoever shall eat this bread and drink this cup of the Lord unworthily... (I Cor. 11: 27)

(NOTE: Did the author of the *Book of Mormon* recognize the difference between an adverb and an adjective?)

3. Grow old when the Lord comes or be changed:

And he that liveth when the Lord shall come...children shall grow up until they become old... (Doc. & Cov. 63:50,51)

...that we which are alive and remain unto the coming of the Lord...shall be caught up together with them in the clouds...(I Thess. 4:15,17)

4. Joel's prophecy fulfilled or not:

He also quoted the second chapter of Joel, from the twenty eighth verse to the last. He also said that this was not yet fulfilled, but was soon to be...(Joseph Smith 2:41, *Pearl of Great Price*)

But this is that which was spoken by the prophet Joel...(Acts 2:16-21)

5. John the Apostle still lives or not:

And the Lord said to me: Verily, verily, I say unto thee, because thou desirest this thou shalt tarry until I come in my glory...(Doc. & Cov. 7:3)

Then went this saying abroad among the brethren, that that disciple should not die: yet Jesus said not unto him, He shall not die; but, If I will that he tarry till I come,what is that to thee? (John 21:23)

6. Melchizedek had a father as king or not:

But Melchizedek, having exercised mighty faith, and received the office of the high priesthood...did reign under his father. (Alma 13:18)

For this Melchizedek, king of Salem, priest of the most high God... without father, without mother, having neither beginning of days nor end of life...(Hebrews 7:1-3)

7. Know of Moses' burial or not:

Behold, this we know, that he was a righteous man; and the saying went abroad in church that he was taken up by the Spirit, or buried by the hand of the Lord, even as Moses. But behold the Scriptures saith the Lord took Moses unto himself; and we suppose that he has also received Alma in the spirit, unto himself; therefore, for this cause we know nothing concerning his death and burial. (Alma 45:19)

So Moses the servant of the Lord died there in the land of Moab... and he buried him in a valley in the land of Moab, over against Bethpeor, but no man knoweth of his sepulchre unto this day. (Deut. 34:5-6)

8. Darkness before or after Jesus' death; lasting three days or hours:

And it came to pass that there was thick darkness upon the face of the land...and it came to pass it did last for the space of three days that there was no light seen. (III Nephi 8:20-23)

And when the sixth hour was come there was darkness over the whole land until the ninth hour. (Mark 15:33)

9. Church established in Old Testament days or after Jesus' life:

And they were called the church of God, or the church of Christ, from that time forward. (Mosiah 18:17)

...and upon this rock I will build my church... (Matt. 16:18)

(NOTE: Footnote says this was about B.C. 147)

10. When the name "Christian" was first used:

And those who did belong to the church were faithful...took upon them gladly the name of Christ, or Christians as they were called, because of their belief in Christ who should come. (Alma 46:15)

And the disciples were called Christians first in Antioch. (Acts 11:26)

11. The King James use of "charity" as "love" or not:

And faith, hope, charity and love, with an eye single to the glory of God... (Doc. & Cov. 4:5)

And now abideth faith, hope, charity, these three; but the greatest of these is charity. (I Cor. 13:13)

12. Use of Greek words "Alpha and Omega" in the Old Testament:

I am the light and the life of the world. I am Alpha and Omega, the beginning and the end. (III Nephi 9:18)

And he said unto me, It is done. I am Alpha and Omega, the beginning and the end. (Rev. 21:6)

(NOTE: Here is a statement about the Greek language from Joseph Smith: "The error I speak of, is the definition of the word 'Mormon.' It has been stated that this word was derived from the Greek word mormo. This is not the case. There was no Greek or Latin upon the plates from which I through the grace of God, translated the Book of Mormon."[9]

13. Time of change of Abram's name to Abraham:

Now the Lord had said unto me: Abraham, get thee out of thy country, and from thy kindred, and from thy father's house, unto a land that I will show thee. (Abraham 3:3, *Pearl Of Great Price)*

Neither shall thy name any more be called Abram, but thy name shall be Abraham; for a father of many nations have I made thee. (Gen. 17:5)

(NOTE: This was five chapters after his call to leave his country and kindred, Gen. 12:1-4).

14. Abram's age when he left Haran:

...and I, Abraham, was sixty and two years old when I departed out of Haran. (Abraham 3:14, *Pearl Of Great Price*)

...and Abram was seventy and five years old when he departed out of Haran. (Gen. 12:4)

15. Christ appeared after His ascension to people on earth or not:

...insomuch that soon after the ascension of Christ into heaven he did truly manifest himself unto them — showing his body unto them, and ministering unto them... (III Nephi 10:18-19)

Therefore being by the right hand of God exalted...sit thou on my right hand until I make thy foes the footstool of thy feet...(Acts 2:34-35)

And he shall send Jesus Christ, which before was preached unto you: whom the heaven must receive until the times of restitution of all things, which God hath spoken by the mouth of his holy prophets since the world began. (Acts 3:20-21)

16. Either God or Abraham told Sarai to lie about their marriage:

And it came to pass when I was come near to enter into Egypt, the Lord said unto me...Let her say unto the Egyptians, she is thy sister...and it came to pass that I Abraham, told Sarai, my wife, all the Lord had said unto me... (Abraham 3:22-25, *Pearl Of Great Price*)

And it came to pass, when he came near to enter into Egypt, that he said unto Sarai his wife...Say, I pray thee, thou art my sister... (Gen. 12:11-13)

Some Conclusions

Do we need any more proof? There are hundreds more such contradictions that can be found in these books. If they were from God, all of them would agree. All the books of both Old and New Testaments agree; why not agreement with all the books which the Latter Day Saints claim to be inspired from God?

It is obvious they do not agree. Therefore it is obvious that one has a choice: accept the Old and New Testaments, or accept the contradictory books of Mormonism with all their contradictions.

It is an insult to God to accept such books. It is an insult to one's intelligence to gloss over such blatant contradictions as if they were not there, or as if they meant nothing. It is as Orson Pratt said: either the *Book of Mormon* is true, or it is a monstrous lie, dooming many believers to destruction.

FOOTNOTES

1. Orson Pratt, *Introduction To Divine Authenticity To The Book of Mormon*, p. 124-125 (as quoted by Roy H. Lanier, *Mormon Doctrine* tract, privately published.)
2. Latayne Colvett Scott, *The Mormon Mirage*, (Grand Rapids, Mich., Zondervan Publishing House, 1979), p. 63.
3. Jerald and Sandra Tanner, *Mormonism-Shadow or Reality?* (Salt Lake City, Utah, Modern Microfilm Co., 1972 Enlarged Edition), p. 89.
4. William Brodie Crouch, *The Myth of Mormon Inspiration*, (Shreveport, La., Lambert's Book House, 1968), pp. 248-268.
5. Alexander Campbell, *Millennial Harbinger* (Bethany, Va., published by the Editor, reprinted by Harbinger Book Club, Nashville, Tenn.), Vol. II, p. 93.
6. Latayne Colvett Scott, p. 76.
7. William Brodie Crouch, p. 262.
8. Latayne Colvett Scott, p. 100.
9. Joseph Smith, *Times and Seasons*, Vol. 4, p. 194 (as quoted by Jerald & Sandra Tanner, p. 81).

CHAPTER 12
SOME ABSURDITIES OF MORMONISM

Garland Elkins

The system of religion that Joseph Smith, Jr., originated contains a multiplicity of errors and absurdities. It is our purpose to discuss a few of those many absurdities.

"Mormon" teaching often conflicts with the Bible. Further, "Mormon" teaching often contradicts other "Mormon" doctrine! Since this is the case, it is simply incredible that any informed person would hold to "Mormonism."

If the Bible is true (as this writer confidently believes it to be), then *The Book of Mormon, The Pearl of Great Price,* and *The Doctrine and Covenants* are all false. If these books are true, then the Bible is false. **There is no middle ground!**

The Absurdities of Joseph Smith's "Prophecies"

Joseph Smith, Jr., claimed to utter a number of prophecies, any one of which could be successfully used to prove that he was not inspired. For our purpose we shall confine our investigation to a series of prophecies which Smith uttered with reference to the building of a city to serve as headquarters for "Mormons" as Jerusalem had served the Jews. The following from one of Joseph Smith's "inspired" books informs us **where** Mr. Smith prophesied the temple would be built: "Hearken, O ye elders of my church, saith the Lord your God, who have assembled yourselves together, according to my commandments, in this land, which is the land of Missouri, which is the land which I have appointed and consecrated for the gathering of the saints. Wherefore, this is the land of promise, and the place for the city of Zion. And thus saith the Lord your God, if you will receive wisdom here is wisdom. Behold, the place which is now called Independence is the center place; and a spot for the temple is lying westward, upon a lot which is not far from the court-house" *(Doc. & Cov.* 57:1-3) (1923 edition). "And, behold, there is none other place appointed than that which I have appointed; neither shall there be any other place appointed than that which I have appointed, for the work of the gathering of my saints" (*Doc. & Cov.* 101:20). So, according to Joe Smith, "Jackson County, Missouri" (*Doc. & Cov.* 124:51-52), was to be the place.

Another important question is: **When** would the city and temple be built? Hear Joseph Smith's "inspired" prophecy on this point: "Verily this is the word of the Lord, and the city New Jerusalem shall be built by the gathering of the saints, beginning at this place, even the place of the temple, which temple shall be reared in this generation. For verily this generation shall not all pass away until an house shall be built unto the Lord, and a cloud shall rest upon it, which cloud shall be even the glory of the Lord, which shall fill the house...Therefore, as I said concerning the sons of Moses—for the sons of Moses and also the sons of Aaron shall offer an acceptable offering and sacrifice in the house of the Lord, which house shall be built unto the Lord in this generation, upon the consecrated spot as I have appointed" (*Doc. & Cov.* 84:4,51 84:31). Attention is called to the fact that Smith prophesied that the city and temple were to be built "**in this generation**." When we remember that Joseph Smith prophesied that "this generation shall not all pass away until an house be built unto the Lord" (*Doc. & Cov.* 84:4-5) in "Jackson County, Missouri" (*Doc. & Cov.* 124:51,52), and when we observe that none of this came to pass, we readily discern the absurdities of "Mormonism." **Not only does the failure of this prophesy to be fulfilled show the absurdities of "Mormonism," but beyond doubt it exposes Joseph Smith as a false prophet!**

God instructs us as to how we can know a false prophet: "When a prophet speaketh in the name of the Lord, if the thing follow not, or come to pass, that is the thing which the Lord hath not spoken, but the prophet hath spoken it presumptuously: thou shalt not be afraid of him" (Deut. 18:22). Let us observe that:

1. If Joseph Smith, Jr.'s prophecy failed to come to pass, then he was a false prophet.
2. His prophecy failed to come to pass.
3. Therefore, Joseph Smith, Jr., was a false prophet.

Also observe that:

1. If Joseph Smith, Jr., was a false prophet, then the entire "Mormon" religion is a false religion.
2. Joseph Smith, Jr., was a false prophet.
3. Therefore, the "Mormon" religion is a false religion.

The Absurdities of Joseph Smith, Jr.'s Teaching Concerning Plural Marriages

Mr. Smith sought to justify plural marriages on the ground that David and Solomon had many wives. He wrote, "David also received many wives and concubines, and also Solomon and Moses my servants, as also many others of my servants, from the beginning of creation until this time; and in nothing did they sin..." (*Doc. & Cov.* 132:38). Jesus taught that, though the Lord tolerated some things relative to marriage in the Old Testament because of "the hardness of your hearts," yet He made it crystal clear that no longer would such abuses of marriage be permitted. Though Matthew 19:3-9 discusses the putting away of wives, it also refutes polygamy, for Jesus said, "For this cause shall a man leave father and mother, and shall cleave to his **wife:** (not wives, GE) and the **two** shall become one flesh" (Mt. 19:5). Jesus clearly taught a man should have but **one** wife. Paul taught this same truth in Romans 7:2,3. It is an absurdity of "Mormonism" that Joseph Smith Jr., taught a doctrine relative to marriage which contradicts Jesus and Paul!

Not only does Joseph Smith contradict Jesus and Paul, but in two of his so-called "inspired" books, Joseph Smith contradicts Joseph Smith. Note the contradictions:

In his *Doctrine and Covenants* book he says, "David also received many wives and concubines, and also Solomon and Moses my servants...and in nothing did they sin..." (*Doc. & Cov.* 132:38). However, in his Book of Mormon he says, "But the word of God burthens me because of your grosser crimes. For behold, thus saith the Lord: This people begin to wax in iniquity; they understand not the scriptures, for they see to excuse themselves in committing whoredoms, because of the things which were written concerning David, and Solomon his son...Wherefore, my brethren, hear me, and hearken to the word of the Lord: For there shall not any man among you have save it be one wife; and concubines he shall have none; For I, the Lord God, delight in the chastity of women. And whoredoms are an abomination before me; thus saith the Lord of Hosts...For behold, I, the Lord, have seen the sorrow, and heard the mourning of the daughters of my people in the land of Jerusalem, yea, and in all the lands of my people, because of the wickedness and abominations of their husbands...Behold, the Lamanites your brethren, whom ye hate because of their filthiness and the cursing which hath come upon their skins, are more righteous than you; for they have not forgotten the commandment of the Lord, which was given unto our fathers—that they should have save it were one wife, and concubines they should have none, and there should not be whoredoms committed among them" (Jacob 2:23,27,28,31; 3:5).

It is interesting that the U.S. Government forced the "Mormons" to give up their practice of plural marriages, as far as was publicly known, though some continue to practice it.

The present generation of "Mormons" for the most part doubtless live in obedience to the law of the land in regard to this matter. However, if they do so, according to Joseph Smith, Jr., they would be violating an "everlasting covenant" and will be "damned," for he said, "For behold, I reveal unto you a new and everlasting covenant; and if ye abide not that covenant, then are ye damned; for no one can reject this covenant and be permitted to enter into my glory" (*Doc. & Cov.* 132:4). Note 132:38.

When the authorities commanded the apostles to cease preaching in the name of Jesus, they said, "We must obey God rather than men" (Acts 5:29). Can the U.S. Government prevent the "Mormons" from practicing an "everlasting covenant?"

If the "Mormons" do practice plural marriages, they would not only be in violation of the law of the land, but would also be engaging in a very sinful practice. Jesus restored marriage to its original ground (Mt. 19:8,9). He previously said, "Have ye not read, that he who made them from the beginning made them male and female, and said, For this cause shall a man leave his father and mother, and shall cleave to his **wife**; and the **two** shall become one flesh?" (Emphasis mine. GE).

It is very apparent that Joseph Smith, Jr., experienced great difficulty in an attempt to convince his wife, Emma, that it was proper for him to marry additional wives. It is revolting and disgusting to the extreme degree to read this so-called "revelation" from his pen to his wife on this matter: "And let mine handmaid, Emma Smith, receive all those that have been given unto my servant Joseph, and who are virtuous and pure before me" (*Doc. & Cov.* 132:52).

The Wives of the Prophet

In the book *No Man Knows My History, the Life of Joseph Smith, the Mormon Prophet,* by Fawn M. Brodie, Brodie makes a number of statements in regard to Smith's wives. If Brodie's statements are true, then Smith's conduct was adulterous, revealing, disgusting, and sinful.

"Probably no one will ever know exactly how many women Joseph Smith married. Brigham Young said quite frankly to William Hepworth Dixon in 1866: 'I myself sealed dozens of women to Joseph.' One Mormon historian drew up a list of twenty-seven wives, but it is clear from all the available published and manuscript records that the number may have reached or even exceeded fifty.*

"In January 1846, eighteen months after his death, thirty women were sealed to the prophet 'for eternity' in the Nauvoo temple, and to various other men 'for time.' Since it is clear from other records that more than two thirds of these women had already been married to Joseph during his lifetime, it can be assumed that for all thirty women the sealing was simply a new solemnization of an earlier ceremony. It was felt that a marriage 'for eternity' was not truly binding unless sanctified within the temple, which had not been completed in Joseph's lifetime.

"In later years in Utah, scores of women were sealed to the prophet posthumously, but since it is impossible to determine how many of these had been married to him during his life-time, they are not included here. The following list, therefore, is possibly incomplete. It contains, however, the names of several women whose relationship to the prophet is admittedly little more than presumable.

"The first thirty-six wives listed here are arranged in the approximate chronological order of their marriage to Joseph Smith. The remainder, where no marriage date can even be guessed at, are listed alphabetically. Since for most of these latter the date of birth is available, and since Joseph married

*See William Hepworth Dixon: *New America* (Philadelphia, 1867), p. 225. Andrew Jenson, formerly assistant historian of the Utah Mormon Church, listed twenty-seven wives in the *Historical Record,* Vol. VI, May 1887, but he gave only the barest details, usually listing them by their maiden names and seldom providing documentation. It is clear that he did not even canvass all the Mormon sources, for he omitted several wives mentioned later by Orson F. Whitney in his *Life of Heber C. Kimball* and many other wives listed in the Nauvoo Temple Record. In the accompanying list question marks indicate where the data are doubtful. For complete documentation on every wife see Appendix C.

most of his wives during 1843 and 1844, it is possible to suggest the approximate age of each woman when married.

Name	Age When Married	Date of Marriage
"1. Emma Hale	22	January 18, 1827
2. Fannie Alger	17?	1836
3. Lucinda Pendleton Morgan Harris, wife of G. W. Harris	37?	1838?
4. Prescindia Huntington Buell, wife of Norman Buell	29?	1839?
5. Nancy Marinda Johnson Hyde, wife of Orson Hyde	24?	1839?
6. Clarissa Reed Hancock, wife of Levi W. Hancock	35?	1840?
7. Louisa Beaman	26	April 5, 1841
8. Zina Diantha Huntington Jacobs, wife of Henry B. Jacobs	20	October 27, 1841
9. Mary Elizabeth Rollins Lightner, wife of Adam Lightner	24	February 1842
10. Patty Bartlett Sessions, wife of David Sessions	47	March 9, 1842
11. Delcena Johnson Sherman, widow of Lyman R. Sherman	36?	Before June 1842
12. Mrs. Durfee	?	Before June 1842
13. Sally Ann Fuller Gatty, wife of Samuel Gatty	26?	Before June 1842
14. Mrs. A**** S****	?	Before June 1842
15. Miss B****	?	Before June 1842
16. Eliza Roxey Snow	38	June 29, 1842
17. Sarah Ann Whitney	17	July 27, 1842
18. Sarah M. Kinsley Cleveland, wife of John Cleveland	54?	1842?
19. Elvira A. Cowles	29?	Before December 1842
20. Martha McBride	38	Summer 1842
21. Ruth D. Vose Sayers, wife of Edward Sayers	34?	August 1842?
22. Desdemona Wadsworth Fullmer	33	1842
23. Emily Dow Partridge	19	March 4, 1843
24. Eliza M. Partridge	23	March 1843
25. Almera Woodward Johnson	31	April 1843
26. Lucy Walker	17	May 1, 1843
27. Helen Mar Kimball	15	May 1843
28. Maria Lawrence	19	Spring 1843

29. Sarah Lawrence	17	Spring 1843
30. Flora Ann Woodworth	17	Spring 1843
31. Rhoda Richards	59	June 12, 1843
32. Hannah Ells	30?	Summer 1843?
33. Melissa Lott	19	September 20, 1843
34. Fanny Young Murray, wife of Roswell Murray	56	November 2, 1843
35. Olive Grey Frost	27-8?	After April 1843
36. Mary Ann Frost Pratt, wife of Parley P. Pratt	34-5?	After April 1843
37. Olive Andrews	25-6?	1843-4?
38. Mrs. Blossom, wife of Edward Blossom	?	?
39. Elizabeth Davis	52-3?	1843-4?
40. Mary Hustin	25-6?	1843-4?
41. Vienna Jacques	55-6?	1843-4?
42. Cordelia Calista Morley	20-1?	1843-4?
43. Sarah Scott	?	?
44. Sylvia Sessions	25-6?	1843-4?
45. Nancy Maria Smith	?	?
46. Jane Tibbets	39-40?	1843-4?
47. Phebe Watroud	38-9?	1843-4?
48. Nancy Maria Winchester	15-16?	1843-4?
49. Sophia Woodman	48-9?	1843-4?

"It will be seen that at least twelve were married women (with living husbands), although the evidence for Mrs. Levi Hancock is only word-of-mouth tradition in the Hancock family. The ages of Joseph's wives varied all the way from the fifteen years of Helen Mar Kimball, daughter of Heber C. Kimball, to the fifty-nine years of Rhoda Richards, spinster sister of Joseph's secretary Willard Richards. The prophet married five pairs of sisters: Delcena and Almera Johnson, Eliza and Emily Partridge, Sarah and Maria Lawrence, Mary Ann and Olive Grey Frost, and Prescindia and Zina Huntington. Patty and Sylvia Sessions were mother and daughter.

"The majority of the prophet's wives fall into three general categories: first, the group of married women to whom Joseph was sealed between 1838 and the expulsion of Bennett in June 1842; and second, the leading women in the Nauvoo Relief Society, who were married to the prophet during the furor that followed Bennett's departure. The third group consists of the dozen or more unmarried women whom he married in the spring and summer of 1843. Most of them were quite young. Helen Mar Kimball was fifteen; Nancy Mariah Winchester (who may be identical with Nancy Maria Smith) was fifteen or sixteen; Lucy Walker, Sarah Lawrence and Flora Ann Woodworth were seventeen. Maria Lawrence and Melissa Lott were nineteen.

"Six of the girls Joseph took as wives lived at various times as wards in his own home. These were the Partridge sisters, the Lawrence sisters, Eliza R. Snow, and Lucy Walker. One of these, the seventeen-year-old Lucy Walker, who had moved into the prophet's home after the death of her mother, described Joseph's whirlwind courtship. She thereby revealed not only her own ingenuousness but also Joseph's sophistication. Late in April 1843 Emma Smith went to St. Louis to make purchases for the Mansion House, accompanied by Lucy's brother, Lorin Walker, who was one of Joseph's business aides. During their absence Joseph asked Lucy to become his wife.

"'I have no flattering words to offer,' he told her after the usual preliminaries. 'It is a command of God to you. I will give you until tomorrow to decide this matter. If you reject this message the gate will be closed forever against you.'"[1]

Additional Absurdities

Note some additional absurdities of "Mormonism."

1. They contend that some books of the Bible have been lost. This is an absurd contention, for the Bible teaches that by the time Peter wrote his second letter, "all things that pertain unto life and godliness" had been revealed (II Pet. 1:3). Jesus promised that His word would be preserved. "Heaven and earth shall pass away, but my words shall not pass away" (Mt. 24:35). Peter also affirms its preservation. "But the word of the Lord abideth for ever. And this is the word of good tidings which was preached unto you" (I Pet. 1:25).

2. The "Mormons" attack the all-sufficiency and inerrancy of the Bible by claiming that the text of the Bible, as we have it, is not an infallible guide. The truth is no "Mormon" can put his finger on his alleged "corruptions in the Hebrew or Greek originals!"

3. "Mormonism," in making the above attack on the Bible, by implication makes an attack upon the Father, Son, and the Holy Spirit, for Jesus said that He would pray the Father and He would send the Holy Spirit (Jno. 14:16). He also stated that the Holy Spirit would teach the apostles "all things" and assured them that He would bring "all things" to their remembrance (Jno. 14:26). Both Peter and Jude wrote by inspiration that this occurred before their deaths (II Pet. 1:3; Jude 3). Paul never heard of the *Book of Mormon,* yet, he said that the man of God was completely furnished unto every good work through the word (II Tim. 3:16,17). John knew nothing of the *Book of Mormon,* yet, he closed the Revelation with an inspired prohibition against anyone adding to or taking from the words (Rev. 22:18,19)! John taught that anyone that goes beyond the doctrine of Christ does not have God (II Jno. 9-11).

4. "Mormonism" teaches the absurdity that remission of sins was fully accomplished approximately five hundred years before Jesus died on Calvary. "And the Lord God hath sent his holy prophets among all the children of men, to declare these things to every kindred, nation, and

tongue, that thereby whosoever should believe that Christ should come, the same might receive remission of their sins, and rejoice with exceeding great joy, even as though he had already come among them" (Mosiah 3:13). The Bible teaches that remission of sins was not obtained until after Jesus was crucified and that remission of sins began in Jerusalem. "And that repentance and remission of sins should be preached in his name among all nations, beginning at Jerusalem" (Lk. 24:47). "And from Jesus Christ, who is the faithful witness, the firstborn of the dead, and the ruler of the kings of the earth. Unto him that loveth us, and loosed us from our sins by his blood" (Rev. 1:5). Therefore, "Mormonism" teaches that the scheme of redemption was made known centuries before Jesus came to earth (Mosiah 3:13). The New Testament teaches, "which in other generations was not made known unto the sons of men, as it hath now been revealed unto his holy apostles and prophets in the Spirit" (Eph. 3:5).

5. "Mormonism" teaches that God has changed and that He was not God from eternity. "God himself was once as we are now, and is an exalted man...It is necessary that we should understand the character and being of God, and how he came to be so; for I am going to tell you how God came to be God. We have imagined and supposed that God was God from all eternity. I will refute that idea, and will take away and do away with the vail so that you may see...God himself, the Father of us all, dwelt on an earth, the same as Jesus Christ himself did...And you have got to learn how to be Gods yourselves" (Joseph Smith, Jr., in sermon in Nauvoo, April 6, 1844, from *Journal of Discourses,* v. 6, pp. 3,4).[2]

"The Father has a body of flesh and bones as tangible as a man's; the Son also; but the Holy Ghost has not a body of flesh and bones, but is a personage of Spirit" (*Doctrine and Covenants* 130:22—accepted as inspired by LDS).

"The mind or the intelligence which man possessed is co-equal with God...The intelligence of spirits had no beginning, neither will they have an end...for they are co-equal with our Father in heaven...This is good doctrine. It tastes good. I can taste the principle of eternal life, and so can you. They are given me by revelation of Jesus Christ" (*Journal of Discourses,* v. 6, pp. 6,7).[3]

They say of Adam, "He is our Father and our God." Observe what Joseph Smith said on this matter: "When our father Adam came into the Garden of Eden, he came into it with a celestial body, and brought Eve, one of his wives, with him...He is our Father AND OUR GOD, and the ONLY GOD WITH WHOM WE HAVE TO DO" (*Journal of Discourses,* v. 1, p. 50).[4] We read from the scriptures: "For I am the Lord, I change not; therefore ye sons of Jacob are not consumed" (Mal. 3:6); "And changed the glory of the incorruptible God for the likeness of an image of corruptible man, and of birds, and four-footed beasts, and creeping things" (Rom. 1:23). The teaching of "Mormonism" is blasphemy!

6. The "Mormons" claim to have "apostles." However, they cannot name one of their "apostles" who has the qualifications for an apostle. To be a true apostle of Christ, it was essential that one be "A witness of his

resurrection" (Acts 1:22). Paul informs us that he was the last man who could and did meet that qualification for being an apostle of Christ. He was the last man to be made an apostle by Christ. He said, "And last of all he was seen of me also" (I Cor. 15:8).

True apostles could speak in languages they had never been taught (Acts 2:1-47). They could survive, unharmed, the fangs of deadly serpents. They could drink deadly poison, and it would not hurt them (Mk. 16:17,18; Acts 28:5). "Mormonism" dares not allow its "apostles" to be tried, examined, and tested in these matters. The Lord's church in the first century tried false apostles and found them false, even as the "Mormon apostles" when tried are found false! (Rev. 2:2).

7. "Mormonism" not only contradicts the Bible when they teach their doctrine on baptism for the dead (i.e., that live people are baptized for dead people), but their baptism-for-the-dead doctrine contradicts their Book of *Mormon.*

"For behold, this life is the time for men to prepare to meet God; yea, behold the day of this life is the day for men to perform their labors. And, now as I said unto you before, as ye have had so many witnesses, therefore, I beseech you that you do not procrastinate the day of your repentance, unto the end; for after this day of life, which is given us to prepare for eternity, behold, if we do not improve our time while in this life, then cometh the night of darkness wherein there can be no labor performed. Ye can not say, when ye are brought to that awful crisis, that I will repent, that I will return to my God. Nay, ye can not say this; for that same spirit which doth possess your bodies at the time that ye go out of this life, that same spirit will have power to possess your body in that eternal world. **For behold, if ye have procrastinated the day of your repentance even until death, behold, ye have become subjected to the spirit of the devil, and he doth seal you his; therefore the Spirit of the Lord hath withdrawn from you, and hath no place in you, and the devil hath all power over you; and this is the final state of the wicked**"(Alma 34:32-35). (Emphasis mine. GE).

"Therefore as they had become carnal, sensual, and devilish, by nature, this probationary state became a state for them to prepare; it became a preparatory state...Therefore, according to justice, the plan of redemption could not be brought about, only on conditions of repentance of men in this probationary state, yea, this preparatory state; for except it were for these conditions, mercy could not take effect except it should destroy the work of justice. Now the work of justice could not be destroyed; if so God would cease to be God" (Alma 42:10,13).

8. They contradict the Old Testament prophet who predicted that Jesus would be born at Bethlehem (Micah 5:2). "Mormonism" says, "And behold, he (Jesus) shall be born of Mary at Jerusalem (Alma 7:10). This contradicts the inspired writing of Luke. "And Joseph also went up from Galilee, out of the city of Nazareth, into Judaea, to the city of David, which is called Bethlehem, because he was of the house and family of David; to enrol himself with Mary, who was betrothed to him, being great with child. And it came to pass, while they were there, the days were fulfilled that she

should be delivered. And she brought forth her firstborn son; and she wrapped him in swaddling clothes, and laid him in a manger, because there was no room for them in the inn" (Lk. 2:4-7).

9. They claim that spiritual gifts continue until the end of time. Paul taught that such miraculous gifts were temporary and were to "fail," "cease," and "vanish (be done) away" (I Cor. 13:8-13; Eph. 4:8-13).

10. "Mormonism" teaches that Jesus' kingdom is of this world, but Jesus teaches that His kingdom is not of this world (Jno. 18:36).

11. "Mormonism" contradicts Hebrews 8:4 which teaches that Jesus would not be a priest on earth.

12. Joseph Smith taught that the Bible is not supreme authority. He taught (and his followers still believe) that the Bible is not the final word of God. Joseph Smith taught that one was a "fool" who thought the Bible is sufficient. He said, "And because my words shall hiss forth—many of the Gentiles shall say: A Bible! A Bible! We have got a Bible, and there cannot be any more Bible. But thus saith the Lord God: O fools, they shall have a Bible; and it shall proceed forth from the Jews, mine ancient covenant people. And what thank they the Jews for the Bible which they receive from them? Yea, what do the Gentiles mean? Do they remember the travels, and the labors, and the pains of the Jews, and their diligence unto me, in bringing forth salvation unto the Gentiles? Thou fool, that shall say: A Bible, we have got a Bible, and we need no more Bible. Have ye obtained a Bible save it were by the Jews? Wherefore, because that ye have a Bible ye need not suppose that it contains all my words; neither need ye suppose that I have not caused more to be written" (2 Nephi 29:3,4,6,10). Brother G. K. Wallace has well said, "*The Book of Mormon* opens with a contradiction of the Bible. In the middle of *The Book of Mormon* it contradicts the Bible. You can open it in the middle and read it both ways and it contradicts the Bible either way you read it. Then as you come to the last chapter you will note that it closes with a flat contradiction of the Bible."

Thus, *The Book of Mormon, Doctrine and Covenants,* and *The Pearl of Great Price* not only contradict the Bible, but they frequently contradict each other!

Conclusion

Joseph Smith was a false "prophet," an originator of a false, and therefore, a dangerous religion. This error will cost millions their souls!

Doubtlessly, many of the followers of Joseph Smith are sincere and truly believe that "Mormonism" is of God. According to the Lord, great numbers of sincere, but deluded, followers of false religions will stand before the Lord in judgment truly thinking that they have done God's will. I simply emphasize the Lord's words in this connection. "Not every one that saith unto me, Lord, Lord, shall enter into the kingdom of heaven; but he that doeth the will of my Father which is in heaven. Many will say to me in that day, Lord, Lord, have we not prophesied in thy name? and in thy name have cast out devils? and in thy name done many wonderful works?

And then will I profess unto them, I never knew you: depart from me, ye that work iniquity" (Mt. 7:21-23).

The only safety for any and all is found in the sage words of Peter to Christ, "Simon Peter answered him, Lord, to whom shall we go? thou hast the words of eternal life" (Jno. 6:68). Let us all remember the solemn, serious and sobering words of Jesus Christ: "He that rejecteth me, and receiveth not my words, hath one that judgeth him: the word that I have spoken, the same shall judge him in the last day" (Jno. 12:48).[5]

FOOTNOTE

1. Brodie, Fawn M., *No Man Knows My History, The Life of Joseph Smith, The Mormon Prophet* (NY, Alfred A. Knopf, 1954), pp. 334-337.
2. Lanier, Roy H., *Mormon Doctrine - True Or False* (Memphis, TN, Getwell Church of Christ).
3. *Ibid.*
4. *Ibid.*
5. Also of great value in the study of Mormonism is *The Spiritual Sword,* Vol. 7, No. 1. *Mormon Doctrine - True Or False* by Roy H. Lanier is excellent material concerning the errors of Mormonism. This sixty-page tract may be ordered from Getwell Church of Christ.

CHAPTER 13
MORMON DOCTRINE OF GOD VERSUS THE BIBLE DOCTRINE OF GOD

John H. O'Neal

Inevitably, when man devises his own religious system, he sets aside the truth about God. No man-made system of religious doctrine can exist without perverting the nature of God, without limiting God in some way. Mormonism is no exception. The religious system of Mormonism is false, because the god of Mormonism does not have existence anywhere, except as a figment of the imaginations of men.

The Bible View of God

The nature of God is revealed to us. The Bible teaches that there is one God. "For there is one God" (I Tim. 2:5; Eph. 4:6). Yet the one God, the divine nature, is made up of three distinct personalities. The **Father** is called God, "yet to us there is one God, the Father" (I Cor. 8:6). The **Son** is called God, as the Hebrews writer explained, "but of the Son he saith, Thy throne, O God, is forever" (Heb. 1:8). Luke records that Peter identified **the Holy Spirit** (Holy Ghost-KJV) as God when he accused Ananias of telling a lie (Acts 5:3, 4). **How** these three distinct personalities comprise the one God is not revealed, but the Bible does teach that there are three persons in one Godhead. Men can come to a knowledge of this because the scriptures teach it! God is a **spirit** (John 4:24; Job 9:11), invisible (I Tim. 1:17; I John 4:12); He is not flesh and bones (Luke 24:39), "dwelling in light unapproachable; whom no man hath seen nor can see" (I Tim. 6:16). God is **immutable,** unchangeable (Mal. 3:6; Heb. 6:17, 18). He is not progressive in his nature, for with God there "can be no variation, neither shadow that is cast by turning" (James 1:17; Psm. 102:26, 27). God is **omniscient,** all knowing, unlimited in knowledge (I Sam. 2:3; I Sam. 40:13, 14), as He declares, "I am God, and there is none like me; declaring the end from the beginning, and from ancient times things that are done" (Isa. 46:9, 10). God is **infinite in wisdom** and understanding, for "Great is our Lord, and mighty in power; His understanding is infinite" (Psm.147:5; Job 9:4). God is omnipresent, everywhere present, "Am I a God at hand, saith Jehovah, and not a God afar off? Can any hide himself in secret places so that I shall not see him? Saith Jehovah" (Jer. 23:23, 24; Psm. 139:7-10). God is **omnipotent,** all powerful. He is "God almighty" (Gen. 17:1). Jeremiah prayed, "Ah Lord Jehovah! behold, thou hast made the heavens by thy great power and by thine outstretched arm; there is nothing too hard for thee" (Jer. 32:17). Further, God is **self-existent.** He exists in and of himself and does not depend on anything else. He is the Self-existing One. He is the "living God" (Josh. 3:10; I Tim. 3:15). To ask the question, "Who made God?", is to misunderstand the very nature of God. Existence is His nature. "What He is, is that he is."[1] God conveyed to Moses to tell the children of Israel, "I AM THAT I AM" (Ex. 3:14,15). He transcends, is outside of, the limitations of time (II Pet. 3:8). He is "from everlasting to everlasting" (Psm. 90:2).There is nothing like God. Moses told the Israelites, "Unto thee it was showed, that thou mightest know that Jehovah he is God; there is none else besides him (Deut. 4:35). There is none to whom we can compare God (Psm. 89:6; Isa. 40:18). "To whom will ye liken me, and make me equal, and compare me, that we may be like?" (Isa. 46:5). Since there is none to whom we can compare God, He is often referred to in the scriptures under human forms and human passions. These are only figures of speech whereby we are enabled to refer to Him and are not to be taken literally.[2] As the Self-existing One, it is to Him that we and all that is in nature owe our existence (Gen. 1; Acts 17:24-28). He is Loving (I Jn. 4:8), Just (Deut. 32:4), Merciful (Eph. 2:4, 5), Good (Mk. 10:18), Holy (I Sam. 2:2; Psm. 5:4), unlimited in all His characteristics and attributes. Truly God is the one, infinite, eternal, self-existing reality who has created all that exists other than himself, and has revealed himself to us.

The Mormon View of God

At first glance, the Mormon view of God might **appear** to be consistent with the Bible. The closing statement of *The Testimony of Three Witnesses,* Oliver Cowdery, David Whitmer, and Martin Harris, as found in the opening pages of the Book of Mormon, states, "and the honor be to the Father, and to the Son, and to the Holy Ghost, which is one God." From the Book of Mormon, we learn concerning God, "I am without beginning of days or end of years"[3]..."there is no God beside me"[4]..."Now Zeezrom said: Is there more than one God? And he answered, No"[5] "...he is that Great Spirit, and he created all things both in heaven and in earth."[6]..."I am the same yesterday, today, and forever"[7] "...for I know that God is not a partial God, neither a changeable being; but he is unchangeable from all eternity to all eternity"[8] "...knowing all things, being from everlasting to everlasting."[9] *Doctrine and Covenants* tells us, "From eternity to eternity, he is the same."[10] But let us not be deceived into thinking that the Mormon doctrine of God harmonizes with the Bible. For, these passages do not accurately represent the Mormon view of God and any references to them only camouflage their actual views!

God, An Exalted Man

At the April conference of the Mormon Church, 1844, in a funeral sermon known as "The King Follett Discourse," Joseph Smith expressed his views on God:

> God himself was once as we are now, and is an exalted man, and sits enthroned in yonder heavens! That is the great secret. If the

veil were rent today, and the great God who holds this world in its orbit, and who upholds all things and all words by his power, was to make himself visible, — I say, if you were to see him today, you would see him like a man in form — like yourselves in all the person, image, and very form as a man; for Adam was created in the very fashion, image and likeness of God, and received instruction from, and walked, talked and conversed with him, as one man talks and comments with another.

In order to understand the subject of the dead, for consolation of those who morn for the loss of their friends, it is necessary we should understand the character and being of God and how he came to be so; for I am going to tell you how God came to be God. We have imagined and supposed that God was God from all eternity. I will refute that idea, and take away the veil, so that you may see. These are incomprehensible ideas to some, but they are simple. It is the first principle of the gospel to know for a certainty the character of God, and to know that we may converse with him as one man converses with another, and that, he was once a man like us; yea, that God himself, the Father of us all, dwelt on an earth, the same as Jesus Christ himself did; and I will show it from the Bible.[11]

In his "Observation on the Sectarian God," Joseph Smith explains, "That which is without body parts and passions is nothing. There is no other God in heaven but that God who has flesh and bones."[12] Parley P. Pratt, one of the original twelve apostles appointed by Joseph Smith declared in his book *"Key to the Science of Theology,"* concerning God being a Spirit, "Such a God could never be seen, heard, or felt by any being in the universe. There never has been a visible idol worshiped among men that was so powerless as this God without body parts, or passions."[13] He represents Christ as "possessing the same attributes as his Father, in all their fulness; a God not only possessing body and parts, but flesh and bones and sinews, and all the attributes, organs, senses, and affections, of a perfect man."[14] Concerning our understanding of God, this same Mormon apostle held, "that which we may know and comprehend or express of him should be divested of all mystery and should be as clearly conceived, expressed, and conveyed as any other item of truth or of science."[15] One-time Mormon apostle and author of the fourth most beloved book to the Mormon mind, *"The Articles of Faith,"* writes, "from the evidence already presented, it is clear that the Father is a personal being, possessing a definite form, with bodily parts and spiritual passions."[16] From the *Doctrine and Covenants,* 130:22, we learn, "The Father has a body of flesh and bones as tangible as man is; the Son also; but the Holy Ghost has not a body of flesh and bones, but is a personage of Spirit." Parley P. Pratt agrees, teaching, "However, the Holy Ghost does not possess a body of flesh and bones, as do both the Father and the Son, but is a personage of spirit."[17] It is very interesting to note the condition in which this leaves the Holy Spirit for, according to Joseph Smith's doctrine, "The great principle of happiness consists in having a body. The devil has no body, and herein is his punishment."[18] The Holy Spirit misses out on the great principle of happiness "and is made to suffer the same punishment the devil suffers," while being a member of the Godhead. This is the foolishness of men!

According to Mormon doctrine, Almighty God is nothing more than "an exalted man." Modern day Humanism holds that man is ultimate reality, and the god of Mormonism ultimately amounts to the same thing. In order to try to avoid the absurdity of calling God an exalted man, Joseph Fielding Smith, long time church historian and later a President of the Mormon church, tries to pass it off by saying, "Naturally there are many things that we will not comprehend while in this mortal life and we will not be able to fathom all the difficulties that lie before us. Our understanding is limited and we judge according to the things we know and with which we are familiar."[19] But Joseph Smith, founding President, and Parley P. Pratt, Mormon apostle, both affirm that the first principle of the gospel is to know for a certainty the character of God, and our knowledge, comprehension and expressions of him should be divested of all mystery and be made as clear as any other item of truth. Obviously, Joseph Fielding Smith did not think things were quite so crystal clear and felt the need to admit some difficulty after all. Joseph Smith created more problems than he ever hoped to clear up! He plunged into the depths of folly when he said he would tell us the origin of God, how God came to be God. He claims that it is only imagination and supposition that "God was God from all eternity." Joseph Smith was deluded! Did he never read Isaiah's description of God as "the high and lofty One that inhabiteth eternity, whose name is Holy" (Isa. 57:15)? God has always existed. "God is not a man" (Num. 23:19). All of God's characteristics and attributes are affected by such a perverted view. The omnipresence of God is rejected when God is viewed as a man. James E. Talmage so affirms, "His person cannot be in more than one place at any one time."[20] Parley P. Pratt falls right in line with these words, "It is, therefore, an absolute impossibility for God the Father, or Jesus Christ, to be everywhere personally present. The omnipresence of God must therefore be understood in some other way than of his bodily or personal presence."[21] Espousers of this doctrine, professing themselves to be wise, became fools, and changed the glory of the incorruptible God for the likeness of an image of corruptible man, and have stored up for themselves the wrath of God (Rom. 1:18-23). Once God is brought down to the level of a man, it becomes easy to make all men into gods. That brings us to our next point of the Mormon view of God.

A Plurality of Gods

It was noted earlier that Joseph Smith taught that God dwelt on an earth, the same as Jesus Christ. He carries the doctrine further, "Here, then, is eternal life — to know the only wise and true God; and you have got to learn how to be Gods yourselves, and to be kings and priests to God, the same as all Gods before you, namely, by going from one small degree to another, and from a small capacity to a great one...."[22] The *Doctrine and Covenants,* 132:19, 20, tells how men may become gods and verse 37 tells us that Abraham, Issac, and Jacob became gods. James E. Talmage informs us, "In his mortal condition man is a God in embryo."[23] Joseph Fielding Smith further explains, "Joseph Smith taught a plurality of gods, and that man by obeying the commandments of God and keeping the whole law will eventually reach the power and exaltation by which he also will become a god."[24]

They can write about it from now to the end of time and it will not change the fact that, as we have already seen, the Bible teaches there is only one God. He is "the Holy One" (Isa. 40:25). Joseph Smith elaborates on the progression of God and His place in the world:

> The first principles of man are self-existent with God. God himself, finding he was in the midst of spirits and glory, because he was more intelligent, saw proper to institute laws whereby the rest could have a privilege to advance like himself."[25] "Where was there ever a son without a father? And where was there ever a father without first being a son? When did a tree or anything spring into existence without a progenitor? And everything comes in this way....Hence, if Jesus had a Father, can we not believe that He had a Father also? I despise the idea of being scared to death at such a doctrine, for the Bible is full of it."[26] "God never had the power to create the spirit of man at all."[27] "The mind or the intelligence which man possesses is co-equal with God himself."[28] "We say that God himself is a self-existent being. Who told you so? It is correct enough; but how did it get into your heads? Who told you that man did not exist in like manner upon the same principles? Man does exist on the same principles.[29]

Further, Joseph Smith explains his view of creation, stating, "God had materials to organize the world out of chaos — chaotic matter, which is element, and in which dwells all the glory. Element has existence from the time he had."[30]

In these statements there is a complete disregard for the word of God. From the Bible we learn that God does not progress, and advance, but rather is immutable, unchangeable, as noted earlier. The same passage that teaches us that God is not a man, tells us that God does not have a father, "God is not a man, that he should lie, neither the son of man, that he should repent" (Num. 23:19). He exists in and of himself and does not depend on anything or anyone else. In other words he is self-existent. God is not simply a cause of change within nature, e.g. rearranging materials, spirits, and intelligence, but, rather, He is the **cause** of nature. He is the bestower of existence to both the material and spiritual, to all things other than himself

(Gen. 1:1; Heb. 12:9).[31] It is a logical contradiction to affirm God is self-existent and also to affirm that man, intelligence and the elements are all self-existent as well. Yet, Joseph Smith did it, even though, the Bible plainly states, there is none beside God. Joseph Smith even went so far as to say that it is in chaotic matter, elements as he calls it, in which all the glory dwells. Truly, he thought more of the physical creation, the creature, than the Creator. Paul declared of God, "To him be the glory forever" (Rom. 11:36).

Conclusion

In the *Book of Mormon,* Ether 3:16-20, the omniscience of God is cast aside. Again in the *Book of Mormon* and the *Pearl of Great Price,* God is made responsible for sin and thus all evil.[32] We have not begun to exhaust all of the conflicts between the Mormon view of God and the Bible.

There are not many religions to which one can go to find, in the name of religion, so thorough a disregard for God's existence, character, and His word, as that which is found in Mormonism. May all those who presently embrace it, repent and turn to the gospel of our Lord and savior Jesus Christ, which has been made known unto all nations unto obedience of faith (Rom. 16:25, 26). To espouse Mormonism is to reject God and His word, the Bible.

Footnotes

1. Samuel M. Thompson, *A Modern Philosophy of Religion,* Chicago, Henry Regnery Co., 1955, p. 340.
2. These figures of speech, anthropomorphism and anthropopathy, can be found in any good dictionary.
3. Moses 1:3 (BM).
4. Moses 1:6 (BM).
5. Alma 11:28, 29 (BM).
6. Alma 22:9-11 (BM).
7. II Nephi. 29:9 (BM).
8. Moroni 8:18 (BM).
9. Moroni 7:22 (BM).
10. *Doctrine & Covenants,* 76:4.
11. *Teachings of the Prophet Joseph Smith,* compiled by Joseph Fielding Smith, Deseret Book Co., 1977, pp. 345, 346.
12. Ibid., p. 181.
13. *Key to the Science of Theology,* Parley P. Pratt, Classics in Mormon Literature, Deseret Book Co., Salt Lake City, 1979, p. 18. (Reprinted & changed from original 1855 edition.)
14. Ibid., p. 20.
15. Ibid., p. 19.
16. *Articles of Faith,* James E. Talmage, Church of Jesus Christ of Latter Day Saints, 1970, 12th ed., p. 41.
17. Ibid., p. 160. Cf. also p. 24, *Key to Science of Theology.*
18. *Teachings of the Prophet Joseph Smith, p. 181.*
19. *Doctrines of Salvation,* vol. 1, Joseph Fielding Smith, compiled by Bruce R. McConkie, Bookcraft, Salt Lake City, 1954, pp. 10, 11.
20. *Articles of Faith,* p. 43.
21. *Key to Science of Theology,* pp. 23, 24.
22. *Teachings of the Prophet Joseph Smith,* pp. 346, 347.
23. *Articles of Faith,* p. 530.
24. *Doctrines of Salvation,* vol. 1, p. 98.

25. *Teachings of the Prophet Joseph Smith,* p. 354.
26. Ibid., p. 373.
27. Ibid., p. 354.
28. Ibid., p. 353.
29. Ibid., p. 352.
30. Ibid., p. 351.
31. For a concise treatment of Gen. 1:1, Cf. *Questions and Answers, Open Forum, Freed-Hardeman College Lectures,* by Guy N. Woods, pp. 15, 16. This material exposes the commentary that Joseph Smith made on Gen. 1:1.
32. II Nephi. 2:22-25 (BM); Moses 5:10, 11 (PGP).

CHAPTER 14
THE SEVENTH-DAY ADVENTISTS DOCTRINE OF GOD

George L. Herring

The doctrine of God is of fundamental importance to any religious body. An understanding of the kind of being God is, and His relation to the world forms the basis for worship and practical living. In discussing the doctrine of God according to the Seventh-Day Adventist view, we shall consider: (1) the nature and attributes of God, (2) the evidences of existence or revelation of God, and (3) the work of God. The "official" positions of the Seventh-Day Adventists in their publications and the actual practice of the religious group sometimes appear contradictory, but as it is our purpose to represent accurately the Seventh-Day Adventist basic teachings on the doctrine of God, this study will consist largely of quotations from representative Adventist writings.

The Nature of God

Anthony A. Hoekema, in his book *The Four Major Cults,* states, "On the doctrine of the being of God Seventh-Day Adventists do not differ from historic Christianity." [1] Unlike the Mormons, Christian Scientists, or Jehovah's Witnesses, Seventh-Day Adventists clearly affirm the Trinity.

The second statement in the "Fundamental Beliefs of Seventh-Day Adventists" as presented in the *Seventh-Day Adventists Church Manual,* which sets forth the official discipline and doctrinal position of the denomination, reads as follows:

> That the Godhead, or Trinity, consists of the Eternal Father, a personal, spiritual Being, omnipotent, omnipresent, omniscient, infinite in wisdom and love; the Lord Jesus Christ, the Son of the Eternal Father, through whom all things were created and through whom the salvation of the redeemed hosts will be accomplished; the Holy Spirit, the third person of the Godhead, the great regenerating power in the work of redemption (Matt. 28:19; Isa. 44:6; 48:13; Matt. 12:32; II Cor. 13:14; Rev. 1:8,11).

The above statement clearly sets forth the personality and infinity of God the Father, as well as the personality and full deity of the Holy Spirit and Jesus Christ.

Leo Rosten, editor of *Religions in America* , in discussing the Seventh-Day Adventists, says:

> Reverently they worship Father, Son, and Holy Spirit, "three Persons in one God." And they do so because they believe this to be the teaching of the Bible concerning God in his relation to this world and the human race.[3]

It is interesting to note that early Seventh-Day Adventist anti-Trinitarians opposed the Trinitarian concept because they felt that such a belief was contrary to common sense and to New Testament statements indicating Christ's subordination to the Father, that it was of pagan origin, and that it depreciated the personality of Christ and the importance of His vicarious death. The writings of Ellen G. White, beginning as early as 1869 and increasing in the 1870's and 1880's, were largely responsible for the final prevailing of the Trinitarian view.[4]

The Adventist writers in *Questions on Doctrine* express the belief that quotations from early, out-of-date literature, and often taken out of context, have presented a distorted picture of the beliefs and teachings of the Seventh-Day Adventist Church of today. They make the following statement:

> All this has made it desirable and necessary for us to declare our position anew upon the great fundamental teachings of the Christian faith, and to deny every statement or implication that Christ, the second person of the Godhead, was not one with the Father from all eternity, and that His death on the cross was not a full and complete sacrificial atonement. The belief of Seventh-Day Adventists on these great truths is clear and emphatic. And we feel that we should not be identified with, or stigmatized for, certain limited and faulty concepts held by some, particularly in our formative years.[5]

It will now be our purpose to consider specific character traits of God, according to the teachings of the Seventh-Day Adventists.

One of the basic attributes of God is **love.** The writings of Ellen G. White frequently refer to the love of God. In her *Steps to Christ* she speaks of the "loving-kindness of God...the benevolence, the fatherly tenderness, of His character."[6] In the same book she declares, "His thoughts are thoughts of mercy, love, and tenderest compassion."[7] The *Seventh-Day Adventist Encyclopedia* speaks of God's love which manifests itself in His care and concern for the happiness and well-being of created beings.[8]

God is **self-existent.** Dr. Richard Rice, Adventist theology professor, asserts in his book, *The Openness of God,* "God is self existent. He is the one being who would exist whether anything else existed or not."[9] In the *Seventh-Day Adventist Encyclopedia* it is stated, "God is self-existent. All other life is from Him, as a gift."[10]

God is **eternal.** In *Speaking Well of God,* Dr. Edward Vick, Adventist theologian, avers, "God is eternal. This is not a simple denial that God does not die. Rather, it affirms that God transcends the limitations of time."[11]

The *Seventh-Day Adventist Encyclopedia* points out that God is both **faithful** and **immutable** (Mal. 3:6; Deut. 7:9). It also states that God is **omniscient, omnipresent,** and **omnipotent.** His knowledge is complete and perfect, and He is ever near; man cannot escape from God's presence. God is sovereign ruler over all, and his power is absolute and infinite.[12]

God is **holy** (Hos. 11:9). God alone can be absolutely holy, for He alone has an infinite comprehension of absolute perfection of character.[13]

All serious students of the scriptures would agree that God is the giver of life and that love and immutability are also divine attributes, but these characteristics have particular significance in our study of the distinctive Adventist doctrine concerning eternal punishment. According to the writers in *Questions on Doctrine,* there are three primary reasons for the rejection of the doctrine of eternal torment by Seventh-Day Adventists:

(1) Because everlasting life is a gift of God (Rom. 6:23). The wicked do not possess this—they "shall not see life" (John 3:36); "no murderer hath eternal life abiding in him" (I John 3:15).

(2) Because it seems to us to provide a plague spot in the universe of God throughout eternity, and would seem to indicate that it is impossible for God Himself ever to abolish it.

(3) Because in our thinking, it would detract from the attribute of love as seen in the character of God, and postulates the concept of a wrath which is never appeased.[14]

Man has always been tempted to make God and His teachings conform to his own limits and interpretations. In *The Kingdom of the Cults,* Walter Martin observes:

> It is my opinion that Seventh-Day Adventists have done just this; first by predicting that a God of love would not eternally punish a conscious being, and second by attempting to force the Scriptures into their frame of thought while seeming to ignore context, hermeneutics, and exegesis.[15]

The author of *Theology of Seventh-Day Adventism,* Herbert Bird, ably expresses the same idea:

> It has not been given to us to determine how sinful is sin, or to fix the degree of punishment which is due those who are in a state of rebellion to God, who then are we to say that infinite love and eternal retribution are incompatible concepts?[16]

What a pity it is to take the beautiful concept of God's love and distort it into a doctrine which is contrary to His Holy Word!

Revelation of God

The Seventh-Day Adventists believe that God has revealed Himself in (1) nature, (2) the written Word, (3) providence, and (4) the incarnation of His Son.

Ellen G. White observes in *Education,* "Upon all created things is seen the impress of the Deity. Nature testifies of God."[17] She further notes, in *Steps to Christ,* that God is seeking to make Himself known to us in many ways and that nature speaks to us without ceasing.[18]

The Bible is, in the opinion of the Adventists, an important source of revelation to humanity. Warren H. Johns, associate editor of *Ministry* magazine, asserts, "It is our conviction that the Bible, composed of Old and New Testaments, is the written revelation of God's will and character and that it has reached mankind in its final form through a process of inspiration."[19] In *Steps to Christ* Ellen White affirms her belief in the revelation of God's character through His word.[20]

It is appropriate, at this point, to refer to the writings of Ellen G. White in connection with the written revelation of God. An examination of her writings will show that Mrs. White considered herself to have received special revelations from God. In her thinking, although her messages were from God Himself and were completely authoritative, they were not to be considered an addition to the canon of Holy Scripture, but as an aid to the understanding and application of its teachings.

The importance of Ellen G. White's writings to the Adventists as an instrument of revealing God's nature and will cannot be discounted. Milton V. Backman, Jr., author of *Christian Churches of America,* in speaking of Ellen G. White, observes, "God, they [Adventists] claim, has relayed his desires and admonitions to mankind through this messenger, and the counsel and writings of Ellen G. White have served as a major factor in maintaining doctrinal unity in the church."[21] The editor of *Ministry* states in the March, 1981, issue:

> Recently, at its General Conference session of April, 1980, the church reaffirmed its confidence in this unique role for Ellen White. Among the fundamental beliefs voted there, number 17 reads: "One of the gifts of the Holy Spirit is prophecy. This gift is an identifying mark of the remnant church and was manifested in the ministry of Ellen G. White. As the Lord's messenger, her writings are a continuing and authoritative source of truth and provide for the church comfort, guidance, instruction, and correction."[22]

In addition to the general revelation in nature and the special revelation of God's word, Adventist writings teach that God reveals Himself through His providence. Two quotations will document this affirmation. From Ellen G. White:

> God speaks to us through His providential workings, and through the influence of His Spirit upon the heart. In our circumstances and surroundings, in the changes daily taking place around us, we may find precious lessons, if our hearts are but open to discern them.[23]

Warren H. Johns, writing in *Ministry,* states:

> God is continually revealing Himself by His providential intervention in human affairs. But while He is thus inter-

> acting at all times within the ebb and flow of human events, He especially intervenes on particular occasions (such as at the Exodus from Egyptian bondage) to reveal Himself in a marked manner.[24]

The supreme revelation of God centers in Jesus Christ, His Son. Dr. Edward Vick emphasizes this point in his book, *Speaking Well of God.* He says, "The Christian points to Jesus as the place within human history where and from which God may be known."[25] Warren Johns also stresses the importance of Jesus as God's revelator:

> Far surpassing the revelation of God in types and symbols, in dreams and visions, or in the prophet's voice is the revelation of Himself in human form. By precept and example, Jesus Christ, the incarnate revelation of God, taught truths about His father that could not be learned in any other way. The revelation centered at the cross is the highest form of revelation, and the knowledge of "Jesus Christ and him crucified" (I Cor. 2:2) far excels any other form of knowledge.[26]

Work of God

Seventh-Day Adventists believe that God is the **creator** and **preserver** of the universe. Indeed, they have been quite vocal in opposing evolutionary teachings. Point one of the denomination's "Statement of Fundamental Beliefs" reads, "[We believe] that God is the Sovereign Creator, upholder and ruler of the Universe and that He is eternal, omnipotent, omniscient and omnipresent."[27] It is further stated, "That God created the world in six literal days; we do not believe that creation was accomplished by long aeons of evolutionary processes."[28]

Prominent current Adventist scholars and authors attest to the belief in God as creator and sustainer, as does Ellen G. White in her publications. Richard Rice speaks of God's creative activity as being the first and most fundamental description of God in the Bible. The Biblical doctrine of creation refers to both the origin of the world and the continuing relation of God to the earth and its creatures as sustainer and preserver.[29] Edward Vick declares that God created everything and is the purpose behind what happens in the world. Therefore, all finite beings are dependent upon the Infinite.[30]

In *Steps to Christ,* Ellen G. White describes God's care for the sparrow, as well as the vast worlds, and for man in all his specific activities. She says, "And God cares for everything and sustains everything that He has created."[31]

The emphasis upon the observance of the Sabbath by the Seventh-Day Adventists is closely related to God's work as creator. In *Christian Churches of America,* Milton Backman points out that they teach "that this seventh day is sacred because it was designed to be a memorial to God's creative power and is a sign of his authority."[32] Ellen G. White, in *The*

Story of Patriarchs and Prophets, observes that God sanctified the seventh day that He might reflect upon God's great work of creation. In placing His blessing upon the seventh day in Eden, God set up the memorial of His work of creation. The observance of the Sabbath "was to be an act of grateful acknowledgment, on the part of all who should dwell upon the earth, that God was their Creator and their rightful Sovereign; that they were the work of His hands and the subjects of His authority."[33]

A study of God's work or His dealings with man, according to Adventist doctrine, would not be complete without at least a brief mention of the relation between grace and the law in God's plan for man's salvation. Adventists have, from their beginning, put great stress upon "the law of God," making a distinction between "ceremonial ordinances" and "the moral law of God—the Decalogue." Walter Martin points out that "by virtue of the fact that they obey the Fourth Commandment as well as the other nine, Adventists maintain that they alone are God's commandment-keeping church."[34] However, Seventh-Day Adventists insist that they believe that salvation is by the grace of God. In *Questions on Doctrine,* it is stated:

> There has been regrettable misunderstanding as to our teaching on grace, law, and works, and their interrelationships. According to Seventh-Day Adventist belief, there is, and can be, no salvation through the law, or by human works of the law, but only through the saving grace of God.[35]

The eighth point in the "Fundamental Beliefs of Seventh-Day Adventists" in their church manual contains the following statement: "We are justified, not by ordinance to the law, but by the grace that is in Christ Jesus."[36] In the words of current Adventist leaders:

> While works are not a means of salvation, good works are the inevitable result of salvation...there is really no actual valid conflict between grace and the law—the Ten Commandments; each serves its special purpose in the plan of God. Grace, as such, is not opposed to the law, which is God's standard of righteousness; neither is the law opposed to grace. Each has its specific functions, and neither trespasses on the functions of the other. One thing is certain, man cannot be saved by any effort of his own...Salvation is wholly of grace; it is the gift of God (Rom. 4:4,5; Eph. 2:8).[37]

On this matter we shall let the Seventh-Day Adventists speak for themselves!

Before leaving God's plan for man's salvation, perhaps we should call attention to two other statements showing the Adventist belief. In *Questions on Doctrine* it is stated:

> We believe that man is free to choose or reject the offer of salvation through Christ; we do not believe that God has predetermined that some men shall be saved and others lost.[38]

In *Steps to Christ,* Ellen G. White says:

> The government of God is not, as Satan would make it appear, founded upon a blind submission, an unreasoning control...God does not force the will of His creatures. A mere forced submission would prevent any real development of mind or character; it would make man a mere automaton. Such is not the purpose of the Creator.[39]

Finally, in discussing the work of God, it should be stated that, in keeping with their belief in premillennialism, point twenty-two of the church manual of the Seventh-Day Adventists says, "That God will make all things new. The earth, restored to its pristine beauty, will become forever the abode of the saints of the Lord."[40]

Conclusion

In conclusion, as we consider the doctrine of God, we find that Seventh-Day Adventist beliefs concerning the Trinity; the attributes of God; revelation of God; God as the creator and preserver of the Universe; God as the author of salvation through His grace and the free moral agency of man are all largely consistent with generally accepted views. However, thorns of error have sprouted from roots of truth. It is paradoxical that the Seventh-Day Adventists should freely admit that the Bible is objectively the authoritative Word of God, and yet turn to Ellen G. White's writings subjectively as "a lesser light to lead men and women to the greater light." It is regrettable that the Seventh-Day Adventists' rejection of eternal torment for the wicked should be based on their concept of a "loving God"; that the observance of the Sabbath has its roots in their acknowledgement of God as Creator; that the "keeping" of the Ten Commandments and other portions of the Mosaic law today is, in their view, a sign of obedience to God; that God has been assigned the work of "making all things new" according to the Adventist theory of premillennialism. Seventh-Day Adventist views on the doctrine of God contribute directly toward making Seventh-Day Adventists a distinctive religious sect.

FOOTNOTES

1. Anthony A. Hoekema, *The Four Major Cults,* (Grand Rapids, Michigan: William B. Eerdmans Publishing Company, 1963), p. 108.
2. *Seventh-Day Adventist Church Manual,* (Issued by the General Conference of Seventh-Day Adventists: Revised 1976), p. 32.
3. Leo Rosten, editor, *Religions in America,* (New York: Simon and Schuster, 1952), p. 179.

4. Don F. Neufeld, editor, *Seventh-Day Adventist Encyclopedia,* volume 10, (Washington, D.C.: Review and Herald Publishing Association, 1976), p. 287.

5. *Questions on Doctrine,* Prepared by a representative group of Seventh-day Adventist leaders, Bible teachers, and editors, (Washington, D.C.: Review and Herald Publishing Association, 1957), pp. 31-32.

6. Ellen G. White, *Steps to Christ,* (Washington, D.C.: Review and Herald Publishing Association, 1921), p. 21.

7. Ibid., p. 56.

8. *Seventh-Day Adventist Encyclopedia,* p. 521.

9. Richard Rice, *The Openness of God,* (Nashville, TN.: Review and Herald Publishing Association, 1980), p. 23.

10. *Seventh-Day Adventist Encyclopedia,* p. 521.

11. Edward W. H. Vick, *Speaking Well of God,* (Nashville, Tennessee: Southern Publishing Association, 1979), p. 104.

12. *Seventh-Day Adventist Encyclopedia,* p. 521.

13. Ibid., p. 522.

14. *Questions on Doctrine,* p. 543.

15. Walter R. Martin, *The Kingdom of the Cults,* (Minneapolis, Minnesota: Bethany Fellowship, Inc., Publishers, 1965), p. 412.

16. Herbert S. Bird, *Theology of Seventh-Day Adventism,* (Grand Rapids, Michigan: Wm. B. Eerdmans Publishing Company, 1961), p. 62.

17. Ellen G. White, *Education,* (Mountain View, California: Pacific Press Publishing Association, 1903), p. 99.

18. White, *Steps to Christ,* p. 87.

19. Warren H. Johns, "Scripture Is by Inspiration of God." *Ministry* 54, 3, (March 1981), p. 16.

20. White, *Steps to Christ,* p. 89.

21. Milton V. Backman, Jr., *Christian Churches of America: Origins and Beliefs,* (Provo, Utah: Brigham Young University Press, 1976) p. 171.

22. J. Robert Spangler, "Ellen G. White—Plagiarist?" *Ministry,* 54, 3, (March 1981), p. 21.

23. White, *Steps to Christ,* p. 89.

24. Johns, "Scripture Is by Inspiration of God," p. 17.

25. Vick, *Speaking Well of God,* p. 112.

26. Johns, "Scripture Is by Inspiration of God," p. 17.

27. *Questions on Doctrine,* pp. 21-22.

28. Ibid., p. 24.

29. Rice, *The Openness of God,* p. 22.

30. Vick, *Speaking Well of God,p. 89.*

31. White, Steps to Christ, p. 88.

32. Backman, *Christian Churches of America: Origins and Beliefs,* p. 171.

33. Ellen G. White, *The Story of Patriarchs and Prophets,* (Mountain View, California: Pacific Press Publishing Association, 1958), pp. 47-48.

34. Martin, *The Kingdom of the Cults,* p. 412.

35. *Questions on Doctrine,* p. 135.

36. *Seventh -Day Adventist Church Manual,* p. 34.

37. *Questions on Doctrine,* pp. 141-142.

38. Ibid., p. 23.

39. White, *Steps to Christ,* p. 46.

40. *Seventh-Day Adventist Church Manual,* pp. 38-39.

CHAPTER 15
THE SEVENTH-DAY ADVENTIST DOCTRINE OF THE SOUL

James W. Boyd

This study is an investigation of the doctrine of man, his nature, the soul, immortality and future punishment as taught by Seventh Day Adventist church (SDA)[1] and its variance from Biblical revelation. It is not unfair to say at the start that the SDA doctrine today may not be what it was in the past or might be in the future because the SDA contends that the unfolding of Bible truth is still progressive. They have never driven in formal creedal stakes but teach new light will ever be revealed with more yet to shine.

In answer to the question, "What is man?" SDA teaches that "man is a unity, and that that unity in a body is a complex of parts, drawing their life and activity from a breath-soul, which has no existence apart from the body." Man is wholly mortal with no entity capable of surviving death. In death he is as if he had never been. After the body decays he has no existence whatever. Neither whole nor part of man is inherently immortal and has no innate immortality. Man is a creature subject to death with possibility of eternal life only because Christ paid the penalty.

SDA doctrine contends that immortality only applies to God, citing I Tim. 1:17; 6:16. The passage teaches, however, that only God can give immortality and only God has the power of immortality, just as only God has the power to forgive sins. It teaches the immortality of God. But one must ignore other Biblical teaching to assert immortality applies "only" to God.

SDA makes much of Job 4:17, "Shall mortal man be more just than God?" But Job did not speak this, but rather Eliphaz, who is described in Job 13:4 as forger of lies and a physician of no value. Shall such a one be the deciding witness regarding the nature of man?

SDA cites I Cor. 15:53, "mortal puts on immortality," as if the passage refers to the soul of man. The context demands that it refers to the body, that which is corruptible and goes to the tomb.

Immortality of the righteous is not really an issue with SDA, with one exceptional point that shall be discussed later. SDA says that the righteous shall be resurrected and given immortality. But such nature did not belong to any inherently because they are human beings. The reward of the saints is immortality, but a reward only to the saints. Before the resurrection and judgment none had immortality in any sense. One is admonished to seek immortality (Rom. 2:7) and one does not seek what he already has, SDA contends. But notice how this clashes with Biblical revelation concerning the nature of man.

Paul wrote of the outward and inward man (II Cor. 4:16). He mentioned the "earthly house" and a building not made with hands, eternal (II Cor. 5:1). Solomon said the body returns to dust but the spirit to God (Eccl.

12:7). Dan. 7:15 reads, "I Daniel was grieved in my spirit in the midst of my body." Our physical parents give us our physical bodies, but God is the "Father of spirits," (Heb. 12:9). SDA contends the spirit is only our breath. When Christ said, "Into thy hands I commend my spirit," (Luke 23:46), did He simply blow His breath back to God? Paul admitted the possibility of one being out of the body (II Cor. 12:1-4). All these passages show that man is not the kind of unit as SDA says, but there is a distinction between body, the soul and spirit of man. Space prohibits a discussion of all such passages that prove this, but listed are several others for study (Matt. 10:28; I Cor. 6:20; 15:44; II Cor. 5:1; 12:2,3; I Thess. 5:23; Heb. 4:12; James 2:26).

As for the soul or spirit of man, SDA teaches that the words of both the Old and New Testaments do not remotely imply a conscious entity that is able to survive the death of the body. They say the words "nephesh, psuche" refer only to the person, the individual, a unit of life that humans have in common with animals, and nothing more. The basic meaning is said to be that of breathing. The soul is not a constituent of the body but only breath. Breath is to the body as gasoline is to an engine, namely, only that which keeps it running.

We are forced to ask, "What part of the body thinks? At death and the loss of breath, why cannot the dead think? Breath does not think, therefore the thinking capacity should abide. What part of the body has intelligence? Since the body is matter, does the matter think? If SDA positions are true, then the larger the body the greater the intelligence."

While SDA says the Bible writers never had inherent immortality idea in mind at all, we must ask again, "What did Peter mean when he admonished a 'quiet spirit'? Did he mean breathe quietly?"(I Peter 3:4). Does a "familiar spirit" (Lev. 20:27) refers only to breath? Is "troubled spirit" (John 13:21) only troubled breath? Is the "filthiness of flesh and spirit" (II Cor. 7:1) a reference to offensive breath? To ask is to point out the absurdity of contending the spirit of the Bible is merely breath.

SDA teaches that death is no more than cessation of physical life, a departure of the breath from the body. SDA says death refers almost exclusively to physical death and is annihilation and a cessation of existence. But the Bible teaches that death is the separation of the body from the spirit (James 2:26). You are not dead simply because the breath is knocked out of your body. SDA confuses the reality of physical and spiritual deaths. They deny that Adam died in any way except physically, even though the Scripture said that God warned, "In the day that thou eatest thereof thou shalt surely die" (Gen. 2:17). Adam did not die physically until hundreds of years after he ate the forbidden fruit. But God said he would die that day. In some sense Adam died other than merely physically.

Jesus said, "Let the dead bury the dead" (Matt. 8:22). Was He saying to let those who have ceased to exist bury those who also have ceased to exist? Reference to spiritual death is obvious in John 11:26; I John 3:14, and many others. Those who convert the sinner from the error of his way do not save a person from physical death (James 5:19,20). One can be dead even while he is physically alive (I Tim. 5:6). Abraham long ago died physically but Jesus said he was still alive and that God was the God of the living (Luke 20:37,38). One cannot grasp the truth when he contends that there is but the physical death and not a spiritual death.

Scripture shows that man is a creature that is both body and soul (Matt. 10:28). Sometimes he is presented as body, soul and spirit (I Thess. 5:23). Man does have a body made of the dust of the earth that will decay after death. Man also possesses a characteristic in common with the beasts of the field, namely, there is life, animation, movement. But man is unique and distinct from all other creatures that God brought into being by the power of His creative Word. Man is created in the image of God (Gen. 1:27). Jesus said God is Spirit (John 4:24). Herein is the quality of man that shows he is immortal. He is spirit as God is Spirit and the Spirit of Deity is immortal. Remove this unique distinction from the human family and humans become nothing more than what evolutionists and all other materialists would have us believe, nothing more than a highly developed animal, that and that only. Other consequences of such a doctrine will be presented toward the conclusion of the study.

Actually, the SDA do not believe in a resurrection of anybody, even though they say they do. Their doctrine prohibits any resurrection. While they say the righteous will be resurrected and given immortality, if they are right about death being a cessation of existence and annihilation, then there is nothing to resurrect. There must be a re-creation to have anyone to whom immortality could be given. The Bible teaches resurrection, not re-creation. So the SDA definition of death is at variance with the Biblical definition.

The SDA doctrine regarding the definition of death means that the wicked, at death, cease to exist and there is nothing good, bad or otherwise in their future. And even the righteous have to be re-created to benefit from that which God gives the righteous because they would cease to exist at death also.

SDA teaches that when one dies he enters into a totally unconscious state, one of silence, inactivity—dead sleep. When one dies he rests in the tomb until the resurrection morning. Just how one can be raised after he has ceased to exist and is totally annihilated is just one of the inconsistencies of SDA doctrine. The doctrine of soul-sleeping is a part of the SDA materialistic view of man. One can easily see that it also reduces man to the level of a beast. But soul-sleeping is consistent with SDA doctrine that man is wholly mortal and death is the end of existence. Any consciousness whatsoever at anytime thereafter would contradict their basic teaching regarding the nature of man. But the Bible does contradict soul-sleeping.

SDA points to Eccl. 9:5,6 where it reads, "but the dead know not anything." But the very next phrase gives that doctrine problems because it also reads, "neither have they anymore reward." The righteous also die physically. They are among the dead. If Eccl. 9:5,6 teaches entire unconsciousness, it also teaches no reward to any who die, including the righteous.

The truth of the passage is not complete until one considers the rest of it. The dead know not anything, have no reward, their love, hatred, envy have perished, and they have no more portion, "under the sun." The reason for this is obvious. They are no longer under the sun. They have left this life under the sun. But the passage does not teach unconsciousness elsewhere.

Romans 2:7-9 presents the recompense of the contentious as "tribulation and anguish." Many who are contentious enjoy this life to the fullest. Tribulation and anguish are after this life as surely as the rewards for the righteous, "glory, honor immortality, eternal life," come after this life. But if one is entirely unconscious and annihilated, dead asleep, how can he suffer tribulation and anguish? That requires a consciousness. So soul-sleeping is not Biblical.

If in death there is nothing but silence and unconsciousness, one cannot explain the presence of the righteous like Moses and Elijah with Jesus in Matt. 17 at the mount of transfiguration. But they were there and very conscious.

Luke 16, of which we shall have more to say, has Abraham telling the right man to "remember." That requires consciousness.

Rev. 6:9,10, the martyred souls that were crying, "How long, how long," were very conscious even though dead physically. This was prior to the resurrection.

John 5:28,29, in which Jesus assures the resurrection of both the good and the bad and the rising to life and damnation, requires consciousness. It absolutely refutes death as annihilation.

SDA doctrine relies heavily on what is not said. They refer to the fact that whose who were called forth from the tomb or raised to life miraculously during the Bible times never said anything about what was on the other side. Whether they said anything or not we do not know. Nothing is recorded. But an argument from such silence is leaning on a broken reed. They also rely heavily on what men have thought through the ages. In fact, the book, *Questions on Doctrine,* published by SDA, devotes twice as much space in the chapter as to what men have thought on these things as in the presentation of any phase of these doctrines.

To the SDA, hell, sheol, hades, all simply refer to the grave. There is no other punishment except the grave. They deny any other punishment because they contend it is inconsistent with God's love and mercy. But wicked people live this life fully indulging themselves with joy in sin, while the righteous suffer because of their righteousness. If there is no punishment for their evil, what does this do to the love, mercy of God for the righteous as well as to His standards of justice? Allowing the wicked to just cease to exist and nothing more, but permitting good people to suffer is simply another instance of inconsistency in SDA doctrine.

If the grave is the hell for the wicked, then only those who forget God ought go to the grave. But all go to the grave. Hell (gehenna), sheol or hades are not simply the grave. These words refer to eternal punishment and/or the unseen state of the dead. The rich man and Lazarus went there. Jesus and the thief went there. They did not go into annihilation, a cessation of existence. There is no punishment for wickedness if hell is only the grave. It would be more of a relief for the wicked to get out so easily.

To the SDA, while claiming they believe in eternal punishment, they say death is that punishment, and it is eternal only in the sense that it is final. But they deny any endless process involving punishment. Sin and sinners will be blotted out of existence and will not suffer punishment throughout eternity. How does this compare with Scripture?

"I fail to see why any good man desires to convince people that wickedness would not meet a terrible punishment," wrote David Lipscomb in the *Gospel Advocate* in 1901. But what saith the Scripture?

Matt. 25:30 speaks of weeping and gnashing of teeth, which demands consciousness. Luke 12:4,5 teaches there is something to fear after death. If death means annihilation, there is nothing to fear. Luke 12:47,48 mentions few stripes and many stripes. SDA denies that there are any stripes at all. How could Christ speak of it being "more tolerable" for Sodom than the cities of His day if all that any of them suffer would simply be physical death? All of the following passages demand consciousness: Matt. 25:46; Mark 9:44; II Thess. 1:6-9; II Peter 2:9; Rev. 14:11; 21:8; Dan. 12:2. There can be no escape from the Biblical teaching that one does not enter total annihilation, soul-sleeping, silence, inactivity, etc. upon physical death. There can be no escape from the Biblical teaching that speaks of punishment. Now let us look to the "eternal" nature of that punishment.

According to Mark 9:48, Jesus says of hell,"...where their worm dieth not, and the fire is not quenched." Now, SDA contends that this refers only to the process of **annihilation.** But we must ask, "Once the body is annihilated, does the worm continue to live, as Jesus said, or does it die?" If the worm dies, Jesus spoke falsely. If man is annihilated and the worm lives you have the peculiar doctrine of the immortality of the worm but not the man who has been created in God's spiritual image. Furthermore, the fire is not quenched. If man is simply burned up, ceases to exist, etc. what fuels the fire? It would cease to burn by virtue of no fuel. Matt. 18:8 refers to everlasting fire.

In Hebrews 10:28,29 we learn that violators of Moses' law died physically. But those who violate Christ's law would suffer "much sorer punishment." But if such wicked violators only die physically and there is nothing more than that, in what way would they suffer a "sorer punishment?" One cannot read of the description of the punishment of the wicked in Rev. 14:9-ll and believe SDA doctrine.

Matt. 25:46 twice uses a word, "aionios," meaning eternal or everlasting. It is used with reference to duration and it modifies both life and punishment. The punishment of I John 4:18 is defined also as torment, the same word as punishment in Matt. 25:46. How could there be torment in a state of unconsciousness, in total annihilation, in soul-sleeping, in cessation of existence?

In II Thess. 9, destruction means "the loss of a life of blessedness after death, future misery," (Thayer, p. 443). Heb. 9:27 teaches we are appointed once to die, and after that the judgment. If SDA doctrine is true, the judgment is only for the righteous, who must be re-created to even face that. The wicked no longer exist. Why the judgment in the first place? Matt. 25 shows it is for the separation of the good for the evil, wheat from chaff, sheep from goats. But if SDA doctrine is true there remains no evil, or chaff, or goats anywhere from which anyone could be separated.

We have only briefly mentioned Luke 16, a passage which refutes this doctrine. But SDA attempt to explain away Luke 16 by saying it is only a "parable." They contend the meaning of the "parable" is simply the uncertainty of riches, the responsibility of the rich for their money, that this life is the only time to prepare, that selfishness is wrong, and the Scriptures sufficient to make us wise unto salvation. That such lessons are found therein none would take issue. But why omit one of the most prominent ones, the existence of life after death, consciousness after death, punishment after death except it would destroy their materialistic doctrines?

Luke 16 is not called a parable. It teaches the truth even if it is a parable. Man will and can "remember." The wicked shall be punished and the righteous will be rewarded.

Ellen G. White, founder of SDA, said that Christ was merely meeting people on their own ground in Luke 16. Many held the view that there was consciousness between death and the resurrection and He merely framed His "parable" to inculcate important truths through these preconceived, even though erroneous, opinions. He never bothered to correct them, either. He simply used the prevailing opinions to convey the idea He wished to make prominent, according to White.

Friend, that makes our Lord a party to perpetuating false doctrine. It would then raise the question, how much else did He accomodate in His teaching and teach error, or allowed error to stand without correction? Do you suppose His teaching on the resurrection was merely accomodating preconceived views and not really true after all? What of anything else He taught? White's view is blasphemy against the Son of God.

SDA are modern-day Sadducees in many respects, with later-day materialism. Their doctrines have a comforting sound to the wicked. If at death the soul sleeps, and death ends it all, and there is no punishment other than the grave, and there is no immortality, then if we choose to live wickedly we are really no worse off than before. We were not immortal nor shall we ever be. We fail to gain heaven, but we suffer no hell of eternal punishment. We cannot lose in this life, even though we might fail to gain.

SDA doctrine means we really will not be held accountable for our deeds whether good or evil because, if evil, we will never be around to answer for anything since we will not exist. We shall never hear the words, "Depart from me," because we cannot hear anything since we would be annihilated. Evil men are really nothing more than beasts and men have nothing more to fear than do beasts if they choose a wicked life.

But "He hath appointed a day, in the which he will judge the world in righteousness by that man whom he hath ordained; whereof he hath given assurance unto ALL (emphasis, JWB) men, in that he hath raised him from the dead" (Acts 17:31). Acts 24:15 teaches, "that there shall be a resurrection of the dead, both of the just and the unjust." We had better believe it and prepare for it. If we do not believe it while here on earth, there will be a time when we will be convinced, but it will then be too late to prepare.

FOOTNOTES

1. Seventh Day Adventist doctrine is presented as taught in their book, *Questions on Doctrine,* prepared by a representative group of Seventh-Day Adventist leaders, Bible teachers and Editors, published by Review and Herald Publishing Association, Washington, D.C., copyright 1957.

CHAPTER 16
THE SEVENTH DAY ADVENTIST DOCTRINE OF "THE SABBATH"

Wendell Winkler

Introduction

Legion are they who still believe in the keeping of the sabbath. Among these are the thousands composing the Adventist movement, along with the additional thousands who are followers of Herbert W. Armstrong and his son, Garner Ted Armstrong. In addition, there are others of lesser notoriety. Accordingly, it is most appropriate that we engage in this present study concerning, "what saith the Lord" relative to sabbath keeping.

I. Passages And Observations Showing That We Are No Longer Under The Law Which Commanded Sabbath Keeping

Study carefully

(1) **Romans 7:1-7.** This passage teaches us that we have become dead to the law (vs. 4) and delivered therefrom (vs. 6). Then, according to verse 7, the law to which we have become dead, and from which we have been delivered, is the law that states, "Thou shalt not covet." This was the ten commandment law! Therefore, we are no longer under — yea, we have been delivered from—the law that requires man to observe the sabbath. Incidentally, this point forever exposes the Adventist position that only the ceremonial law (offering sacrifices, etc.) has been done away, while the moral law (the ten commandment law) is still binding. Too, notice in this passage, according to Paul's analogy, that if a person seeks to be joined to the old law, he is guilty of spiritual adultery.

Study carefully

(2) **Colossians 2:14-17.** According to this passage, something was (a) blotted out, (b) was taken out of the way, and (c) was nailed to the cross. But, what? Paul answers, "the handwriting of ordinances." But, to what does this have reference? By reading Exodus 31:18 (the law was written with the finger of God) and Deut. 4:13 (the ten commandments were written upon tables of stone), and Exodus 24:12 (God's law and commandments were written by him), we can readily see that "the handwriting of ordinances" referred to the old law; yea, the ten commandment law. Furthermore, let us notice the word "ordinances." Ordinances are "things ordered." And, according to Numbers 19:2, the sabbath was ordered; thus, making it an ordinance. Now, with said law having been blotted out, taken out of the way, nailed to the cross, the text concludes by saying that no one is to judge us (bind upon us) certain things. The things that are not to be bound upon us have to do with yearly ("holyday"), monthly ("the new moon"), and weekly ("the sabbath days") observations. Thus, we can readily see that the law which has been abrogated is the law that involves the sabbath.

(3) **Study carefully II Corinthians 3:6-11.** Upon reading II Cor. 3:7, we can see that reference is made to "the ministration of death, written and engraven in stones" which was given on the occasion of the time when Israel could not stedfastly behold the face of Moses for the glory of his countenance. By reading Ex. 34:28-35, we observe, that what was given on that occasion were "the tables the words of the covenant, the ten commandments." Now concerning such, in the text presently being discussed, Paul says such "was glorious;" but, "which glory was to be done away" ("which glory was passing away," ASV). Then, we observe in verse 11 that the "was glorious" thing "is done away." Thus, unquestionably, we can readily see that the ten commandment law is no longer binding today.

(4) **Study carefully Zechariah 11:10-13.** In this passage Zechariah prophesies of the death of Christ by saying, "And I took my staff, even Beauty, and cut it asunder,..." Then, the prophet tells us the reasons for his death: "**that** I might **break my covenant** which I had made with all the people. And it was broken in that day." Thus, when Jesus died on the cross, the covenant that God had made was broken. Accordingly, no wonder Col. 2:14-17 teaches us that the law was abrogated at the cross.

(5) **Study carefully Ephesians 2:13-16.** "Having abolished" is the clear and definite affirmation of Paul in this text concerning "the law of commandments contained in ordinances." Furthermore, he identifies "the law of commandments" in this passage as being "the enmity." Then, in verse 16, he teaches us that this enmity has been slain. Too, Paul teaches us that this abolishing and slaying took place "in his flesh," or "by the cross." And, with the law having thus been abrogated, Jew and Gentile can be reconciled each to the other, and in turn both can be reconciled to God. Thus, this passage gives us the "what," the "when," and the "why" of the abrogation of the law.

(6) **Study carefully a number of passages in the Galatian epistle. First,** observe Galatians 3:16-19. According to this passage, the law was added "till the seed should come." Then, verse 16 identifies the seed as Christ. Accordingly, with the coming of Christ, the law was done away. **Secondly,** observe Galatians 3:23-26. This passage teaches us that the law was our schoolmaster to bring us to Christ, that we might be justified by faith. Then, Paul affirms, "after that faith is come, we are no longer under a schoolmaster (the law)." Then, in verse 26, he teaches us that faith has come! **Thirdly,** observe Gal. 4:21-31. Here is Paul's well known allegory of Hagar and Sarah, said allegory graphically and illustratively teaching us that the law has been abrogated. In the allegory, he identifies Hagar as representing the covenant from Mount Siani. Then, he observes, "Nevertheless what saith the scripture? Cast out the bondwoman and her son." How could Paul have made the matter clearer? **Fourthly,** read Gal. 5:4. Here Paul says, "Christ is become of no effect unto you, whosoever of you are justified by the law; ye are fallen from grace."

(7) **Study carefully a number of passages found in the Hebrew epistle.** (a) Heb. 7:12. According to this text, the priesthood and the law stand or fall

together. Accordingly, with the priesthood having been changed (Christ is a priest after the order of Melchisedek, rather than the Levitical system), there is a change also of the law. Thus, if the law is still binding, we still have the Levitical priesthood in effect. (b) **Heb. 8:6-13.** Here, the Hebrew writer quotes that famous prophecy from Jeremiah 31:31-34, said prophecy referring to the abrogation of the old law. In fact, according to verse 13 of this text, we read that the law was becoming obsolete even in Jeremiah's time (600 years before Christ)! That is, all these years, the old system, the old law, was decaying and destined to pass away. Yet, our sabbatarian friends want to maintain that it is new, fresh, and still very much binding on men in the 20th century. (c) **Heb. 10:9.** Herein the writer affirms, "He taketh away the first (law), that he may establish the second (New Testament)." This passage not only clearly teaches that the first testament has been taken away, but it also teaches that it is impossible for both the old and new testament to exist bindingly at one and the same time.

II. Proof Texts And Arguments Used By Sabbatarians Examined And Refuted

(1) **Sabbatarians affirm that the sabbath law was given from the beginning of time.** Gen. 2:2-3 is used as a proof text. However, be it observed that in this passage there are three references to the "seventh" day; but, not one reference to the sabbath! Too, in this passage there are three references to God, but none to man! The passage is simply telling us what God did! How weak a system must be to depend upon a major proof text for the validity of the sabbatarian system, when neither **man** nor the **sabbath** are mentioned. Furthermore, the sabbath is not mentioned in the first 65 chapters of the Bible. In fact, it is not until Israel had been delivered from Eqyptian bondage, and shortly before the Sinai assembly that the first reference is ever made of the sabbath (Ex. 16:23). If the sabbath was a universal law given from the beginning, is it not strange that the preceding obtained? That the sabbath was not mentioned for the first 25 centuries of man's existence? Is it not strange a universal law would be in existence for such a lengthy time and there not be a single reference or utterance concerning the same? Again, we ask, why? The answer: the sabbath law was not given from the beginning! Deut. 5:1-14 teaches that the law, which involved keeping the sabbath (vs. 12) was made in Horeb (vs. 2) and that this law was not made with the fathers (vs. 3); but, rather, was made with the Israelites who were there alive that day (vs. 3)! Furthermore, Neh. 9:13-14 teaches us that "upon Mount Sinai" God "madest known" his "holy sabbath." We cannot make known what is already known. Hence, the sabbath law was not given from the beginning. Also, according to Ex. 16:4ff, the Israelites, on the sixth day, gathered together twice as much of the "bread from heaven," as they did each day. God said that he made this arrangement "that I may prove them." However, if the sabbath observance had obtained from the beginning, they would already have been proven!

(2) **Sabbatarians affirm that the law to keep the sabbath was given to all mankind; thus, that it was a universal law.** But, again, observing Deut. 5:1-

14, we observe that "Moses called **all Israel,** and said unto them, hear, O **Israel** the statutes and judgments that I speak in your ears this day, that you may learn them, and keep, and do them. The Lord thy God made a covenant with **us** (that is, Israel) in Horeb. The Lord made not this covenant with our fathers, but with **us** (that is, Israel), even **us** (that is, Israel), who are all of **us** (that is, Israel) here alive this day." Furthermore, Deut. 5:15 teaches us that the sabbath was to those who were delivered from Egyptian bondage (hence, the Israelites). In fact, the text says, "**therefore** (because thou wast a servant in the land of Egypt, and that the Lord thy God brought thee out thence") the Lord thy God commanded thee to keep the sabbath day." Furthermore, by studying carefully Ex. 31:13, 17; Neh. 9:13, 14; and Ex. 20:10-12, we can readily and inescapably conclude that the sabbath law was given to the Israelites only.

(3) **Sabbatarians affirm that the law to keep the sabbath was to last forever.** It is true that Ex. 31:12-17 states that the sabbath observance was "a sign between me (God) and the children of Israel forever." However, in the same text, the Lord stated that the observance of the sabbath was to be "throughout your generations (thus a limitation)." Also, Ex. 12:14 teaches us that the Passover was to be kept by the Israelites "forever." Then, the feast of the tabernacles was commanded "forever" in Lev. 23:41. Also, Pentecost was to be observed "forever throughout your generations," according to Lev. 23:21. Is the Passover, the Feast of Tabernacles, and Pentecost still to be observed? Remember, they were "forever" ordinances. No, they are not to be observed. (Then, why make the sabbath binding today, since it was spoken of as a "forever" ordinance? Then, in the text presently being discussed (Ex. 31:12-17), Adventists make a play on the sabbath being "for a perpetual covenant (vs. 16)." However, Ex. 30:8 speaks of "perpetual incense throughout your generations," as being commanded. Why do sabbatarians reject all of these "perpetuals" and "forevers" when applied to other matters, but refuse to have the same attitude when applied to the sabbath? Here is the truth of the matter: these matters were to be observed "forever" and "perpetually" throughout the **designated time frames;** that is, their observances were not to cease during the designated time or era in which God had arranged that said ordinances were to be observed.

(4) **Sabbatarians affirm that Christ kept the sabbath; hence, that we should keep the sabbath.** Yes, Christ did keep the sabbath. However, let us remember that he was born and lived under the law that commanded such (Gal. 4:4). But, you and I were not born under, nor do we live under, this same law. Also, Christ kept the Passover (Lk. 22:7-14). Are our sabbatarian friends going to begin to keep the Passover? Consistency would demand the same.

(5) **Sabbatarians make a division in the old law; they say that the ten commandment law (binding the sabbath) is the law of God and is to last forever, whereas the law commanding incense and the observance of feast days, was the law of Moses and has been abrogated.** This arbitrary division of the old law will not stand scriptural scrutiny. Rom. 7:4-7 teaches us that

we are dead to the law (vs. 4); then, by reading verse 7 we can see that the law to which we are dead is the law that includes the commandment "thou shalt not covet." This was the law which also said, "thou shalt keep the sabbath day holy." Hence, the law to which we are dead (separated, James 2:26) is the law that involved the commandment to keep the sabbath! Furthermore, in John 7:19, Christ said that the law that forbade killing was the law that Moses gave; yet, according to sabbatarians, this law ("thou thalt not kill," etc.) is the law of God. Hence, their arbitrary distinction and designations will not stand. Then, by reading Neh. 8 carefully, it can be readily seen that the terms "law of God" and "law of Moses" are used interchangeably. This is an additional fact that shows the distinction that sabbatarians make in the law is not a valied one.

(6) **Sabbatarians also use Isaiah 66:22-26 as one of their prooftexts.** However, this text just assuredly teaches the same about the feast of the new moon! Are sabbatarians going to begin advocating the keeping of this? Let us remember that, according to Col. 2:14-17, the law involving weekly (sabbath days), monthly (new moon) and yearly (holy days) has been abrogated. Is. 66:22, 23 was fulfilled in the return of the Jews from captivity.

(7) **Sabbatarians also observe that Paul preached on the sabbath in the synagogues (Acts 13:14-44), and that this is an apostolic example for sabbath keeping.** However, just because one preaches the gospel on Saturday (as we frequently do in gospel meetings) does not prove that we are keeping the sabbath any more than preaching the gospel on Thursday proves that we are observing Thursday as a holy day. Paul preached on the sabbath in the synagogues because this afforded a very fine opportunity to preach the gospel of Christ, since so many people would be gathered at this place and at this time. We humbly and kindly extend this challenge to our sabbatarian friends: let them advance just **one** example of any apostle keeping the sabbath day **as** the day of Christian worship.

(8) **Sabbatarians also use Matt. 5:18 as a proof text, stating that this text shows that the sabbath requirement of the law is still in force.** The key word of this text is "till" in the statement "till all be fulfilled." This passage is really teaching that the law **will** pass away when, "all be fulfilled;" that is, when the law would have accomplished its purposes for having been given. And, the books of Romans and Hebrews clearly and undeniably teach that said purposes have been fulfilled. Accordingly, instead of Matt. 5:18 teaching that the law is still binding, it is a strong text affirming the abrogation of the law. Philip Schaff says, " 'till' implies that after the great events of Jesus' life, and the establishment of his kingdom, the old dispensation, as the dispensation of the letter and yoke of bondage...will pass away, and has passed away (Eph. 2:15; Col. 2:14; Heb. 8:13)."

(9) **There remaineth therefore a rest to the people of God (Heb. 4:9) is also used as a proof text by sabbatarians.** However, the context of this passage (Heb. 4:8-11) will show that the "rest" of this passage is the **heavenly** rest. Consequently, the passage has no reference whatsoever to the weekly sabbath.

(10) **Sabbatarians argue that if the sabbath is no longer binding, then why did the Lord say, "But pray ye that your flight be not in the winter, neither on the sabbath day" (Matt. 24:20).** The fact that our Lord taught his disciples to pray that their flight be not on the sabbath day, with relation to the destruction of Jerusalem, does not teach that the sabbath is a sacred day of worship. He also taught them to pray that their flight be not in the winter. Does this teach that winter is a sacred and holy season? Our Lord knew that if they had to flee during the winter season or on the sabbath day, that such would make their departure far more difficult. Bad weather could so easily characterize the winter season. Then, because the unconverted Jews would have the gates of Jerusalem closed on the sabbath day, our Lord knew that if the disciples had to flee from Jerusalem on the sabbath that such would be, as just observed, far more difficult.

(11) **Sabbatarians also affirm that the sabbath is binding due to the fact that the Lord told the rich young ruler, "Keep the commandments" (Matt. 19:17).** However, Jesus could thusly instruct the young ruler since the law was still in effect at that time. During his lifetime, our Lord taught men to keep the law (Lk. 5:14, Matt. 23:23).

(12) **Sabbatarians ask, "Well, if the ten commandment law has been abrogated, then why is it not all right to steal, to murder, etc.?"** Surely these matters are wrong, definitely wrong. However, such obtains because these restrictions are found in the New Testament. We do not observe them because they are part of the Old Testament law. To illustrate, it was wrong to murder under the colonial law. This law is no longer binding. Now, we do not commit murder. Why? Not because this was prohibited under colonial law; but, rather, because such is a part of the law under which we now live.

III. The First Day Of The Week Is Now The Authorized Day Of Worship

From the following study, it will become crystal clear that the first day of the week is now the day upon which Christians are to meet and worship God. Furthermore, the following information will forever answer the sabbatarian false claim that, "The sabbath was changed to Sunday by the authority of man, namely by an edict of Emperor Constantine in A.D. 321."

(1) **Acts 20:7.** According to the context (vs. 6), Paul was in Troas **seven days.** Hence, he was present in that city on the sabbath. However, there is no mention of the sabbath or of Paul meeting with the brethren on that day! Rather, it is specifically stated that he met with the brethren on "the first day of the week." And, according to Exodus 20:10, the sabbath is the **seventh day** — not the first day — of the week!

(2) **I Cor. 16:2.** According to this text, the New Testament church in the city of Corinth observed "the first day of the week."

(3) **Mark 14:25.** According to this text, our Lord promised the disciples, "I will drink no more the fruit of the vine (Lord's supper), until that day that I drink it new in the kingdom of God." Observe the "until **that** day" of

the text. Yes, the word "that" of this passage is most significant. This word implies a given day; not just any day. Now, the kingdom of God (in which the Lord says the Lord's supper is to be observed), was established on the day of Pentecost (Mark 9:1; Acts 1:8; Acts 2:1-4, 47). And, according to Lev. 23:15, the day of Pentecost always came on the first day of the week! Hence, the Lord's supper (here is the day of worship) is to be observed on the first day of the week. Such obtaining, we better appreciate Acts 20:7: "And upon the first day of the week, when the disciples came together to break bread." Also, we can appreciate the fact that the Corinthian brethren observed the Lord's supper when they came together (I Cor. 11:20); and, according to I Cor. 16:2, they came together upon the first day of the week.

(4) **History tells us that the early Christians worshiped upon the first day of the week.** (a) "But Sunday is the day which we all hold our common assembly, because Jesus Christ, our Savior, on the same day rose from the dead" (A.D. 140. Justin Martyr: *Seventh-Day Addventism Renounced,* D. M. Canright).

(b) "We keep the eight day with joyfulness, the day also on which Jesus rose again from the dead" (A.D. 120. Barnabas).

(5) **When we observe the wonderful and noble events that have occurred upon the first day of the week, we can better appreciate the fact that this is certainly the day that Christians are to meet upon to worship God.**

(a) Our Lord arose from the dead on the first day of the week (Mk. 16:9).

(b) The church of our Lord, the kingdom of Christ, was established upon the first day of the week (Mk. 9:1; Acts 1:8; Acts 2:1-4, 47). Remember, according to Lev. 23:15, that the day of Pentecost always came upon the first day of the week.

(c) The New Testament, the law of Christ, went forth from Jerusalem, and became operative, the first day of the week (Acts 2; Acts 2:1-4; Lk. 24:47).

(d) The first gospel sermon proclaiming remission of sins in the name of Jesus Christ was preached upon the first day of the week (Acts 2:1, 22-36).

(e) The apostles began to use the keys of the kingdom upon the first day of the week (Matt. 16:18; 18:18; John 20:23; Acts 2:1, 37-47).

(f) The Great Commission began to be preached and became operative upon the first day of the week (Matt. 28:18-20; Mark 16:15, 16; Luke 24:46-49; John 20:21-23; Acts 2:1-47).

Conclusion

May the preceding study help us to see clearly that the sabbath is no longer binding; but, that the first day of the week is the authorized day of worship for men today. Furthermore, in the study just pursued, may we have sufficient information to help our sabbatarian friends to see the error of their way, to turn therefrom, and to come to know the joy of salvation that is in Christ.

Also, may there be a revival of dedication to the Lord's day among members of the church of our Lord. Let us be reminded that it is the Lord's **day,** and not the Lord's hour (Rev. 1:10).

CHAPTER 17

THE SEVENTH-DAY ADVENTIST DOCTRINE OF PUNISHMENT (HELL)

J. Noel Merideth

Though William Miller (1782-1849) never joined the Seventh-day Adventist movement, the history of Seventh-day Adventism has its roots in Miller's work. William Miller began to preach that the end of the world was at hand, that a fiery conflagration would usher in the new heaven and the new earth, and that the date for this would be sometime between March 21, 1843 and March 21, 1844. The movement weathered its first disappointment when the deadline passed; another date was set: October 22, 1844. The new date passed and the early Millerite fervor was largely diminished.

A group of "Millerite" believers had gathered at the home of Hiram Edson in New York and were disappointed when the Lord did not return on October 22, 1844. Later Edson had an alleged vision in which he said he saw the Lord, the High Priest, enter into the second apartment of the sanctuary and that he had a work to perform in the most holy before coming to this earth.

Still another person prominent in the early history of the Seventh-day Adventist movement was Joseph Bates. Bates concluded that the Sabbath (Saturday) was to be kept today and that the Papacy had changed the day for worship.

And then we come to Ellen G. White (1827-1915). Her maiden name was Ellen Gould Harmon. After the family heard the lectures of William Miller in 1840 and 1842 they accepted his teachings and were disfellowshiped from the Methodist church. It was after the Great Disappointment of 1844 that Ellen had her first alleged vision. On August 30, 1846, she married James White, a young Adventist preacher who had been active in the Millerite movement. Soon there was a sizable group who began to conclude that Mrs. White was being uniquely guided by the Holy Spirit. Mrs. White's husband stated that during the earlier part of her ministry she had from one hundred to two hundred "open visions" in twenty-three years. These visions, however, decreased as the years passed. Almost every aspect of the belief and activity of the Seventh-day Adventists was encouraged or inspired by a vision or word from Mrs. White. Thus, in February of 1845, she had a vision of Jesus entering into the holy of holies of the heavenly sanctuary, confirming Hiram Edson's vision received in the preceding year. On April 7, 1847, she supposedly had a vision in which she was taken first into the holy place, and then into the holy of holies of the heavenly sanctuary. There she supposedly saw the ark and the Ten Commandments in the ark, with a halo of glory around the Sabbath commandment. This confirmed Bates' teachings about the seventh day.

The attitude of present-day Seventh-day Adventists toward Mrs. White is seen in the *Church Manual,* Issued by the General Conference of Seventh-day Adventists, page 34: "That the gift of the Spirit of prophecy is one of the identifying marks of the remnant church...They recognize that this gift was manifested in the life and ministry of Ellen G. White."

The Adventist group headed by Hiram Edson in New York; the group in New Hampshire with Bates; and, the group in Maine with Ellen G. White fused to form the Seventh-day Adventist denomination. In 1860 the name Seventh-day Adventist was adopted and in May 1863 the first General Conference was held in Battle Creek, Michigan. 1863 is the date of the official organization of the Seventh-day Adventist denomination.

Seventh-day Adventists are against the idea that man consists of two aspects—a physical aspect called body, and a non-physical aspect called soul or spirit. Their writers say that there is nothing in the word soul which implies a conscious entity that can survive the death of the body. They say that man is a soul. They also conclude that the word spirit does not denote a separate entity capable of conscious existence apart from the physical body. Adventists believe that "the condition of man in death is one of unconsciousness. That all men, good and evil alike, remain in the grave from death to the resurrection" (*Church Manual,* p. 31). Adventists believe that the return of Jesus to earth will be literal and personal and will precede a period of 1,000 years during which time the saints of all ages will live with Christ in heaven. Adventists also believe that the end of this 1,000 year period—the millennium— the wicked of all ages, who did not share in the first resurrection, will be resurrected only to be immediately destroyed by fire from heaven. "In the conflagration which destroys Satan and his host, the earth itself will be regenerated and cleansed from the effects of the curse. Thus the universe will be purified from the foul blot of sin" (*Church Manual,* p. 35).

Seventh-day Adventists believe that "there shall be a resurrection both of the just and of the unjust. The resurrection of the just will take place at the second coming of Christ; the resurrection of the unjust will take place a thousand years later, at the close of the millennium...That the finally impenitent, including Satan, the author of sin, will, by the fires of the last day, be reduced to a state of nonexistence, becoming as though they had not been, thus purging the universe of God of sins and sinners" (*Church Manual,* p. 32). Seventh-Day Adventists thus reject the teaching of the Bible on hell.

We shall note a couple of passages where the word soul (**psuche**) is obviously used to designate that aspect of man which continues to exist after death. The first is Matthew 10:28, "And fear not them which kill the body, but are not able to kill the soul: but rather fear him which is able to destroy both soul and body in hell." In this passage soul cannot be another name for the whole person (compare the Seventh-day Adventist position that man does not have a soul but is a soul); for, if so, the soul would be dead when the body is killed. Jesus teaches that there is something about man which those who kill men cannot touch. That something is that aspect of man which continues to exist after the body is lowered into the grave. A second instance is Revelation 6:9,10, "And when he had opened the fifth seal, I saw under the altar the souls of them that were slain for the word of

God, and for the testimony which they held: and they cried with a loud voice, saying, How long, O Lord, holy and true, dost thou not judge and avenge our blood on them that dwell on the earth?" It is obvious that souls here cannot simply mean living creatures or persons, for it makes no sense to say, "the people of those that had been slain" or "the living creatures of those that had been slain." That these souls are in a conscious state is evident from the fact that they cry out and that they are spoken to.

On the word spirit we note a few examples to show that there are instances when the word refers to that which survives death. Luke 23:46 "Father, into thy hands I commend my spirit." Arndt and Gingrich give the following various meanings of spirit: wind, breath, life-spirit, soul, the spirit as a part of the human personality, state of mind, a spirit as an independent being, the Spirit of God, the Spirit of Christ, the Holy Spirit. To commend one's breath to the Father is meaningless. To commend one's state of mind also make no sense. By a process of elimination we note that the only meanings of spirit that make sense here are soul, or spirit as a part of the human personality. In Acts 7:59 we read of dying Stephen saying "Lord Jesus, receive my spirit." What would be the point of Stephen's asking Jesus to receive his spirit if his spirit simply ceased to exist at death? In Hebrews 12:22,23 we read of the "spirits of just men made perfect." How could that which has gone out of existence be made perfect?

Seventh-day Adventists teach that, after Satan's final assault on the "camp of the saints," fire will come down from heaven and will annihilate Satan, his evil angels, and all the wicked. Before this happens, however, those to be annihilated will be subjected to gradations of suffering, depending on the guilt of the persons or demons involved; Satan himself will suffer the longest and will therefore be the last to perish in the flames. At the end of this period of suffering, however, all those who have rebelled against God will be wiped out of existence.

But the doctrine of annihilation of the wicked is not in accord with the teaching of the Bible. Seventh-day Adventists claim that destroy means annihilate. Seventh-day Adventists are wrong. The word for destroy is **apollumi**. The word has various meanings but in no instance does it mean annihilate. Sometimes **apollumi** simply means to be lost as in the three lost parables in Luke 15 but it does not mean to annihilate. **Apollumi** may be applied to something that has become useless as the skins of Matthew 9:17, but it does not mean annihilate. Sometimes **apollumi** is used to mean kill as in Matthew 2:13 where Herod sought to destroy or kill the child, but it did not mean annihilate. In Luke 9:24 we read that the person who shall lose his life shall save it. If **apollumi** meant annihilation then the person who would enter into a state of annihilation would be the saved person! In light of these usages of the word when one comes to the passages where **apollumi** is used to describe the future destiny of the wicked we can understand that the word does not mean annihilation. It means "to devote or give over to eternal misery" (J. H. Thayer, *Greek-English Lexicon,* p. 64).

Seventh-day Adventists teach that the word **Gehenna**—hell, refers to the fires of destruction which shall finally annihilate the wicked. In Matthew

18:9, however, the phrase the Ghenna (or hell) of fire is parallel with the expression, "the eternal fire" in verse 8. So the fire of Gehenna is not a temporary one but an eternal or endless one. If the fire of Gehenna is eternal, we must conclude that the punishment of which the fire is connected will also be eternal. For what would be the point of keeping the fire of Gehenna burning as a punishing fire if the wicked had been annihilated by it? Note further that in Mark 9:43 the word **gehenna** occurs in parallel construction with the expression, "the unquenchable fire." If the fire of Gehenna is unquenchable fire, will it not be an everlasting fire? Observe also that in Mark 9:48 Gehenna is described in words quoted from Isaiah 66:24 where it is said their worm dieth not, and the fire is not quenched. These expressions mean that there is no end to the punishment of Gehenna. Adventists and others often speak much of these statements just being figurative and symbolic. It is true that these descriptons are figurative, but the figures are intended to convey meaning. They are symbols of something real, namely, that the punishment of the wicked will be horrible beyond expression and it will be everlasting. Also, the Biblical descriptions of Gehenna rule out annihilationism, for creatures who have been annihilated cannot be everlastingly punished. Annihilation would be punishment for only a few seconds or ever how long it would take to burn them up; but the punishment of hell is everlasting.

Adventists often allege that the wicked will be "destroyed" and cite the Greek word **olethros**. But when **olethros** is applied to future punishment of the wicked as in II Thessalonians 1:9 where they are said at the judgment to receive "everlasting destruction" the word simply means "the loss of a life of blessedness after death, future misery" (J. H. Thayer, *Greek-English Lexicon,* p. 443). The word does not mean the annihilation of the wicked.

A simple, plain, and clear passage that describes the eternal destiny of the righteous and wicked is found in Matthew 25:46 where we have the judgment described: "And these shall go away into everlasting punishment: but the righteous into life eternal." The word "punishment" is translated from **kolasis** and is understood to mean punishment by Thayer, Arndt & Gingrich, and Moulton and Milligan. Josephus, who lived from A.D. 37-100 says the Pharisees of his day believed in the eternal punishment of the wicked and so since we know Jesus did not correct them but rather affirmed this as we read in the New Testament then this position is correct. The Sadducees were the ones who denied that man had a spirit and so denied eternal punishment and Jesus said they did err not knowing the scriptures. Note that the punishment of the wicked will be "everlasting" from the Greek **aioonios**. **Aioonios** is applied to God in Revelation 4:9, where God is said to live for ever and ever. When the word **aioonios** is used to describe future time, it denotes time without end (Arndt and Gingrich, p. 28; Thayer, p. 20; and H. Sasse, "**Aioonios**," in Kittel, I, 209). So the eternal punishment is for ever and ever. Also, eternal punishment will last as long as eternal life for the same word describes them both. Now Seventh-day Adventists will admit that **kolasis** means punishment and that **aioonios** means endless but they say that the expression "eternal punishment," just as in "eternal redemption" and "eternal judgment," the Bible is referring to all eternity—not as of process, but as of result. They allege it is not an endless process of punishment, but an effectual punishment, which will be final and forever. By way of refutation we note that in the parallel expression "eternal life" in Matthew 25:46 the word **aioonios** is used to picture a life which is not just everlasting in its result, but everlasting in its duration or continuance. Seventh-day Adventists admit that eternal life is everlasting in its duration since they hold that the righteous will be given life forever. But if **aioonios** in the last part of Matthew 25:46 means endless in duration, what right do they have to restrict the meaning of **aioonios** in the first part of the same verse to endless in result? This is inconsistent and incorrect. Eternal punishment will last just as long as eternal life and eternal life will last as long as eternal punishment. Both are eternal.

A further consideration against annihilation is the fact that the New Testament speaks of degrees in the punishment of the wicked: Luke 12:47,48, "And that servant, which knew his lord's will, and prepared not himself, neither did according to his will, shall be beaten with many stripes. But he that knew not, and did commit things worthy of stripes, shall be beaten with few stripes." It is here taught that not all the lost will be punished in the same way. If, however, the wicked are annihilated, how can there be degrees of punishment? There cannot be degrees of annihilation.

In conclusion we take note of the Lord's words about Judas in Matthew 26:24, "woe unto that man by whom the Son of man is betrayed! it had been good for that man if he had not been born." If death means the extinction of being, why should life be worse for him, Judas, than any other wicked traitor? Never to have been born means never to have come into existence. If death means going out of existence, then never to have been born and to die are equivalent conditions; they would mean the same thing—non-existence. Why, then, did the Lord say it would have been good not to come into existence? Why did he not say (seeing the man was born and there was no use in wasting regrets over his birth)—why did he not say, "It will be good for that man when he dies, for when he dies he will then be just as if he had never been born—non-existent?

But death does not mean the end of existence. The teaching of the Seventh-day Adventists on the annihilation of the wicked is contrary to the Scripture and robs the proclamation of the gospel of its deepest earnestness. The punishment of the wicked in hell is not going to be for just a few seconds, hours or days. The punishment will not be just for a little while and then all be over. The punishment of the wicked in hell will be for ever and ever. It is the serious realization of this fact that should make us ponder the path of our feet and obey the Lord. Knowing the goodness and the terror of the Lord, we persuade men.

CHAPTER 18
A GENERAL LOOK AT SOME FALSE DOCTRINES OF THE UNITED PENTECOSTAL CHURCH

Guy N. Woods

In recent years several small groups of the "holiness" persuasion have attracted to themselves considerable attention by the militancy with which they have advocated the view that there is but one Person—Jesus—in the Godhead. Sometimes styled the "Oneness people," or the "Jesus only" folks, there are three separate and distinct groups known to this writer which subscribe to this question. These are, "The United Pentecostal Church," "The Church of the First-born," and the "Pentecostal Assemblies of Jesus Christ." While minor differences obtain among them regarding other issues, their position is the same touching the nature of the Godhead.

In common with the whole "Pentecostal" movement, they claim the baptism of the Holy Spirit, the ability to speak in tongues, and the power to perform miracles. Limitations of space make it necessary that we deal herein with the distinctive doctrines of the "Oneness" people only. Excellent material is already available on the baptism of the Holy Spirit, tongues and miracles. Brother W. Curtis Porter is the author of a fine booklet on "Divine Healing," and Brother Gus Nichol's work in the Nichol-Weaver Debate is a most thorough refutation of such matters. It is absolutely conclusive on the issues treated.

Believe Jesus Alone Constitutes Godhead

It is the view of the "Oneness" people that Jesus alone constitutes the Godhead, the various names designating the Father, the Son and the Holy Spirit being nothing more than *titles* of the same person and thus applicable only to *Him*. The theory takes on a practical aspect from the fact that its adherents teach that baptism—water baptism—is to be administered *in the name of Jesus only*, by which they mean that it is not to be administered "into the name of the Father, and of the Son, and of the Holy Spirit," as set forth in the Great Commission. (Matt. 28:18-20). When their attention is directed to the fact that it was the Lord himself who commanded that it be thus done, they reply that inasmuch as Jesus is God, Christ and the Holy Spirit—all in one—baptism in the name of Jesus (baptism administered under this "formula") is, in reality, in the name of the Father, the Son and the Holy Spirit!

Their Proof Texts

This position they seek to sustain in the following fashion: Jesus said: "I and my Father are one" (John 10:30). In response to Philip's request, "Shew us the Father," Jesus answered, "Have I been so long time with you, and yet hast thou not known me, Philip? *he that hath seen me hath seen the Father;* and how sayest thou then, Shew us the Father?" (John 14:8, 9). The watchword of Israel was, "Hear, O Israel, the Lord our God is one Lord" (Deut. 6:4). The prophet Isaiah repeatedly asserted in chapters 43, 44 and 45 of his prophecy that God is *one;* that there is no God before or after Him; that He *alone* created the heavens and the earth. Zechariah declared that His name *is one.* All emphasis is given to the name Jesus in the New Testament, the apostles having preached in it, baptized in it, magnified it, performed miracles in it, etc. From all of which they conclude that Jesus is the whole of the Godhead revealed in the Scriptures.

The usual arguments against the traditional view of three persons in the Godhead, often advanced by the Jews, are repeated: such is a denial of the unity of God; it necessitates the conception that not *one,* but *three* gods exist, and is, therefore, a repudiation of the Biblical doctrine of Monotheism, and an acceptance of Polytheism, the doctrine of many gods!

Much emphasis is given to Paul's statement, "For in him (i.e. Christ) dwelleth all the fulness of the Godhead bodily" (Col. 2:9) and from it the conclusion is drawn and since Christ possesses the fulness of the Godhead, he must then be the Godhead alone!

Finally, with much confidence, they cite Job's words of reproof to his "friends": "Will ye speak wickedly for God? and talk deceitfully for him? Will ye accept his *person*? will ye contend for God?...He will surely reprove you, if ye *secretly accept persons.*" (Job 13:8, 10). The implication of course being that God is a "person" (singular), but that we accept *persons* (plural).

An Ancient Heresy

The heresy that there is but one person in the Godhead is an ancient one, having first begun to attract attention in the second century of the Christian era. Of it the scholarly Moshiem writes:

> "The numerous evils and discords which arose from combining Oriental and Egyptian philosophy with the Christian religion began to be increased about the middle of this century by those who brought Grecian philosophy with them into the Christian church. As the doctrines held by the Christians respecting the Father, Son and Holy Spirit and respecting the twofold nature of the Savior, were least of all in agreement with the precepts of this philosophy, they first endeavored so to explain these doctrines that they could be comprehended by reason. This was attempted by one Prazeas, a very distinguished man and a confessor at Rome. **Discarding all real distinction between the**

> **Father, Son, and Holy Spirit,** he taught that the whole Father of all things joined himself to the human nature of Christ...They denominated the **man** Christ, the Son of God, and held that to this Son the Father of the Universe of God so joined himself as to be crucified and endure pangs along with the Son." (Book One, Century two, Part 2, chapter 5, page 149).

This ancient heresy, in slightly revamped form, is precisely that which is being advocated so vigorously by certain holiness sects among us today.

Examining The Proof Texts

We shall examine first the passages offered in support of the view, and then go on to other considerations revealing the falsity of the position.

John 10:30

1. Jesus asserted that he and his Father are *one* (John 10:30). Until it has been shown that by this Jesus intended to teach that he and his Father *are one person* the relevancy of the passage has not been established. A man and wife are one, but not *one person*! If such were so, when a man gets sick, his wife could take the medicine, and he'd get well! Jesus said, "For this cause shall a man leave father and mother, and shall cleave to his wife; *and they twain shall be one flesh* (Matt. 19:5), i.e. one in purpose, end and aim, but still "twain" (two).

John 14:8,9

2. He who saw Jesus saw the Father (John 14:8, 9). This can mean only one of two things: to see Jesus was to see the Father either *actually,* or representatively. That he did not intend to convey the idea that to see him was to see God *actually* follows from the fact that John said, "No man hath seen God at any time; the only begotten Son, which is in the bosom of the Father, he hath declared him." (John 1:18). No man has actually seen the Father, but Jesus declared him, revealed him, made him known to man. To see Jesus was, therefore, to see God representatively. In no other fashion can sinful man see God and live (Deut. 33:20).

Deuteronomy 6:4

3. The "Shema," Israel's great watchword, "Hear O Israel, the Lord our God is one Lord," (Deut. 6:4), often cited by the Jews in their arguments with Christians by which they attempt to prove that the acceptance of the deity of Jesus is a repudiation of the unity of God as here and often elsewhere taught, instead of being a refutation of our position, is an affirmation of it! The "Shema" takes its name from the first word, in Hebrew, of the sentence, *"Shema Yisrael, Yehovah Eloheinu Yehovah achad."* On it Adam Clarke comments,

"Many think that Moses teaches in these words the doctrine of the Trinity in Unity. It may be so; but if so, it is not more clearly done than in Genesis 1, to which the reader is referred. When this passage occurs in the Sabbath readings in the synagogue, the whole congregation repeats the last word 'achad' (the Hebrew word for **one** (G. N. W.) for several minutes together with the loudest vociferations. This I suppose they do to vent a little their spleen against the Christians, for they suppose the latter hold three Gods, because of their doctrine of the Trinity; but all of their skill and cunning can never prove that there is not a plurality expressed in the word **Eloheinu,** which is translated **our God;** and were the Christians, when reading this verse, to vociferate **Eloheinu** for several minutes as the Jews do **achad** it would apply more forcibly in the way of conviction to the Jews of the plurality of persons in the Godhead than the word **achad** (one) against any pretended false tenet of Christianity, as every Christian receives the doctrine of the unity of God in the most conscientious manner. It is because of their rejection of this doctrine that the wrath of God continues to rest upon them, for the doctrine of the atonement cannot be received unless the doctrine of the Godhead is received too."

Mr. Clarke significantly adds:

> **"Some Christians have joined the Jews against this doctrine, and some have even outdone them, and have put themselves to extraordinary pains to prove that Elohim is a noun of the singular number. This has not yet been proved. It would be as easy to prove that there is no plural language."**

In Gen. 1:1, the word for God is *elohim,* the plural form of *El* (God). To it is attached the singular verb *bara,* "he created," to forestall any conclusion of Polytheism (many Gods) from this passage. This construction, not characteristic of the English language, is often observable in connection with this noun, in Hebrew. Literally rendered, Gen. 1:1, runs, "In beginning Gods, he created, the heavens and the earth." Here is plurality clearly taught with a caution against any conclusion of divergent personalities. Again comments Mr. Clarke,

> "The original word **Elohim** (God) is certainly the plural form of **El, or Eloah,** and has long been supposed by the most eminently learned and pious men to imply a plurality of persons in the divine nature...He must be strangely prejudiced who cannot see that the doctrine of a Trinity, and of a trinity in unity is expressed in the above words. The verb **bara,** he created, being joined in the singular number with this plural noun, has been considered as pointing out, and not obscurely, the unity of the divine persons in this work of creation."

Without adopting what all men have affected to see in the doctrine of the Trinity as incorporated in the creeds, we nevertheless accept as conclusive the foregoing reasoning by this eminent Hebraist.

The Doctrine Of The Anti-Christ

Despite the claims of the Jews, Unitarians, Oneness Holiness, etc., we shall show that only those who subscribe to the plurality in unity thus taught accept the doctrine of the Unity of God. The word *God* simply means deity, from the Greek *theos,* God. The Scriptures ascribe deity to all the persons in the Godhead: The Father is called God (I Cor. 8:6); the Son is called God (John 1:1); the Holy Spirit is called God (Acts 5:3, 4). *Deity* is the essence of God; all possess this deity; hence, all are God. To deny to any one or more of them deity is to *deny God!* This, indeed, is the spirit of the antichrist: "He is antichrist that denieth the Father AND THE SON." (I John 2:22). To escape the spirit of antichrist one must receive the doctrine of the Father *and* (a co-ordination conjunction with the force of the plus sign) *and* the Son." That by this John intended to convey the idea that the Father and the Son are distinct personalities, follows from the fact that in this same letter he wrote, "No man hath seen God at anytime," (I John 4:12), yet two verses later he wrote, "And *we have seen* and do testify that the Father sent the Son to be the Savior of the world." (I John 4:14). Though no one had ever seen God, they had seen Christ and bore witness of Him. Obviously, the One they had seen was not the One no man can see. Christ and His Father are thus seen to be two distinct personalities. To deny this is the spirit of antichrist. This is precisely what advocates of the "Oneness Holiness" do!

Colossians 2:9

5. Christ does indeed possess all the fullness of the Godhead bodily, but this does not mean that there is but one person in the Godhead. An examination of the context of Col. 2:9, will reveal that the apostle is contrasting the fullness that is in Christ with the emptiness and vanity of the heathen systems of philosopy in vogue at the time. The actual attributes of the whole Godhead dwell in Jesus bodily—i.e. actually, and not typically or symbolically. The words were penned to caution the brethren against accepting any of the current philosophies, assuring them that in Christ the divine nature abode so that in him was available all that the God head contained, and that they stood in need of nothing from the heathen systems or the Jewish law who had accepted him. The passage, designed to establish clearly the deity of Jesus, does not support the view that there is but one person in the Godhead.

Job 13:8, 10

6. Job 13:8, 10, could scarcely apply to us because we certainly make no secret of the position we occupy touching the nature of the Godhead. The

context reveals that Job reproved his "friends" because they affected to be interested in God's defense, whereas they were only flatterers, secretly plotting a course that would bring them into favor with whomsoever they dealt. (See R.V. It omits the words *person* and *persons.*)

Under the foregoing heads may be summed up every argument made in support of the "Oneness Holiness" position.

II
Refutations Of The Oneness Theory

We shall now engage to show that the theory under review is false from other considerations.

1. We have seen that the name of God in Gen. 1:1 is plural. Plural *pronouns* are often used in connection with God's name: "And *God* said, Let *us* make man in *our* image, after *our* likeness." (Gen. 1:26). Who are embraced in the pronouns *us,* and *our* of this passage? "And the Lord God said, Behold man is become as one of *us*" (Gen. 3:22). "Go to let *us* go down, and there confound their language." (Gen. 11:6, 7). "And I heard the voice of the Lord saying, Whom shall I send, and who will go for *us*?" (Isa. 6:8). This usage necessitates the conviction that there is a plurality in the Godhead.

2. The *person* of pronouns likewise points to this conclusion.

1st. per. The Father—I, me, my, mine (Heb. 1:5).

2nd. per. The Son—Thee, thy, thine (Heb. 1:5ff).

3rd. per. The Holy Spirit—He (John 16:13).

3. As there was plurality in the Godhead in *creation,* the same forces are observable in *salvation.* The "us" of creation is also seen in the "us" of redemption. John 14:16: "And I will pray the Father, and he shall give you another comforter that he may abide with you forever. Even the Spirit of truth; whom the world cannot receive, because it seeth him not, neither knoweth him: but ye know him; for he dwelleth with you, and shall be in you." The function of each was as follows:

CHRIST—"I will pray"—INTERCESSION

FATHER—"I will send"—DONATION

HOLY SPIRIT—"I will comfort"—CONSOLATION.

4. There are three that bear record in heaven: (1) the Father; (2) the Word; (3) the Holy Spirit. There are three that bear record on earth: (1) the Spirit; (2) the water; (3) the blood. (I John 5:7, 8). As the Spirit, the water and the blood differ from each other on earth, so the Father, the Word and the Spirit differ from each other in heaven!

5. The name of the Father and the name of the Son are often declared to be different: "And I saw, and behold, the Lamb standing on mount Zion, and with him a hundred forty and four thousand, *having his name* and the *name of his Father,* written in their foreheads." (Rev. 14 R.V.) (See, also, Prov. 30:4; John 3:13; Rom. 10:6,7).

6. The Father is often distinguished from the Son: "The kings of the earth set themselves, and the rulers take counsel together *against Jehovah*

and *against his anointed,* saying, let us break *their* bands asunder, and cast away *their* cords from us" (Psm. 2:13-3; cf. Acts 4:25-27).

7. The seven *unities* of Eph. 4, necessitate the conclusion that each member of the Godhead is distinct from the other. There is one body, one Spirit, one hope, one Lord, one faith, one baptism, one God. As the apostle distinguishes between the one body, the one hope, the one faith, and the one baptism, so he distinguishes between the one Spirit, the one Lord, the One God. One might as sensibly insist that the body, the hope, the faith, and the baptism were all identified with one act, as to insist that the Father, the Son and the Spirit of the passage are the same person!

8. "For Christ is not entered into the holy places made with hands, which are the figures of the true; but *into heaven itself,* now *to appear in the presence of God* for us." (Heb. 9: 24). (1) Christ entered into heaven; (2) he entered into heaven to appear in God's presence; (3) to do this he left the earth. If God and Christ are the same person, did he enter into his own presence? If they are the same, why did he go to heaven to enter into the presence of God? Was he not already in the presence of God while here on earth?

9. Christ is now reigning at God's right hand, having been raised up to sit on David's throne. (Acts 2:30). He is to reign until the last enemy is destroyed. (I Cor. 15:26). Thereupon he is to deliver the kingdom up to his Father (I Cor. 15:24), henceforth himself to be subject to Him. (I Cor. 15:28). Is he to deliver the kingdom to himself, and thereafter to be subject to himself? Will he not still possess it after he delivers it up? If so, how did he deliver it up?

10. Christ *sat down* at the right hand of the Father. It would be quite a feat, would it not, to *sit down on one's own right hand?* Stephen saw Jesus *standing* at the right hand of the Father in the heavens. (Heb. 1:1-14; Acts 7:55). Was Jesus *standing* on his own right hand?

11. The Holy Spirit was poured out on the day of Pentecost. (Acts 2:1-4). Jesus had already ascended and was at God's right hand. Moreover, at the baptism of Jesus (Matt. 3:15), God was in heaven, Christ was on earth being baptized, and the Holy Spirit came from heaven to earth in the form of a dove. How could one person be in three places at the same time?

12. Jesus often declared he would eventually ascend to the Father. (John 14:28). To do this he had to leave the earth. If he is the Father, why did he have to ascend to go to the Father? Following his death, he said he had not ascended to his Father. (John 20:17). It follows then, that he is not the Father. Moreover, Jesus declared that his Father was greater than he. (John 14:28). If he is the same person as the Father, was he not greater than himself? He said that he did not speak of himself, but of the Father. But if he is the Father, he did speak of himself, and his statement is false. In the shadows of Gethsemene and on the cross, Jesus prayed to the Father. Did he pray to himself? On the cross he delivered up his spirit to the Father. Did he still retain it? If so, did he die?

13. Jesus promised the disciples that he would send them *another* Comforter—the Holy Spirit. (John 14:16). But, if he is the only comforter

they ever had, why did Jesus call the Holy Spirit *another* comforter? If Jesus and the Holy Spirit are the same person did not they possess the *same* comforter, and not *another?*

14. God knows some things the Son does not: "But of that day and that hour knoweth no man, no, not the angels which are in heaven, *neither the Son,* but the Father." (Mark 13:32). If the Father and the Son are the same person, then does not the Son know some things he does not know?

15. In the model prayer of Matthew 6:19-13, Jesus taught the disciples to pray: "Our Father which are in heaven..." If Jesus is the Father, was not the Father *on earth,* at this time, and *not in heaven?*

16. Jesus prayed to the Father that his disciples might be one, "as thou, Father, art in me, and I in thee, that they also may be one in us: that the world may believe that thou hast sent me." (John 17:21). If Jesus and the Father are the same person, since Jesus prayed that his disciples might be one as he and his Father are one, did he pray that all Christians might be fashioned into one giant Christian?

17. Christ came not to do his own will, but the will of his Father. (John 6:38). If he is the Father, he did come to do his own will, and his statement is, therefore, false. Jesus did not bear witness of himself; God bore witness for him. (John 5:3). But, if he and the Father are the same person, he did bear witness of himself. There are three which bear witness in heaven. (John 5:7). How can *three* testify (bear witness) if there is but one person? Jesus is the only begotten Son of the Father. If he is the Father, did he beget himself? If so, did he not then exist before he existed? Christ offered himself up without spot to God. (Heb. 9:14). Did he offer himself up to himself?

18. God does not love those who deny the difference between the Father and the Son: "For the Father himself loveth you, because ye have loved me, and have believed *that I came forth from the Father.* I came out from the Father, and am come into the world, and go unto the Father." (John 16:27, 28).

Much more of the same type of evidence is available, but this will suffice to show the absurdity of the position that would seek to identify as one person the members of the Godhead.

III
Baptism In The Name Of Jesus Only

The "Oneness Holiness" teach that baptism is to be administered "in the name of Jesus only," by which they mean that the names of the Father and the Holy Spirit are not to be pronounced in the baptismal act. When their attention is directed to the fact that Jesus, in the Great Commission, (Matt. 28:18-20), commanded that baptism be administered "into the name of the Father, and of the Son, and of the Holy Spirit, they reply that inasmuch as the names of the Father and the Spirit are but different designations of Jesus, to baptize in the name of Jesus is, in effect, to baptize in the name of the Father and the Son and the Holy Spirit. Their theory assumes a degree of plausibility from the fact that, despite the nature of the command as set forth in Matthew's account of the Commission, there is no clear-cut instance of the use of the terms there designated, in Luke's record of the apostlic age. Adherents of the theory make much of the fact that this arrangement is nowhere to be found in that historic recital. They forcefully point out that in the instances where baptism is mentioned in connection with the *name,* it is declared to have been done "in the name of Jesus" without exception. These references are, Acts 2:38; 8:16; 10:48 and 19:5. From the premises thus adduced it is alleged that this was the uniform pattern of the apostolic age, and the formula intended for us today.

An examination of these passages, however, produces the definite conclusion that the uniformity claimed for them is wanting. If the first of these—Acts 2:38—be offered as a model, "...be baptized..in the name of *Jesus Christ,"* it must follow that Peter and John in Samaria, Peter at Caesarea and Paul in Ephesus, (Acts 8:16; 10:48, and 19:5), did not adhere to the prescribed formula. *In the four instances where baptism and the name of Jesus are associated, there are three different arrangements of the name, thus indicating conclusively that no definite design for the order of words was intended.* Obvious even to the English reader, the variety is more striking in the Greek:

Acts 2:38: **kai baptistheto...epi to onomati Iesou Christou.**
Acts 8:16: **bebaptismenoi...eis to onoma tou Kuriou Iesou.**
Acts 10:48: **baptisthenai en to onomati tou Kuriou.**
Acts 19:5: **ebaptisthesan eis to onoma tou Kuriou Iesou.**

Note the absence of uniformity in the use of the name:
Acts 2:38: Jesus Christ.
Acts 8:16: The Lord Jesus.
Acts 10:48: The Lord
Acts 19:5: The Lord Jesus.

Note, too, the variations in the prepositions used to show relation between the name and the baptismal act:
Acts 2:38: **epi to onomati** (literally, upon the name.)
Acts 8:16: **eis to onoma** (into the name).
Acts 10:48: **en to onomati** (in the name).
Acts 19:5: **eis to onoma** (into the name).

Thus out of four occurrences where baptism is said to have been in the name of Jesus, there are three variations in the Greek Testament. From this induction, it becomes apparent that no uniformity in the use of terms occurs, and the conclusion from such alleged uniformity is fallacious. *There is no instance of baptism performed in the name of Jesus only!*

The Great Commission, under which the apostles were sent forth to labor, is clear and explicit touching the manner in which they were to baptize: "And Jesus came to them and spake unto them, saying, All authority hath been given unto me in heaven and on earth. Go ye therefore, and make disciples of all the nations, baptizing them into the name of the Father, and of the Son and of the Holy Spirit: teaching them to observe all things whatsoever I commanded you: and lo, I am with you always, even unto the end of the world."(Matt. 28:18-20). The Lord authorized baptism to be performed in this manner—any other arrangement is without his authority.

"In The Name" Equals Baptizing As Authorized

One acts in the name of another when his acts have been authorized. To baptize *in the name of Jesus,* is to baptize as Jesus authorized. This, as we have seen, is to baptize *into the name of the Father, and of the Son, and of the Holy Spirit."*

One acts in the name of another when his acts have been authorized. To baptize *in the name of Jesus,* is to baptize as Jesus authorized. This, as we have seen is to baptize *"into the name of the Father, and of the Son, and of the Holy Spirit."* Hence, only those who baptize into the name of the Father and of the Son and of the Holy Spirit baptize in the name of Jesus. Any variation thereof is unauthorized and, therefore, not in his name.

Advocates of the theory here under consideration are not informed of, or else ignore, the vital and significant difference of the statements, (1) in the name of Jesus; and (2) into the name of the Father, and of the Son, and of the Holy Spirit. To be baptized "upon the name" or in the name of Jesus suggests the *ground* or *occasion* for the baptism. The name, in the Sacred writings, often denotes the sum of the divine attributes of the Person named—all that is involved in the Being Whose name is thus designated. "Into the name" denotes *union* or *communion with.* Thayer says that "by a usage chiefly Hebraistic the name is used for everything the name covers...to do a thing in the name of another—that is, by one's command and authority, acting on his behalf, promoting his cause." Thus, acting by the authority of Christ from the relationship we sustain to him as our Redeemer and Lord, we are baptized into a state of union and communion with God, the Father; Jesus Christ, the Son; and the Holy Spirit. (Brethren who are accustomed to follow the erroneous translation of the King James' Version, "baptizing them *in* the name of the Father, etc., should ponder these facts well, and bring their practice into conformity therewith.)

Not What Is Said But What Is Done

The name, as Vincent has well said "is not the mere designation, a sense which would give to the baptismal formula merely the force of the charm. It is equivalent to his *person.* When one is baptized into the name of the Trinity, he professes to acknowledge and appropriate God in all that he is and in all that he does for man." (Word Studies, Vol. 1, page 150). One word is objectionable in the foregoing quotation, the term *formula.* Here indeed is the basic error of the "Oneness Holiness" people on this question. *It is not what the preacher says that is significant; it is what is actually done for the candidate!* The words, "into the name of the Father, and of the Son and of the Holy Spirit," or indeed, *in the name of the Lord Jesus,* do not constitute a charm, the pronouncement of which amounts to an essential formula. *It should never be lost sight of* that it is something *done,* rather than something *said* that makes baptism valid. Unless the act is authorized, and performed as Jesus commanded, regardless of what the preacher says the baptism is not properly administered.

Thus, when the true significance of the expression, "in the name of Jesus," is grasped, it becomes clear that the practice of the apostolic age, touching the proper procedure in the baptismal act, followed the instructions delivered by our Lord in the Great Commission. When Paul came to Ephesus (Acts 19:1ff), he found certain disciples who had been baptized by Apollos when that preacher was mistakenly preaching the baptism of John after it had ceased to be valid. Paul inquired of them: "Have ye received the Holy Ghost since ye believed?" They answered: *"We have not so much as heard whether there be any Holy Ghost."* Immediately Paul asked, "Unto (Revised Version, *into*) what then were ye baptized?" Why did Paul think of *baptism* on being informed that they had not heard of the Holy Spirit? It became immediately apparent to him that their baptism was defective if they had never heard of the Holy Spirit, seeing that they could not have been baptized with the baptism of the Great Commission without hearing of it, i.e. by being baptized into the name of the Holy Spirit. The baptism of John was not "into the name of the Holy Spirit." Having, in this fashion, discovered that their baptism was invalid, he commanded them to be baptized "in the name of the Lord Jesus," i.e. as Jesus had commanded. This command reads, "Baptizing them into the name of the Father, and of the Son and of the Holy Spirit!" (Matt. 28:18-20).

Inasmuch as this command was to be continued until the end of the age, any other arrangement is unauthorized, and an officious intermeddling with the will and way of the Lord himself. Those who insist that baptism is to be administered into the name of "Jesus only," are in the position of denying that this manner of procedure *ever began,* that the Pentecostians were baptized thus, or anyone else by divine commandment. It is idle for them to deny this. Scriptural practice is to adhere without variation to the arrangement thus prescribed. A question the "Oneness Holiness" people should carefully consider is this: *"If it is wrong to follow the arrangement as set forth in Matthew 28:18-20, who misleads us?"*

—from **What Is Wrong?** Thomas L. Campbell, editor.

CHAPTER 19
THE MANUAL OF THE UNITED PENTECOSTAL CHURCH

Bill Jackson

The Apostle Peter tells us that the scriptures came into being as "...men spake from God, being moved by the Holy Spirit" (II Pet. 1:21). Thus, the scriptures are INSPIRED OF GOD (II Tim. 3:16). In telling us how this came to be given to men, Paul told the Corinthians of the message: "Which things also we speek, not in words which man's wisdom teacheth, but which the Spirit teacheth..." (I Cor. 2:13). Now, these are sufficient to let us know that in the Bible we have the message from God, and the message inspired of God, and the message provided in a form suited for man's use - in words. In a passage already cited, we're told that man is thus FURNISHED COMPLETELY unto every good work (II Tim. 3:17). And this being so, we're not surprised that Paul presented only "Jesus Christ, and him crucified" (I Cor. 2:2), nor that John gave the warning that "Whosoever goeth onward and abideth not in the teaching of Christ, hath not God..." (II John 9). This warning stands at the very heart of our present study.

From Heaven or From Man?

The all-sufficiency of that which the Lord has provided us was given emphasis by the Lord when men asked about his authority. He then referred to the baptism of John, and asked the Jewish leaders, "The baptism of John, whence was it? From heaven or from men?" (Matt. 21:25). The question at hand, and all others of that day and of this, and the question in the whole world of religion, is the question of matters either standing on the basis of THE AUTHORITY OF GOD, or THE AUTHORITY OF MAN! If a thing is from God, then the all-sufficient word of God will provide for it; if the thing is of man, then men will have to spurn the word and provide some other means of making it known, regulating it and "justifying" it. One of the more prominent forms of promoting the doctrines of men is through the creeds of men, whether verbal or written. Most religious denominations have a creed in written form, be it manual, discipline, confession of faith, articles of faith, or catechism. In our present study, we'll be examining the creedbook of the United Pentecostal Church. Its title is: Manual of the United Pentecostal Church, International.[1]

A Creed-Bound World

No one phrase more accurately describes the religious situation today than this: men are creed-bound. The great tragedy is that the devil works in men to make them more zealous of their creed than they are of the Bible! Added to this tragedy is that many are in support of human creeds and do not know of it; their leaders do, but many of the people in the pews do not, and feel that they are really in support of the Bible. In the very area of human creeds, and man's support of them, the Lord said, "But in vain do they worship me, teaching as their doctrines the precepts of men" (Matt. 15:9). This, in the context where he accuses them of transgressing the commandment of God, and making void the word of God, because of their human traditions (vs. 3,6). The situation there noted by Jesus has been duplicated many, many times over to bring us to see, today, a religious world completely creed-bound! We shall now see, by way of illustration, to what extent.

The United Pentecostal Manual

This manual, issued annually, is identified on the cover as being the "Manual, United Pentecostal Church, International" and further marked as being the "Articles of Faith - Constitution," and issued by the "Headquarters, Hazlewood, Missouri, U.S.A."[2] The very first glance at the manual identifies the book, the United Pentecostal Church and everything about, as NOT being the New Testament church! We have correctly shown, down through the years, that Jesus' church has no manual or creed and the proof has been given in the verses already cited to the effect that the Bible is the volume furnishing man completely unto all good works. The same point is made concerning the manual as containing the "Articles of Faith" and the "Constitution" of the church, and based on the same scriptures. A further point is the noting that Jesus' church is headquartered from heaven, where the head of the Church, Jesus Christ, is at the right hand of the Majesty in the heavens (Heb. 8:1). That's where the ruling power of Jesus' church happens to be, and not, as stated by the manual, in Hazelwood, Missouri, U.S.A.! We believe that the UPC Manual, examined just by its cover, brands that body as being something OTHER than the church of the New Testament. But, let us look inside the manual.

Beginning on page 2 of the manual, we find men who compose the "Board of General Presbyters," the "Regional Executive Presbyters," the "District General Presbyters" and "Honorary Presbyters." Thus, we find officers, offices and titles, with accompanying works, completely foreign to anything in the New Testament of Jesus Christ. Those who were truly presbyters in the New Testament operated within the local congregation-" the flock...among you..." (I Pet. 5:2). None of these had any position of any general, regional, district or honorary sort. Again, from the basic organization, we see that the UPC cannot be the church of Jesus Christ! The simple organization of Jesus' church can be found in one verse: Phil. 1:1.

The Claims of the Men Behind the Manual

In the "Foreword" to the UPC Manual, attention is immediately given to the baptism of the Holy Ghost, and this is introductory to the claims that the founders of the UPC also received Holy Ghost baptism. The claim is given thusly:

> During the last 21 days of the 19th century, a band of earnest, hungry-hearted ministers and Christian workers in Bethel Bible College, Topeka, Kansas, called a fast, praying

> earnestly for a great outpouring of the Holy Spirit, which, to their joyful surprise, came upon them in the early hours of the morning, on January 1, 1901.[3]

This claim of the baptism of the Holy Spirit is then said to be "...just as it had happened on the day of Pentecost in the year 30 A.D."[4] Of course, men having this baptism could then be directed in their labors in a supernatural fashion, and, as in the case of those in Acts 2, could then speak and write through inspiration. In this regard, it is most interesting to note that in previous editions of the manual the date of the Holy Ghost baptism is given as "January 1, 1900."[5] If one claims an error in typing, it is inconceivable that an inspired typist could make the error, or that an inspired proofreader would overlook it, or that a church of inspired men would overlook it and have it repeated again and again! The manual this is seen, again, to be in error, and hardly the kind of work produced by Holy Ghost-directed men.

The Manual and Latter-Day Revelation

While the claimed outpouring of the Holy Spirit came in 1901 (or, in 1900), the manual's "Foreword" tells us that it was not until 13 years later that "revelation" came on doctrinal matters now so heavily stressed by the United Pentecostal Church. Here is the statement: "In the year 1914 came the revelation on the name of the Lord Jesus Christ. The pivotal doctrines of the absolute deity of Jesus Christ and the baptism in His name became tenets of faith."[6] It is then very plain that these prime points of Pentecostal doctrine were NOT matters of faith until 1914 and that as of that year these matters BECAME tenets of faith! In fact, the very next statement is that "God marvelously confirmed our message as the Gospel was preached in its fulness."[7] Then, by their claims the fulness of the gospel was not possessed by men in the first century, nor at any time until "revelation" came to these in 1914. Their position has the Holy Spirit baptizing men, and then letting them remain in, teach and support error for 13 years!

It is in the "Preamble" to the manual that we find a statement which itself renders the manual as an addition to the will of God. The first paragraph of the Preamble quotes II Tim. 3:16 and affirms that the Bible is inspired of God and is the infallible Word of God. Then, the second paragraph begins with this: "The Bible is the only God-given authority which man possesses..."[8] Here is the statement in the United Pentecostal Manual which is absolutely true! The Bible IS the only God-given authority; that being so, then what place does the manual serve?

A pertinent question here, and one usually aggravating to members of the United Pentecostal Church, is this: "With your claims of latter-day revelation, what distinguishes your claims, and makes them authentic, as opposed to similiar claims made by the Mormons, Catholics, Adventists, other Pentecostals who believe in three persons in the Godhead, etc., etc.?" And, it is a question they cannot answer! In making the only reply they can make, they make other claims: Holy Spirit baptism and speaking in tongues. And yet, these are the very same "evidences" these other groups give! All of them claim latter-day revelation, all of them claim the same powers, all of them claim Holy Spirit guidance, and none of them are in fellowship with one another nor would accept one another's "revelations!"

All of them DO have one thing in common: their claims of such revelation conflict with the words of the apostles! The Bible speaks of its all-sufficiency (II Tim. 3:16,17) and of the fact that upon revelation being completed, the attendant miraculous gifts then would have ceased (I Cor. 13:8-13).

Precious wording passed on to us from the Restoration period is here repeated: If the UPC Manual teaches more or less than the Word of God, it then teaches either too much or too little; and if the UPC Manual teaches exactly what is found in the Word of God, then it is a superflous document, and certainly not needed at all! The UPC Manual then stands condemned.

The Manual And The Terms Of Pardon

In their "Articles of Faith," and under the heading, "Repentance and Conversion," we find this: "Pardon and forgiveness of sins is obtained by genuine repentance, a confessing and forsaking of sins. We are justified by **faith in the Lord Jesus Christ (Romans 5:1)."[9] No mention is here made of** baptism at all; pardon is based on one's penitence, confession and forsaking of sins. In the following section of the "Articles of Faith," entitled "Water Baptism," they speak of water baptism by immersion and to be administered according to Acts 2:38, etc., but the stress is not on the purpose of the baptism but on the "name of the Lord Jesus Christ."[10] By their doctrine, this means with the word "Jesus" being verbally used in the baptismal ceremony. Thus, baptism FOR the remission of sins is not given emphasis by them, and we are sure this is so for one reason: their stress of Holy Spirit baptism!

In their Article of Faith entitled, "Fundamental Doctrine," it is said: "...the Bible standard of full salvation, which is repentance, baptism in water by immersion in the name of the Lord Jesus Christ for the remission of sins, and the baptism of the Holy Ghost with the initial sign of speaking with other tongues as the Spirit gives utterance."[11] Here, while baptism for the remission of sins was not mentioned earlier, under "Conversion," now it is included when "full salvation" is discussed. Still, the matter of baptism of the Holy Spirit is their rallying point. We are plainly told that for FULL salvation, one must receive the baptism of the Holy Ghost and speak with tongues. In religious discussion with UPC ministers, they have been asked: "Is Holy Ghost baptism essential to being a Christian — to being saved?" And the answer has been, "I can say, without reservation, 'Yes'!"[12] So, by their doctrine, and by their creed-book, one would not be saved, and thus would not be a Christian, until he received the baptism of the Holy Spirit. Yet, noting again the Foreword to their creed, it was "...a band of earnest, hungry-hearted ministers and Christian workers..." who were meeting, and praying for, and claiming to receive, Holy Spirit baptism in either 1900 or 1901 as they began their movement! On the one hand, they state that these were already Christians who had not received Holy Spirit baptism, and on the other hand they state that one must receive Holy Spirit baptism in order to become a Christian! Again we see that there is no way that men can be in support of a human creed and then keep from contradicting the Word of God!

But even more: they state that one must speak in tongues in order to be a Christian, and yet we are plainly shown that not every child of God spake in tongues in the New Testament (I Cor. 12:8-10,30)! Again, the UPC Manual is in contradiction to the New Testament of Jesus Christ!

Is The Manual Authoritative?

We have noticed, down through the years, that one of the first responses made, when men are asked about their human creed, is to deny that such exists. Then, having been confronted with it, the next response is a denial that it is followed — a denial that it is authoritative. Regarding the United Pentecostal Church, debates with their representatives have shown us that many of their members are not familiar with the creed, and we may be going a long way toward opening their eyes by throwing the spotlight on it. The creed very definitely has an authoritative hold on them!

In the UPC Manual, under "Local Church Government - Membership - Section 1. Eligibility," we have this: "Anyone believing in and accepting the Apostolic doctrine as set forth in our Articles of Faith is eligible to become a member."[13] In discussion after discussion with them, these men have been pressed on this matter. In one discussion, the UPC minister was asked, since he said the creed was not authoritative, to publicly disavow it. When further pressed on this, his response was: "I will not publicly disavow the doctrine that the apostles shed their blood for...we will not disavow this."[14] This type response simply means that either the apostles provided the UPC Manual, or that they did not and that he was going to follow his human creed anyway. By points we have previously made, we can see that he is going to do the latter: follow the human creed, regardless!

Further discussion with the UPC reveals that, when pressed, they will claim that in the UPC Manual, only the Articles of Faith are endorsed by them, and considered binding, and that the rest of the creed is not of a binding nature. They usually prefer to state this matter privately, for with the hold they have on their members, it would not be wise to advertise that any aspect of their relationship with their members wasn't of a binding nature.

In the UPC Manual, we note that beyond the "Articles of Faith" is the "Constitution," and then rules for "Local Church Government." We wonder if these men really know what a Constitution happens to be? The very nature of a Constitution, anywhere, in any type organization, is to set forth rules whereby those in the organization are to be governed! Can you imagine someone claiming to be a faithful citizen of the United States, and then disclaiming our Constitution? A standard oath given in our nation is to the effect that the Constitution will be protected and defended! The Constitution, by its very naure, is authoritative!

It matters little whether the UPC ministers try to divide the UPC Manual into "binding" and "non-binding" sections. We have seen that even the section they admit is "binding" is contrary to the New Testament! But just taking a look into the Constitution reveals rules regarding: purpose of the church and membership (p. 28), church officers (p. 29f), qualifications and ordaining of ministers (p. 36f), matters of discipline and penalty (p. 41f), matters regarding marriage-divorce-remarriage (p. 43f), instances of immoral conduct (p. 44f), general church discipline (p. 117f), and the fact that the local UPC pastor has "...the oversight and superintendence of all interests of the church and of all departments of its work, both spiritual and temporal..." (p. 119). Amazingly, the UPC preachers will claim that their Constitution is not authoritative, when rules by the score are found there, with the threat of discipline and disfellowship set forth! It should be stressed to them that matters relating to morality, discipline and marriage are matters of doctrine set forth in the Bible, and their Constitution affects to emphasize the Bible, and then they would claim it is not binding!

Conclusion

We have thus reviewed the United Pentecostal Church Manual, and we have seen it to be a human document, produced by men in error and designed to keep men in error by its authoritative hold. We have seen that which is always typical of a creed: it will contradict the Word of God over and over again! Let us do all that we can to familiarize ourselves with this creed, and use every opportunity we have to teach these zealous people the way of the Lord more perfectly!

FOOTNOTES

1. United Pentecostal Church Manual, Pentecostal Publishing House, 8855 Dunn Road, Hazelwood, Missouri 63042.
2. Ibid., cover.
3. Ibid., p. 12.
4. Ibid., p. 12.
5. Op. cit., 1968 & 1969 editions.
6. Ibid., p. 13.
7. Ibid., p. 13.
8. Ibid., p. 18.
9. Ibid., p. 20.
10. Ibid., p. 21.
11. Ibid., p. 22.
12. Jackson-Bayer Debate on Pentecostalism, Sowing the Seed Books, 8900 Manchaca Rd., Austin, Texas 1980, p. 8.
13. United Pentecostal Church Manual, p. 116.
14. Jackson-Bayer, p. 72.

CHAPTER 20
THE UNITED PENTECOSTAL CHURCH'S DOCTRINE OF THE GODHEAD

Alan E. Highers

In order to understand the doctrine of the United Pentecostal Church with reference to the Godhead, it is necessary to examine the history of the movement and its claim to special revelation.

History of the United Pentecostal Church

The first meeting of the United Pentecostal Church as a new organization occurred on September 25, 1945, but the roots of its beginning go back to a Pentecostal camp meeting in 1913 located just outside Los Angeles, California. Although the UPC claims that "a great outpouring of the Holy Spirit" came on January 1, 1901 (or, 1900, depending upon which edition of the UPC Manual one reads), it was not until the Arroyo Seco camp meeting that the distinctive "oneness" identity began to take shape.

During the camp meeting a man named R. E. McAlister spoke on the subject of water baptism and at the conclusion of his address he remarked that the apostles always baptized in the name of Jesus Christ and never with the words Father, Son, and Holy Spirit. One of those who listened to McAlister, John G. Scheppe, spent the night in prayer and in the early morning hours ran through camp, shouting that God had revealed to him the truth on baptism in Jesus' name. Frank J. Ewart, one of those present in the camp meeting, later met and studied with McAlister and he became one of the early leaders of the oneness movement.

The oneness position spread rapidly among Pentecostal groups and caused considerable contention, but it was not until 1916 that the lines of fellowship were drawn and the Assemblies of God forced out the "Jesus only" adherents. The oneness people formed their own organization in 1917 at Eureka Springs, Arkansas, and through the years they went through a number of organizational changes until finally, in 1945, a merger of the most prominent groups resulted in the formation of the body known as the United Pentecostal Church.

The United Pentecostal Church is today a very militant organization in promoting its view of "baptism only in the name of Jesus" and "only one person in the Godhead." From its history, however, we may make the following observations:

(1) It is an organization founded upon a supposed "revelation" rather than upon the teaching of the scriptures.

(2) It is a human institution, resulting from various mergers, consolidations, and councils of men.

(3) It was born of contention and disagreement among men, all of whom claimed to have the miraculous outpouring of the Holy Spirit.

Claim of Special Revelation

In the "Foreword" of the United Pentecostal Church Manual, it is said: "In the year 1914 came the revelation on the name of the Lord Jesus Christ." The scriptures, of course, did not change in 1914; whatever the scriptures revealed, they revealed both before and after 1914. If the revelation "came" in the year 1914, then it did not exist prior to that time. The so-called "oneness" doctrine originated, therefore, not as the result of scriptural teaching, but due to an alleged latter-day special "revelation."

There is a concentrated effort by UPC writers and debaters to avoid any reference to this special revelation. If one examines the polemic and apologetic treatises on the subject, he will not find any defense based on divine revelation in the year 1914. No writer says, "We teach there is only one person in the Godhead and that baptism must be administered only in the name of Jesus Christ because we received this teaching as a direct special revelation of God in the year 1914." Why not? The answer seems to lie in the fact that once doctrines are conceived by alleged special revelations, they are then defended on the basis that this is what the scriptures said all the time! The UPC aggressively defends its doctrine on the Godhead by elaborate scriptural citations, but the Adventists do likewise with reference to their doctrine on the sabbath-day. One must not forget, however, that the initial force behind the doctrine is the claim of **special revelation,** and that the search for **scriptural support** of the revelation comes in the aftermath.

A doctrine which originated upon a claim of special revelation is indefensible by the scriptures. The fact that men may now seek to defend it by the scriptures does not make it a scriptural doctrine. If a doctrine was not revealed in the scriptures before 1914, then of course it did not suddenly appear in the scriptures **after** 1914. The Bible is the same as always. The UPC doctrine on the Godhead and baptism, therefore, is not Bible doctrine.

Scriptural Teaching on the Godhead

The scriptures clearly teach that there is more than one person in the Godhead. There is only one Deity, but there are three divine persons in that one Deity: namely, the Father, the Son, and the Holy Spirit.

(1) There are several passages in which three are all mentioned in the same verse (Matt. 28:19; II Cor. 13:14; I Pet. 1:2).

(2) Plural pronouns are associated with the Deity (Gen. 1:26; 3:22; Isa. 6:8). "Let **us** make man..."

(3) Jesus said he was not alone, thereby distinguishing between himself and the Father. "For I am not alone, but I and the Father that sent me" (John 8:16). See also John 8:17, 18; 8:29; 16:32.

(4) Words are used with reference to the Godhead which demand a plurality. (a) **Both** (II John 9). (b) **Another** (John 14:16). (c) **Two** (John 8:17, 18).

(5) The Father-Son relationship necessitates more than one in the Godhead. "I came forth from the Father, and am come into the world: again, I leave the world, and go to the Father" (John 16:28). In II John 3 the Lord Jesus Christ is called "the Son of the Father."

(6) The baptism of Jesus clearly manifests the truth of three persons in the Godhead (Matt. 3:16, 17).

(7) In Ephesians 4:4-6 Paul names seven items of which he says in each case there is **one:** one body, one Spirit, one hope, one Lord, one faith, one baptism, and one God and Father of all. Among these he mentions **one** Spirit, **one** Lord, and **one** God which, when added together, make **three.**

(8) Jesus sits at the right hand of the Father (Acts 2:33; Eph. 1:20; Col. 3:1).

(9) The Father and Son are one "even as" believers should be one; therefore, not one in person, but in unity (John 17:20-22).

(10) There are certain "scriptural impossibilities" if Father and Son are the same person. (a) "My father is greater than I" (John 14:28). (b) "For the Father judgeth no man, but hath committed all judgment unto the Son" (John 5:22). (c) "The word which ye hear is not mine, but the Father's which sent me" (John 14:24). (d) "For I came down from heaven, not to do mine own will, but the will of him that sent me" (John 6:38). (e) "But of that day and that hour knoweth no man, no, not the angels which are in heaven, neither the Son, but the Father" (Mark 13:32).

Some Special Considerations

One who expects to refute Pentecostal doctrine on the Godhead should be aware that many Pentecostals endeavor to avoid the force of scriptures against their doctrine by arguing that "Father" refers to the Spirit and "Son" to the flesh. They also contend that "person" means the human fleshly being. Therefore, they argue that Jesus is the only "person" in the Godhead, that is, he is the only human fleshly form of the Godhead. This line of argument is obviously an attempt to dodge the consequences of their position. When we affirm that there are three **persons** in the Godhead, we certainly do not mean that there are three **fleshly** beings; and further, when the oneness people affirm that there is **only one person** in the Godhead, they do not mean simply that there is only one who came in the flesh. They believe and teach that there is only one individual being in the Godhead, period; and they should be required to face up to their doctrine and to defend it without being allowed to escape exposure by the use of obscure and artificial definitions. It is crucial, therefore, in any discussion with the oneness advocates, to establish the meaning of the word "person."

It may be shown that Father, Son, and Holy Spirit all possess the attributes of **persons** and that all are addressed with **personal pronouns:**

1ST PERSON — "I" (FATHER) — Hebrews 1:5
2ND PERSON — "THOU" (SON) — Hebrews 1:5
3RD PERSON — "HE" (HOLY SPIRIT) — John 16:13

Each has mind, or intellect, and is consequently capable of "knowing" or possessing knowledge. (See, for example, Matt. 6:32; John 2:25, Rom. 8:27). Father, Son, and Holy Spirit are, then, all "persons" in the true and proper sense of the word; hence, it is scriptural and right to speak of "three persons in the Godhead."

Some oneness defenders appear to equate "person" and "Son" which, in each instance, they apply to the **flesh.** This they do in order to explain such passages as, "My Father is greater than I" (John 14:28). The usual explanation is, "My Father (the Spirit) is greater than I (the flesh)." If this is the correct understanding of "person" and "Son" (and it is **not**), then Pentecostals are in error in affirming that Jesus is the **only person** in the Godhead because, according to their position, there is **no person** in the Godhead today unless Jesus is still in the flesh! Further, Jesus would not be the **Son of God** today and, in fact, there would be **no** Son of God today unless Jesus were still in the flesh today! So, in an effort to escape one dilemma, the oneness people get into two more. The very existence of their plight is evidence of the strong scriptural proof against them and their doctrine of the Godhead. The United Pentecostal Church's doctrine of the Godhead has been weighed in the balances and found wanting.

CHAPTER 21
THE BAPTISMAL FORMULA OF THE UNITED PENTECOSTAL CHURCH

W. Ray Duncan

May I first of all express my appreciation to the Getwell church of Christ and all those connected with making these annual lectureships possible. While I am fearful that even this effort is not enough to supply our present needs in the brotherhood, it is at least a wonderful effort to do a great service.

In a West Palm Beach meeting on March 3, 1967 Willard Collins quoted Batsell Barrett Baxter as saying, "The church of Christ will face greater struggles in the next fifty years than it has faced in the last two hundred years." And also, "A former President of the Southern Association of Schools said, 'by the year 2000 there will be no Christian colleges in the United States because religion will lose its influence! Only 4 to 5% will worship, hence there will be no interest in Christian Schools.' "

Paul's "Every wind of doctrine, by the slight of men, and cunning craftiness, whereby they lie in wait to deceive;" has descended upon the church of the Lord in these days in all its fury!

I have a limited acquaintance with several churches from San Diego to Savannah and from Miami to Minneapolis, and there are few congregations, if any, that have not had to deal with serious problems in the church today not only of loose morals but even the doctrine is being attacked!

In view of the tremendous shifting of the foundations of faith in so many congregations, the divisions that have come, the complete apostasy of some congregations, and a general surge of anxiety among informed members of the Lord's church, I approach my subject with carefulness and prayer.

From all that I have observed and read I believe that the elements of this neo-Pentecostalism that is now sweeping through the church with visible results like a whirlwind in a dry cowpasture is the most devasting and disturbing thing to strike the church in this century.

In this lectureship the "Spiritual Sword" is dealing with "Some Modern Cults and World Religions," and my part is to deal with the "Baptismal Formula" of the United Pentecostal Church.

If it can be shown that the UPC is wrong in their concept of [1] the Church, [2] God, [3] Christ and [4] the Holy Spirit it would be a simple matter to show that a formula requiring an audible pronouncement, "I baptize you in the name of Jesus Only," is wrong!

Gen. 3:15 is the first indication in the Bible that a Savior would come.

Deut. 18:15-22 clearly states that the time would come when power or authority would pass from one PERSON to ANOTHER.

Acts 3:19-24 records that this exact prophecy was fulfilled in the coming of the Messiah and that God's authority has passed to him. Furthermore Luke said that "all the prophets from Samuel and those that follow after, as many as have spoken..." so understood the prophecy. Now it seems to me that to read these two Scriptures and misunderstand or misapply them would take some expert help! The UPC, in their Articles of Faith, page 17 [1952 edition] says no authority has ever changed hands because there is only one God with different manifestations! Jesus said it did happen [Matt. 28:18; Dan. 7:14]. Which do you think told the truth?

IF those "hungry-hearted ministers [Foreword, par. 6] and Christian workers in Topeka, Kan., knew of these two Scriptures on the morning of Jan. 1, 1900, I am not surprised that "they were surprised" when they thought they got a conflicting message from the Holy Spirit! (Ibid.) In fact they tacitly admit in this very paragraph that their experience is exactly 1870 years too late to agree with Peter's application of "these days" in A.D. 30. Or, the only alternative I can see for them is that Peter and the prophets were wrong, and the UPC is right! If this is correct then Peter and "all the prophets from Samuel on down..." missed which days were "these days" by 1870 years. Can you believe it?

Daniel 2:44 not only says the kingdom would be established in the days of the Roman kings but that the government would NOT be left to other people. Jesus said the "apostles would sit on twelve thrones judging the twelve tribes of Israel." [Matt. 19:28] Furthermore the Spirit would guide **them** into **all truth** and bring all things to **their** remembrance [John 14:26; 16:13] The UPC Manual says that Jesus nor the Spirit guided them into ALL TRUTH because these "hungry-hearted ministers" discovered TRUTHS that no man knew till 1914! [Foreword, par 7] They must have been hungry indeed to fabricate a story like this - and eat it! Imagine, if you can, that Jesus lied to the apostles by telling them "I will send the Spirit and he will guide you into ALL TRUTH, and bring ALL THINGS to your remembrance." Peter testified that he did it by saying, "According as his divine will **hath given** us all things that pertain unto life and godliness..."[II Pet. 1:3] The Bible is right and the fabrication of the UPC to the contrary has to be wrong. Imagine, not a single apostle nor any inspired man knew the proper way to baptize a penitent believer until these "hungry-hearted" ministers discovered this truth (?) in 1914.

In Matt. 16:18 the Lord promised to build his church, and in Mark 9:1 he said it would be established in that generation. The UPC did not get into full swing till 1906 in an old building on Azusa Street in Los Angeles, Calif. [Ibid.] The Lord's church got into full swing on Pentecost day in Jerusalem in A.D. 30, according to Luke 24:46-47 and Acts 2. Three thousand heard, believed and obeyed the gospel that day and were "added to the church."

[Acts 2:47] Nothing is said about a baptism formula, it simply records what Peter told them to **do** to be saved, not what he **said** when they were baptized!

The Bible Vs The UPC On The Godhead

The very first "Article of Faith" in the UPC Manual [1952] concerns their view of the Godhead. I doubt not that they believe what the Manual says but they are grossly in error on this point, and from this error stems their false teaching on a baptism formula. They strongly insist that God is limited to ONE PERSON [they don't use the word person] and only one! They do believe that he looked and acted different on different occasions, but in reality they are claiming it was a deception! He really in fact was never a Father of anyone in particular, nevertheless He did reveal himself as a Father as pertains to redemption. He never was in reality any one's Son, although he did reveal Himself as such in the scheme of redemption! He revealed Himself by "emination" as the Holy Spirit [Webster's New World Dictionary says 'emination' means, [1] an eminating; coming forth. [2] something that comes from a source; thing emitted.] but they fail to tell us from what the Holy Spirit emitted! I have always believed that God was eternal, that he did not come forth from anything.

There Is But One God [I Cor. 8:6]

I believe you will discover or discern the Bible truth about the Godhead by looking at the chart below and checking the Scriptures at your convenience.

Matt. 11:25
John 8:41,42
Rom. 15:6
I Cor. 8:6
Eph. 4:6; 1:17

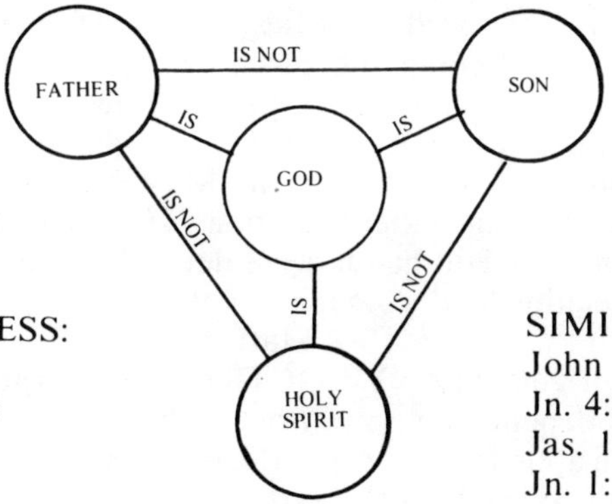

John 1:1,2
John 20:28
Phil. 2:6
Col. 2:9
Heb. 1:8
Acts 20:28

DISTINCTNESS:
Matt. 3:16,17
John 14:16,26
John 15:26
John 16:13ff
John 17:1-8

SIMILARITY:
John 1:18; 14:9
Jn. 4:24; Lk. 24:39
Jas. 1:13; Heb. 4:15
Jn. 1:1; I Jn. 1:1-3
II Pet. 3:9; Lk. 19:10

The FATHER......PLANS
The SON......PERFECTS
The SPIRIT......REVEALS

If the above is a true picture of the Biblical view of the Godhead then I affirm that it is impossible to administer water baptism in any other way except "into the name of the Father, and of the Son, and of the Holy Spirit!" No matter what is said or if anything is said, it has to be authorized by God, Christ and the Holy Spirit.

John 7:16 Every doctrine Jesus taught was authorized by his Father.

John 8:28 Jesus **never** did anything of himself, his Father provided the plan.

John 12:49 He never spoke of himself, he repeated only what his Father said.

Such Scriptures could be multiplied, but these should be sufficient.

Jesus Spoke With All Authority

Because God had given him authority without measure he exercised power over all the elements in heaven and on earth. [Matt. 28:18; John 3:34] Not one time did his power fail on anything! He exercised power over the bodies of men by raising the dead, unstopping deaf ears, opening blind eyes, loosing dumb tongues, casting out demons, stilling storms at sea, commanding the fish of the sea into service for his disciples. No man ever exercised such authority. He even took away the sin of the world; praise God for such a Redeemer!

Thus when Jesus commanded baptism in water for the forgiveness of sins it was the Father's command and is irrevocable and unchangeable. [Mark 16:15, 16; Matt. 28:18-20] Without the authority of his Father there never would have been the command!

The Plenary Power Of The Holy Spirit

Albeit Jesus never appeared in the flesh to any of the early Christians yet they were to speak and command certain things in his name or by his authority. The early Christians had no printed New Testament from which to quote, hence the apostles were given the baptism of the Holy Spirit whereby they could teach inerrantly the Master's will and also transfer some of this ability to some other Christians. However the apostles as well as those on whom they laid hands were dependent upon that direct and spontaneous revelation and guidance of the Holy Spirit in those early formative years of the church. [See Matt. 10:19; II Pet. 1:21; II Tim. 1:6] The Spirit never originated ANY DOCTRINE nor surpressed any, he was wholly and solely dependent upon Christ for his instructions[John 16:13]. Hence neither the apostles nor inspired Christians could speak for Christ except by the Holy Spirit. [Check Matt. 10:19-20; John 14:24; 16:13; I Pet. 1:22; I Cor. 14:37; II Pet. 1:3; Rom. 8:14; Gal 5:18.]

CONCLUSION: Thus, it would seem that any unbiased and unprejudiced mind could soon determine that without the work and authority of the Holy Spirit no preaching would have been done; without Christ's authority directing the Spirit he would have been silent; and Christ never exercised any authority nor gave any command that did not come from his Father. Hence I firmly affirm the impossibility of performing Scriptural baptism at all except "into the name of the Father, and of the Son, and of the Holy Spirit" (Cf.: Acts 2:38).

Furthermore, before Jude laid down his pen of inspiration [The UPC to the contrary notwithstanding] he said, "The faith (was) once for all delivered to the saints." [Verse 3] So, the "heart-hungry ministers" in California were left out of God's plan completely. They are strictly a 20th century cult with no authority higher than a bunch of zealous uninspired men meeting in an old house of Azusa Street in Los Angeles in 1906.

The UPC Doctrine Of The Holy Spirit Is Wrong

In conclusion I want to point out as strongly as possible that the UPC is as wrong on their doctrine of tongue-speaking and divine healing which they say accompanies salvation [UPC Manual, 1952, page 21, par. 4,5] as they are on the doctrines of the Godhead and the Baptism Formula.

On May 26-29, 1953 I met Mr. D. L. Welch, one of the most able defenders of the UPC doctrines to be found anywhere, in Hohenwald, Tenn. Oddly enough there was a death in his congregation in Miami at the time for the debate to begin and he did not appear the first night. He "sent his son," and this was so announced to an audience of approximately 2000 people. It was apparent to many of us [I think Garland Elkins was present] that the son was woefully lacking in preparation for the debate. The Spirit had apparently left him with quite a deficiency and a poor memory - if indeed he ever had it! Mr. Welch was ill at ease on the second night when I chided him for not having the death of his member postponed till after the debate, or else to have raised the deceased from the dead. If his doctrine is demonstrable he **could have** either raised the dead and **would not,** or else he **would have** raised the dead and **could not!** In either instance he was in the tights!

Secondly I pressed the argument to his embarassment that he actually did not "send his son," but only a manifestation of himself! If God used the very same identical language concerning His son and did not really mean it, how could the audience accept Welch's statement that he "sent his son"? The prevailing circumstances had a devastating effect on every speech Welch made. [Of course I had one of the best moderators a debater could have - Boone Douthitt.]

Thirdly I challenged him with all my might to prove that every miracle (so-called) in the UPC was not either ACCIDENTAL, INCIDENTAL or CIRCUMSTANTIAL! I challenged Mr. Welch to PICK, NAME, SELECT, SPECIFY or IDENTIFY his very next miracle, and have competent people to judge that the affliction, blindness, lameness or whatever was an organic situation, but Mr. Welch was indisposed to attempt to produce such a miracle. I have made the same offer on the KNOW YOUR BIBLE television program which I have conducted for twenty years - and no healer (?) has had sufficient faith in his doctrine to attempt to name, pick or specify the next miracle he expects to perform -

especially if it must be certified by competent witnesses that there is indeed an organic affliction. However, be it said to their credit (if it is a credit) that a member of Ben Franklin's church [Christ's Center] in San Diego did go to a funeral parlor one Saturday morning with others of like faith and make every attempt they could to raise a dead man! I was there making pictures which I still have, and I'll tell you right now IF that dead man had arisen I would have been more surprised than that bunch of "hungry-hearted ministers" in California!! I asked Ben why he did not accompany the group, and if he believed the dead man would get up. He said he thought it possible if the petitioners had sufficient faith, but that his faith was not that strong, so he just stayed at home! I tell you, brethren, this miracle working, tongue-speaking, charismatic movement is a hoax, a deception and there is not one thing they can perform with their doctrine that cannot be duplicated and improved by the science of HYPNOSIS! Indeed there are strange things that happen today, and many of them we may not understand, but there is no evidence in the Bible nor proof outside the Bible that God is still performing miracles today. In fact the greatest demonstration of unbelief in the Scriptures is from all those who are insisting that God must still "be confirming His word by signs, and miracles" in this present day.

I knew that neither Mr. Welch nor any of his group could perform a miracle, but at brother Douthitt's suggestion I pleaded with Mr. Welch to give the audience just a little demonstration, like dousing his face with india ink, or just common school-type ink — and show the audience how he could miraculously make it disappear. Mr. Welch was most uncooperative to the suggestion!

Gifts Of The Spirit

I am submitting a chart that I have used effectively with several Pentecostal preachers in debate. Before displaying the chart I tell the audience that I can anticipate every argument that he will produce for claims to miraculous powers, and that even before he makes his arguments I will identify, classify, and locate by book, chapter and verse every argument that he will make for his tongues, divine healing and miracles. I will also show in advance his misapplication of these Scriptures and the falseness of his doctrine even before he speaks. [We may find it necessary to use the chart on several of our own brethren nowadays.]

(What follows in the rest of this chapter is the chart which I used.)

GOD
Holy Spirit

TONGUES, MIRACLES, Etc

ALL CHRISTIANS RECEIVE COMMON GIFT:
Acts 5:32; Gal. 4:6; Acts 2:38f; Jude 3.

Never miraculously attended. Acts 2:41; Rom. 8:9; Eph. 3:16; 1:13-14; II Cor. 5:2-6; Possible to be "clothed with Spirit" and found naked. Gen. 3:21; Rom. 8:6-10; Gal. 5:16-22.

LAYING ON OF HANDS GIFT:
Acts 6:6; 8:6-7; I Tim. 4:14; II Tim. 1:6; I Cor. 12:1-11. Spirit of Word of Wisdom; Word of Knowledge; Faith; Gifts of Healing; Working of Miracles; Prophecy; Discerning of Spirits; Divers Kinds of Tongues; Interpretation of Tongues.

APOSTLES — BAPTISMAL MEASURE:
Acts 1:8, 5, 26; 2:1-7; 11:15-17; Luke 24:49; Matt. 3:11. Devils — Diseases, Luke 9:1. New Tongues. Mark 16:17; I Cor. 14:21-22. Signs, Mark 16:20; Raise Dead, Acts 9:40; 20:9-12; Healing, Acts 5:12-16.

CHRIST WITHOUT MEASURE:
Devils — Diseases. Matt. 17:14-21; Death, John 11:43-44; Elements, Mark 4:37-41. Signs, Jno. 20:30-31.

OTHER MIRACLES:
Simon, Acts 8:9-11. Elymas, Acts 13:6-11; Theudas & Judas, Acts 5:36-37. Spirits of Devils, Rev. 16:13-14; Gal. 1:8, 9; Heb. 13:8.

a. ALL CHRISTIANS RECEIVE COMMON GIFT.

Just as certain as a child partakes of the spirit and nature of an earthly father so the "Father of spirits" imparts an element of Himself into each of his children. The Scriptures say, "And because ye are sons [not to make you a son], God hath sent forth the Spirit of his Son into your hearts, crying, Abba, Father" (Gal. 4:6). This is in perfect harmony with Acts 2:38, when certain conditions are met, "ye shall receive the gift of the Holy Ghost." If the receiving the "remission of sins" is conditional, then in the same verse to the same audience the receiving of the Holy Ghost is conditional. When the brother of our Lord referred to the ones who had been thus redeemed he spoke of "the common salvation" characteristic of God's people. Acts 5:32 seems to indicate that God has never let an obedient child of his inherit a common salvation without also giving him a common gift of the Holy Spirit. When the UPC manual says that with obedience in baptism one also gets the speaking in tongues gift he is saying what the Bible does not teach!

b. LAYING ON OF HANDS MEASURE.

Some of the early Christians (S E C) had the ability to speak in tongues and to perform miracles, but no example of such can be cited but that it is evident that they had been so qualified by the laying on of the hands of the apostles. In fact Timothy was reminded that he had received his gift from God by the laying on of the hands of Paul (II Tim. 1:6). No one can doubt but that some of the members of the church at Corinth had various gifts and did some marvelous things, but these gifts were not common to the Spirit or provided indiscriminately to the people, but the Spirit "dividing to every man severally as he will" (II Cor. 12:11). If these nine gifts had been common to all the people there would have been no room for arguments and jealousies among the members! The Pentecostal preachers today cannot find one among all their members who can do anything characteristic of the workings of the Holy Spirit in this category. Let him try it!

c. BAPTISMAL MEASURE TO THE APOSTLES.

The apostles were certainly short of exercising the power of the Spirit as did the Master, but at the same time they were far ahead of anything that any of the members could do who were not apostles. Each of the apostles could "bind or loose" in the name of the Lord. Inspired members were limited to reiterate what had already been announced by an apostle. The apostles could speak new truths to the world and unlock the mysteries of the kingdom. Other members could only speak what the apostles had already declared. In fact the apostle Paul made a point on this very subject by saying that either man or angel who would alter or change what had been spoken by the apostles would be accursed (Gal. 1:6-9). Jesus had promised the apostles the baptism of the Holy Spirit, Peter said they received it, and Luke records the reception in the second chapter of Acts — and that should settle the matter for those who respect the Book!

d.GOD GAVE CHRIST THE SPIRIT WITHOUT MEASURE.

The outer ring on the chart is intended to show that Christ exercised more power by the Spirit than any other. No finite mind can begin to describe infinite power. It was by him, for him, and through him that all creation exists. Indeed he said, "Before Abraham was, I am." John describes him as the Alpha and the Omega, the first and the last, he had the first say — and will have the last say — and it doesn't really matter what anybody else may say! Truly he was God manifested in the flesh and has offered the scheme of redemption that will save to the uttermost all who will come unto God through him. The words that he has spoken will be our judge in the last day. Rightly divide and obey the Word of truth and he will save you. Pervert the message of the cross — and you must take the consequences.

CHAPTER 22
TWO BAPTISMS ACCORDING TO UNITED PENTECOSTAL DOCTRINE

Winfred Clark

When one speaks of the doctrine of the United Pentecostal Church, of what does he speak? He speaks of that group formed by a merger of two groups in 1945. These were the Pentecostal Assemblies of Jesus Christ Inc. and the Pentecostal Church Inc. This merger was brought about by those who had adopted the "oneness" doctrine. Among these groups this idea first took shape in the Arroyo Seco Camp meeting in 1913. It is supposed that a man by the name of John G. Scheppe, claimed that God revealed to him the truth on baptism in Jesus' name. By that they mean one must have the name of Jesus called over him at the time of his baptism.

The headquarters of this group is found in St. Louis, Missouri or more specifically, Hazelwood, Missouri.

Thus, when we speak of the doctrine of the United Pentecostal Church, we speak of this group, and the doctrine peculiar to that which they teach and support.

"Two Baptisms" Are Asserted

One has but to read the literature of this group to see that they assume that there are indeed "two baptisms." In their manual, 1978 edition, one finds stated the following: Under "Articles of Faith," "The basic and fundamental doctrine of this organization shall be the Bible standard of full salvation, which is repentance, baptism in water by immersion in the name of the Lord Jesus Christ for the remission of sins, and baptism of the Holy Ghost with the initial sign of speaking with other tongues as the Spirit gives utterance." Surely one can see by this a very bold assertion of both water baptism and Holy Spirit baptism. They declare that such is a basic and fundamental doctrine.

The preachers of this group will teach this by writing and word oi mouth. For example, "Water baptism is an essential part of New Testament salvation: and not as some teach, 'Just an outward form of an inward cleansing.' Without proper baptism it is impossible to enter into the kingdom of God (God's true church, the Bride of Christ) and therefore, it is not merely a part of local church membership." So says one of their writers.

Notice also. "The baptism of the Holy Ghost is the birth of the Spirit (John 3:5). That spiritual baptism is necessary to put anyone in the kingdom of God (God's true church, the Bride of Christ), and is evidenced by speaking in other tongues (other languages) as the Spirit of God gives utterance."

In view of the quotes afore mentioned, could one deny the assertion of both water baptism and Holy Spirit baptism being necessary according to United Pentecostal doctrine? They assert that both are necessary before one can enter God's true church, the Bride of Christ. This is plainly stated. Surely one would say it is necessary for one to be a part of the Bride of Christ. But these will tell you that you can only become a part of that Bride by being baptized both with water and the Holy Spirit. There is then no question as to the assertion of "two baptisms" by the United Pentecostal Church.

"Two Baptisms" Are Argued

They not only assert that there are "two baptisms," but try to set forth what they consider to be arguments to prove such. One has but to read the manual of the United Pentecostal Church to see this. In their articles of faith they set forth such passages as Matthew 3:11, Acts 1:5, Acts 2:4, Acts 2:38, 39 as passages that support their teaching that the baptism of the Holy Spirit is for all believers today! Also, concerning water baptism, they use such passages as Acts 2:38, 8:16, 10:48, 19:5. These passages enable one to obey Matthew 28:19, they say.

Anyone who has encountered any of this group would know that they affirm the baptism in water for the remission of sins. They argue their case from the aforementioned passages and others. In public debate they will affirm that Holy Spirit baptism is for all believers today. This can be seen in the Jackson-Bayer and Ramsey-Hicks debates.

They use the terms, "baptized with the Holy Ghost and fire," "filled with the Spirit," and "gift of the Holy Ghost" as synonymous. When they use a term like this it means but one thing, the baptism of the Holy Spirit. Also, remember that they argue that the evidence of such a baptism is the power to speak in tongues.

One finds abundant evidence of the United Pentecostals arguing that John 7:38-39 promises the baptism of the Holy Spirit to all believers today. Of course, anytime they see the Holy Spirit it means to them the baptism of the Holy Spirit.

Such passages as John 14:16-17, 26; 15:26; 16:6-7; 16:13 are used to argue that men can expect the baptism of the Holy Spirit even today. No matter that this was spoken to the apostles and about their work, they still insist that these passages promise such for today. Again, the United Pentecostal will use what John said, "I indeed baptize you with water...but he that cometh after me...he shall baptize you with the Holy Ghost, and with fire..." (Matt. 3:11,12). They think this promises the baptism of the Holy Spirit to all believers for all time. They argue that this was not limited to the apostles.

An effort is made to say that not just the apostles were baptized with the Holy Ghost on Pentecost. This is done by referring to Luke 24:33-49 and Acts 1:13, 14. In this argument, they seek to include all the one hundred and twenty in Acts 2:1-4.

Also, an argument is presented based on the prophecy of Joel as quoted by Peter in Acts 2:17-18. The United Pentecostal will ask, "Are we living in the last days?" Also, they will ask were any of the apostles handmaidens. By these methods they seek to find support from these passages for their position.

"The gift of the Holy Spirit" in Acts 2:38, is to the United Pentecostal, Holy Spirit baptism. He will argue that the word "gift" in Acts 10:45, 11:17 refers to Holy Spirit baptism and thus it refers to Holy Spirit baptism in Acts 2:38. They, thus have "two baptisms" in this one verse, at least they think they do.

In addition to Acts 2:38, they will argue that Acts 2:39 makes the promise of Holy Spirit baptism for all. They argue that the "promise" of Acts 2:39 includes the baptism of the Holy Spirit for all today.

Acts 8:15-17 is cited as a proof text to Holy Spirit baptism because it speaks of the Holy Spirit "falling upon them." They argue that the Holy Spirit fell on those in Acts 10:44, that this was Holy Spirit baptism, then when it says, "For as yet he was fallen upon none of them" (Acts 8:16), that would mean Holy Ghost baptism.

Add to this Acts 19:1-6. They have no reluctance to claim this supports their teaching that these in Ephesus were baptized with the Holy Ghost. This is done because they "spake with tongues."

The United Pentecostals will argue that John 3:5 involves both water baptism and Holy Spirit baptism. They say, "If water means baptism then Spirit means baptism." Some will go so far as to call this "cooperate baptism." It is a feeble effort to try to make the two one. This is done in an effort to make the "two" fit the one baptism of Ephesians 4:5. Their argument would say that two elements are required for the one baptism of Ephesians 4:5. In this way they try to adjust their doctrine to what the Bible has to say on this important subject.

They will argue that John spoke of water and Spirit (Mk. 1:8), that Peter preached water and spirit (Acts 2:38), and Paul preached such in Acts 19:1-5. In all of these they assume that one has both water and Holy Spirit baptism. Thus, to them, the two elements are of the one baptism.

"Two Baptisms" Answered

Every false doctrine is answered by the Bible and this one is no exception.

Paul, in inspiration, said, "There is one body, and one Spirit, even as ye are called in one hope of your calling; one Lord, one faith, one baptism" (Eph. 4:4-5). Can one say there are "two baptisms" and remain true to the scriptures? If he can, he can do so by denying what the scriptures have to say. How can a man deny what inspiration has to say and be in harmony with God who gave such by inspiration? Suppose one were to say "There are two callings approved of God." Do you know of anyone that would say such a person is faithful to the Bible? Surely not. Neither could one be considered to be in harmony with Holy Writ and say there are "two Lords" or "two faiths" with God's approval. Such just cannot be the case. How, then, could the United Pentecostal Church say water baptism is to be practiced AND Holy Spirit baptism is for today? All will agree that water baptism and Holy Spirit baptism are not the same. One who is baptized in water would not claim that he was, by such, also baptized with the Holy Spirit. Even the United Pentecostals will say these are two separate events. They would have to admit this. For example, John spoke of his baptizing those to whom he spoke with water, but one who came after him would baptize them with the Holy Spirit (Mark 1:8). These events were separated by a period of perhaps three years. The promise was not fulfilled until Acts 2:1-4. It is then obvious that water baptism is not Holy Spirit baptism, nor is Holy Spirit baptism water baptism. There was the baptism of the Holy Spirit AND water baptism. No inspired man ever claimed that they were one.

The commission of Jesus Christ sets forth only one baptism. Matthew's record shows that those who were to go and teach were to baptize those who were taught (Matthew 28:19). It is obvious to all that these could not baptize with the Holy Spirit. They would know, as did John the Baptist, that Jesus was the one who baptized with the Holy Spirit (Matthew 3:11).

The baptism of the commission was in the name of the Father, and of the Son, and of the Holy Spirit (Matthew 28:19). Yet, Holy Spirit baptism is in no such names.

The practice of the apostles under the commission shows that the baptism of the commission was commanded. One can well see this by reading such passages as Acts 2:38. Here they were told, by Peter and the rest of the apostles, "to repent and be baptized." Surely one would argue that repentance is a command. It surely is as stated by Paul, "and the times of this ignorance God winked at; but now commandeth all men everywhere to repent" (Acts 17:30). Baptism is joined by the conjunction "and" to enforce the fact that it is also a command.

Peter set forth baptism as a command at the house of Cornelius, "and he commanded them to be baptized in the name of the Lord..." (Acts 10:48). This Peter would do as he operated under the commission of the Lord as set forth in Matthew 28:19-20; Mark 16:15-16. One must conclude that the baptism of the commission was commanded. It was not optional.

The baptism of the Holy Spirit was a promise. As one goes back to Joel 2:28-29, he will see such. John declared that such was a matter of promise (Matthew 3:11; Mark 1:8). Repeatedly, Jesus assured his apostles that the Holy Spirit would come upon them. Such passages as John 14:26, 15:26, 16:7, 16:13, all announce the promise of the Holy Spirit being sent to the apostles. He would guide them into all truth and assist in other ways. This was said by the Lord to comfort his disciples, from whom he would be separated.

Surely one can see the nature of this promise in these words, "For John truly baptized with water; but ye shall be baptized with the Holy Ghost not many days hence" (Acts 1:5). It is, indeed, a promise. Jesus referred to the Holy Spirit's coming as "the promise of my Father" (Luke 24:49).

From these passages it should be abundantly clear that water baptism falls in the category of a thing commanded, while Holy Spirit baptism was a promise. But, remember that the baptism of the commission, given by our Lord, was commanded. Thus, the baptism of the commission was water baptism. It could not be Holy Spirit baptism since such was a promise and not a command.

Also, one must conclude that one is saved by the baptism of the commission. This Jesus declared by his statement, "He that believeth and is baptized shall be saved" (Mark 16:16). This is the commission Peter was under when he commanded repentance and baptism in Acts 2:38. One would note that the baptism of Acts 2:38 is for the remission of sins. How could it be otherwise if it were the one under the great commission? But remember, Holy Spirit baptism is not a command, but a promise. Thus, Holy Spirit baptism is not the one baptism of the commission of our Lord.

The United Pentecostal doctrine makes Holy Spirit baptism necessary to salvation. In fact, if Holy Spirit baptism is a part of the new birth, then one cannot be born again until he is baptized with the Holy Spirit. They will argue that if water in John 3:5 means baptism, the Spirit of the same passage means baptism. By this, they mean Holy Spirit baptism. They argue that it takes both Holy Spirit baptism and water baptism to have the one birth.

Now, if Holy Spirit baptism is necessary to salvation, who is the administrator of Holy Spirit baptism? Surely one would say, "Christ." If one were not then baptized of the Holy Spirit it would be because Jesus had not baptized one with the Holy Spirit. What then of all those who have been baptized in water, who seek the baptism of the Holy Spirit, and do not receive it? They do not show the evidence of such by speaking in tongues. This is what the United Pentecostals will say. They argue that the evidence of the baptism of the Holy Spirit is speaking in tongues. Thus, when one seeks such but does not receive such, whose fault would that be? Wouldn't that make Jesus responsible for their not being saved?

They argue that water baptism is for the remission of sins but then turn around and make the baptism of the Holy Spirit necessary to salvation. Such an argument leaves one only "half saved" as it were. For example, Peter told those in Acts 2:38 to "Repent and be baptized for the remission of sins." If they did that they would obtain the remission of sins. Peter also told those who would do this that they would "receive the gift of the Holy Spirit." To the United Pentecostals this can mean but one thing. That they were baptized in water in the first part of the verse and baptized with the Holy Spirit in the last part of the verse. Yet, if Holy Spirit baptism was essential to salvation, and this was a case of Holy Spirit baptism, then it would not be, "You shall receive it," but, "You are commanded to do it." That only would fit the Pentecostal doctrine of the "two baptisms!" It would not be something one received but rather something commanded.

Look at the case in Acts 8. Phillip had gone to Samaria and preached to the people. Some believed what he preached and were baptized (Acts 8:5-12). But one learns that they had not received the Holy Spirit as of yet for when the apostles in Jerusalem heard that Samaria had received the word of God they sent Peter and John (Acts 8:14). When they arrived, they prayed for them that they might receive the Holy Ghost. It is noted that as yet he was fallen on none among them, only they were baptized into the name of the Lord Jesus (Acts 8:14-15). Now, according to Pentecostal doctrine, they were just half saved for they had not received the Holy Spirit. Yet, these people will argue that water baptism is for the remission of sins, per Acts 2:38. Yet, their doctrine places them in a position that they must deny the very thing they affirm concerning Acts 2:38. If one is not saved until he is baptized of the Holy Spirit then he is not saved by being baptized in water. He does not have the remission of sins by water baptism if he isn't saved until he is baptized with the Holy Spirit. He couldn't be. Yet, these folks will argue that baptism is the remission of sins but turn around and say one must be baptized with the Holy Spirit. They can't have it both ways.

The truth is that the reception of the Holy Spirit in Acts 8 comes by the laying on of the hands of the apostles (Acts 8:17). That is not the baptism of the Holy Spirit. In fact, not every time the word "Spirit" is used does it mean "baptism of the Spirit." If this were the baptism of the Spirit why did Peter and John have to go and lay their hands on them? Even Simon saw that it was through the laying on of the apostle's hands that the Holy Spirit was given (Acts 8:18). Paul wanted to go to Rome to impart some spiritual gifts (Romans 1:11). If this does not differ from the baptism of the Holy Spirit, why must an apostle be present for the reception of such?

This doctrine says one must speak in tongues before he is saved. This is a conclusion that must be accepted, for if it takes Holy Spirit baptism to complete the one birth, in addition to water baptism, and the initial evidence of the baptism of the Holy Spirit is speaking in tongues, then only those who speak in tongues are saved. Now look at the consequence of this doctrine. Not all in the church at Corinth spoke in tongues (I Cor. 12:30). This is obvious by the question Paul asked. For example, "Are all apostles?" What is the answer? Surely not. "Do all speak with tongues?" What is the answer to this? Surely not. But they had all been baptized into the one body (I Cor. 12:13). Now, if they were all baptized into the one body were they not saved? Surely they were. But, if Pentecostals are right, they must be baptized with the Holy Spirit to be saved and if they are baptized with the Holy Spirit they speak with tongues. One would thus have people in the body, having been baptized into such, who were not saved because they did not speak with tongues. This is a part of the consequence of this doctrine.

Conclusion

One would hope that the United Pentecostal doctrine of "two baptisms" would be abandoned. Surely the consequences of this doctrine can be seen by honest investigation.

Footnote

1. UPC Manual, pp. 23-24.

CHAPTER 23
PENTECOSTALISM — ITS DOCTRINE OF HOLY SPIRIT BAPTISM AND MIRACULOUS GIFTS IN GENERAL

Ralph Stout

The Pentecostal movement is on the growing edge of religious movements. While many may deny the propriety of the movement and question its propelling force, none can deny that the movement is growing. The movement is among us and with increasing numbers as well as in the significance of its influence in religion, even to be seen within the ranks of the New Testament church.

The international Pentecostal movement embraces an increasingly integrated, articulate self-conscious body of individuals, congregations and denominations in what is variously called evangelical, holiness, revivalist or conservative wing of the religious community. Most are loosely represented in the Triennial Pentecostal World Conference generally outside the ecumenical movement. While some groups were received into the World Council, most of the bodies consider membership in an unfavorable light and take a negative posture toward unitive movements.

Theologically, the adherents of the Pentecostal movement unite around an emphasis upon the "experience" of the Holy Spirit in the life of the individual believer. They do not care to distinguish themselves from other evangelicals but crucial for them is their faith in the supernatural, extraordinary, and visible work of the Holy Spirit in the post conversion experience of the believer as, they would insist, in the days of the Apostles.[1]

The distinctive teaching of the Pentecostal movement concerns the experience, evidence and power of what they call the baptism of the Holy Spirit, the first reception of which they believe to be recorded in Acts 2, and from that they get their name. A side effect of this Holy Spirit baptism is their estimation and practice of the spiritual gifts noted in I Cor. 12-14. They wish to be understood as an experiential Christianity.

There are theological differences within the movement but they nevertheless are bound together through their common views and doctrines. "...to these first belongs the concern for the direct experience of the presence of the divine spirit."[2] It is worthy to note that they stress, not the doctrine, but the experience. One of its major leaders said, it consists "purely of a powerful, individual, spiritual experience."[3]

The Pentecostal feels an absence of "power" in the contemporary church. He feels the difference between the church of Acts and the church of today could be characterized as the difference between a church which emphasized the Spirit and a church which has neglected the Spirit as an experience in contrast to a doctrine.

The Pentecostal believes the baptism in the Holy Spirit is something which every believer can and should experience giving him a power and sensitivity which no ecclesiastical rite, ceremony or ordination can give. He feels that this power is given, not because it is a declaration, or a promise, but because it is an experience: tangible, physical, confirmable and personal.

There is another characteristic of the Pentecostal conviction that may be called the contemporaneity of apostolic christianity. In one Pentecostal's words, "the New Testament is not a record of what happened in one generation, but it is a blue-print of what should happen in every generation until Jesus comes."[4]

These concerns taken together — power, the individual, the Spirit experience — construct an introductory profile of the phenomenon of Pentecostalism. More specific areas, debatable, will be pointed up as we proceed in our study.

In a study of the Holy Spirit, I readily confess that there are a variety of views held, even within the church. Some of our greatest men are not in perfect agreement. Consequently, I do not consider myself above them either in scholarship or in knowledge. However, these things to be set forth I believe to be Biblical truth and such conclusions to be drawn must be in harmony with the body of truth revealed.

Of the manifestation of the Holy Spirit, John 4:34 states plainly that the Christ has the Spirit **without measure.** This is to be expected for He is Deity, and Deity is infinite in every respect. Implied though is that the Holy Spirit is given to men **by measure.** I Cor. 12:4-6 supports this in that there are diversities of gifts, differences of administration, and diversities of operation.

Then as relates to man there are three degrees or manifestations of the Holy Spirit. These are (1) Baptismal, (2) Laying on of hands of an apostle, and (3) the **ordinary** degree, or measure. All of these are called "gifts" (Acts 11:17; Rom. 1:11; Acts 2:38).

There are two instances in the scriptures of the baptismal measure of the Holy Spirit. Each of these must have any conclusions drawn from the entire narrative rather than from a false exegesis.

1. The twelve apostles received it (Acts 1:1-5, 26; 2:1-4). The apostles were the recipients of it as it was promised **to them** and it was evidenced by them (Acts 2:1-4). One is mistaken who assumes that the 120 received it. It was not promised to them and the antecedent of "they" in Acts 2:1 is the apostles, not the 120 disciples.

2. Cornelius and his house also received the Holy Spirit in Acts 10 as the apostles did in Acts 2. From Acts 11:17, 18, this context shows the purpose of that reception by the Gentiles was to convince the Jews and all people for all time that the Gentiles were accepted of God even according to the extent of the great commission as well as the statement of Peter in Acts 2:39.

This degree or measure of the Holy Spirit gave to the apostles power to perform all manner of miracles. They were able to speak so that fifteen nations heard in their own language. They were able to heal the sick (Acts 5:12-16). Also they could raise the dead as Peter raised Dorcas and Paul raised a young man in Acts 26. Such constituted the signs of an apostle spoken of in II Cor. 12:12.

Second in the manifestation of the Holy Spirit is that measure giving power to and gifts derived from the laying on of hands. There are four instances of this measure recorded. The seven selected in Acts 6; The Samaritans, given by Peter and John in Acts 8; The twelve Ephesians by Paul in Acts 19; and Timothy by Paul's hands referred to in II Tim. 1:6. The evidence is that none but an apostle had the power or gift to confer the Holy Spirit by this measure of the laying on of hands. The church at Rome, not having been founded by an apostle, had no spiritual gifts and Paul longed to be with them that they might receive some such gift (Rom. 1:10, 11). From Acts 8, Phillip was without such power as was evidenced by Peter and desired by Simon. Even though one had had an apostle's hands laid on him, he could not in turn impart such a gift (cf. Acts 6:6; 8:12-17).

Thirdly, there is the general gift of the Holy Spirit. If it seem demeaning to refer to this gift as general, I use the term only to differentiate between measures. This gift of the Holy Spirit is promised to all those who obey the gospel. Substantiated by other passages, none is clearer than Acts 2:38; 5:32. As a result the Holy Spirit dwells in us. Paul says that the Spirit of God dwells in us (Rom. 8:9), and in the same verse that the Spirit of Christ dwells in us. Isn't it strange that some would place such an unusual and dogmatic emphasis on the one and practically neglect or ignore the other? Evidence of our reception is not a miraculous manifestation but rather by our manner of life (Gal. 5:22, 23).

We could get stymied on the definition of the word "miracle" as the manifestations or the laws of nature are mysterious, even birth itself. However, within the context of our study, I think there will be no misunderstanding as I state that miracles have ceased. Or, miraculous manifestations of the Holy Spirit have ceased to be in evidence.

Stated briefly, 1. the **purpose** of miracles being performed no longer exists, 2. the **means** of performing miracles no longer exists, (the apostles and those on whom they laid their hands have long since died), and 3. the **fact** of miracles no longer exists. Lying frauds are in abundance but bonafide miracles are not seen today as in New Testament times.

First let's establish that this cessation is a matter plainly declared by scripture rather than a thought pulled from the air by this writer.

I Corinthians 12 notes nine manifestations of the Spirit. Some of these contributed more to ostentation than others, and seemed to be the ones more to be desired in that day as well as in this. Paul tried to instill some rationality (I Cor. 14:19). Without the dividing into chapter 13 from 12 of first Corinthians, Paul continues with his subject. He said, specifically of those nine manifestations, prophecies would fail, tongues would cease and knowledge would vanish away. Then he places all in its proper perspective noting that the time of partial relevation required an imperfect knowledge. As the man is the mature manifestation of the child, the completion of God's revelation was the maturity of that partial revelation supplemented by the miraculous. Those things of childhood are put away in manhood. The supplemental miracles are "put away" with the complete revelation. How wonderful as that partial knowledge was replaced by a knowledge so complete as to be compared to his knowledge of himself.

Shall cease!` When? When the revelation is complete. It surely is complete today furnishing a man completely and giving all things that pertain to life and godliness (II Tim. 3:16-17; II Pet. 1:3). As the scaffolding so essential to the creation of a building is at the proper time, that is when it is no longer needed, pulled down, so the miraculous, so essential to the establishment of truth was at the proper time, caused to cease.

Now back to our previous thought, why we teach that miracles have ceased. We noted first that the **purpose** of the miraculous no longer exists. Why were miracles ever performed? Either to confirm the word and/or validate the messenger. Even Jesus himself needed and relied on such a confirmation (John 14:11). God also confirmed the apostles and their teaching (Mark 16:20).

The apostles didn't perform miracles indiscriminately. Paul didn't heal Epaphroditus (Phil. 2:25-27), nor Trophimus (II Tim. 4:20) and instead of healing Timothy, suggested he use wine medicinally. In fact as the New Testament writings increased, the signs decreased.

Today, the Lord, the apostles and their word **have been** confirmed. Consequently the purpose of miracles no longer exists. God has no thing to walk with aimless feet, even miracles.

Then we noted that the **means** of performing miracles are no longer with us. The baptism of the Holy Spirit promised only to the apostles, also given to Cornelius' house in an especial case, and the laying on of the hands of the apostles, the only ones who could, are simply no longer available.

The **fact** of miracles no longer is with us. Lying frauds abound. Or, "I know someone who knew someone who said that he had heard of an authentic miracle." That's about as close as it gets. In how many instances have the "Healers" been tried and found wanting? In every case.

Such a lacking can't be contributed to an absence of faith for in New Testament times, miracles were performed on objects incapable of faith (Mk. 11:20, 21) and upon individuals before they believed (Acts 3:1-9). The church at Rome had a faith spoken of throughout the world (Rom. 1:8) and yet had no spiritual gifts (Rom. 1:11). Timothy with unfeigned faith (II Tim. 1:5) had to take medicine (I Tim. 5:23). No, the absence of the miraculous today cannot be blamed upon a lack of faith but rather because it was a part of God's plan that they would cease to be — and they have.

Matthew 7 gives a strong denunication of those who would claim such power. In verse 21 Jesus will call them "workers of iniquity." Verses 21 and 22 teach that working miracles is not doing the will of the Father. Many will try to save themselves by performing miracles, verse 22. And verse 23, Christ will tell such to depart from Him.

Pentecostalism is destroyed with an understanding of Paul's letters to the Corinthians — not only the Holy Spirit experience but that which subtly moves people of God to "stand out" for their Spirituality. Christcenteredness is the answer. Man must be turned from that spirit which boasts to that spirit which builds. From being impressed and impressing with one's own spiritual relevance and power to being concerned with finding a lowly and patient relevance to Christ and His church.

The church from its start has been filled with problems because it has been filled with people. If people would look at Christ singly and serve him simply they would find life in their weakness and find the fullness of the Spirit it wrongly seeks and minister to the Lord and His church we need so badly.

Our Lord died to give the purchase price for His church to be the body of all redeemed persons. Too great the price and too precious the church for it to be divided assunder and to destroy its influence in the world and upon the individual in cultism.

May each dedicate himself to the task of never contributing to the alienation of believers through dogmatism but ever endeavor to keep the unity of the Spirit in the bond of peace.

Footnotes

1. *The Religious Bodies of America* (Concordia Publishing House, 1956).
2. *Pentecostal Preaching* (Vantage Press, 1957).
3. *The Pentecostal Movement,* Donald Gee.
4. *Pentecost,* DuPlessis.

CHAPTER 24

THE CHRISTIAN SCIENCE DOCTRINE OF THE GODHEAD, EVIL, AND PHYSICAL ILLNESS

Roy Deaver

Introduction

In Luke 1:26-38 we have the Bible record of how Jesus would be born. The record makes it clear —

1. That God sent the angel Gabriel to talk with Mary;
2. That Mary was a virgin;
3. That she was betrothed to a man named Joseph;
4. That she was of the house of David;
5. That the angel explained —
   (1) That she was highly favored in the sight of God;
   (2) That she was to become the mother of a child;
   (3) That the child would be named "Jesus";
   (4) That the child would be great;
   (5) That the child would be called the "son of the Most High";
   (6) That the son would occupy the throne of his father David;
   (7) That he would reign over the house of Jacob forever;
   (8) That the child would not have a human father, but would be miraculously begotten; and
6. That Mary yielded herself completely to God's will.

This divine record shows forcefully Mary's relationship to God and to Jesus.

Based upon this reading, and upon this background, we are engaging in a study from the general field of "Christology," and out of which general field this specific thought as assigned: **Was Jesus the Offspring of Mary's Self-conscious Communion With God?** It shall be our purpose to completely refute the position suggested in the specific thought, and with the objective of helping all to have a better understanding of the erroneous position involved, and consequently to better appreciate the truth regarding the birth of Jesus.

Frequently, the most powerful **refutation** is **explanation.** I believe firmly that if I can succeed in **explaining** Christian Science doctrine on the origin of Jesus that I will have succeeded in large measure in **refuting** that doctrine.

The standard authority in Christian Science is "Science and Health With Key to the Scriptures," by Mary Baker Eddy. The quotations which shall be used in this study are from this book, the edition bearing the copyright date of 1906. This book has a number system for each line on each page. hence, in our study 35:12-15 will mean page 35, lines 12 through 15.

The Position of Christian Science

The question which constitutes the title for this study relates to the actual position of Christian Science. This religious system was founded by Mary Baker Glover Patterson Eddy. Mrs. Eddy claimed for her system "divine revelation." She says: "In the year of 1866, I discovered the Christ Science or divine laws of Life, Truth, and Love, and named my discovery Christian Science. God had been graciously preparing me during many years for this reception of this final revelation of the absolute divine Principle of scientific mental healing" (109:1-6). This system emphatically declares: "Jesus was the offspring of Mary's self-conscious communion with God" (29:31).

My Task

It is not my task to discuss Christian Science in general, with all its atheistic aspects; nor to discuss the teachings of Christian Science concerning Jesus Christ in general. Rather, it is my task to deal only with one phase of the teaching of Christian Science regarding Jesus.

Discussion
The Background for This Position

The doctrine of the Christian Science on the origin of Jesus actually grows out of the fundamental tenets of the system.

First — Christian Science teaches that all is Mind, and Mind is all, and denies the very existence of matter. This point is stated over and over. The phraseology is often changed, but the thought remains the same. The terms Truth, Love, Spirit, Mind, Principle, Divine Principle are all used as synonyms for God, and these terms are often used in developing the thought of the **allness** of mind and the **nothingness** of matter. Consider carefully the following quotations: "My discovery...led up to my declaration of the proposition that Mind is All and matter is naught as the leading factor in Mind-science," (108:30-109:3). "The starting-point of divine Science is that God, Spirit, is All-in-all, and that there is no other might nor Mind — that God is Love, and therefore He is divine Principle. To grasp the reality and order of being in its Science, you must begin by reckoning God as the divine Principle of all that really is...Divine metaphysics, as revealed to spiritual understanding, shows clearly that all is Mind, and that Mind is God...Hence all is in reality the manifestation of Mind," (275:6-24); "God is Mind, and God is infinite; hence all is Mind," (492:25); "Hence all is Spirit and spiritual," (331:24); "Matter and Mind are opposites. One is contrary to the other in its very nature and essence; hence both cannot be real. If one is real, the other must be unreal," (270:5-7); "Life is neither in nor of matter. What is termed matter is unknown to Spirit, which includes in itself all substance and is Life eternal. Matter is a human concept," (469:1-4); "The realm of the real is Spirit. The unlikeness of Spirit is matter, and the opposite of the real is not divine, — it is a human concept. Matter is an error of statement," (277:24-26). "Divine metaphysics explains away matter. Spirit is the only substance and consciousness recognized by divine Science. The material senses oppose this, but there are no material senses, for matter has no mind. In Spirit there is no matter, even as in Truth there is no error, and in good no evil. It is a false supposition, the notion that there is real substance-matter, the opposite of Spirit," (278:3-10). "That matter is substantial or has life and sensation is one of the false beliefs of mortals, and exists in a supposititious mortal consciousness. Hence, as we approach Spirit and Truth, we lose the consciousness of matter," (278:12-16). "Spirit, the synonym of Mind, Soul, or God, is the only real substance" (468:21, 22).

Second — Christian Science teaches the doctrine of mental generation, that reproduction is possible and even desirable through mental effort, and without physical union. Christian Science actually plans to abolish marriage. It holds that "heaven" means "Harmony; the reign of the Spirit; government by divine Principle..." (587) as the consequence of Christian Science, and that "resurrection" means "Spiritualization of thought;...material belief yielding to spiritual understanding" (593), and that in the resurrection there will be "no marrying nor giving in marriage," (64:17ff). Mrs. Eddy uses the Lord's statement "Suffer it to be so now" as proof that he conceded to "material methods" in some cases (56:1-6), and Christian Science looks upon marriage as a "material method" regarding which concession must be made until men are resurrected through Christian Science!

Mrs. Eddy further says, "Matrimony, which was once a fixed fact among us, must lose its present slippery footing, and man must find permanence and peace in a more spiritual adherence. The mental chemicalization, which has brought conjugal infidelity to the surface, will assuredly throw off this evil, and marriage will become purer when the scum is gone" (65:25-32). Also, "Proportionately as human generation ceases, the unbroken links of eternal, harmonious being will be spiritually discerned..." (68:30-32).

Christian Science holds that God is all, that God is Mind, that therefore all is mind, that therefore nothing is material, and that consequently generation is possible through mental effort and without physical union. Notice carefully: "Until it is learned that God is the Father of all, marriage will continue...Spirit will ultimately claim its own, — all that really is, — and the voices of physical sense will be forever hushed" (64:26-33). "Those instructed in Christian Science have reached the glorious perception that God is the only author of man" (29:14-16).

In June of 1890 a son was born to a Mrs. Woodbury, one of Mrs. Eddy's most devoted followers **at that time.** Mrs. Woodbury claimed her son was without human father, and was mentally conceived.

This is the two-point background upon which Christian Science declares that "Jesus was the offspring of Mary's self-conscious communion with God." Mary was simply a good Christian Scientist! She understood that all is mind, that matter is non-existent, and that generation is possible through mental effort!

An Important Factor In Christian Science

It should be pointed out that Christian Science, and Mrs. Eddy in particular, is very adept in using usual terms with unusual meanings. This, as in modernism, is a very basic factor. Assuming the right to define her terms, Mrs. Eddy can prove anything. Does Christian Science believe in God, Christ, the Holy Spirit, heaven, hell, sin, the atonement, the death of Christ, the entombment of Christ, the resurrection, the ascension? Yes, but only as Christian Science defines these, and in **no instance** is their definition in harmony with the Bible meaning.

Is Christian Science Christian? Is it a science? Yes — if Mrs. Eddy is allowed to define the terms; no — if the terms are considered from the view point of the Bible and an English dictionary.

Christian Science is fully aware of the importance of this aspect of the system. It will take a word commonly used and found in scripture, strip it of its common meaning, attach to it a meaning demanded by Christian Science, and claim this attached meaning (new meaning) to be the original meaning. Notice carefully: "In Christian Science, we learn that substitution of the spiritual for the material definition of a Scriptural word often elucidates the meaning of the inspired writer. On this account this chapter is added. It contains the metaphysical interpretation of Bible terms, giving their spiritual sense, which is also their original meaning" (579:1-7).

In Christian Science "Adam" means error, the belief in original sin, sickness, and death (580:15). "God" means Divine Principle, Love, the universal cause (331:18). "Heaven" means harmony, the reign of Spirit, government by divine Principle (587:25). "New Jerusalem" means Divine Science, which means Christian Science (592:18). "Mortal mind" means nothing claiming to be something, a suppositional material sense (591:25). "Children" are "sensual and mortal beliefs...material suppositions of life, substance, and intelligence" (583:1-4). And on and on we go.

A Study of the Statement of the Position

This brief study of Christian Science and terminology will help us to better understand the statement of Christian Science regarding the origin of Jesus. This statement we need to analyze carefully. The Christian Science position on the origin of Jesus is clearly declared in 29:14-32, which reads as follows: "Those instructed in Christian Science have reached the glorious perception that God is the only author of man. The Virgin-mother conceived this idea of God, and gave to her ideal the name of Jesus — that is Joshua, or Saviour.

"The illumination of Mary's spiritual sense put to silence material law and its order of generation, and brought forth her child by the revelation of Truth, demonstrating God as the Father of men. The Holy Ghost, or divine Spirit, overshadowed the pure sense of the Virgin-mother with the full recognition that being is Spirit. The Christ dwelt forever an idea in the bosom of God, the divine Principle of the man Jesus, and woman perceived this spiritual idea, though at first faintly developed.

"Man as the offspring of God, as the idea of Spirit, is the immortal evidence that Spirit is harmonious and man eternal. Jesus was the offspring of Mary's self-conscious communion with God" (29:14-32). Let us notice the component parts of this statement.

"Those instructed in Christian Science have reached the glorious perception that God is the only author of man."

1. This grows out of the basic tenet that God is all, that God is Mind, that hence all is Mind, and therefore there is no such thing as matter.

2. Based upon the notion that nothing is matter Mrs. Eddy developed the doctrine that generation is possible through mental effort without physical union.

3. Since God is all, and God is Mind, and God is the only author of man, then generation must come from Mind!

4. "Only author" is designed to convey the thought that no physical union is necessary in generation.

"The Virgin-mother conceived this idea of God, and gave to her ideal the name of Jesus — that is, Joshua, or Saviour."

1. "The idea of God" — the idea that God is the only author of man, that all is Mind, that nothing is matter, and that generation is mental.

2. "Conceived" — Does Christian Science teach that there was an unusual conception in connection with the birth of Jesus? It does. Does Christian Science teach the same kind of conception the Bible teaches? Emphatically, no. What kind of conception was it? A mental conception — a perception of a basic tenet of Christian Science. "Mary's conception of him was spiritual..." (332:26).

3. "And gave to her ideal the name of Jesus — that is Joshua, or Saviour." Note that Jesus was simply an ideal — the ideal of Mary, which resulted from her mental conception of the idea that God is the only author of man, and that generation can be mental and without physical union.

"Jesus" in Christian Science does not mean what you and I have in mind in connection with that name. It's the name of an ideal! Christian Science is careful to make a distinction between "Jesus" and "Christ." "Christ is the true idea voicing good, the divine message...incorporeal, spiritual...the divine idea of God" (332:9-20). "Jesus" was the name of this idea. Consider the following: "The invisible Christ was imperceptible to the so-called personal senses, whereas Jesus appeared as a bodily existence. This dual personality...continued until the Master's ascension, when the human, material concept, or Jesus, disappeared, while the spiritual self, or Christ, continues to exist..." (334:10-20). Note also: "Christ is the ideal Truth, that comes to heal sickness and sin through Christian Science, and attributes all power to God. Jesus is the name of the man who, more than all other men, has presented Christ, the true idea of God...Jesus is the human man, and Christ is the divine idea..." (473:10-16).

"Jesus" means "Saviour." In what sense is Jesus Saviour, according to Christian Science? "Jesus," Mary's ideal, saves from sin, sickness, death, and disease, by helping people, who do not actually exist, through Christian Science, to understand that there is no such thing as sin, sickness, death, disease, and matter. Note: "Sin, sickness, and mortality are the suppositional antipodes of Spirit, and must be contradictions of reality" (335:29-31). "Matter is a human concept," (469:3). "Spirit, the synonym of Mind, Soul, or God, is the only real substance" (468:21, 22). "Therefore the only reality of sin, sickness, or death is the awful fact that unrealities seem real to human, erring belief, until God strips off their disguise" (472:26-29).

Christian Science builds its entire case on healing. It teaches that suffering (supposed) causes one to turn to Divine Love (God), implies that without this suffering one would not seek God, yet denies the existence of the sufferer, and of the suffering. See 322:26ff. Yet, there are no contradictions in Christian Science — Mrs. Eddy says so (345:13). Christian Scientists must "Expose and denounce the claims of evil and disease in all their forms, but realize no reality in them" (447:20-22).

"The illumination of Mary's spiritual sense put to silence material law and its order of generation, and brought forth her child by the revelation of Truth, demonstrating God as the Father of men."

1. The illumination of Mary's spiritual sense is the same thing as her **mental conception** of the idea which produced the ideal which she named Jesus.

2. This illumination put to silence the "order of generation" which demands physical union. This illumination enabled Mary to perceive that generation was mental!

3. Her child was brought forth. What was her child? Jesus, the Christ, the Son of the Living God? Emphatically No! Her son was the **ideal,** the consequence of her mental conception, which she named Jesus.

4. Is God the father of men? Certainly so. But not in the sense used in this statement. Here (in Christian Science) God is simply and only: Mind, Truth, Love, Principle. In this statement "Father of men" means "mental generation."

"The Holy Ghost, or Divine Spirit, overshadowed the pure sense of the Virgin-mother with the full recognition that being is Spirit."

1. What is the "Holy Ghost"? Christian Science (588:7). The "Comforter" means Christian Science (55:27). When the disciples received the Holy Ghost it means they were roused to a better understanding of Christian Science (46:30).

2. Did the conception take place in the womb of Mary? No, just in her "pure sense."

3. Did the Holy Spirit, in the Bible sense, overshadow Mary? No — it was Christian Science.

4. Mary understood that "Being is Spirit" — that is, that all is Mind, that Mind is all, that there is no such thing as matter! The only substance which exists is Spirit (468:22).

"The Christ dwelt forever an idea in the bosom of God, the Divine Principle of the man Jesus, and woman perceived this spiritual idea, though at first faintly developed."

1. God is Mind, God is all, all is Mind. (492:24). Mind has a bosom. In this bosom dwelt an idea. This idea was Christ. This idea was the Principle

of the man Jesus! Or, as stated elsewhere, "Jesus demonstrated Christ" (332:19).

2. Woman (Mary) perceived, faintly at first, the spiritual idea that Christ was an idea in the bosom of God (Mind), and that this idea was the Divine Principle of the man Jesus! This blasphemous statement is an outright insult to Mary.

"Man as the offspring of God, as the idea of Spirit, is the immortal evidence that Spirit is harmonious and man eternal."

1. "Man as the offspring of God" is simply another way of saying mental generation.

2. In Christian Science the terms God, Divine Principle, Truth, Love, Mind, Spirit — are all used synonymously.

3. Note that man is simply an idea. The thought that man is an **idea** of Mind is frequently taught in the writings of Mrs. Eddy: "Man is idea, the image of Love; he is not physique" (475:13). "...And man is the idea of God" (476:10).

4. "That Spirit is harmonious" — the thought here is: God is All; God is good; God is Spirit; Spirit is good; All is good! Therefore — there's no such thing as matter, sin, sickness, disease, and death!

"Jesus was the offspring of Mary's self-conscious communion with God."

1. There was God. Not God as you and I think of God, but God as Mind, Principle.

2. There was Mary. **The very existence of Mary nullifies the doctrine of Christian Science,** for it emphatically declares that there is no such thing as matter. Mary therefore was simply an **idea** of God.

3. There was "self-conscious communion." If God is all, and all is Mind, and Mary was an idea of God, then the "communion" could hardly be anything other than "self-conscious." "Self-conscious" means "conscious of one's acts or states as belonging to, or originating in, oneself."

4. There was Jesus, the offspring. What kind of offspring? Mental, an ideal. Jesus — the same as the Christ? No! Christ the Principle, and Jesus the manifestation of that Principle!

5. Here then is what we have? **Mind** (God) **had an idea called Mary, which idea** — being immortal mind, since mortal mind is "the belief that man is the offspring of mortals" (592:5) and since Mary had no such belief (?) — in turn mentally **communed** (self-consciously) **with mind, and produced** (offspring) **an ideal** which the idea Mary **named Jesus,** and **which** Jesus **was the representation of the Divine Principle called Christ!**

According to This Blasphemous Doctrine —

1. There is no such thing as the God of the Bible. Think for a moment about God according to Christian Science. God is all; God is Mind; therefore, All is Mind. Hence, there is no such thing as matter, sin, sickness, death, and disease. Such non-realities as matter, sin, sickness, disease, and death only seem to be so; they are "suppositional." "That

which seemeth to be and is not" is "error" (472:19). Note carefully therefore that matter, sin, sickness, death and disease are errors of mind, which is God. Hence, **according to Christian Science God is nothing more than defective Mind trying to heal itself!**

A more blasphemous doctrine never was written. Personally, I subscribe to the view that the mental defect is to be found somewhere else.

2. There's no such thing as the Christ of the Bible. Jesus the Christ, the anointed one, the Prophet, Priest, and King, the Messiah, the Son of the Living God — nothing more than an ideal, synonymous with God, which is synonymous with Mind!

3. There's no such thing as the "Jesus" of the Bible, for in Christian Science "Jesus" is simply the name which Mary gave to her ideal.

4. Jesus and Christ are not the same. Christian Science holds that Christ was the ideal and that Jesus was the name of that ideal. Every New Testament passage which refers to "Jesus Christ" and/or "Christ Jesus" is a fatal blow to Christian Science.

5. There is no such thing as the Holy Spirit of the Bible. In Christian Science "Holy Ghost" and "Comforter" mean Christian Science. See 588:7; 55:27.

6. There is no such thing as man, for man is simply an idea of God.

7. Jesus Christ has no physical existence. Yet the Bible declares that he was born; that he grew; that he ate, drank, slept, walked, and talked; that he had flesh and bones; that he had a body. Note carefully: "Since then the children are sharers in flesh and blood, he also himself in like manner partook of the same..." (Heb. 2:14). "But a body didst thou prepare for me" (Heb. 10:5). "By which will we have been sanctified through the offering of the body of Jesus Christ once for all" (Heb. 10:10).

8. There's no such thing as the death of Jesus Christ. If Christ is simply Principle, and if Jesus is simply the name of an ideal and had no bodily existence, and if there is no such thing as death, then there could be no such thing as the death of Jesus Christ. Christian Science speaks of the death of Jesus, but it does not mean what we mean, and what the Bible means. Mrs. Eddy refers to the "supposed" death (598:10) and his "seeming" death: (45:11).

9. There was no such thing as the Lord's burial. According to Mrs. Eddy the Lord was only **hiding** in the tomb, and the disciples believed him to be dead, but he was alive (44:28, 29).

10. There was no such thing as the Lord's resurrection. If there was no actual death then there was no actual resurrection.

11. There was no ascension. Ascension in Christian Science means coming to a higher understanding of Christian Science.

12. The disciples did not receive the Holy Spirit. In 46:30 Mrs. Eddy says, "His students then received the Holy Ghost. By this is meant...they were roused to an enlarged understanding of divine Science...."

13. There's no such thing as the inspiration of the Bible.

14. The Bible is not sufficient. In fact, according to Christian Science, the Bible cannot be understood without Mrs. Eddy's additional revelation:

Science and Health with Key to the Scriptures. Every passage (Such as Acts 20:32 and II Tim. 3:16, 17) which shows the all-sufficiency of the scriptures is a fatal blow to Christian Science.

15. Luke's record of the approaching birth of Jesus (Luke 1:26-38) is all wrong. The angel said, "Thou shalt conceive in thy womb...," whereas according to Christian Science the conception was in Mary's "pure sense." The angel said the conception was to be a conception in the womb, whereas Christian Science holds that the conception was strictly mental. The angel said, "And shalt bring forth a **son**..."; Christian Science says Mary had an **Idea** and an **ideal.** The angel said the **son** would be called Jesus. Christian Science says Jesus was the name of Mary's ideal. According to Luke (1:34) Mary knew that generation required physical union, but according to Christian Science Mary believed that generation was strictly mental. According to Luke the Holy Spirit was to come upon Mary, and the Power of the Most High was to overshadow her. But, according to Christian Science there was nothing more than Mary's self-conscious communion with Mind.

16. Luke 2:7 is all wrong. Luke says "She brought forth her firstborn son." Christian Science says she had an idea and an ideal. Luke says, "She wrapped him in swaddling clothes." Imagine — a mental ideal in swaddling clothes! Luke says, "And laid him in a manger" — a mental ideal wrapped in swaddling clothes, and laid in a manger!

17. Luke 2:11 is all wrong. Luke says the angel said to the shepherds, "For there is born to you this day in the city of David a Saviour, who is Christ the Lord." According to Christian Science the angels were mistaken, for the offspring of Mary was not Christ, but Jesus who was the manifestation of Christ, Divine Principle.

18. Matt. 1:18 is all wrong. Matthew says, "...She was found with child of the Holy Spirit." Christian Science says Self-conscious mental communion.

Conclusion

Christian Science teaches that all is Mind, and denies the existence of matter. It teaches the doctrine of mental generation. It defines common terms to suit itself. And upon this background it declares that Mary understood the all-ness of mind, the nothing-ness of matter, mental generation, the difference between Christ and Jesus, and that she therefore mentally produced an ideal which she named Jesus.

Christian Science is a system of atheistic blasphemy. It blasphemes God, Christ, the Holy Spirit, the Bible, Man. It denies every point of Bible teaching while claiming to respect the Bible.

"Beloved, believe not every spirit, but prove the spirits, whether they are of God; because many false prophets are gone out into the world. Hereby know ye the Spirit of God: every spirit that confesseth that Jesus Christ is come in the flesh is of God; and every spirit that confesseth not Jesus is not of God: and this is the spirit of the anti-christ whereof ye have heard that it cometh; and now it is in the world already" (I Jno. 4:1-3).

CHAPTER 25
"THE UNITY IN DIVERSITY" THEORY OF THE DISTINCTION BETWEEN "GOSPEL" AND "DOCTRINE"

Joe Gilmore

"Unity means 'oneness'." "The state of being one." "Unity" must be important for Christ prayed for it (Jno. 17:20, 21).

We are now living in the second century of a movement for the restoration of New Testament Christianity and for all the "Unity" of the religious people of the world on the basis of the New Testament. It is obvious that the religious world has been aroused to the importance of this movement. The news media is alive and humming with the voices of religious leaders suggesting the absolute necessity of "getting together."

One of the first things we need to understand is this: Christ did not pray for, nor does the Bible teach the "Unity of all denominations." There can never be such a thing as uniting all denominations into another large denomination. Modern denominations were not on earth when Jesus prayed for "Unity." Neither were they here when the New Testament was written.

Seven gospel "Unities" are enumerated in Eph. 4:1-5. (1) There must be "Unity" in worship because there is **one** God. (2) There must be "Unity" in authority because there is **one** Lord. (3) There must be "Unity" in message because there is one faith. (4) There must be "Unity" in organization because there is **one** body, or church. (5) There must be "Unity" in practice because there is **one** baptism. (6) There must be "Unity" in life because there is **one** Spirit, one Guide (Jno. 14:26; Jno. 16:13). (7) There must be "Unity" in desire and expectation because there is **one** hope. We will have "Unity" if these seven points are accepted. Paul states the problem in this manner: "Endeavoring to keep the "Unity" of the Spirit in the bond of peace" (Eph. 4:3). This means more than not to cause strife. We must actively seek and maintain harmony. Paul did not have in mind just any kind of "Unity." He said: "Unity of the Spirit." When one omits the teaching of the Spirit, then the Spirit is left out.

Paul defines "Unity" as being perfectly joined together in the same mind and the same judgment, all speaking the same thing, no divisions (I Cor. 1:10). Many today believe the opposite of Paul's definition. They assert that there is "Unity in diversity," and claim that this is the only way that there can be "Unity."

What Is This Teaching Of "Unity In Diversity"?

It is the "doctrine" that doctrine is not important. This means that numerous contradictory beliefs and practices are valid. This idea suggests that there is some other ground for "Unity" rather than truth for no error is wholly wrong. In the past we often heard preaching about "**The Man,** not the plan" doctrine. These preachers failed to see that the Lord's "plan" was in the New Testament. They were preaching "Unity in Diversity" which meant that "differences do not break up fellowship." Where is scripture for the "Unity In Diversity" doctrine?

The Doctrine That Doctrine Is Not Important

Such a doctrine does not make for a strong faith. People who preach or believe this "Unity In Diversity" idea will compromise the truth. They will mix truth with all kinds of error. Paul told Timothy to: "...keep that which is committed to thy trust" (I Tim. 6:20). If the "Unity In Diversity" doctrine is correct, then why guard something that is not important? When people believe and practice alike "Unity" will follow. The doctrine in question will also produce inactivity because people will not put out much effort for that which is not very important. Also, the "Unity In Diversity" doctrine will keep people from obeying the truth, one cannot be taught wrong and be baptized right. The souls of people are in danger when they follow courses that are not set forth in the New Testament. All error must look alike. We must wage war on error. Christ does not reign over a divided kingdom. No one who loves the truth will belittle sound doctrine.

The Bible Commends Unity And Condemns Division

It is recorded in I Cor. 12:25, "That there should be no schism in the body; but that the members should have the same care one for another." When people believe, teach and practice different doctrines how can they have the same care one for another? John 10:16, is often used to teach "Unity In Diversity" or "denominationalism": Other sheep I have, which are not of this fold: them also I must bring, and they shall hear my voice; and there shall be one fold, and one shepherd." The church of our Lord was not yet established. The "other sheep" referred to were the Gentiles, not members of denominations. If the passage applied to different denominations, it would also be teaching "Unity," because when they hear His voice they shall come out of them and be in one fold of which Christ is the Shepherd. Notice I Cor. 1:12, 13: "Now this I say, that every one of you saith, I am of Paul, and I of Apollos; and I of Cephas; and I of Christ. Is Christ divided? Was Paul crucified for you? Or were you baptized in the name of Paul?" Paul rebukes the sectarian "Unity In Diversity" spirit by asking these questions: (1) "Is Christ divided?" This is a way of saying that He is not divided. When people are divided they are not in fellowship with Christ or with each other. Christ was not divided, and since they were all baptized into Christ, how could they be divided without doing injustice to Christ? (2) "Was Paul crucified for you?" Since Christ was crucified for all, all should be for Christ. (3) "Were you baptized in the name of Paul?" Since all were baptized in the name of Christ, all should wear His name. It is wrong to wear the names of men—such as Paul, Apollos, John the Baptist,

Wesley, Luther, or any other except Christ. Division is an evidence of carnality. "And I, brethren, could not speak unto you as unto spiritual, but as unto carnal...For ye are yet carnal; for whereas there is among you envyings, and strife, and divisions, are ye not carnal and walk as men?" Why were they carnal (worldly, fleshly) minded? The reason given is that "There is among you envyings and strife and divisions." Paul says: "For to be carnally minded is death." (Rom. 8:6). The "Unity In Diversity" doctrine is responsible for much of the infidelity, indifference, heartaches, disappointments, squandered time, money and energy in the world today. We cannot prevent the jealous, warring, sectarian disposition existing today as long as the different doctrines, names, and practices which produced it, exist and are recognized and adherred to.

The "Unity In Diversity" Doctrine Did Not Originate With The Apostles

There were twelve apostles. They were selected by the Lord and were to preach the Gospel in all the world. When the church was established on the first Pentecost following the resurrection of Christ they were in the city of Jerusalem. When persecution came the saints were scattered. This included the apostles. Did all apostles preach the same thing? Did they continue as members in the same body, or church? Since the apostles started together and stayed in the same religious faith then the "Unity in diversity" doctrine did not come from them. In order to prove this teaching one would have to show that the apostles taught conflicting doctrines and labored to establish different churches. The apostles all preached and taught the same things and urged others to do the same (I Cor. 1:10). Conflicting religious groups cannot exist unless conflicting doctrines are taught. The apostles knew but one church (Eph. 4:4; I Cor. 12:27; Col. 3:15).

Christ came to destroy the works of the devil (I Jno. 3:8). Now let some good brother tell us if denominationalism is the work of Christ!

Things That Christians Cannot Fellowship

Christians cannot fellowship a movement which ignores or rejects God's word such as: (1) That one is saved at the point of faith and is born into the family of God without water baptism (Jno. 3:5). (2) That people can please God and be divided in doctrine and practice (Jno. 17:20, 21; I Cor. 1:10-13).

Christians cannot endorse and pray for a religious effort where sinners are not told what Jesus commanded that people should believe and do (Mark 16:16; Acts 2:38). How can we fellowship a group promising salvation to people out of Christ (Gal. 3:26, 27)?

Christians cannot worship unless what is done is authorized by Christ (Col. 3:17; Matt. 7:21-23).

There is not a scriptural way to assist a course or movement that will not renounce spiritual error and moral sins (Gal. 1:6-8). Only a false teacher would advocate sympathy for false institutions. It is sinful to give aid and comfort to enemies of the Lord's church.

Christians cannot assist a movement which suppresses any part of Christ's gospel or doctrine (II Jno. 9-11). Vincent defines fellowship as: "A relation between individuals which involves a common interest and a mutual, active participation in that interest and in each other." The common interest is the doctrine of Christ. Fellowship is the mutual agreement and cooperation of individuals in a common cause. Can there be "fellowship" or "Unity" among antagonistic beliefs. Efforts are often made to show that II Jno. 9 does not apply today as this disfellowship refers only to the denial of the "Deity" of Jesus. They cite II Jno. 7. Notice verses six and nine: "And this is love, that we walk after **his commandments**," "Whosoever transgresseth, and abideth not in the **doctrine** of Christ hath not God." "Deity" is just one of the facts concerning Christ. Hence, the doctrine of Christ includes all the other things about Christ. The "Deity" of Christ is nullified when His authority is rejected. To reject the apostles (Lk. 10:16; II Cor. 5:20) is to reject Christ and in so doing one rejects His "Deity." If anyone adds to any part of the apostles doctrine (Acts 2:42; I Jno. 4:6) he violates (II Jno. 9).

The Lord's people cannot fellowship others if we must stretch that fellowship beyond God's word. Any fellowship we must pay for with compromise is not worth the price (I Cor. 16:13). In New Testament days some walked in such ways that heaven's order was to withdraw from them. The division that is the legitimate result of preaching the gospel is not to be considered in Paul's command. The division Paul condemns is that which is contrary to the doctrine. "Now we command you, brethren, in the name of our Lord Jesus Christ, that ye withdraw yourselves from every brother that walketh disorderly, and not after the tradition which he received from us (II Thess. 3:6). To obey this command necessitates a division, a separation from the ones who walk disorderly. The faithful ones cannot fellowship the disobedient ones. Again: "Now I beseech you, brethren, **mark** them which cause divisions and offences contrary to the doctrine which ye learned: and turn away from them" (Rom. 16:17). This command must be obeyed just as much as any other command of the Lord. When we get to the point where we obey only those commands of God that please us, the word of God has lost its power in our lives. The "marking" and "turning away" must be done by someone, or Paul's command is ignored. It is the nature of the physical body to throw off all impurities. It is one of God's laws in the natural world. It is the will of the Lord that the church, the body of Christ should be kept pure, and throw off all impurities. But some congregations, by neglect refuse to do so, keeping ungodly people for years in their number or on their rolls. It is strange that some fail to learn from nature and revelation.

We cannot fellowship those who are not faithful (Eph. 5:11; II Thess. 3:6-14; Matt. 18:15-17). Paul made baptism a test of fellowship (Acts 19:1-6). In II Tim. 2:16-18 we find some believed in the resurrection. However, they believed and taught the wrong thing about it. "Saying that the resurrection is past already; and overthrow the faith of some" (II Tim. 2:18). Fellowship then is based on common elements of belief. Try preaching (Acts 2) today in denominational meetings. The unitarians would not fellowship you for preaching the "Deity" of Christ. The Baptists would have nothing to do with you after they heard Acts 2:38 preached. The materialists would disfellowship you for preaching the kingdom now exists, and the reality of heaven and hell and that the soul survives the shock of the death of the body. People argue about many issues. However, the real issue is New Testament authority.

We cannot fellowship those who say and do things that are unsound in doctrine: the unsound in doctrine is put in the class of murderers, whoremongers, etc., (I Tim. 1:9, 10; II Tim. 1:13). The "Unity in Diversity" crowd often tells us that love demands the toleration of false doctrines. They are wrong in this for love demands the correction of false doctrines. It was false doctrine that Jesus said that he hated in Rev. 2:15. Also, Paul said to Elymas, "Wilt thou cease to pervert the right ways of the Lord" (Acts 13:10). Here doctrine is meant!

Some Things To Believe

Jesus said: "Believest thou this?" (Jno. 11:26). We may apply this statement to many principles to be believed and taught. We believe: (1) In a trinity: Three persons in the Godhead (I Jno. 5:7; Matt. 28:19). (2) The Bible is the word of God. No other rule needed (II Tim. 3:16-17). (3) There are two covenants, New and Old (Heb. 8:13). The old was made with Israel and was abolished at the cross (Isa. 31:31-34; Col. 2:14; Heb. 10:9). (4) Man is a two-fold being. He possesses body and soul (Zech. 12:1; Job 32:8; Job 14:22). Spirit survives the death of the body (Eccl. 12:7; Matt. 10:28). (5) Man is lost because of his own sin; not born a sinner (Matt. 18:3; Matt. 19:14). Sin is a voluntary act (I Jno. 3:4). We become sinners by going astray (Isa. 53:6). (6) Man is a free moral agent. He has power to come to Christ (Jno. 5:40; Rev. 22:17); not lost because of some unchangeable decree (II Pet. 3:9). (7) Provision is made for all men to be saved (Heb. 2:9; II Cor. 5:14; Matt. 28:19; Mark 16:15). (8) The Gospel is God's power to save. It is sufficient to produce faith (Rom. 10:17). Able to save (Isa. 1:21; Rom. 1:16). (9) There is one plan of salvation for all; a plan that requires conditions (Matt. 7:21; Rev. 22:14). The conditions stated are: Faith (Acts 16:31); Repentance (Acts 17:30); Confession (Rom. 10:9, 10); Baptism (Acts 2:38); Faithfulness (Matt. 24:12, 13). (10) There is one baptism. Holy Spirit baptism was to the apostles (Acts 1:5). Water baptism is to all (Matt. 28:19). Performed by a burial (Rom. 6:3, 4). (11) The church is a New Testament institution: built by the Lord (Matt. 16:18), not existing before, not a non-essential institution (Acts 20:28). It should be called by scriptural terms (Acts 20:28; Rom. 16:16). (12) The first day of the week, Sunday, is the day for worship. The Sabbath is no longer binding (Col. 2:14-17; I Cor. 16:1, 2). (13) Simplicity in worship. No effort should be made to entertain. Only vocal music should be used (Eph. 5:19). The Lord's supper should be kept every week (Acts 20:7). (14) The second coming of Christ will be a personal coming (Acts 1:9-11; Rev. 1:7); coming to judge the world (Jude 14, 15). (15) There are two places of eternal destiny (Matt. 25:46).

There is an old Scottish proverb that says the devil's boots do not creak. Satan does not wave banners, blow trumpets or beat drums as he goes forth to destroy the church. His strategy is to "divide and conquer" from within. Let us resolve to be united with Christ and each other. It is high time to wage war on error. We must be unwilling to take human statements for authority. Let us always insist on a "Thus saith the Lord."

CHAPTER 26
THE "UNITY IN DIVERSITY" THEORY OF NO DISFELLOWSHIP ON THE BASIS OF "DOCTRINE"

J. Pat McGee

"How forcible are the words of uprightness" (Job 6:25). But on the other hand, error is an egregious evil which the Bible identifies as "damnable heresies" (II Pet. 2:1). The theories of men can not and could not bring lost man to God for they have no power or ability to so do (Cf. Romans 1:16; Heb. 4:12). The Bible says, "We are of God; he that knoweth God heareth us. Hereby know we the spirit of truth, and the spirit of error" (I Jn. 4:6). Only the words of truth and uprightness have divine power (James 1:21).

The Bible speaks of "damnable heresies" (II Peter 2:1) and certainly the grievous error under study at this time is worthy of such a description. The so-called "unity in diversity movement" is nothing less than a damnable heresy! No more dangerous error confronts the Lord's church today. Brother Goebel Music has stated it perfectly. "The great and beloved body of Christ today is being ripped apart by the sawblade of insidious doctrines, one such being that of 'Unity in Diversity.' This is one of the most treacherous, double-tongued, underhanded, delusive, guileful, cunning, slippery, intriguing, crooked, questionable, fishy and deceitful doctrines and must be met with a head-on onslaught! It is totally unbiblical, completely sectarian and has nothing at all to do with New Testament Christianity."[1] Amen!

What exactly does the "Unity In Diversity" doctrine teach? This cult-like movement owes most of its original impetus among churches of Christ to the influence of the Ketcherside-Garrett sect. This radical departure into Neo-Liberalism began over two decades ago and is gaining ground and prominence throughout the brotherhood. As every error, it thrives and grows on ignorance and indifference on the part of brethren. It shall be the purpose of this brief chapter to define and Biblically expose this seditious deceit which if unchecked and unchallenged will "eat as doth a gangrene" (II Tim. 2:17) until the faith of many be overthrown (II Tim. 2:18). This is a deliberate and planned effort now taking place across the brotherhood in order to create a false fellowship. This false fellowship is born by a new hermeneutic, subtle human philosophy and the spirit of compromise.

Of course, the Bible teaches that unity is the ideal goal to be reached (John 17:21; Eph. 4:3; Psalms 133:1). In spite of the fact of what the Bible teaches concerning the desire of God for unity the Bible does not teach unity at any price i.e., at the price of truth! God has made it clear in his word that true fellowship is contingent upon belief in and practice of the truth according to the gospel. All men must recognize unity and fellowship on the basis of what God says in his word and only on this basis. Imitation is an essential unifying agent. The development of a close-knit group is inconceivable without a total diffusion of uniformity on all matters of faith. As we shall later demonstrate this total uniformity is based on the doctrine of the gospel of Christ.

Denominationalism, liberalism and cultic movements have always had their slogans. Ketchersideism has, of course, it's slogans and pet phrases i.e., "Fraternity based upon common paternity." "Fellowship is greater than orthodoxy." "We do not fellowship things, ideas, or doctrines but persons." "Fellowship is not endorsement." "Every Christian is free." "Fellowship is not harmony." "Nothing a test of fellowship which God has not made a condition of salvation." "One act...one fact." "Gospel — yes, Doctrine — no." "We're all brothers in error." And then among these and others that could be mentioned is, "Unity in Diversity" which is the subject of this study. The current false teachers parrot and echo the same old canards and profoundly propose the same old conundrums that sectarians, digressives, dissenters and renegades have been howling for more than a hundred years. The false teacher can be "sweetness" in public but in private all sarcasm and bitterness. Having read *Mission Messenger, Restoration Review,* and other sources of Carl Ketcherside's writings for over twenty years I know that he is a most cunning manipulator of words, phrases and slogans. Some of the above mentioned statements witness to that. But what brother Ketcherside has done in his attempts at "unity" is to confuse **unsectarianism** with **all-sectarianism** and philosophy with sound doctrine. His is a Neo-ecumenical movement which he has attempted to foster upon churches of Christ in the spirit of so-called love and unity. I am convinced that he is succeeding much more than most are willing to admit or recognize. This movement poses a very serious threat to the Lord's church across the country as we go into the latter part of this century. It is time that the issues were studied and that eyes were opened.

The Ketcherside view of "Unity and Fellowship" are succinctly set out in the words of the following quote,

> **The Ketcherside Concept**
>
> The second erroneous concept of fellowship which I want to review is that one which is proposed by Carl Ketcherside and promulgated in his paper, *Mission Messenger*. It can be chiefly characterized in this short quote which is most often stated by brother Ketcherside: **"Fraternity based upon common paternity."**
>
> This view is quite similar to the one just reviewed. Being similar in content, if not in form, the errors of it will also be similar. While this author so far has carefully avoided plain statements of modernistic faith concerning the scriptures — something which Mr. Morrison makes no attempt to do — personally, I have little doubt that his disciples will eventually arrive at this position. Any teaching which rationalizes truth sooner or later must affirm that truth itself is relative and not absolute.

According to brother Ketcherside's own testimony, he has spent a good part of his life contributing to the problem that he is now trying to solve. An admission of wrong is greatly to be admired. Because the author has walked on "both sides of the street," so to speak, he has a decided advantage in knowing the arguments both pro and con. I would also like to divide the schemata of this system into strategy and tactics.

The Strategy of His Plan

The Ketcherside strategy has two basic parts:

(1) **To make no test of fellowship what is not a condition of salvation.** The author means by this, for example, since what one believes about mechanical music in worship is not essential to salvation, what one believes will not determine fellowship in the things of Christ. This view obviously requires the author to formulate some basis upon which it may be determined what is essential to salvation and what is not.

(2) **To define sonship and brotherhood only in terms of faith in the Divinity and confession of the Lordship of Jesus Christ.** To sustain this proposition the author has come up with the concept of "the child of God in prospect." This novel view of sonship will be discussed later in this lesson.

This system has been carefully thought out as well as carefully explained. The author has not been in a hurry to put it out all at one time. It has been developed in various phases over a period of years. Having admittedly been a sectarian for many years, and having a close association with those he now so stigmatizes, he knows full well the soft and vulnerable spots of the opponents he wars against. Granting him sincerity of heart (which I do), this brother's ideal is lofty and needed. Division deserves the attention of concerned Christians; unity requires a full effort of Christ's fellows. Its intent is appealing to all who love peace and hate war. It is essentially attractive to a generation of young people who see only the signs of carnage, having never stopped to learn what caused the war.

The Tactics of His Plan

We are now ready to consider the tactics essential to carrying out this strategy.

(1) The first tactic is **to separate clearly between "gospel and doctrine."** The author declares: "Not a single one of the New Testament epistles is a part of the gospel." He believes that the gospel relates only to the facts of Christ's death, burial, and resurrection. The doctrine is what one is taught after one becomes a Christian. His conclusion is that belief in the gospel is the requirement of salvation; belief in the doctrine is not. This point is essential to point number one in his strategy, namely: "To make no test of fellowship what is not a condition of salvation."

(2) **The second tactic is to limit fellowship to relationship.** He denies that fellowship is ever something which man extends or withdraws. It is only relationship which results necessarily from individuals obeying the gospel. "Fellowship has nothing to do with things or ideas. It is a relationship between persons." This tactic is necessary to justify sharing with fellow Christians where there is serious doctrinal disagreement.

(3) **Fellowship does not constitute endorsement.** The point here is that being in the same relationship — sons of God — does not mean that one approves of all that one's brothers do. Proof of this is offered from the analogy of human kinship. Two boys are brothers because they have the same father. Their kinship is established because of the fact and not because either or both recognize that they are brothers. This same point is true, it is argued, among the sons of God. In explanation of this point, the author has said, "I am in fellowship with my brother whether I like it or not."

(4) **Unity in diversity.** "The unity that the Bible speaks about is not a unity of blind conformity, but a unity of diversity." The point here is that men are united in spite of differences; the union results from the diversity. Once again, human analogy is offered as proof. The body has many members, the members are different in form and function, yet the body is one. Or, another analogy is offered. Physically, men and women are different. It is this difference which enables them to unite and produce a child. The author has said, "Diversity is essential to unity as much in the fellowship of Christ as it is in the marriage or an orchestra."

(5) The fifth and most fundamental tactic is to speak of persons being children of God either in actuality or in prospect. The author of this view interprets the Biblical phrase "begotten of God" to mean "child of God in prospect." This novel interpretation is absolutely essential to the whole theory. "I regard every sincere, conscientious person on the facc of the earth who believes in Jesus as the Son of God as God's child in prospect. He is God's child because he has been begotten of my Father, but he has not been born in the family relationship yet. Therefore my task toward such a person is to act as an O. B. or midwife to bring him to the place of delivery; and until he has been born, I cannot invite him to participate in the services anymore than I could invite my son, while being carried in his mother's womb, to play baseball with me. So he is my brother in prospect, and God's child by the 'begetting process'" (*Firm Foundation,* September 25, 1962).

This means that one who believes that Christ is God's son — whether he has expressed his faith in gospel obedience or not — is God's child in a prospective sense. Because he has not been immersed into Christ, he is therefore not "born" and thus, he cannot be invited to eat at the Lord's table — or enjoy other privileges of God's actual child. But, he is considered to be God's son in the prospective sense.[2]

Although rather lengthy the above statement does bring before the eyes of the reader a fair and adequate account of the New Unity Movement now gaining ascendancy in the brotherhood. It will serve as a good framework upon which may be built a basis to evaluate the dangerous error currently under consideration.

To the above may we add in the words of brother Ketcherside himself what he considers to be his "Plea."

Summary of Our Plea

For the benefit of those who may wish to petition for a just and open hearing of our contention for fellowship, and who may be new to *Mission Messenger,* we offer the following ten-point program as a mere skeleton of our plea.

1. Fellowship in Christ Jesus is a state or condition into which we are called by the gospel. Every person on this earth who properly responds to the gospel by belief in Jesus and immersion in his name is in the fellowship.

2. Fellowship of those in Christ is not contingent upon agreement or conformity. We are not in the fellowship because we are in harmony, but we strive for harmony because we are in the fellowship. It is a sin to make anything a test of fellowship which God has not made a condition of salvation.

3. The flock of God is still a scattered flock rather than a gathered flock. There are children of God dispersed among the various sects. To deny that they are his children is to reflect against their paternity and insult the Father.

4. In our present divided state no sect, faction, or party among us, is the "loyal church" to the exclusion of all others. We must establish association and communication across all of these lines in order that our lives be leavened and leaven others. And we must associate as brothers in the same family.

5. Men and women in all of our parties must be granted and guaranteed their freedom in Christ Jesus. This means freedom to read what they wish without censure, freedom to attend any meeting or forum without attack, and freedom to participate in any conference or conclave without fear of partisan pressure of factional exclusion.

6. We must not expect to arrive at recognition of brotherhood by settling all of our problems and differences first, for brotherhood is not based upon seeing everything alike, but upon having the same father and mother. We must begin with brotherhood, which means love for all of our brethren, wherever they are. And we must demonstrate that love openly and unashamedly, recognizing their equal right to communicate with us and with our common Father.

7. To achieve unity we cannot wait until all of us reach maturity and usher in an ideal state. We must begin where we are and work together where we can. Unity is a command of God, not a matter of choice with us. Certainly we can work together up to the point where we disagree, and by ardently laboring together to that extent when and where we can, our area of disagreement may shrink and the time of our distinction be postponed.

8. We must reject partisan debate by professional "disputers of this world" as offering any hope for producing unity in our day. Such debate widens the chasm instead of reducing it. We must substitute dialogue for debate and meet as equals in our failure to keep the peace. In debate one is thinking what to say to the other man, in dialogue he is thinking of what the other man says to him. We must approach our problems looking for a solution and not seeking for vindication. Bridges must always be built from both ends!

9. We must purge our thinking of the basic fallacies adopted by our fathers when confronted with innovations. These fallacies have fragmented us into fighting factions. They are two in number. The first is that purity of doctrine can only be maintained by separating from brethren; the second is that division is the God-ordained way of dealing with differences in the family. These two vicious horns have been used by religious opportunists and politicians to gore the body into a shameful and bloody mess.

10. We must re-examine and scrutinize carefully and critically every passage of the written word which we have used to divide brethren from one another. Those who trust in Jesus were meant to be one. He died to make that unity possible. We need always to be reluctant to apply the scriptures in such a manner as to defeat the very purpose of their author.[3]

Just what are the consequences of this "diversity" philosophy? Where will it lead? The answer is that ultimately it will destroy the gospel and turn the Lord's church into denominationalism. In the meantime the church will be infiltrated with compromise, uncertain sounds and a softening on the importance of sound doctrine along with a belittling of issues such as the use of instruments of music in Christian worship. Witness the following two quotes in demonstration of this very point:

You Mean, Exactly Correct?

Someone says, "Does that mean then that if I really tried to follow the Bible, and I honestly wanted to serve God, but I misunderstood an important concept here or there that God would destroy me?" Of course, that's up to God. The answer to this is beyond my depth. But are we forced to assume that God

> has that kind of a harsh, legalistic approach to things? My whole salvation is based on the truth that **God's mercy is broader than God's law.** Why? Because I am not intelligent enough to understand all of it or good enough to obey all of it. The only hope I have is His mercy, His grace.[4]

And again,

> What we in the Church of Christ lack is the honesty to "de-essentialize" our beliefs and see if some tertiary (third-rate-PM) doctrine has been elevated to the front burner where it does not belong. One has lost his sense of doctrinal priority altogether, for example, if he seriously thinks that the question of instruments of music has the same weight as the Resurrection and Atonement of Christ. The tragedy of such a distorted hierarchy of doctrinal priorities is that Christians waste time and energy championing a secondary belief and never join hands with their brethren in spreading the Gospel.[5]

These sad and grievous declarations of error are but clear illustrations of the results of the "unity in diversity" doctrine. This is where it leads.

Concerning "Unity in Diversity" as we have discussed it above the question now to be addressed is, "What does the Bible teach?" Inasmuch as we must have Biblical authority for everything believed, taught and practiced in true religion (Col. 3:17), this is a most important query.

Let us keep the question of this study before us. We are not asking, "Can the church digress and practice unity in diversity," for the answer to that is yes. We are not asking, "Have congregations started practicing unity in diversity," for the answer to that is yes. We are not asking, "Are the denominations and sects practicing unity in diversity," for again the answer is yes. Nor are we asking, "Is the church in grave danger of being taken over by this theory," for again the answer is yes. What we are asking is, "Does the Bible teach that we ought to practice unity in diversity." "Is it a doctrine authorized by the Bible" (which, if it is, according to Ketcherside's own presupposition, since it is **doctrine** and not **gospel,** it wouldn't matter anyway and could not be made a test of fellowship. It would be interesting to hear how brother Ketcherside would extract himself from such a dilemma).

A clear and true statement of what the Bible teaches is that in all matters of faith (matters of non-option) there must be unity i.e., no diversity. In fact the words unity and diversity are contradictory and the concept of unity in diversity involves one in a logical fallacy to say nothing about a tragic conflict with the Scriptures. The Bible teaches that truth leads to unity but error leads to diversity. Unity is truth and diversity is error. Brother Thomas B. Warren has asked a question that none of the proponents of this view could answer i.e., "Should there be 'unity in diversity' in regard to the theory of 'unity in diversity'?" Certainly brother Ketcherside and his followers would find it more than a task to deal with this. In fact they could not answer it without completely contradicting themselves.

The "Unity in Diversity" doctrine fails to recognize the following matters:

1. The authority of the scriptures in all things.
2. The hermeneutical principles of how the Bible authorizes or teaches.
3. What the Bible teaches on law and grace, gospel and doctrine.
4. That the Bible teaches there are degrees of error.
5. What the Bible teaches on the extents and limits of true fellowship.
6. That it is self-contradictory and involves one in a logical fallacy.
7. It fails to answer the question, "Diversity in what?" Eg. Inspiration? Existence of God? Blood of Christ? Deity of Christ? Return of Christ?
8. God has never allowed diversity in any dispensation or age. If he did not permit it under Patriarchy and he did not tolerate it under Moses why would he now so condone it?
9. The Bible teaches that the New Testament law is more strict than the Old Testament and that God will judge with much sorer punishment under Christ (read Heb. 2:1-2; 10:26-31; 12:25).
10. God is not a God of confusion (i.e., division or diversity) but a God of peace (I Cor. 14:33).

The Bible instructs Christians to believe the same thing (I Cor. 1:10), walk by the same rule (Phil. 3:16), to give all diligence to keep the unity of the spirit, the unity of the faith (Eph. 4:3, 13) and to teach the same thing as was taught by the inspired apostles (II Tim. 2:2). The men among us who are so convinced on this theory of "unity in diversity" would have a hard time convincing Nadab and Abihu (Leviticus 10:1-2) of its values. These two tried to practice a little "diversity" but God wasn't impressed. We are persuaded he has not changed (Heb. 13:8).

FOOTNOTES

1. Goebel Music, "The Challenge of Unity In Diversity," *The Spiritual Sword,* Vol. 12, No. 1, p. 19, Oct. 1980.
2. Harry W. Pickup, Jr., *The Fellowship of Jesus Christ Our Lord,* (Atlanta, Ga.: Publishers Systems Inc. 1974), pp. 25-29.
3. Carl Ketcherside, "The Moment of Truth" *Mission Messenger,* Vol. 26, No. 10, pp. 150-51, Oct. 1964.

Please note also the following sources which the reader may wish to note as further documentation of this error presently under study as given from the view of liberal brethren among us. It is hoped this will impress upon all how serious and widespread this false doctrine is spread among "our" colleges, churches, papers, preachers, etc.

Goebel Music, "The Challenge of Unity In Diversity," *The Spiritual Sword,* Vol. 12, No. 1, p. 19-21, Oct. 1980; *Voices Of Concern* edited by Robert Meyers (Mission Messenger, St. Louis, Mo.), pp. 5, 257; M. F. Cottrell, *Refocusing God, The Bible And The Church, p. 118; G. C. Brewer, As Touching Those Who Were Once Enlightened,* (Gospel Advocate Company, Nashville, Tenn.), p. 12; Pat Boone, *Dr. Balaam's Talking Mule,* (Son-Rise Books, Van Nuys, Cal.), p. 39; Francis A. Schaeffer, *The Mark of the Christian,* (Inter-Varsity Press, Downers Grove, Ill.), p. 33; Leslie Eugene Fooks, *Fellowship Of Believers,* (Pioneer Book Publishers, Inc.), pp. 36-37; Leroy Garrett, "The Ancient Order," *Restoration Review 1978,* pp. 83, 192; *One Great Chapter, Mission Messenger, 1971,* "Unity With Diversity" by Patrick M. Phillips, p. 75; *Thoughts On Unity* edited by Stanley Paregien, (Mission Messenger, St. Louis, Mo.), p. 80; *The Twisted Scriptures, Reprint Edition, Mission Messenger 1965,* p. 97; Donald H. McGaughey, "Following Jesus," Mission July

1967, p. 19; Carl Herbert Stem, "Unity and Fellowship in the Congregation," *Mission, October, 1967,* p. 26 (126); Thomas H. Olbricht, "W. Carl Ketcherside," *Mission, July, 1968,* p. 24. John McRay, "Undenominational Christianity," *Mission, December, 1968,* p. 16 (176); Arthur L. Miley, "There Are *Two* Churches," *Mission, October, 1971,* p. 7 (103); R. Lanny Hunter, "The Three Hundred And One Cubit Ark," *Mission, December, 1971,* pp. 12-13; David H. Bobo, "Worship And Unity," *Mission, February, 1972,* p. 12; Neal Buffaloe, "Frauds, Fools and Freedom," *Mission, May, 1972,* p. 18 (338); Everett Ferguson, "Theological Foundations of Unity," *Mission, November, 1972,* p. 12 (140); Don Haymes, "Church of Christism," *Mission, April, 1972,* p. 12; Wayne Willis, "The Plight of the Church of Christ Liberal," *Mission, June, 1973,* p. 8 (360); Victor L. Hunter, "Sharing At Shiloh," *Mission, January, 1973,* p. 24 (248); Victor L. Hunter, "Openness And Growth: The Belmont Experience," *Mission, March, 1973,* p. 21 (277); Everett Ferguson, "The Validity Of The Restoration Principle," *Mission, August, 1973,* pp. 6 (38)-7 (39); *Fellowship, Restoration Review,* Leroy Garrett, Editor, Vol. 15, No. 2, February, 1973, pp. 22-29; Hoy Ledbetter, "Interpretation: How Much Diversity Can Fellowship Bear," *Mission, March, 1978,* pp. 15-18.

4. Lynn Anderson, "Misunderstandings About The Church," *The 20th Century Sermons Series — Steps To Life,* 1977, p. 71, (Biblical Research Press, Abilene, Tx.).

5. Arlie J. Hoover, "Our Lingering Legalism," *What Lack We Yet?* (Biblical Research Press, Abilene, Tx., 1974), p. 124.

CHAPTER 27
THE "UNITY IN DIVERSITY" MOVEMENT AND ITS DOCTRINE OF DISFELLOWSHIP RE "GOSPEL" ONLY — NOT "DOCTRINE"

Jackie M. Stearsman

From the earliest days of the church, the subject of Christian fellowship has been controversial. It is essential that every generation of the Lord's people be taught the Biblical limits or extent of fellowship. Without understanding the bases for fellowship, fellowship becomes purely a subjective matter. Without an objective standard by which to measure fellowship, everything is endorsed and nothing may be objectively opposed. With an objective standard, consideration must be given to what is specified in order that those in error are not fellowshipped, endorsed, and encouraged, and that those who should be fellowshipped are not excluded.

There is a movement alive within our brotherhood that would reduce the practice of Christian fellowship to the subjective likes and dislikes of individuals. The only test for fellowship that some are making is baptism, some even rejecting what the Bible teaches on repentance. Most, if not all, immersed persons would be considered in fellowship. Some would go beyond this and include among the saved (thus in fellowship) nonimmersed individuals as long as they are ignorant of what the Bible teaches or have strong reservations against the essentiality of baptism. For example:

> Should...anyone...ask any of us in the Church of Christ if we believe that baptism is essential to salvation (going to heaven), I think we should say **no,** or at least **yes** and **no,** depending on where one is. We should say **no** because we speak as the scriptures speak, and the Bible nowhere says that baptism is essential. Or we might say **yes** and **no,** in that even...[some individuals] concede that baptism is a command, and if one understands it to be a command for him, then it is essential for him to do it.[1]

Among the longtime and most vocal spokesmen for this movement are Carl Ketcherside and Leroy Garrett. For years brethren have been opposing the Garrett-Ketcherside movement that would make doctrinal matters unimportant in the subject of fellowship.[2] Others, who may not endorse in every detail the approach of Garrett and Ketcherside, arrive at the same destination, ignoring and/or explaining away doctrinal difficulties and appealing for brethren to "agree to disagree," or to have "unity in diversity."

"The Twisted Scriptures"

Brother Ketcherside in his efforts to sustain the theory that there is a distinction between gospel and doctrine, has written a book entitled *The Twisted Scriptures.* The book is now out of print, but I was able to locate a copy with the help of brother Tom L. Bright, and quote from it as follows:

> "The gospel is addressed to unbelievers and not to believers." (p. 46) "The intent of the good news is to convert aliens into citizens. It is a message to the unsaved and never to the saved..." (p. 63) "The 'doctrine of the apostles' consists of a course of instruction designed to bring citizens of the kingdom to a constantly increasing sense of maturity and responsibility...The gospel brings men into Christ, the doctrine helps them to grow up in him." (p. 63)
>
> "Fellowship results from the gospel growth within the fellowship is the aim of doctrinal development." (p. 63) "So long as men seek to make fellowship in Christ Jesus contingent upon conformity of opinion, deduction, understanding and apprehension of apostolic doctrine, rather than upon faith in Him through the facts of the gospel, that long will they be purveyors of partisan loyalties and fomenters of factional strife." (p. 63)
>
> The "gospel" is not a message for the saved but for the lost. It is never addressed to saints but to sinners. It is never proclaimed to the church but to the world." (p. 33)

Brother Ketcherside asserts that there is a clear-cut distinction between "gospel" and "doctrine." Then he affirms, "Obedience of the gospel is an act once for all, while partaking of the bread of life is a daily performance. The gospel produces life, the doctrine is for the training and discipline of the children after they are born." (p. 50) Applying this theory to fellowship, we have something Ketcherside calls "gospel" preached to the unbeliever and something he calls "doctrine" restricted to the believer; and no matter how wild one's conclusions be doctrinally, if he has obeyed Ketcherside's "gospel" he is to be accepted into fellowship. An interesting question may be posed here: Is Ketcherside's theory of doctrine a part of the gospel or a part of the doctrine? Does he preach it to the unbeliever and the believer? Can one be a Christian without accepting Ketcherside's "doctrine"?

The Bible and "Ketcherside Doctrine"

Ketcherside asserts that gospel and doctrine are never mixed or interchanged. Gospel must always be preached to the unbeliever, and doctrine always preached to the saved, the believer. What say the scriptures?

(1) Doctrine, didache

In John 7:17 Jesus states that if any man willed to do His will, he would know of the teaching (doctrine, didache) whether it was of God or not. Clearly, here is doctrine having application to the unbeliever (non-Christian). The Sanhedrin accused the apostles of having "filled Jerusalem with their teaching," (didache) (Acts 5:28). The same Greek term is used, and here again we have the apostles doing what Ketcherside says they must not do — preaching doctrine to the non-Christian. Barnabas and Saul were teaching Sergius Paulus and, when Elymas the sorcerer opposed them, Paul rebuked him for perverting the right ways of the Lord. In Acts 13:12, "The proconsul, when he saw what was done, believed, being astonished at the teaching (doctrine, didache) of the Lord." Again, Ketcherside's doctrine fails to harmonize with the Bible. In Acts 17:18 certain philosophers confronted Paul, and verse 19 states: "And they took hold of him and brought him unto the Areopagus, saying, may we know what this new teaching is, which is spoken by thee?" Obviously, the teaching (doctrine, didache) was being presented to the unbeliever. Paul affirmed that the saints in Rome had become obedient to the "form of teaching" (doctrine, didache). Thus, again, doctrine was preached to the non-Christian.

(2) Gospel, kerugma

We now show that Ketcherside's doctrine on the "gospel" will not harmonize with the teaching of the Bible and thus is false doctrine. In Romans 16:25 Paul addresses some remarks to the saints in Rome, stating that God is able to establish them by the preaching (kerugma) of Jesus Christ. In Acts 20:25 Paul speaks of having gone about among the elders at Ephesus preaching (karusso) the kingdom. "The word 'preaching' is the Greek 'karusso,' which is the root word behind 'kerugma.' 'Kerugma' would be the cognate of 'karusso,' just as 'didache' is the cognate of 'didasko.'"[3]

(3) Ketcherside's Conclusion Does Not Follow

> Even if these brethren were right in their unscriptural distinction between "gospel" and "doctrine" it does not follow that there can be no withdrawal of fellowship in matters of "doctrine." What is there about **this** distinction that leads to **this** conclusion? This would be parallel to saying: the command to be baptized applies to the non-Christian (and is a matter of gospel). The command to contribute of one's means applies to the Christian (and is a matter of doctrine). Therefore, if one refuses to contribute of his means he cannot be disfellowshipped! What is there in the information at hand that forces this conclusion? The conclusion just does not follow.[4]

(4) Mark and Turn Away From Those Promoting Doctrinal Error

The New Testament teaches in Acts 2:42 that the early church continued steadfastly in the apostles' teaching (doctrine, didache). Paul demands that we mark the ones causing division and occasions of stumbling contrary to the doctrine (didache) and turn away from them; and this would include such doctrines as Ketcherside's (Rom. 16:17). This must be done for those who will not abide in the teaching (didache) of Christ have neither Christ nor the Father, hence cannot be fellowshipped with God's approval (II Jno. 9-11).

Different Roads — Same Destination

A person does not have to accept the "gospel" and "doctrine" distinction of Ketcherside in order to arrive at his position — "unity in diversity," "agreeing to disagree," etc. One of the methods used to arrive at the same position is to show a number of inconsistencies of which brethren have been guilty and then to affirm that, since we have been, and still are, inconsistent on some issues, then just continue to practice our inconsistencies and there can be "unity."[5] For example, brother Bales in *Not Under Bondage,* p. 7, states: "If my position is right they are guilty of making a law where Christ did not make one. They are shutting the kingdom against some people, and they are home wreckers." On page 9, in the same section of the Introduction, he says: "I no more make this issue a matter of fellowship than I do the war question."

I cannot believe that our brethren are so unconcerned that they would permit people to enjoy the fellowship of the church who are guilty of: (1) making laws where Christ did not make them; (2) shutting the doors of the kingdom against those whom the Lord admits; (3) wrecking homes; (4) throwing a blanket of fellowship over any and every conceivable position held on Marriage, Divorce, and Remarriage.

That the manner in which one arrives at his position on fellowship is not so important as his arriving at the point of "unity in diversity," "agreeing to disagree" may be seen in the following. First, note Leroy Garrett's statement in the *Restoration Review* (February, 1978), page 37:

> Moreover, when I was in Searcy, Arkansas recently J. D. Bales of Harding College told me that he is changing the position he has held on divorce and remarriage, and he indicated that this has already brought some fire from the right. If the fire came from the right (and does it ever really come from the left?) it must have been at close range, for one doesn't get very far to J. D.'s right! But I say bully for J. D. It is wise men who change their minds.

Now read what Hoy Ledbetter says in *Integrity* (October, 1979):

> Although we risk adding to his grief by taking his side, we feel an obligation to speak out on behalf of James D. Bales. The veteran teacher at Harding College has been under heavy fire from some who like to lord it over the faith of others because of his position on divorce and remarriage. In a recent article in *Firm Foundation* (9/11/79) he says, "At least four people have

disfellowshipped me because of my position. I am not their conscience, and have no desire to dictate to them. If they disfellowshipped me, I shall continue to love them and if we both make it to heaven I hope they feel differently about the matter then!"

....

Bales further says, "It is my judgment that some brethren who disagree with me, but who believe that fellowship should be maintained in spite of our differences, ought to speak out and say so....I think it may discourage some individuals from trying to split the church over these matters."

His judgment is correct. And, since we meet his qualifications for doing so, we are happy to speak out. But some, we suspect, will be less than open in this matter because sectarianism, no less than conscience, "doth make cowards of us all." **There is a danger that if we tolerate differences regarding such important ethical questions as war and divorce, we may begin to make allowances in organizational and liturgical disputes** [Emphasis added]. And if we do that, our sects will sink into the church at large, and we will have no reason to go on. People who walk by the party spirit regard trying to split the church as a virtue, and we need not expect those who are under this delusion to be reasonable or to do right. (pp. 50, 64)

Please observe very carefully that brother Ledbetter recognizes that brother Bales needs defending by the likes of him, and the likes of him are those who maintain open fellowship with the Christian Churches and those of almost any other sectarian persuasion. Note particularly the last paragraph states that by the same kind of "reasoning" that we accept contradictory positions on ethical matters such as war and divorce, we can allow for organizational divergencies and liturgical differences.

Concluding Exhortation

To accept the **false** doctrine of the "unity in diversity" movement would mean that "fellowship" would include such diverse and contradictory elements as the following: (1) All immersed individuals who believe in Jesus; (2) Unimmersed individuals who believe in Jesus as long as they are ignorant of what the Bible teaches or sincere in their opposition to immersion for the remission of sins; (3) Premillennial brethren, for this would be justified under the "doctrine" as revealed by Ketcherside; (4) Home wreckers; (5) Those who make laws where Christ did not — this would include the most "anti" of the "anti's"; (6) Those who would shut the doors to the Kingdom; (7) Those in any and every conceivable marriage situation; (8) Those who would restructure the church in organization and worship to include women elders and preachers, instrumental music, etc., etc.; (9) Those who reduce all "truth" to mere subjectivism — what it means to me does not have to mean what it does to you, etc.; (10) Those practicing immorality. Since morality is a matter of doctrine and doctrine must be understood subjectively, then whatever one felt, liked, or believed would be right — pray tell what could be forbidden? Behold the "beauty" of "unity in diversity."

Brethren who have "withdrawal-of-fellowship phobia" had better awaken while there are still those who respect the truth, walk in truth, and are willing to be fellow-workers for the truth (III Jno. 1-4, 8). Can we not see that to accept "unity in diversity" is to destroy New Testament Christianity and place us at one with the denominational world? Do we believe Paul's words?

> For we are not bold to number or compare ourselves with certain of them that commend themselves: but they themselves, measuring themselves by themselves, and comparing themselves with themselves, are without understanding (II Cor. 10:12). For not he that commendeth himself is approved, but whom the Lord commendeth (II Cor. 10:18).

Footnotes

1. Leroy Garrett, ed., "Is Baptism Essential," *Restoration Review,* XXII (Nov., 1980), pp. 169-171.

2. Helpful in exposing and refuting the gospel-doctrine controversy are:

Tom L. Bright, "The Twisted Scriptures," *Contending for the Faith,* X (June, July, Sept., Nov., 1979); Roy Deaver, "Gospel, Doctrine, and Fellowship," *Biblical Notes,* VII (April, 1974), pp. 125-129; Alan Highers, "The Fellowship Question," *Gospel Advocate,* CXV (June 7, 1973), pp. 364-365; Roy H. Lanier, Jr., "II John 9-11; The Grave Question of Fellowship and 'The Doctrine of Christ,'" *Difficult Texts of the New Testament Explained* (1981 Fort Worth Lectures), Wendell Winkler, ed., pp. 385-389; Roy H. Lanier, Sr., "The Denver Unity Meeting," Nos. 1, 2, 3, 4, 5, *Firm Foundation,* LXXIX (Sept. 11, 18, 25, Oct. 2, 9, 1962); Goebel Music, "The Challenge of 'Unity in Diversity,'" *The Spiritual Sword,* XII (Oct., 1980), pp. 19-21; G. K. Wallace, *A Critical Review of a New (Old) Modernism and A Plea for Unity: A Review of W. Carl Ketcherside.* "The Influence of the Ecumenical Movement of the Chruch," *The Church and Fellowship: 1974 Freed-Hardeman College Lectures, pp. 58-62. "Instrumental Music and Fellowship," Ibid,* pp. 63-68. "The Twisted Scriptures in the Unity Movement," *Ibid,* pp. 76-78; Thomas B. Warren, *Keeping the Lock in Wedlock,* esp. Ch. X, "There Is One — And Only One — Body of Doctrine for Men Living Today: The Gospel of Christ (the Law of Christ)." "The Bases of Fellowship," *The Church and Fellowship: 1974 Freed-Hardeman College Lectures,* pp. 32-42. "The Church Versus Denominationalism," *Gospel Advocate* CXII, (No. 1, May 21, pp. 324-325; No. 2, July 30, pp. 481, 486; No. 3, Aug. 13, p. 117, 1970); William Woodson, "Fellowship — Noun and Verb — And a New Unity Movement," *Gospel Advocate,* CXV, (No. 1, May 10, p. 296ff.; No. 2, May 24, pp. 332-333, 1973). "Gospel, Doctrine, and the New Unity Movement," *Gospel Advocate,* CXV (No. 1, Jan. 11, pp. 24-26; No. 2, Jan. 18, pp. 43-44; No. 3, March 15, pp. 165-166, 1973). "The New Unity Movement in Perspective," *The Church and Fellowship: 1974 Freed-Hardeman College Lectures,* pp. 43-57.

3. I am indebted to brother Roy Deaver for the material in this section, *Biblical Notes,* X (April, 1974), pp. 125-129. For more detailed discussion of these terms, see Thomas B. Warren, *Keeping the Lock in Wedlock,* Ch. X.

4. Deaver, *Ibid.*

5. James D. Bales, "Before You Disfellowship," *Firm Foundation,* XCVIII (Sept. 11, 1979), p. 5.

CHAPTER 28
"UNITY IN DIVERSITY" AND DENOMINATIONALISM

Tom L. Bright

"Unity in Diversity" is dangerous, deceptive and destructive. It is dangerous in what it will do to the cause of Christ, deceptive in its subtlety and clouding of the real issue, and destructive in that it will break down all inspired barriers that inspiration has established.

If Unity in Diversity is followed to its logical end, the distinctiveness of New Testament Christianity will be devastated, utterly wiped from the earth. If this theory is accepted by New Testament Christians, the second generation following will not know the Lord's Church as it now exists. There will once again be the need to restore New Testament Christianity.

Unity in Diversity is not unity. It is an amalgamated conglomeration of toleration, "freeness" and unadulterated compromise. In principle, Unity in Diversity is not one whit behind the ecumenicalism of the liberal denominations, specifically those that represent the National Council of Churches.

Moreover, if Unity in Diversity is followed to its ultimate goal, those who espouse it will soon be flying the tainted colors of the Social Gospel of liberal denominationalism. And why not, they will not be able to preach THE gospel of Christ in all of its pristine beauty and simplicity while continuing to advocate Unity in Diversity. Yet, they will preach A gospel, they will preach some message and I am convinced that it will be the Social Gospel. Notice the following from the pen of an atheist:

> What would happen if Christians should discover that their leader was not an incomparable guide? Absolutely nothing at first. Those accustomed to lead a moral life would continue to do so. Members of Christian churches are the very people who most wish to do what is right. They will not lose their character because Jesus has lost his fictitious divinity. On the contrary, they will search for the most elevating principles to substitute for the personality that has been found deficient. It is difficult for people to be superior to their gods. **These same church-going individuals, when freed from the fetters of antiquated supernaturalism, will gradually learn to serve mankind with the same devotion they now render to a misunderstood God. They will no longer be limited by the defects of their paragon in their efforts to make the most of life. They will seek to solve modern problems in a rational way**....For the first time they will make their decisions according to the best knowledge obtainable today"[1] (emp. mine, T.L.B.).

Now, this is exactly the path that has been followed by liberal denominationalism and it is, in principle the same path that the advocates of Unity in Diversity will follow.

The Lord's Church is made up of people, just as is liberal denominationalism. We are not immune to following the same course they have taken. Now, if we accept and promulgate the same philosophy as they, what will keep us from ending up in the same camp? Absolutely nothing!

Now, watch this thought: If Unity in Diversity is accepted by the Lord's people, the evidence is already overwhelming — the Lord's Church will be filled with agnosticism! This might sound strange to many, but it is true nonetheless. Unity in Diversity will bring one to nothing less than rank agnosticism, if followed to its final and logical destination.

Defining the Terms

It is necessary to define the terms as used here. Thayer defines unity as "unity, i.q. unanimity, agreement."[2] Arndt-Gingrich simply has "unity."[3] Webster has some good thoughts: "1. the state or condition of being one; oneness; singleness; being united. 2. concord; agreement; harmony; oneness of sentiment, affection or the like."[4] One authority, in discussing the synonyms of this word states, "unity implies the oneness, as in spirit, aims, interests, feelings, etc., of that which is made up of diverse elements or individuals."[5]

Thus, from the above definitions, we see that when we speak of unity, of oneness, we do not mean the concept of little robots running around waiting for someone to flip a switch so all will do the same thing at the same time. We do not have in mind the concept of mass production wherein all things are interchangeable, with every Christian a carbon copy, a look alike, of every other Christian. And when one portrays my advocacy of unity in this light, it is not a true representation of what is meant by "unity."

Therefore, when I speak of unity, I mean the idea of oneness of spirit, aims, purposes, goals, interests, feelings, etc., of individuals. I do not affirm that the unity of Eph. 4:3 means that if one limps, all must limp; if one is right-handed, all must be right-handed, or because I dislike breakfast, that all must dislike breakfast. The charge is laid at our feet that when we speak of unity, we mean that all must goose-step to the same drum beat, all are little tin soldiers that must kow-tow to some dictatorial command from someone higher up; I assert that this is fabricated nonsense. It makes for good liberal sermons whereby "Church of Christers" can be castigated, but it is a far cry from the truth.

We do affirm, however, that under the concept of "unity" as defined above, there is a certain amount of latitude (allowed freedom of opinion, conduct, or action). But we completely reject the idea of "diversity" we are examining here.

The word "diversity" is found in the King James Version in the plural form in I Cor. 12:4, 6 (the word "diversities" in v. 28 is translated from another word). The original word is also found in verse five, translated "differences." Thayer says "distinction, difference...; in particular, a distinction arising from a different distribution to different persons."[6] Arndt & Gingrich says "allotments of spiritual gifts."[7] Webster says "quality, state, fact or instance of being diverse; different, dissimilitude... variety; multiformity."[8]

It is interesting to note that one authority, in listing the antonyms of "unity," lists the word "diversity."[9] Now, we all know that an antonym is a word that is opposite in meaning. In the same list of antonyms, we find such words as discord, separation, severance and incongruity. So instead of affirming Unity in Diversity, we might aver Unity in Discord or Unity in Separation; perhaps we could assert Unity in Severance or even Unity in Incongruity!

Problem Is Much Deeper

This theory that does not have the old Jerusalem ring has caused, and will continue to cause, much damage to the cause of Christ. We must understand, however, that the heart and core of Unity in Diversity goes much deeper than many are aware.

There is in our world that which we call "cause and effect." In other words, for every effect that we see, there is a cause. Now, Unity in Diversity is an effect, it is the result of the philosophy known as Subjectivism.

Subjectivism can be simply defined as the philosophy that Bible Truth is determined by the subjective reasonings of the knower; it exists within the experiencer's mind and is not capable of external verification. In other words, the truth of any proposition is determined by the individual. Truth may vary from person to person. One might study the Scriptures and conclude that premillennialism is true; another may conclude that it is false. Neither is to bind his subjective view of Truth upon the other because each view is a result of the sacred oracles having been filtered through human rational processes.[10] Remember, one subjective view of Bible Truth is just as authoritative as another.

Now, if Bible Truth is determined subjectively and one's view of Truth is as valid as another's (remember, there is no absolute standard of authority which reveals that which is right for every person on every occasion), how do you look upon one whose "views" concerning premillennialism, instrumental music, tongue speaking, etc., differ from yours? You just "play like" you have unity while overlooking the diversity (disparity), and presto! Unity in Diversity.

With this view, you don't have to defend anything, refute anything, stand for anything or stand against anything. After all, Bible Truth is what you, personally, have determined it to be. Since your view of Truth is as valid as mine, even though we may stand at opposite ends of the extreme, I do not have the right to say you are wrong. Though my concept of Truth might be totally different than yours, we still have total unity. How? Unity in Diversity.

Truly, Unity in Diversity is a natural, logical outgrowth of subjectivism. No man can consistently hold to the subjective philosophy, without affirming Unity in Diversity (of course, consistency is the least of the worries of those who hold this view).

Arguments for Unity in Diversity

A subtle argument has been made that since there are differences in the domestic realm and unity is still maintained, this proves that the argument for Unity in Diversity in the Church is valid.

It is stated that unity in the home exists even though the son might prefer a sports car with a stick shift, whereas his mother prefers a bigger car with an automatic transmission.[11] Now, does this really prove Unity in Diversity? Why not argue that because a son likes onions and the mother does not, that Unity in Diversity is substantiated? Or that the son's favorite color is red and his mother's is blue?

Therefore, because of this supposed Unity in Diversity in the home, we are to have it in the Lord's Church, i.e., different brands of coffee are parallel to the use or non-use of instrumental music in our worship; a stick shift vs. an automatic transmission is equivalent to the acceptance of, and teaching of, premillennialism. Anybody who will accept that will accept anything, and anybody who will teach that will teach anything!

Certainly there is freedom of opinion in the home. But this fact does not prove that every single relationship in the home falls into this area.

Is only the wife obligated to conform to God's law of fidelity in the marriage relationship? Is the husband free to commit adultery? Of course not. Is this not conformity in the home? Indeed it is.

Is there latitude as to whether the wife is subject to the husband or not? Must the wife be subject to her husband? Surely all will agree that she must be subject to her husband. Is this not conformity to God's law?

Now, if the fact that there is latitude in certain areas in the home proves the liberal claim of Unity in Diversity in the Church, then I can argue that since there is conformity in certain areas in the home, this proves there is conformity in every area of the Church!! And my argument for "conformity" would be as reasonable as the argument for Unity in Diversity.

A similiar argument is given by using the governmental realm.[12] It is stated that Unity in Diversity exists in such areas as tariffs, taxes, legislative programs, executive power or Supreme Court prerogatives. Of course there are differences of opinion. In all of these areas there are those who would disagree with me. But does any have the right to pay only those taxes which appeal to him? Or abide by only those tariffs that he likes? Or function in only those legislative programs which suit him? Or abide by only those Supreme Court decisions with which we agree? The point that is missed by the above argument is that all law-abiding citizens must abide by the same taxes, tariffs, etc.

No one would deny differences in various aspects of the home or governmental realm, but this latitude does not exist in every single aspect of the home or government. Differences in brands of coffee certainly do not prove the right to adultery, nor use of mechanical instruments of music in our worship. The differences in the governmental realm do not prove the right to commit treason or to teach premillennialism as a part of "the faith."

Another argument given to substantiate Unity in Diversity is the diversities of the spiritual gifts in the early Church. It is argued that "What was said of gifts bestowed supernaturally will also be true of gifts derived naturally."[13] Who would deny that different gifts were given? But does this prove the "diversity" advocated by our liberal brethren? I think not.

We need to realize that although there were different gifts given, they were given for the fulfillment of ONE purpose, for one goal, for only one reason. The very context of I Corinthians 12 shows that Paul wrote this portion to correct an abuse of God's intended purpose for spiritual gifts. According to the thinking of some, Paul should have never written that portion of Scripture, he should have allowed them to continue in their "diversity," to go their separate ways, misusing and abusing God's purpose for these "diversities of gifts" (I Cor. 12:4).

Now, if what is said of the gifts bestowed supernaturally will also be true of gifts received naturally, then one would not be wrong in affirming that what is said of the **purpose** of gifts received supernaturally, will also be true of the **purpose** of the gifts received naturally; and the purpose of gifts was for unity in the body of Christ, not disparity!

We see then, that this argument on the diversity of spiritual gifts to confirm Unity in Diversity is no argument, but a subtle attempt to prove the unprovable.

Another simplistic argument in favor of this fanciful theory is that in Corinth there was a diversity in understanding.[14] Of course there was a diversity of understanding. But the situation at Corinth does not confirm Unity in Diversity. In actuality it negates the whole argument. It was this "diversity of understanding" that Paul condemned so forthrightly in his first epistle to them. In fact, it can be said that there was not a diversity of understanding as much as there was a **gross misunderstanding.** It was to this "diversity of understanding" to which Paul wrote, "What will ye? shall I come unto you with a rod, or in love, and in the spirit of meekness?" (I Cor. 4:21). It was to this "diversity in understanding" that Paul wrote when he said, "What shall I say to you? shall I praise you in this? I praise you not" (I Cor. 11:22). Is it not very clear that Paul wanted this "diversity in understanding" corrected? Indeed it is.

No Latitude

In II Pet. 1:5-7, the inspired writer lists seven attributes that each Christian is to add to his life. Now, there is no freedom as to whether these things are added to one's life or not. It is imperative that each Christian add them to his life.

In verse 11 Peter writes "For so an entrance shall be ministered unto you abundantly into the everlasting Kingdom of our Lord and Saviour Jesus Christ." Look at the word translated "for so." Thayer says "By virtue of its native demonstrative force it refers to what precedes; in the manner spoken of; in the way described; in the way it was done; in this manner; in such a manner."[15] Then, in referring specifically to this passage, he says, "things having been thus settled, this having been done, then."[16] Therefore, Peter is saying, "These previously mentioned things having been added by you, an abundant entrance shall be ministered unto you." Now, is there latitude as to whether these things are added by the individual to his life or not? Of course there is no latitude, these attributes must be in each Christian's life. We have no choice.

Before some would impugn our thought here, let us assert that there is unity here, there is conformity; all must attain to the degree and to the extent to which he is capable. I think Jesus said it so well, "She hath done what she could..." (Mark 14:8). The parable of the talents further clarifies this thought. "And unto one he gave five talents, to another two, and to another one; to every man according to his several ability..." (Matt. 25:15). Did each receive the same? No. But some would want us to make them receive exactly the same number of talents in order to have unity. And since they did not receive the same number, some will argue that this is Unity in Diversity. But this is untrue, each received according to his individual ability. And when each receives according to his individual ability, this is UNITY, not "union in compromise and toleration."

We must understand that the unity for which we plead allows latitude, freedom in many areas. But we further affirm that there are limitations to this latitude (some would call it "diversity"). There is a point to which this freedom can be taken, but no further.

This latitude does not extend into the area of what one would teach as "the doctrine" (I Tim. 4:16), or "the faith which was once delivered unto the saints" (Jude 3), allowing one to preach "another gospel" (Gal. 1:6). There is no latitude as to whether premillennialism is taught and practiced. This doctrine is false to the core and denies the Sovereignty and the Majesty of the great I AM. There is no freedom in the area of the direct operation of the Holy Spirit. It is irresponsible to affirm that one has received tongues if he subjectively determines that he has. It is sinful to use mechanical instruments of music in worship to God; there is no freedom here. The doctrines of Faith Only and Umbrella Grace are the doctrines and commandments of man and there can be no Unity in Diversity here.

Conclusion

Unity in Diversity is nothing more than the warmed over denominational ecumenicalism that has virtually destroyed denominationalism. If this anti-scriptural theory is allowed to go unchecked, it will lead those professing New Testament Christianity into the same thing. And should this happen, it ceases to be the Lord's Church and becomes a denomination among many denominations.

Unity in Diversity and Denominationalism? Unity in Diversity is denominationalism!!

Footnotes

1. William Floyd, *The Mistakes of Jesus* (The Freethought Press Association, New York, 1932), pp. 15, 16.
2. J. H. Thayer, *Greek-English Lexicon of the New Testament,* (Zondervan, 1977), p. 217.
3. William F. Arndt & F. Wilbur Gingrich, *A Greek-English Lexicon of the New Testament and Other Early Christian Literature,* (University of Chicago Press, 1957), p. 267.
4. Jean L. Mckechnie, ed. *Webster's New Twentieth Century Dictionary of the English Language, Unabridged* (Collins-World, 1975), p. 2000.
5. David B. Guralnik and Joseph H. Friend, ed., *Webster's New World Dictionary, College Edition,* (World, 1968), p. 1592.
6. Thayer, *op. cit.,* p. 137.
7. Ardnt-Gingrich, *op. cit.,* p. 182.
8. Webster's New Twentieth Century Dictionary, p. 537.
9. John Gage Allee, Ph.D., ed., *Webster's Encyclopedia of Dictionaries* (Ottenheimer Publishers, Inc. 1978), p. 504.
10. W. Carl Ketcherside, *The Twisted Scriptures* (Mission Messenger, n.d.), p. 177.
11. W. Carl Ketcherside, *op. cit.,* p. 22.
12. W. Carl Ketcherside, *op. cit.,* p. 22.
13. W. Carl Ketcherside, *op. cit.,* p. 67.
14. W. Carl Ketcherside, *op. cit.,* p. 67.
15. Thayer, *op. cit.,* p. 468.
16. *Ibid.*

CHAPTER 29
"UNITY IN DIVERSITY" AND INSTRUMENTAL MUSIC

Roy Deaver

The Problem

Many among us have subscribed to the doctrine of "Unity in Diversity." This doctrine holds that there can never be real unity upon the basis of a "pattern concept," and that, therefore, the only unity possible is that which comes from agreement to disagree — or, to agree to be united in spite of disagreements.

For example, consider the following: (1) "The Central Church upholds the authority of the Scriptures, the centrality of Jesus, and the unity of all believers. The Church believes that the only unity possible among thinking people is unity within diversity. The Church therefore welcomes all those who have placed their faith in Jesus as Lord and Saviour, regardless of doctrinal differences regarding other matters." (2) "New Testament churches were not churches that had been stamped out like a cookie cutter." (3) "I think the only kind of unity that is possible among **thinking** people is unity within diversity...People can no more think alike than they can look alike." (4) "And, therefore, unity within diversity is the only kind of unity that is possible among **free** people." (5) "I personally intend to embrace as my brother and sister in Christ every person who believes that Jesus Christ is Lord...."

Consequently, there are many brethren who are teaching the false doctrine that there is to be among us **no disfellowship for any cause.** This is a doctrine which has been propagated for many years by Garrett and Ketcherside. And now, they have been joined by many others. I am presently engaged in a written debate on "marriage, divorce, and remarriage" with Dr. James D. Bales. I am persuaded that Dr. Bales is not nearly as concerned about the teaching of Mt. 19:9 as I had thought that he was. Instead, I think that he is using this matter to press the "let-there-be-no-disfellowship-for-any-cause" doctrine. As evidence related to this conclusion I cite the following: (1) With obvious reference to Deaver and Warren he says (in NOT UNDER BONDAGE, page 7): "If my position is right, they are guilty of making a law where Christ did not make one, they are shutting the kingdom against some people, and they are home wreckers." QUESTION: What could be worse than these things? (2) Then, on page 10, he says: "I want to emphasize that I have no uncertainty concerning the position set forth in this book." (3) Then, also on page 10, he says: "I no more make this issue a matter of fellowship than I do the war question."

The Root of the Problem

Certain brethren are striving to make a distinction between "gospel" and "doctrine." They hold that "gospel" relates only to the **outsider,** and that "doctrine" relates only to the **Christian.** They insist that "gospel" is that part of God's message which enables one to **become** a Christian, and that "doctrine" is that part of God's message which enables one, as a Christian to **grow,** to **be edified,** to **remain faithful.** These men insist, therefore, that the "gospel" must be **preached** only to the **outsiders** — that it **cannot** be preached to the **Christian!** They insist that "doctrine" must be **taught** only to the **Christian** — that it **cannot** be taught to the **outsider!** They insist that **any** and **all** persons who have "obeyed the gospel" — who have become Christians — must be fellowshipped, regardless of any and all problems which may arise or exist in the area of **doctrine.** They emphatically declare that there can be **no** withdrawal of fellowship in matters of **doctrine.**

These people are, therefore, stressing the view that (1) those people in the independent Christian churches have obeyed the gospel; (2) that the use of mechanical instrumental music in worship is a matter of **doctrine** — not a matter of **gospel;** (3) that God does **not** demand "unity" in matters of doctrine; and that, therefore, (4) we cannot refuse to extend fellowship to these and to all others in similar circumstances.

This Is No New Distinction

We hasten to emphasize that this distinction between "gospel" and "doctrine" is not a new one. The "ring leaders" of the view described above are the same men who in former days — in their opposition to **located preachers** — made the same distinctions. These men formerly argued that it is **impossible** for one to **preach** to the church — that one can **preach** to the world, but that one can only **teach** the church. They argued that one cannot preach (or teach) the **gospel** to the church — that **the gospel** is for the **outsider** only. They stressed that it is the work of the evangelist to **preach** the **gospel.** From this set of assumptions they declared that it is a sin for a preacher to live and work with a local congregation (for more than 10 days at a time!). We are dealing with the same old erroneous premises — just a new application, a new conclusion. The distinctions **now** relate to a new unity movement.

These Distinctions Are Not Scriptural

We hasten to emphasize that the distinction indicated above between "gospel" and "doctrine" is **not** a scriptural distinction. The English word "doctrine" can be translated from the Greek "logos," or "didaskalia," or "didache." The word about which we are concerned just now is "didache." Some are insisting that "didache" is **always** used in relationship to **the church** — in relationship to **Christians.**

In Jno. 7:17 the Lord said: "If any man willeth to do his will, he shall know of the teaching, whether it is of God, or whether I speak from myself." The word "teaching" is the Greek "didache," and "If any man willeth to do his will" obviously **could** apply to one who is not a Christian but who is interested in becoming a Christian. The Sanhedrin said to the apostles: "...and behold, ye have filled Jerusalem with your doctrine..." (Acts 5:28). The word "doctrine" is the Greek "didache," and in this passage it obviously is **not** limited in its import to Christians only. Further, Barnabas and Saul had attempted to teach Sergius Paulus. Elymas the sorcerer withstood them. Paul severely denounced Elymas for seeking to pervert the right ways of the Lord. Verse 12 (Acts 13) says: "Then the proconsul, when he saw what was done, believed, being astonished at the doctrine of the Lord." Again, the word "doctrine" is the Greek "didache," and here obviously relates to teaching addressed to a non-Christian. According to Acts 17:18 certain philosophers encountered Paul. Verse 19 says: "And they took hold of him, and brought him unto the Areopagus saying, May we know what this new doctrine is, which is spoken by thee?" The word "doctrine" here is "didache," and is **not** restricted to saints only. The saints in Rome had become obedient to the "form of doctrine" whereunto they were delivered. "Doctrine" here is "didache," and certainly relates to persons before they became Christians.

Clearly, the word "doctrine" (teaching) in the sense of the Greek "didache" **cannot** be limited to God's message to those who are already Christians.

Furthermore, it certainly is **not** the case that the word "gospel" relates exclusively to God's message to those who are **not** Christians. The Greek word under consideration here is "kerugma," and it is being insisted by some that "kerugma" applies **exclusively** to the **non**-Christian. In Rom. 16:25 Paul says: "Now to him that is able to establish you according to my gospel and the preaching of Jesus Christ...." The remarks were addressed to the saints in Rome. Paul affirms that God is able to establish them; that God is able to establish them (saints) by the "preaching of Jesus Christ." The word "preaching" here is the Greek "kerugma," and it clearly relates to people who were **Christians.** In Acts 20:25 Paul says: "And now, behold, I know that ye all, among whom I went about preaching the kingdom, shall see my face no more." Paul was speaking to Christians — to elders of the church at Ephesus. Among these, he had gone about **preaching** the kingdom. The word "preaching" is the Greek "kerusso" which is the root word behind "kerugma." "Kerugma" would be the cognate of "kerusso," just as "didache" is the cognate of "didasko."

Clearly, the word "gospel" in the sense of "kerugma" **cannot** be limited to God's message to the **outsider** — the message by which one **becomes** a Christian. It is also God's message to and for the Christian.

It must be obvious, therefore, that the distinction which some are trying to make between "gospel" and "doctrine" is (1) unnecessary, (2) arbitrary, and (3) unscriptural.

But, Even If They Were Right...

Even if these brethren were right in their distinction between "gospel" and "doctrine" it does not follow that there can be no withdrawal of fellowship in matters of "doctrine." What is there about **this** distinction that leads to **this** conclusion? This would be parallel to saying: The command to be baptized applies to the non-Christian (and is a matter of gospel). The command to contribute of one's means applies to the Christian (and is a matter of doctrine). Therefore, if one refuses to contribute of his means he cannot be disfellowshipped! What is there in the information at hand that forces the conclusion that there can be no disfellowship in matters of doctrine? The conclusion just does not follow.

What Saith the Scriptures?

With regard to the Jerusalem church, inspiration records: "And they continued steadfastly in the apostles' doctrine and fellowship, in the breaking of bread and prayers" (Acts 2:42). This passage clearly shows the importance of our continuing steadfastly in the apostles' "teaching." The word "teaching" is the Greek "didache." Is it possible for one to refuse to continue in the apostles' **doctrine**? What is to be done with regard to the one who does not continue in it?

In Rom. 16:17 we have: "Now I beseech you, brethren, mark them that are causing the divisions and occasions of stumbling, contrary to the doctrine which ye learned: and turn away from them." Paul thus refers to certain ones that were causing divisions and occasions of stumbling. Their actions were contrary to the **doctrine** which they had learned. The word "doctrine" is the Greek "didache." Paul says: "For they that are such serve not our Lord Christ, but their own belly; and by their smooth and fair speech they beguile the hearts of the innocent." What are the instructions given? (1) "Mark them," and (2) "turn away from them." It does "appear" that the New Testament teaches that there can be withdrawal of fellowship in matters of **doctrine!**

Consider also, II Jno. 9, 10. The Record says: "Whosoever goeth onward and abideth not in the doctrine of Christ, hath not God: he that abideth in the teaching, the same hath both the Father and the Son. If any one cometh unto you, and bringeth not this teaching, receive him not into your house, and give him no greeting: for he that giveth him greeting partaketh in his evil works." This reading shows clearly the importance of abiding in the "doctrine" (didache) of Christ. It shows just as clearly the sin of lending encouragement to anyone who does not abide in the "doctrine of Christ."

Conclusion

Even though they did not even attempt to set out a precisely formulated, logically sound argument, their effort might be reduced to the following: If (A) it is the case that "gospel" relates only to the outsider; and if (B) it is the case that "doctrine" relates only to the Christian; and if (C) it is the case that God demands unity in "gospel" but does not demand unity in "doctrine"; and if (D) it is the case that mechanical instrumental music in Christian worship is a matter of "doctrine" and is not a matter of "gospel";

and if (E) it is the case that there can be no disfellowship in matters of "doctrine"; then (F) it is the case that there can be no disfellowship over mechanical instrumental music in Christian worship.

This is saying that the conjuncts of A and B and C and D and E **imply** F. Some are affirming these conjuncts, and are concluding: "Therefore F." But, as has been shown, A is false; B is false; C is false; D is false; and E is false. This is an effort to set out a Modus Ponens form argument, but it is **unsound.** Therefore, it does **not** prove the conclusion.

The use of mechanical instrumental music in Christian worship is a practice for which there is no Bible authority, and is a practice which — therefore — stands condemned. There can be no fellowship with those who engage in or who defend such practices.

CHAPTER 30
BINDING - LOOSING - PERVERSION OF SCRIPTURE UNDER THE "TOTAL COMMITMENT" MOVEMENT

W. E. Wardlaw

The theme of this lectureship is "Some Modern Cults and World Religions." The purpose of this lesson is to show how the Total Commitment Movement binds, looses and perverts the scriptures to achieve its goal.

There has been much interest and concern in the last few years regarding the cults of the 70's. It began with a mass murder by the Charles Manson cult in the early seventies and reached its zenith when 900 people committed suicide in Guyana in 1978 under the direction of Jim Jones, their cultic leader. Many other prominent cults in our society today are causing great concern.

Cults do not always have the same characteristics. Sometimes they are completely opposite. Followers of the Charles Manson cult engaged in drugs and sexual perversions. Such is taught against and forbidden by a cult known as the Unification Church. There are things however that are characteristic of all cults. Some of these are:

Strong human leader
Extreme devotion to its leader
Total commitment required to its teachings
High demands made on its members
Separation of follower from family and former friends
Age group most susceptible to the movement

The so-called Total Commitment Movement which is sweeping the church today has all of these cultic characteristics.

The Total Commitment Movement may be defined as a movement that captivates and controls the minds of its converts; demands a strict and unwavering loyalty to its leaders; pressures its followers to be totally committed to rigid activities engaged in by the group, such as, "soul talks," "prayer partners," and "quiet times." A failure to do so marks one as being less than totally committed. A high priority is also placed on recruiting new members to the group. The movement is based on a 126 page book, *The Master Plan of Evangelism,* by Robert E. Coleman. For the movement to be successful it manipulates its follower by perverting the scriptures, binding where God has not bound and loosing where God has not loosed.

The Bible clearly and emphatically warns against anyone trifling with the word of God in any fashion. One is not to add to, take from, or wrest the scriptures. To do so is to bring about one's own destruction (II Pet. 3:16). Both the Old and New Testament abound in warnings against any disregard for the sacred word. Moses warned Israel, "Ye shall not add unto the word which I commanded you, neither shall ye diminish from it, that ye may keep the commandments of Jehovah your God which I commanded you" (Deut. 4:2). "What thing soever I command you, that shall ye observe to do: thou shalt not add thereto, nor diminish from it" (Deut. 12:32). Again, in the middle of the Bible we read the same warning, "Add thou not unto his words, lest he reprove thee, and thou be found a liar" (Prov. 30:6). In the New Testament Paul says, "Now these things, brethren, I have in a figure transferred to myself and Appolos for your sakes: that in us ye might learn not to go beyond the things which are written;...." (I Cor. 4:6). The writer John also testifies that, "Whosoever goeth onward and abideth not in the teaching of Christ, hath not God: he that abideth in the teaching, the same hath both the Father and the Son" (II John 9). The last book and the last chapter in our Bible clearly warns, "I testify unto every man that heareth the words of the prophecy of this book. If any man should add unto them, God shall add unto him the plagues which are written in the book: and if any man shall take away from the words of the book of this prophecy, God shall take away his part from the tree of life, and out of the holy city, which are written in this book" (Rev. 22:18,19). Jesus said, "...and ye have made void the word of God because of your tradition" (Matt. 15:6).

The expression "totally committed" as used by this group does not have reference to being totally committed to the authority of the scriptures. If so, there would be no objection. The Bible teaches that one must "be subject therefore unto God" (James 4:7). Christ claimed that "all authority hath been given unto me in heaven and on earth" (Matt. 28:18). Paul said that "whatsoever ye do, in word or in deed, do all in the name (authority) of the Lord Jesus..." (Col. 3:17). Peter warns that "if any man speaketh, speaking as it were oracles of God..." (I Pet. 4:11).

However, to those in this movement, total commitment has reference to one being faithful to attend all "soul talks," to have an active communication with a senior "prayer partner" and to regularly engage in what is known as "quiet times." One of their instructors stated in one of their workshops:

> "One should attend a soul talk every week. One needs to make a commitment. To attend every other week is not a commitment."

One of the favorite passages of this group is in the book of Luke where Jesus gives several lessons on true discipleship. These lessons are perverted by them in an effort to control the lives of their followers. The first says, "If any man cometh unto me, and hateth not his own father, and mother, and wife, and children, and brethren, and sisters, yea, and his own life also, he cannot be my disciple" (Luke 14:26). They use this passage to encourage young converts to break ties with their families and friends. One caught up in this movement told me that he had learned to hate his wife and children as he thought this passage taught. The verse is perverted by them.

One can come to a better understanding of what Jesus meant by "hate" when a comparison is made with a parallel verse in Matthew. It says, "He that loveth father or mother more than me is not worthy of me; and he that loveth son and daughter more than me is not worthy of me" (Matt. 10:37). Jesus used the word "hate" to mean to love less. This can also be seen in an Old Testament passage. It is stated that Jacob "loved also Rachel more than Leah" (Gen. 29:29). Yet in the next verse it says, "And Jehovah saw that Leah was hated" (Gen. 29:30). The passage in Luke simply means that one should not let anything, not even his loved ones, interfere with his submitting to the authority of Christ. When one is totally committed to the authority of Christ he will obey and honor his parents. Paul said, "Children obey your parents in the Lord: for this is right. Honor thy father and mother..." (Eph. 6:1,2).

The other two lessons are, that a man does not begin to build a tower unless he is confident that he will be able to finish it (Luke 14:28-30), and a king does not go into battle when he is outnumbered and the odds are strongly against his winning, without first trying to settle his differences by sending "an ambassage, and asketh conditions of peace" (Luke 14:31-33).

These verses are used by them to teach that one should not be baptized unless he makes a commitment or statement that he will be totally committed after his baptism. Thus they often refuse baptism to some who desire it because the canidate has not convinced the instructor that he will be totally committed to the movement. This is a perversion of the passage. A proper explanation of these verses was given by the late Bro. N. B. Hardeman a number of years ago when he said:

> "If you contemplate fighting against God, going through life and meeting the judgment in disobedience to Him, you had better sit down and count well the cost."
>
> "If you are marshalling your forces against Jehovah, it would be well to think seriously, and come to a decision to send an ambassy and seek peace while the time and opportunity is yours."
>
> "As a matter of fact, you are certain to be defeated, if you wage war against the authority of God."[1]

Another passage perverted by them is the parable of the vine and branches regarding fruit bearing (John 15:1-8). They give a very strained and narrow interpretation to this passage. To them, fruit bearing is one thing only, that is to win new converts. They conclude that if one is not out winning souls to Christ he is not bearing fruit. Therefore, he will be lost. Thus the followers of the movement are encouraged to invite new prospects to the "soul talks" and in this way, bear fruit. A failure to do so will put his soul in jeopardy. Thus they keep their new converts activated and faithful through a feeling of fear and guilt.

Jesus did not intend to teach a lesson on personal evangelism by his parable of the vine and the branches. The context will clearly show that to bear fruit is to remain in Christ and that means to do **all** that he commands. It is true that teaching others about Christ is among those things commanded, but it does not follow that it is the only way to bear fruit or that every person has to be involved in knocking on doors and having a Bible study with someone.

In Paul's discourse on spiritual gifts he compared the church to the human body (I Cor. 12:1-31). He clearly pointed out that as the various members of the human body do not all have the same function, neither do the members of the spiritual body have the same function. He concludes by asking, "Are all apostles? are all prophets? are all teachers? are all workers of miracles?" (I Cor. 12:29). To ask the question is to answer it in the negative. All members are not to be preachers, elders, teachers, door knockers, etc; but each member functioning in the capacity in which he is best qualified will constitute the whole body wherein God's work will be accomplished.

When we bear fruit we glorify the Father. "Herein is my Father glorified, that ye bear much fruit; and so shall ye be my disciples" (John 15:8). To bear fruit is the same as to "let your light shine before men; that they may see your good works, and glorify your Father who is in heaven" (Matt. 5:16). This includes all that we do as followers of Christ. The apostle Peter is even more specific when he names some works that glorify God. One must "abstain from fleshly lusts...having your behavior seemly among the gentiles...be subject to every ordinance of man...honor all men, love the brotherhood, fear God, honor the king" (I Pet. 2:11-17).

Not only do those who are caught up in the Total Commitment Movement pervert the scriptures, but they also are guilty of binding where God has not bound. Some of the strongest teaching in the Bible is against this practice. Earlier in this lesson several passages of scripture were noticed that warned against adding to or taking from the Word of God. The same condemnation awaits those who add laws where God has not legislated, as to those who refuse to do all he says (Prov. 30:6; Rev. 22:18,19).

Jesus, during his personal ministry, used some of the most scathing language to denounce the Pharisees (Matt. 23). One of the things they were guilty of was "they bind heavy burdens and grievous to be borne, and lay them on men's shoulders..." (Matt. 23:4). Those who are leaders in the Total Commitment Movement are guilty of the same thing the Pharisees were guilty of. In fact, a whole lesson could be and has been given, showing the parallel of this movement to the Pharisees of the First Century.

They do not hesitate to bind on their followers a rigid schedule which involves soliciting for and attending "soul talks," reporting to a senior "prayer partner" on a regular basis, and observing a "quiet time" each day. None of these activities is required by the Lord, yet they make great demands on their followers not to neglect any of these. To do so is to be reprimanded severely. One of the most successful ways to censure those who are guilty is to withdraw love from them.

Followers of the movement are also pressured to confess all their sins, shortcomings, and even their thoughts to a senior prayer partner that they have been assigned to. To convince the convert that he must do so, they quote: "Confess therefore your sins one to another, and pray one for another, that ye may be healed" (James 5:16). "One another" in this passage does not require a prayer partner to confess sins to, any more than "one another" in Col. 3:16 requires a singing partner to teach and admonish. In fact, this verse does not require one to confess his sins to a senior prayer partner any more than it required one to confess his sins to a priest.

According to the philosophy of this movement one is totally committed if he is faithful to attend soul talks, communicate with his prayer partner and observe his quiet times. If he is negligent in these things, then he is not totally committed. The truth of the matter is, one may engage in all of these things very faithfully and still not be totally committed to the authority of Christ. On the other hand, he may never engage in any of these things and still be totally committed to God's authority. Those in the movement are guilty of binding where God has not bound.

Another area where the movement is wrong is that its law makers are guilty of loosing where God has not loosed. This is especially true in the divine organization of the church. The scriptural organization of the local church is elders (Acts 14:23), deacons (Phil. 1:1), and evangelist (II Tim. 4:5). The elders are to oversee the flock (Acts 20:28; I Peter 5:1, 2). Through the years we have consistantly pointed out that one of the errors of denominationalism is that it is wrong in organization. Those in the Total Commitment Movement have changed the organizational setup of the church. Evidently, they do not see the need to be guided by the authority of the scriptures. They loose what God has bound. Their organizational structure is: campus minister, a female counselor, soul talk leader, and senior prayer partner. They cannot defend their position by claiming what they have is no different from a congregation having an educational director or personal work director. These are not parallel. The educational director works within the organizational framework of the local church. He is still under the elders. In the Total Commitment organization, the campus minister is the real overseer. They do not hesitate to bypass the elders. Their own guide book teaches this principle:

> "It is high time that the requirements for membership in the church be interpreted and enforced in terms of true Christian discipleship. But this action alone will not be enough. Followers must have leaders, and this means that before much can be done with the church membership something will have to be done with the church officials."[2]

The record is clear. They have already demonstrated this principle in several places. Elders were removed when they got in the way. They accept an eldership only when it does not interfere or get in the way. Elders of several different congregations have reported that the campus minister had run up a sizable long distance telephone bill to Gainesville, Florida, but never sought counsel or advice from the local elders. The Total Commitment Movement is not the church at work but it is a movement within the church that will ultimately destroy the church if it is not stopped.

Any religion that perverts scriptures, binds where God has not bound and looses where God has not loosed, is destined to cause division. This is the primary reason that the Total Commitment Movement has caused such division throughout the brotherhood. May we all take the admonition of the pioneers of the Restoration Movement to "Speak where the Bible speaks; be silent where the Bible is silent; call Bible things by Bible names and do Bible things in Bible ways." Then the prayer of Jesus, "that we might all be one," may be a reality.

Footnotes

1. N. B. Hardeman, *Hardeman's Tabernacle Sermons,* Vol. III, Gospel Advocate Co., Nashville, Tenn., 1928, p. 231.
2. Robert E. Coleman, *The Master Plan of Evangelism,* Fleming H. Revell Co., Old Tappan, N.J., 1978, p. 60.

CHAPTER 31
THE PEOPLES TEMPLE CHRISTIAN CHURCH

Max Patterson

The Peoples Temple Christian Church began in the mid 1950s and came to a sudden and dramatic halt in November, 1978. James Warren Jones, the founder and leader, ended his leadership and a great number of the movement by killing more than 900, including himself.

The Peoples Temple Christian Church was affiliated with the Disciples of Christ. In fact, it was held up by them as an example in earlier days. In April, 1973, Jerry McHarg, Associate Regional Pastor, Southern California, wrote:

> Peoples Temple is an interracial, vibrant, exciting congregation, called into being by God through its Pastor, Jim Jones, with a unique sense of the servant role of the church...One gets the impression of being in the midst of the human race at its best; a community of people whose primary concern is to love and to serve.[1]

However, from the very beginning of its inception, its ideas and practices were blatant and unmistakable. It displayed every characteristic of the cults at large, and its true side came out and was summed up by Ron Javers, a reporter who survived the attack in November, 1978: "Jonestown is every evil that everybody thought — and worse. We knew that before the shooting started." —San Francisco Chronicle, November 20, 1978.

History

The history of the Peoples Temple Christian Church movement is the history of Jim Jones. As a teenager Jones manifested both the desire and the charismatic ability to manipulate others. His mother, a divorcee, raised Jones to be an agnostic. He married Marceline Boswell, and the both of them had a pronounced interest in people with problems, especially the poor and downtrodden.

After high school Jones went to Indiana University with visions of becoming a doctor. One of his classmates observed of those days, "Jones believed himself then to be a Messiah." He would talk for hours on his religious and social theories at IU to the embarrassment of his associates. Ultimately he left IU and decided to become a faith healer. However, it must be observed, this decision was not on the basis of faith in God. In a 1977 *N. Y. Times* interview, his wife Marceline said that her husband "had not been lured to the ministry by deep religious faith, but because it served his goal of achieving social change through Marxism."

Jones preached first for the Methodist church, then the Pentecostal church, then his own community unity church, later to be called the Peoples Church. Jones held a non-Christian stance describing himself in college as a Unitarian. He needed respectability and courted and won approval to be listed by the Disciples of Christ as a member congregation by 1960. He was ordained a preacher in 1964. Men like Father Divine and Daddy Grace fascinated him, and he envied the devotion, adoration, and absolute loyalty given them by their flocks. On one occasion he threw a Bible on the floor, stomped on it, and shouted, "People are worshiping this thing too much when they should be worshipping me." This scene was to be repeated many times through the years.

Jones built a name for himself through political and social programs. In California Jones made friends with politicians. He set up nursing homes, took in wayward children from the San Francisco area, taught school, was foreman of the County Grand Jury, and the Peoples Temple was Incorporated in the State of California.

In 1977 the *New West* magazine printed an article critical of the temple and its leader. That was when things began to come unglued. Sometime in the early 1970s Jones began to make his first arrangements for an agricultural colony in Guyana. His paranoia, fed by this new criticism, caused him to set his schedule up and he took his followers to his new utopian colony named, of course, Jonestown.

In May, 1978, a group of 57 relatives of the Peoples Temple petitioned Secretary of State Cyrus Vance to do something to save their relatives. The State Department did nothing!

Work hours were eleven or twelve hours a day in blazing sun and drenching humidity with guards on watch constantly. There was no privacy, even for married couples. Rice and gravy was the staple diet. Nightly meetings with Jones' harangues over loud speakers lasted sometimes until 3 A.M. Communications with outsiders, including relatives, were tightly controlled, and monitored. Breaking the rules brought torture, even for children.

U. S. Congressman Leo Ryan accompanied by a news team went to Jonestown. While things were staged to give the best impression, the ragged edge of reality became obvious. When some decided to leave with Ryan, Jones' paranoia got the best of him and he dispatched an assassination crew who killed Congressman Ryan and some of the newsmen, but others escaped. The stage was set. Jones called his congregation together and carried out a plan that had been rehearsed since San Francisco days. 911 died in what has been called the greatest single perverted religious tragedy of our time.

The Theology of Jim Jones

Jones had two theologies: one for observing publicly and quite another for his followers. His idea was plain old pragmatism: if it contributes to control people, use it. Jones was a Unitarian Humanist. He systematically picked apart the Bible, going into tirades against it, yelling and screaming that it was full of lies, tearing out pages, spitting on it, and stomping it. The only true God to Jones was Jones. He claimed to be the reincarnation of Jesus. He also claimed to be Buddha, Lenin, and God Almighty. An example of the songs sung is:

I gotta tell it
I gotta tell it
I gotta tell it
I gotta tell ya how Jim Jones changed my life.
I gotta tell it
I gotta tell it
I gotta tell ya how Jim Jones changed my life.
Once I was burdened
and filled with misery.
Along came this prophet,
and he delivered me.
I gotta tell it.

(This song was repeated by Birdy Marable on December 6, 1978, after the tragic death of the 911).[2]

Jones once faked a shooting of himself and claimed to raise himself from the dead, reaching into his body, removing the bullets, not even leaving a scar. He would cry out in services, "I am God! I am God!" He once flew into a rage when two women sang "Amazing Grace." He said, "I'm the only God you'll ever see."[3]

Former Jones' devotee, Yulanda Crawford, in a notarized affidavit, says, "On numerous occasions I was in the congregation when he told us 'I am God' and 'there is no other God, and religion is the opium of the people.'" Jones claimed people would be reincarnated, a possible factor that has been mentioned in the mass suicides.

His feelings were no doubt socialistic. In fact, he required members to read the book, *Introduction to Socialism.* Some say he wished to supplant the Bible with it. With him, heaven was an ideal to be attained here on earth. Hell was poverty, war, racism, etc. God is love, and this love or good is in us. Jones deified himself, was anti-Christianity, and pro-Marxist.

Jones dreamed of a socialist utopia presided over by Jim Jones. He had an appearance of compassion, especially his public image. He used faith healing and claimed to save many lives by this means. Actually, it was used to control the people.

What Controlled The People?

1. **Sexual Bondage:** According to Sparks,[4] Jones had sex with both women and men and had pictures taken of the acts. He claimed to be the only one fit to have sex relations with others. In fact, it was a well known fact that one had to have sexual relations with Jones in order to be trusted.

2. **Interrogation, Catharsis, Punishment:** From Indianapolis days, Jones had an interrogation committee. The committee was composed of

loyalists of Jones. One could say anything against God, Jesus, the Bible, but criticism of Jones was blasphemy. People were sometimes grilled for hours. Jones sometimes used spies who obtained information on various people and then Jones would have these special revelations. He would keep in bondage by claiming to know all the people did. The catharsis sessions were comprised of putting a person before the whole group and blasting him with the most intimate questions.

Public beatings at one time were common. Teenagers and older people were beaten. In San Francisco Jones had a boxing ring set up. After a person was beaten to a pulp, he had to struggle to the microphone held out by Jones and say "Thank you, Father." Later, children were controlled by an electrical cattle prod.

3. **Money:** Jones put the squeeze on for money, property, or for anything to get his hands on money. One of the more prominent ways was through a nursing home scheme. He would take the checks of old people and put them in cramped quarters. Keeping people poor kept them easier to control.

4. **Control by blackmail:** Members had to write out and sign confessions to crimes. These were kept for possible future use.[5]

Refutation

1. There is no relationship of the views and teaching of Jim Jones and the true form of historic Christianity (John 8:24; 14:1-6).

2. Jones was a false messiah who mixed a false religion with political aspirations (John 12:48).

3. Jones was an immoral, financially dishonest, paranoid who seemed not to stop at anything (I Tim. 4:1-3; II Thess. 1:7-9).

4. "Why refute him! He's dead and gone." It is the highest form of ignorance and naivete to think there are not others capable of doing (and are doing) the same thing (I John 4:1).

5. Jones' religion was supposed to be a religion of brotherhood. Instead it was a tactic of repression and suffering (John 8:32).

Footnotes

1. Jack Sparks, *The Mind Benders* (New York: Thomas Nelson Publishers, 1979), p. 258.
2. *Ibid.*, p. 269.
3. *Ibid.*, p. 270.
4. *Ibid.*, p. 280.
5. For a fuller discussion of many of these points, see *Newsweek*, December 4, 1978, pp. 38-81; *U. S. News and World Report*, December 4, 1978, pp. 23-29 and Jack Sparks, *The Mind Benders*, pp. 257-306.

CHAPTER 32
INTERNATIONAL SOCIETY FOR KRISHNA CONSCIOUSNESS

Max Patterson

The International Society for Krishna Consciousness was founded in 1966 in New York City by A. C. Bhaktivedanta Swami Prahupada. The cults objective is to promote "spiritual enlightenment," and to spread the pure love of God (Krishna) throughout Western society.

Devotees follow a traditionally ascetic Hindu life style. There are about 50 communelike temples in urban areas of the United States. According to the movement itself, there are 10,000 full time devotees.

The cult is very strict, authoritarian, and feel that outside influences, including parents are an evil influence. There are four basic temple rules of conduct: no gambling, no intoxicants, including tobacco, coffee, and tea, no illicit sex, and no eating of meat, fish, or eggs. Other rules that must be strictly observed are: no conversation with others outside the movement; no reading of outside materials; devotees learn how to chant, how to participate in temple ceremonies, and how to prostrate oneself before the deities of wood and marble.[1]

Full membership is attained by stages. First, one tries it by participation. Initiation, usually after about six months, includes being assigned a new name (Sanskrit), and three strands of neck beads to be worn the rest of one's life. After another six months or so, the second rite, brahminical initiation can be performed. In order for this to take place, one must have a good record, and have done everything one was told without questioning, etc.

The next step is sannyasa, a renunciation stage, especially designed for young men. It entails a life-long vow of poverty and celibacy and a commitment to preach and do good works.

Krishna is the Supreme God. Bhakti is loving, selfless service to Krishna. Krishna consciousness is becoming aware of God's will for us by using all our senses for that purpose. A Karmi is a worldly non-member.[2]

The average age of those going into this type of cult is between 18 and 22. They come from average American homes with many experiencing communication problems with their parents. A great number of these have known the pain and deprivation of a single parent home.

A Defense Against Cultism

The best defense is a good offense. Make sure we teach the Scriptures to our children. They need to be able to distinguish false doctrine from the truth. Our children can be taught to defend the Bible doctrines of inspiration, worship, and the exclusiveness of Christianity (Prov. 22:6).

We need to set the proper example. Nothing is rejected faster than hypocrisy. We need to see to it that our children are loved, and that the home to them is a place of security and comfort.

We need to inform ourselves of where the danger is. This enables us to better protect ourselves and our children (I John 4:1; II Cor. 13:5).

Never assume a great leader will always make the right decisions. We need strong leaders and role models, but beware of anyone who elevates himself too highly, and does not take the servant approach to Christianity. We need to constantly examine for self interest and false teaching (Acts 20:28-31; I Tim. 4:1-3).

Acts 17:11 puts strong emphasis on thinking for ourselves. Never should we blindly follow a mere man.

The church must put a strong emphasis on fellowship, care, love, and concern for one another.

The church must be Scripture centered, not leader centered. This is to say, that Christ is the head of the church, not man (Eph. 1:22, 23).

FOOTNOTES

1. Ronald Enroth, *Youth, Brainwashing, and the Extremist Cults* (Grand Rapids: Zondervan Publishing House, 1977), pp. 21, 22.

2. Fuller discussions of all of these areas are found in the following books: Conway, Flo, & Siegelman, Jim. *Snapping*. pp. 15-16, 28. Hefley, James C. *The Youth Nappers*. pp. 33-45. Petersen, William J. *Those Curious Cults*. pp. 139-148. Sparks, Jack. *The Mind Benders*. pp. 91-120.

CHAPTER 32 A
UNITARIANISM

Max Patterson

In May of 1960 a merger was approved between the Unitarians and the Universalists. In May of 1961 the Unitarian Universalist Association was formally launched.

The liberalism and modernism which came out of the Renaissance and Reformation proved to be a foundation upon which Unitarianism in Europe and America could be established. Although there were those characterized as Unitarians before the 19th century, it was not until 1815 that the name Unitarian was accepted. Unitarians consider themselves a voluntary association of independent churches and fellowships mainly in the United States and Canada. Unitarianism in America mostly grew out of Congregational churches in New England.

The Unitarian platform was outlined in 1819 by William Ellery Channing of Boston in a sermon entitled "Unitarian Christianity." The American Unitarian Association, a missionary and publication society, was formed in 1825.

Because of the emphasis given to "free thinking," it is difficult to put down a fixed set of doctrines or ideas. However, some of the ideas that have been formulated by the Unitarians and generally accepted by them are:

1. The unity of God (a rejection of the doctrine of the trinity).
2. The strict humanity of Jesus. Jesus was divine only as all men are divine.
3. The natural character of the Bible. It is not infallible, but on a par with the writings of Buddha, Mohammed, Confucius, and others. Unitarians emphasize the reign of natural law.
4. All men will be saved. However, salvation is only in this life from sin, and not from any punishment hereafter. Eternal punishment is held to be inconsistent with an all-loving, all-powerful God.
5. Heaven is a state, or condition of the soul, not a place.
6. Personal ideologies are encouraged within the bounds of the widest possible freedom. Every person should be free to form his own beliefs.
7. Man is capable of solving his own problems and overcoming any problem by reason. Thus, man is capable of creating a world society based on justice and cooperation.
8. Man rose through a process of evolution. His nature is claimed to be essentially good.
9. Character is the aim of religion.

As one can see Unitarianism is as much a denial of Biblical religion as anything else. Unitarians are humanists. They reject the personal God of the Bible, the Bible as the inspired Word of God, the creation story, the virgin birth, blood atonement, and deity of Jesus, the church as a divine institution, and prayer ("why pray since we live in a world governed by natural law?").

Some of the goals of the Unitarian Universalist Association are:

1. To strengthen one another in a free and disciplined search for truth.

2. To spread universal truths as taught by prophets and humanity, especially love to God, and love to man.

3. To affirm, defend and promote the supreme worth of every human personality, the dignity of man, and the use of the democratic method in human relationships.

4. To implement the vision of a one world community.

5. To serve, promote and strengthen liberal religion.

6. To encourage cooperation with men of good will in every land.[1]

Footnotes

1. For an expanded discussion see: Cassara, Earnest. "Unitarianism," *World Book Encyclopaedia.* XIX, 20. Chorowsky, Carl M. "What is a Unitarian?" *Look* Magazine, March 8, 1955. Martin, Walter R. *The Kingdom of The Cults.* p. 424. Mead, Frank S. *Handbook of Denominations.* p. 209. Van Baalen, J. K. *The Chaos of Cults.* p. 285.

CHAPTER 33
SCIENTOLOGY

Max Patterson

Scientology and the use of "Dianetics" was L. Ron Hubbard's brainchild and was founded by him in the 1950s. Basically, this is a type of psychoanalysis which promotes the theory that one's present problems are caused by prenatal experiences.

At first, the idea of "Dianetics" was one of science. However, Hubbard ran into trouble with the law and turned dianetics from a science into a religion. In this way his scheme was somewhat protected by the law. An Australian official has termed Hubbard's work, "the world's largest organization of unqualified persons engaged in the practice of dangerous techniques, which masquerades as mental therapy."

Hubbard receives ten per cent of all fees collected by Scientology centers, and according to *Time* magazine boasts of seven million stashed away in Swiss bank accounts. *Time* also reported that in 1949 Hubbard had joked to an author's convention, "writing for a penny a word is ridiculous. If a man really wanted to make a million dollars, the best way would be to start his own religion."

The terminology used could only have been dreamed up by a science-fiction writer. Scientology and its peculiar terminology includes such words as orgs, E-Meters, clears, pre-clears, engrams, and thetans. The understanding of these words become clear in the process of going through the program:

First, you are a pre-clear. This means you still have problems and difficulties. A pre-clear goes through an "auditing" or processing counseling session. In this process use is made of the E-Meter, which is a crude lie detector (sometimes nothing more than two tin cans connected to a simple galvanometer). Hubbard divided the mind into two compartments: the analytic (the conscious, rational mind) and the reactive (the storehouse of unpleasant memories — "engrams"). Treatment involved exposing and erasing engrams until the analytic mind gained dominance over the reactive mind.

Very personal questions are asked, and this is supposed to help one get rid of the engrams that are fouling up one's life. It is believed that the source of man's reactive mind can be contacted and erased. Questions like, "Have you done anything your mother would be ashamed to find out," with the auditor looking you in the eye, usually brings the truth out. Some claim to remember back when they were in the uterus of their mother and even the egg waiting to be met by the sperm. It becomes clear that existence before this life is taught. One is urged to search these for those troublesome engrams.

As one is gradually cleared of engrams one moves up through eight grades of clearness until finally he is clear. Obviously, not many make it all the way. One reason for this is the amount charged. Prices vary from fifteen to thirty-five dollars an hour. One ought to get clear from seven to ten thousand dollars. The *Saturday Evening Post* reported on one Florida man who spent $20,000.00 to help be cured of his nervousness. Annual gross income at one time was estimated to be $70 million.

Hubbard's eight dynamics for survival are:

1. To survive as an individual.
2. To survive through sex and family.
3. To survive as a group (school, society, town, and nation).
4. To survive as mankind.
5. To preserve animal and plant life.
6. To preserve the physical universe, including matter, energy, space, and time.
7. To preserve spiritual existence.
8. To preserve immortal existence.

The court system, the American Medical Association, various newspapers and magazines, and many other groups, have vigorously opposed this movement.

Reaction

It is wise to remember that Scientology's highest authority is not Jesus nor the Bible, but a science-fiction writer named Hubbard. The gestapo-like control under which members are kept is not only frightening, but far from the truth of John 8:32. In Scientology God is irrelevant. It deifies man and denies sin. The Bible says, "All have sinned and come short of the glory of God" (Rom. 3:23). Scientology offers nothing to the poor. Everything it offers costs money. Consider also its warped code of ethics. Hubbard says, "Never fear to hurt another in a just cause." He promises to "punish to the fullest extent of my power anyone misusing or degrading Scientology to harmful ends." This is far from "turn the other cheek," and "love your enemies." Scientology deifies man. Man, often spelled with a capital letter, can produce perfect behavior and therefore solve all the problems of the human predicament. This claim is a humanist claim and contradicts Jeremiah 10:23 which affirms that the way of man is not in himself.[1]

In answer to the question, "is Scientology good for anything?" someone answered, "Yes, it is a good money making business and Hubbard is getting rich."

Footnotes

1. An expanded discussion of this material may be found in the following books: Conway, Flo, & Siegelman, Jim. *Snapping*. pp. 16, 25, 28, 73, 161-67. Gruss, Edmond C. *Cults and the Occult*. p. 119. Hefley, James C. *The Youth Nappers*. p. 113. Petersen, William J. *Those Curious New Cults*. p. 87.

CHAPTER 34
THE UNIFICATION CHURCH ("MOONIES")

William Wilder

Its Founder and Leader

Very few movements have made faster strides and attracted broader international attention than has the unified family known also as the Unification church, and more popularly called "the Moonies." In airports, on college campuses, in shopping centers and on the street corners, millions of Americans are constantly confronted by smiling faces of mostly young people who are members of the Moonie movement headed by Sun Myung Moon soliciting funds to support their diabolical cult.

The founder of this cult, Sun Myung Moon, was born in 1920 in Northern Korea. When Moon was about ten, his family was converted to the Presbyterian church.[1] While Moon was in deep meditation in the mountainside of North Korea in 1936, he claims that he saw Jesus, and Christ explained to him that he would complete the mission that Jesus had failed to do. For the next nine years, he prepared himself for the task. Moon left Korea for a few years and attended school in Tokyo studying electrical engineering. In the late 40's he was put in prison for what he claimed were anti-Communist activities. He states that he was tortured by the Communists, and in his booklet, "The Heart of Our Father," Moon's suffering for his faith is likened to the sufferings of Christ.[2] It is claimed that in a small northern Korean town he was severely beaten and left for dead. His followers came and carried his body away to be buried, but someone felt life in him. Within three days he remarkably began to preach. "Others report that he was imprisoned for adultery and bigamy; however, his anti-Communist work was not organized until 1962."[3]

About 1954 Moon erected a church in Seoul. It was called the Tong-il-Kyo and in English "The Holy Spirit Association for the Unification of World Christianity." His doctrine spread like wildfire. People were at this particular time fed up with the norm and were looking for something different. "About 400,000 members are claimed in Korea and Japan. About 6,000 are instilled with his teachings in West Germany and over 30,000 claimed in the United States."[4] "Some 10,000 are full-time workers living in 120 communes."

In 1954 Moon's wife of ten years left him because, he states, "She could not comprehend my mission."[5] Moon claims he only was married once since his first wife had failed to become the perfect wife. Some believe he has been married four times.

In 1972 Moon brought his doctrine to the United States from Korea. An article by George Cornell in the Reader's Digest states, "that in 1975 members of his church collected over ten million dollars through the selling of nuts, candles and flowers."[6] The group has acquired about ten million dollars in property also in and around New York City. They own a ranch in California and run over 150 centers at various college campuses. Here is where they recruit many of their followers. There is a training center located in Barrytown, New York, on 255 acres.

The Moon Movement

Over a period of years, Moon wrote his "Divine Principle," the extraordinary "Bible" of the Unification church.[7] This book is the primary document which contains the basic tenets and doctrines of his false movement. His followers firmly believe that God has imparted revelations to Moon, much of which is written in Divine Principle. Moon believes that in some of these revelations God told him a second Messiah would be born in Korea during a period that included Moon's own birth year, 1920. In 1954, he was known among his followers in Korea as "the Master;" now he prefers to be called "the Father." He was asked if he would turn out to be the second Messiah. "That will be made known in further revelations," said Moon.

Moon teaches that Mother Eve was beguiled by Satan, thus sinned and corrupted the human race. He claims that the missions of Jesus failed because he was to marry a perfect woman and start a **pure** race. However, this was prevented from happening because he was crucified. Moon's mission is to provide physical redemption and perfect the human posterity. He is revered by his followers as the "true parent" even though he has been divorced at least two times.

Moon states in detail in the "Principle of Creation" that "God made two worlds, visible and invisible, and created man to have both spirit and body, in order to have him dominate the two worlds, according to his words of blessing. Nevertheless, due to Adam's fall, man failed to enjoy dominion over these two worlds."[8] Until Christ came, man lamented for his failure. The advent of the Lord was to perfect the dominator of these two worlds, in the capacity of a perfected Adam intending to make all believers in one body with himself by engrafting them to his body. "Nevertheless, due to the Jewish people's rebellion against him, the physical body of Jesus was delivered into the hands of Satan as the condition of ransom for restoration of the Jews and the whole of mankind back to God's bosom; his body was invaded by Satan."

Moon believes that had Jesus not failed in his efforts to restore the kingdom of God on earth, he would have been the True Parent of restored mankind.[9] Moon's theological theory that at the second advent God would raise up a Messiah, coming from Korea, would make him a prime candidate for the position. Moon affirms that man is still in his original sin, for Christ's death on the cross affected only the spiritual. Since Jesus will not come again in the flesh as at first, then it follows, says Moon, "the Second Advent will surely be realized not in a spiritual body but in the flesh..."[10] And, naturally, since Jesus will not appear in the flesh, God then, must raise up someone else in the flesh to be the Messiah to continue the work that Jesus failed to do. The failure as already seen on the part of Christ was due to not marrying an ideal wife and begin the perfect earthly family. Moon puts the blame on the Jews for the failure and he calls it "Collective sin."

The Divine Principle states that about 400 years in advance of Jesus, God sent Malachi to the Jewish nation to prepare them for the coming Messiah.[11] Meanwhile, in Asia, God prepared Buddha and Confucius, in the Hellenist world he prepared Socrates. As Moon states, "All religions and cultures were to unify under the acceptance of Jesus. But God's will was tragically thwarted by the crucifixion of Christ."[12]

Moon Sent to Deliver America

Sun Moon says America is not going to bring the world anything but heartache. The time for the arrival of the Lord of the Second Advent is near and American Christians should be God's champions. However, he further points out that the majority are too busy pursuing their own individual interests and their denominational ties. Moon goes on to teach that it is not the goal of God to save any one church or nation — it is not just Christians whom God wants to save, or just Americans. "God will," says Moon, "sacrifice his special church and his special nation for the sake of the rest of the world." Moon believes that the will of God is to sacrifice the lesser for the greater.[13]

Moon calls for a re-awakening of the American believers. He calls for a pilgrim spirit to carry on the work of its ancestors. "Individualism," he says, "must be bound into a God-centered ideology." "He has come to America," he says, "as a part of God's will." For 6,000 years, God has been working toward the building of the American nation, and the entire future of the world depends on it. Moon believes Christianity and the United States are in a position to create a new one-world system with all the nations joined into one.

It should be clear that Moon sees America as stewards of God — the deposit holders as it were, of His wealth and blessings. The worldwide church is impotent, according to Moon's theory, without a nation to combine with, and America must exist for the whole world.

Moon's theory wants God to combine church and state to his glory. Israel failed and Christianity replaced it; the Roman Empire along with the Popes could have gone forth together to bring about world salvation, but they failed and the blessings intended for these nations were withdrawn from. "Now," says Moon, "Christianity and the United States are supposed to combine to accomplish One World of God." The truth in the matter is Moon was run out of his native land and America was ripe for picking. With his concoctions, the United States is being duped to believe such erroneous teachings.

The 120-day Training Manual makes the following statement about the essential nature of the Unification church. "The mission of the Unification church is to consummate the mission of Christianity. Therefore, the

Unification is different from the Christian church. We must clearly understand the difference between the Unification church and the Christian church...Through unity between sinless father and his sinless bride, there must be born lineal sinless children of the Lord of the Second Advent. Father is sinless, Mother is sinless and their children are sinless. Then a sinless family on earth will be realized." (p. 236)

The Lord of the Second Advent

Another distortion of Holy Writ is readily discerned in the Divine Principle's reference "the first man, Adam, became a living soul. The last Adam became a lifegiving spirit" (I Cor. 15:45). The followers of Moon believe that the last Adam is not Christ our Saviour (verse 57) but the Lord of the second event. The reason for such a ridiculous position is: Jesus, when he came to this earth, did not fulfill God's plan of **total** redemption. This was because of John the Baptist. Their claim for the reason of Christ's death was the failure of the Jews to believe in the Messiah.

As to the location of the origin of the Lord of the Second Advent, the Divine Principle puts together a number of assertions. "First, it argues that 'another angel' is the Messiah and not an actual angel. Second, it asserts that 'from the rising of the sun' is from the East and not from an eastward direction. Third, it argues that the East refers to the Orient and not a more likely location than the Middle East. Fourth, it claims that the East refers to Korea, Japan and China, and not any other oriental nation. Finally, it asserts that Korea is the birthplace of the Messiah."[14] How absurd! To accept Korea as the birthplace is to rest the maximum of faith upon the minimum of logic.

Nonetheless, despite these weaknesses in Sun Moon's teachings, despite their incompatibility with either the Bible or secular thought, many young people are turning to the Unification church.

Seduction Syndrome of Cults

The majority of people who join new-age cults are between eighteen and twenty-two years of age. Many come from homes that have experienced very unstable family relationships. "They are involved in a search for identity and a quest for spiritual reality that provides clear-cut answers to their questions."[15]

These cults not only provide firm answers to every question, but also make promises that appeal to those who need reassurance and confidence to face society. They promise abundant living which means you can be set free from all fear and doubt; delivered from poverty, sickness and poor health; re-saved from condemnation and self-contempt; cured of drugs and sex abuse. Your marriage can be restored and you can enjoy a happy family life where there is no generation gap.

If you have power for abundant living, you can gain self-respect — love your work regardless of what it is. You can overcome all worries and depressions and have real peace of soul. There can always be a positive outlook on life, day by day with no letdown at all. There will be a new purpose in your life, like never before if you have the abundant life. You can have whatever you want if you will let go and get involved in the cult. The Moonies work very hard to recruit people because they believe they are in a movement which is unifying the people of all races and beliefs around love and fraternity.

Their workshops stress the family concept. Soon you realize that you are spoken of as a "spiritual child." Hence, you are not left alone and there soon becomes a very rigid schedule for you so they can begin to indoctrinate you in their teachings. "There are specific times for eating, exercising, playing, singing, listening to lectures and discussing them. You are separated into small groups, led by a team leader who has to have perfect control. You are not to talk to anyone, just listen and conform. All day you are bombarded by ideas and concepts. The family members aim directly at your most vulnerable points: the need to belong, to feel useful, and to feel loved."[16]

The Indoctrination

After committing oneself to the movement, things really begin to happen and change in his life. They give one about two weeks to adjust and then he must turn over **all** his possessions to them. In this procedure one is most vulnerable to the church — he is brainwashed and broke. "A person is taught that everyone who is not a part of this movement is under the power of Satan and that you should mistrust them."[17] So one becomes dependent on the group for any love and positive reinforcement. After alienation is complete, one can leave the training if they care to.

By now one is quite familiar with Moon's doctrine and program. You now speak of him as Master or Father. Through Moon, he claims, God has imparted revelations revealed in the Divine Principle and his sermons. Moon and his wife are the Perfect Parents who dupe their followers into believing they will bring physical salvation to them and the world. To members of this cult Moon is everything.

They are required to adhere to a schedule more rigid than the workshops. You only sleep five to six hours a day. You eat food that is low in proteins. Often you are compelled to fast up to three or four weeks. One is constantly praying and studying the Divine Principle. You work very hard and long in all types of weather, asking for donations or selling flowers, candy or whatever. If you can't sell the product, ask for a donation. If they have no cash, ask for a personal check. They are encouraged to take food stamps for payment. A typical Moonie fund-raising brings in between one and five hundred dollars a day. "You are taught that, because Satan deceives God's children, you are justified in deceiving Satan's children, a doctrine known as heavenly deception."[18]

They say if your body reacts negatively with illness or fatigue, it is a sign of Satan taking over your body. If you slow down in your efforts to "roll in the dough" for the cause, you are selfish and are failing in growing close to

God. If you object to their rules, they say Satan is working through you against God. A person is taught to mistrust his mind. You no longer need to think or evaluate for yourself, but, instead, recall what was taught you for that situation. One almost becomes as a robot. They say if you leave the organization, you will die spiritually. It is claimed that you become so dependent that you will do anything for them and Moon.

Sobering Facts

"He (God) is living in me and I am the incarnation of Himself. The whole world is in my hand, and I will conquer and subjugate the world." — Moon

"I am your brain" statement by Moon in the June 14, 1976 issue of *Time*.

"You must start over again your new life, from that point denying your past families, friends, neighbors and relatives. You must keep yourself pure. If you may have to be stained in some way or another, it is better for you to kill yourself than to remain alive. In restoring man from evil sovereignty, we must cheat." — pg. 49 *Time*, June 14, 1976.

In private meetings, he is the authorization Master Moon who claims to be "greater than Jesus himself" and says, "God is now throwing Christianity away and is now establishing a new religion, and this religion is the Unification church." — *Time Magazine*, Sept. 30, 1974, pg. 68.

"They honor, even pray to, Moon and his wife, as their 'true parent'." — *Time*, June 14, 1976, pg. 49.

"Moon got married in 1944 but left his pregnant wife behind in Seoul to go to preach in the North." — *Time*, June 14, 1976, pg. 49.

"In those days (1950's), say early members of the sect, ritual sex characterized the Moon communes. Since Moon was a pure man, sex with him ("blood cleansing") was supposed to purify both body and soul, and marriages of other cultists were infact invalid until the wives slept with Moon." — pg. 50, *Time*, June 14, 1976.

Conclusion

From the Christian point of view, Moon joins a number of false prophets who, even as the Bible predicts (Matt. 24:24), rise up to discredit the true Messiah, Christ our Saviour. The work of Christ is complete and steadfast, and the Scriptures pronounce a curse on any who would attempt to alter in any way the gospel message. As always, the best defense against any cult or false theory is a thorough knowledge of the Scriptures (John 8:32).

Footnotes

1. *Gospel Advocate*, p. 1, Vol. CXX, 1978.
2. *The Moon Doctrine*, p. 6, J. Isam Yamanoto.
3. *Ibid.*, p. 6.
4. *Reader's Digest*, pp. 97, 98, Feb. 1976.
5. *The Moon Doctrine*, p. 7.
6. *Reader's Digest*, p. 97.
7. *The Spirit of Sun Myung Moon*, pp. 13-17, Zola Levitt.
8. *Divine Principle*, p. 510, Sun Myung Moon.

9. *Ibid.*, p. 511.
10. *Ibid.*, p. 514.
11. *Ibid.*, p. 423.
12. *The Moon Doctrine*, p. 14, J. Isam Yamanoto.
13. *The Spirit of Sun Myung Moon*, pp. 50-51, Zola Levitt.
14. *The Moon Doctrine*, p. 29.
15. *Youth Brainwashing and the Extremist Cults*, p. 150, Ronald Enroth.
16. *Ibid.*, p. 150.
17. *The Moon Doctrine*, p. 34.
18. *Ibid.*, p. 36.

CHAPTER 35
ASTROLOGY

Terry Varner

Astrology can be defined as (1) "the prediction of human character and destiny based on the stars and their constellations"[1] or (2) "a complicated form of divination based on the theory that our lives are governed or influenced by the stars and planets."[2]

Astrology is from the compound word **astros** meaning "star" and **logos** meaning "word, reason, or logic." **Astrology** is not to be confused with **astronomy** which Webster defines as "the science which treats of the celestial bodies, their magnitudes, motions, constellations, etc., a treatise on this science." Astrology is a pseudo-science and astronomy is a legitimate science. Astrology is part of the occult movement; i.e., "hidden, mysterious, secret, super-natural in claims" (Webster).

It is difficult to deny that our lives are benefited by the sun without which there would be no physical life (Gen. 1:14-16; Deut. 33:14; Ps. 136:8; Jer. 31:35) and to a lesser degree by the moon which produces the tides upon the earth (Gen. 1:14-16; Deut. 33:14; Psm. 104:19; 136:9; Jer. 31:35). But, the particular pseudoclaims of astrology on our life by planetary vibrations, as examined and refuted in this study, are rooted in many false premises and assumptions that are open to both scientific and biblical objections.

Some Introductory Matters

The practice of attempting to foretell the future by observing the positions of the stars, the moon, the sun, and the planets arose among the pagan Babylonians who believed the stars and the planets were gods. Later the practice spread throughout other nations and was developed more fully in subsequent generations.

Early astrology devotees believed that the earth was the center of the universe with the stars and planets revolving around it for the sole benefit of mankind. Such appealed and seemed reasonable to the masses. In ancient times armies went to war only at an hour predetermined by the astrologers who studied the position of the planet Mars, which was considered to be the planet of war. The travels of the various kings, the crowning of new rulers, the marriages of members of the royal families were not scheduled until the students of astrology had been consulted. In the system of astrology the sun, considered the giver of life; Venus, the planet of love; and Jupitėr are all believed to have favorable influence upon man; whereas, Mars, Mercury, and Saturn are believed to have unfavorable influence upon man.

Ancient and modern astrology is based upon eight planets: the sun, moon, Mars, Mercury, Jupiter, Venus, and Saturn all revolving around the planet earth. Since 1871, three additional planets have been discovered

— Uranus, Neptune, and Pluto. For the most part these three planets have been ignored by most modern astrologers.

Today in consulting an astrologer for one's horoscope reading, one must know the precise moment of his birth which includes the exact latitude and longitude of his birthplace. Only with this accurate information can an astrologer "cast your horoscope"; that is, determine the configuration of the stars and the planets at the exact time you were born, which supposedly determines your character and influences your future.

Astrologers claim that each person is born under a certain "sign" of the zodiac. The zodiac is an imaginary path in the sky across which the sun makes its yearly journey. The "path" is divided into twelve houses, each named after a stellar constellation. The constellation rising in the east at the time of one's birth is his "sign." The twelve constellations were originally all named after animals; consequently, the term zodiac means the "path of the little animals."[3] The individual born in his given constellation takes on the characteristics of the mythological animal or other object after which that constellation is named.

The traditional zodiac circle contains 12 equal divisions with each division corresponding to one of the 12 constellations lying around the celestial zodiac circle: Aries (the Ram), Taurus (the Bull), Gemini (the Twins), Cancer (the Crab), Leo (the Lion), Virgo (the Virgin), Libra (the Scales), Scorpio (the Scorpion), Saggitarius (the Archer), Capricorn (the Goat), Aquarius (the Waterbearer), and Pisces (the Fishes). Recently, Steven Schmidt published a book, *Astrology 14,* in which he challenged the traditional 12 constellations of the zodiac circle by claiming there are now 14 constellations and by adding: Cetus (the Whale) and Ophichus (the Serpent-Slayer). Yet, others reject both the 12 and 14 constellations of the zodiac circle by admitting only 8 or 10 constellations and some have set forth the idea of as many as 24 constellations.

Astrology's Impact in Society

Astrology is world-wide. Thousands begin each day by consulting their astrological horoscopes and charts to see if it is a good day for shopping, working in the garden, harmonizing family relationships, for business decisions, and etc. Astrological journals abound and carry articles such as, "A Guide To Financial Success," "Keys to a Deeper Romance," "How to Enjoy Better Health," and "Tips to Teens." There are zodiac cookbooks, zodiac autograph books, zodiac coloring books for children and even an *Astrology and Horse Racing* book which the author claims sells about 100,000 copies per year.

According to the "20/20" television program aired on March 21, 1981, it was reported that 15% of all Americans believe in some form of astrology. They estimated that over 1000 books were printed advocating astrology during the decades of the 1970s, that approximately 1 million listen daily to an astrological radio program aired over a Boston station, and that daily horoscopes are published in more than 1000 newspapers in America. In America during 1980, "339,660 people subscribed to horoscope services, paying between $4 and $10 each. The available mailing lists of names of people involved in the occult now stands at 3.8 million."[4]

Astrology is prevalent on our college campuses with over 200 colleges having a 24 hour-a-day computer service that casts horoscopes for the students.[5] *Horoscope and American Astrology* claims a paid circulation of about a half million subscribers. Astrology is so large a business that Petersen claimed in 1973 it employed "12,000 fulltime astrologers and keeps 175,000 part-time astrologers busy."[6] Time Pattern Research Institute, Inc., has a computer programmed to cast "a 10,000 word horoscope reading in two minutes. It set an early goal of 10,000 capacity in a month, with plans for continued expansion."[7]

Astrology and the Bible

The astrologists claim the Bible is sympathetic to their teachings by asserting that (1) Abraham, Joseph, Moses, David, and the biblical prophets were practicing astrologists; (2) the Bible contains astrological symbolism which has never been correctly understood or interpreted by Christians; and (3) the Star of Bethlehem was not a miracle by God but an astrological phenomenon. Through various presuppositions astrologers have attempted to link the 12 signs of the zodiac to the 12 tribes of Israel; that the word **angel** was in reality a corruption of the astrological term **angle;** and that Jesus when writing on the ground (Jn. 8:6-8) He was actually casting a horoscope.[8]

The questions of the Bible containing any evidence (1) that one is correct in consulting astrology and its ways and (2) that the stars and planets influence man's actions and affairs of life can be simply, easily, and accurately answered — NO! Though the Bible indicates an awareness of the existence and practice of astrology by other nations, the faithful children of God through all dispensations did not tolerate or involve themselves in the practice of astrology, but rather condemned it in no uncertain terms.

1. **Astrology is forbidden:** Moses spoke with clarity when he said, (a) "neither shall ye use enchantments, nor observers of times" (Lev. 19:26). "Observers of times" is translated as "augury" (ASV); i.e., one who interprets various omens as being either favorable or unfavorable times to undertake certain actions and etc. (b) "The Lord thy God hath not suffered thee so to do" (Deut. 18:14); (c) "regard not them that have familar spirits, neither seek after wizards, to be defiled by them: I am the Lord your God" (Lev. 19:31); i.e., no honor is to be paid to any who claims such powers; and (d) "and the soul that turneth after such as have familar spirits,....I will even set my face against that soul, and will cut him off from among his people" (Lev. 20:6). In II Kings 23:45 Josiah commanded Hilkiah, the high priest, and the other priests to rid the land of the "idolatrous priests" who "burned incense...to the sun, and to the moon, and to the planets, and to all the hosts of heaven." The King James Version has a footnote reading for the term "planets" as "the signs of the Zodiac" and the American Standard has "twelve signs." The worship of the gods Baal and Asherah, a heaven

cult, was strictly forbidden by Jehovah. Josiah dealt with this violation in accordance with Deuteronomy 7:25 and 12:3 by "burning the vessels" (II Kings 23:4).

2. **Astrology is an abomination:** When Israel entered Palestine she was instructed to "not learn to do after the abominations of those nations" (Deut. 18:9). The "abominations" offended and were abhorred by God of which "obervers of times" (Deut. 18:10, 14) was one. Moses then states that Israel was to "be perfect with the Lord thy God" (Deut. 18:13). Reider states that "the implication is: 'Trust in God and do not seek the assistance of magic forces and demoniacal powers.'"[9] Then Moses re-iterates what he has said with the "Lord they God hath not suffered thee so to do" (Deut. 18:14).

3. **Astrology is idolatrous:** Moses had declared that Israel was to have and was to depend upon no other gods than Jehovah when giving the Ten Commandments (Ex. 20:1-5; Deut. 5:6-9). The beloved apostle John commanded, "Little children, keep yourselves from idols" (I Jn. 5:21). Isaiah stated, "and when they shall say unto you, seek unto them that have familiar spirits, and unto wizards that peep, and that mutter: should not a people seek unto their God? for the living to the dead?" (8:19). Isaiah claims that "seeking" is important but the children of God are to "seek their God" not the stars! Isaiah then emphasizes the importance and all-sufficiency of the message of God in "to the law and to the testimony" (Isa. 8:20). Jeremiah instructs Israel to "hear ye the word which the Lord speaketh unto you,...Learn not the way of the heathen, and be not dismayed at the signs of heaven; for the heathen are dismayed at them" (10:1-2). They are to "seek their God" in the sure and certain "law and testimony" which will give them sufficient direction. They are to "learn not" the way of the heathen and the signs of heaven. The word "learn" is considered by Thompson as implying "becoming a disciple."[10] The ancient Near East religions focused their attention on the astral deities, sun, moon, and stars. That astrology involves idolatry listen to Llewellyn George, a prominent advocate, "I revere the 'voice' (vibrations) of the planets. They are God's messengers and speak in His language; they give us His 'word.'" Astrology encourages men not to consult God for guidance but rather to consult the stars! The children of God have no need of the superstition and fear regarding the position of the sun, moon, and stars! Reliance upon them is idolatrous!

4. **Astrology is futile:** Isaiah chides Babylon of the futility of her astrologers and her other enchantments. Despite her many enchantments they are of no help in diverting the coming disaster upon that nation. He chides, "thou are wearied in the multitudes of thy counsels. Let now the astrologers, the stargazers, the monthly prognosticators, stand up, and save thee from these things that shall come upon thee" (47:13). The assertion is made. Disaster is coming. If there is "truth" and "salvation" in their astrologers and enchantments, these should now come forward and "save thee from these things that shall come upon thee," but their futility is

seen when the prophet states, "none shall save thee" (Isa. 47:15). These are false saviours!

Biorhythms, also called the new astrology, bears out the futility of relying upon such counsel. The theory of biorhythms, as worked out by two German doctors earlier this century, is that

> human behaviour is strongly influenced by three rhythms: a physical cycle repeating every 23 days, and emotional cycle of 28 days, and an intellectual cycle of 33 days. In each of these cycles a person is supposed to be strong in the first half and weak in the second. These cycles are all supposed to start off from zero when you are born and continue without variation to the day you die. Thus calculation of your biorhythmic status at any time is relatively simple if your birthdate is known.[11]

Futility is seen in placing dependence in one's biorhythms. Why should one's cycle begin at birth? A baby is alive at conception or months before he is born. Too, some babies are born prematurely; others are born many days overdue. What evidence is there that all people have the same length cycles? What evidence exists that the length of these cycles is unchangeable? If any cycle varies by even a few tenths of one percent from the 23, 28 or 33 days, then the usual calculations will be worthless for anyone more than twenty years or so old. In some studies that have been made the futility of such a theory is obvious. Reggie Jackson, right fielder for the New York Yankees, hit three home runs in his last three at bats to win the 1977 World Series on a "low" day in his physical cycle. In the January 1979 Super Bowl, physical biorhythms were done on both Terry Bradshaw and Roger Staubach prior to the game. In fact the outcome of the game was predicted from the biorhythm charts. Terry Bradshaw's biorhythm chart showed he was to have a "low" day and Roger Staubach was to have a "high" day. The Pittsburgh Steelers won the Super Bowl on the pin-point passing of Terry Bradshaw.

5. **Astrology ends in ruin:** The prophet Amos predicted the coming Assyrian captivity of Israel because of Israel's sins and idolatry, "But ye have borne the tabernacle of your Moloch and Chiun your images, the star of your god, which ye made to yourselves. Therefore will I cause you to go into captivity beyond Damascus, saith the Lord, whose name is The God of hosts" (5:26-27). Stephen, in using the words of Amos, said, "But God turned and gave them up to worship the host of heaven,..." (Acts 7:42). The sun, moon, stars, and planets are the "host of heaven." The worship of the stars was one of the earliest forms of idolarty in pagan worship. As punishment for their rejection of Him, God allowed Israel to become worshippers of astrology. Moloch, Chiun, and Remphan are considered planetary divinities of the Egyptians, Canaanites, and Assyrians and which refers to "a name of the god of the planet Saturn."[12] Israel's choice to worship the stars brought her to ruin.

Reasons for Rejecting Astrology

Astrology, with its many presuppositions, is antagonistic to the faith of the Christian who believes in the Creator and the Sustainer of the universe (Heb. 1:1-3). A number of reasons exist for rejecting astrology.

1. **Astrology emphasizes the creation rather than the Creator:** Paul denounced those who "exchanged the truth of God for a lie, and worshipped and served the creature rather than the Creator" (Rom. 1:25). The emphasis in astrology is on nature rather than the Lord of nature. The heavens are to declare the glory of God, not the destiny of man (Psm. 19:1-6; Rom. 1:19-20).

2. **Astrology claims "your destiny is in the stars" rather than in our freedom of choice:** A well-known criminal case[13] recently occurred in Florida where a man's defense lawyer attempted to plead his case of rape and robbery charges on the basis that his client was "insane by reason of astrological influence." The defense lawyer claimed his client and others like him are "forced by planetary obedience to lead violent and troubled lives. I want the verdict to prove that an individual has no control over his behaviour." That would be comforting in some ways, IF true, but it is not true! Paul wrote that we must all stand before the judgment seat and give an account (Rom. 14:12; II Cor. 5:10). Our Lord's lesson on the Parable of Talents teaches that we must give an account and thereby determine our destiny (Matt. 25:14-30). Astrology is fatalistic in nature. Christianity involves the working of God's providence in our lives (Rom. 8:28). Shakespeare, also, was correct when he wrote, "The fault, dear Brutus, is not in our stars, but in ourselves..." *(Julius Caesar).*

3. **Astrology is not scientific:** No true scientist places any confidence in astrology which is a curious mixture of superstition, mythology, astrophysics and mathematical formulas. Astronomers and scientists have related numerous scientifically based objections to astrology, none of which has been adequately answered. Astrologers claim a connection between birth dates and a gift for science, but a quick and careful study of a "Who's Who" book called *Men of Science* reveals that scientists are born at all times of the year.

4. **Astrologers predictions often differ widely and are many times contradictory:** Jeane Dixon, one of the better known astrology columnists, wrote that if Virgos (those born between August 23 and September 22) "have anything to sell, now is the time to seek buyers." But, another horoscope columnist advised Virgos, on the same day, to "watch their possessions." The lucky number for Aries born people is 3, according to one astrologist; yet another claims it is 48, still others claim 10, and others, 55. Illustrations as these could be multiplied many times.

5. **Astrology frequently gives very general and obvious instructions:** Common within the horoscope columns is the advice to its devotees to "be considerate," "friendly," "finish what you start," "be patient," and etc. But, we ask why should these things be done only on certain days? Should not such advice and actions be constant? Is this not the teaching of the Bible? (cf., Lk. 9:62; I Cor. 13:4-8; 15:58; Phil. 4: 6-9; etc.).

6. **Astrology claims to predict future events and ignores God and the Bible in seeking to know the future:** There is some evidence to the effect

that Jeane Dixon predicted the assassinations of President John F. Kennedy and his brother Senator Robert Kennedy. But so many of her predictions, and those of others, do not come true. An example in point is: Jeane Dixon predicted President Lyndon B. Johnson would win renomination of his party with ease, but the President refused to run for another term. This and other failures should help us to understand that their predictive powers are **not** from God — predictions of God's prophets **never** fail to be fulfilled. Moses gave the inspired criteria for judging prophets by saying, "When a prophet speaketh in the name of the Lord, if the thing follow not, nor come to pass, that is the thing which the Lord hath not spoken, but the prophet hath spoken it presumptiously: thou shalt not be afraid of him" (Deut. 18:22).

7. **Astrology implies the Scriptures are not all-sufficient:** In our day, the very concept of the authority and all-sufficiency of the Scriptures is being questioned and challenged on every hand. Astrology has done just that with the precious Book divine. Isaiah said long ago, "Bind up the testimony, seal the law among my disciples...To the law and to the testimony" (8:16, 20). Peter calls the Scriptures the "sure word of prophecy" (II Pet. 1:19). Jesus says, "and ye shall know the truth, and the truth shall make you free" (Jn. 8:32) and "sanctify them through thy truth, thy word is truth" (Jn. 17:17). Luke reminds us that we can "know the certainty concerning the things wherein thou wast instructed" (Lk. 1:4). Paul reminds us of the effect of the Word of God in our lives when he writes, "but we have this treasure in earthen vessels, that the exceeding greatness of the power may be of God, and not from ourselves" (II Cor. 4:7).

Reasons People Turn to Astrology

Why the sudden and renewed interest in the occult and astrology? Why should this generation, which claims to be the most enlightened in all of history, seek out guidance and dependence upon astrology? The following reasons are some of the many that can be given in answer to the question.

1. **We live in an age of fear and anxiety:** In facing the unknown future and a present with which man does not feel capable of coping, he looks elsewhere for strength and help instead of our only source — God! David reminds us that "The Lord is my strength and my shield" (Psm. 28:7); "the Lord God is a sun and shield" (Psm. 84:11); "The Lord...a refuge in time of trouble" (Psm. 9:9); and "God is our refuge and strength, a very present help in trouble" (Psm. 46:1). Peter writes, "Casting all your care upon him; for he careth for you" (I Pet. 5:7).

2. **We live in an age in which men have rejected the ultimate standard — the Bible:** Man will have some kind of a standard. It may be himself, some false religion, and with many it is the stars! With the ever-increasing problem of permissiveness and confusion, man has turned to the "host of heaven." The need is to return to the Bible, the ever-tested, all-sufficient Word of God. Paul wrote that the Scriptures are "able to make us wise

unto salvation...and are profitable for doctrine, for reproof, for correction, for instruction in righteousness,..." (II Tim. 3:14-16). Nebuchadnezzar found the wisdom and that the understanding of Daniel and his three friends was "ten times better than all the magicians and astrologers that were in his realm" (Dan. 1:20), but **only** because their wisdom and understanding rested upon the solid rock of God's Word!

3. **We live in an age of great religious confusion:** While the majority of the people have little time for God, seemingly they cannot cease "seeking" for a substitute. Life and religion have become a point of frustration to many. Michel Garquelin writes that "the collapse of religious faith"[14] is one of the major reasons for people turning to astrology. Jeane Dixon[15] concurs and predicted that during the decade of the 1970s many people would find faith in the Lord through ESP (extra sensory perception). Shirley Spencer, an astrologer, admits "that many of astrology's new converts are refugees from religion: 'We're afraid to say no, no, no, to the bearded man upstairs before we have a substitute'."[16] Howard Sheldon, an astrologer, states, "Unlike religion, it gives concrete answers....It offers kids more security than they can find any place else. I have many young clients...finding Big answers in astrology."[17] Yet, all of these quotes are in direct contradiction to the teachings of Paul, who writes, "so belief cometh of hearing, and hearing by the word of Christ" (Rom. 10:17); of Jesus, who said, "the words I speak unto you, they are spirit, and they are life" (Jn. 6:63); of James, who writes, "the engrafted word, which is able to save your souls" (1:21); and of Peter, who says, one is "born again,...by the word of God" (I Pet. 1:23).

4. **We live in an age of great interest in space and the stellar world:** Closely combined with interest in space and the stellar world is the concept of power. America and Russia are both striving for power and dominance in exploration of outer space. Movie moguls have developed this theme in a series of space films. **Star Wars,** and its sequel **The Empire Strikes Back,** dazzled the nation by becoming the largest box-office success in history. Its success was built on — POWER! The films subtly introduce the power of the occult to its captivated audiences. The films are filled with telekinesis and levitation (moving objects with the mind power through seances and occult rituals); apparitions (seeking guidance through communicating with the dead); and clairandiant (hearing spirits for guidance). Interestingly, both the good and bad guys drew upon the same force to demonstrate power: the "white" representative of protection and defense and the "dark" representative of ruthless control over others. Anton Lavey, the black pope of the Church of Satan, says, "Anyone who pretends to be interested in magic or the occult for reasons other than gaining **power** is the worst kind of hypocrite."[18] This is subtle deception used to give credibility to the occult when all displays of occult power are condemned by God (Deut. 18:10; Lev. 19:30; 20:6).

Conclusion

Let us "prove all things, hold fast to that which is good" (II Thess. 5:21).

God wants us to concentrate on doing His will, and He will provide man with the **only** real security there is. We must increase our determination to provide man with the sound alternative which is found in the Word of God. We have the "light that shineth in a dark place" (II Pet. 1:19). In Christ, "all things work together for good" (Rom. 8:28). Moses reminds all of us, "the eternal God is thy refuge, and underneath are the everlasting arms" (Deut. 33:27).

Footnotes

1. Kent Philpott, *A Manual of Demonology and the Occult,* p. 110.
2. Robert C. Newman, "Astrology: A Form of Occult Divination," *Biblical Bulletin.* Vol. VIII, No. 25, July 1978, p. 2.
3. Roy B. Zuck, "What's Wrong With Astrology?", *Moody Monthly,* Nov. 1968, p. 21.
4. *Christianity Today,* February 26, 1981, p. 92.
5. William J. Petersen, *Those Curious New Cults* (New Canaan, Conn.: Keats Publishing Co., 1973), p. 13.
6. *Ibid.*
7. Merrill F. Unger, *Demons in the World Today* (London: Tyndale House Publishers, 1971, p. 60.
8. Karl Anderson, *Astrology of the Old Testament* (Mokelumne Hill: Health Research, 1965), p. 70.
9. Joseph Reider, *Deuteronomy* (Philadelphia: The Jewish Publication Society of America, 1948), p. 181.
10. J. A. Thompson, *The Book of Jeremiah* (Grand Rapids: William B. Eerdmans Publishing Co., 1980), p. 327.
11. Robert C. Newman, "Biorhythms: The New Astrology," *Biblical Bulletin,* Vol. VIII, No. 28, Spring 1979, p. 3.
12. F. F. Bruce, *Commentary on the Book of the Acts* (Grand Rapids: William B. Eerdmans Publishing Co., 1954), p. 155, fn 63; Merrill F. Unger, *Biblical Demonology* (Wheaton; Scripture Press Publications, Inc., 1952), pp. 133-135.
13. "Accused Rapist Pleads He Was Led By Planets" *The Parkersburg Sentinel,* March 19, 1980, p. 15.
14. "Astrology Gaining New Acceptance in Europe" *Los Angeles Times,* November 18, 1971, p. E4.
15. Jeane Dixon, *My Life and Prophecies* (New York: William Morrow and Co., 1969), p. 153.
16. *Time,* March 21, 1969, p. 56.
17. *Los Angeles Times,* March 12, 1972, p. E2.
18. Ron Sunseri, "Starwars and spacefilms...A Lure to Occult Powers!!", *The Church Speaks,* Vol. 32, No. 2, September-October 1980, pp. 1-2.

CHAPTER 36
SECULAR HUMANISM

Robert R. Taylor, Jr.

Overt pride produces Humanism. This is not new on the human scene. A manifestation of this very spirit is exhibited by the prince of Tyre in the era of Ezekiel. Jehovah directed his faithful and fervent prophet to write, "Thus saith the Lord God; Because thine heart is lifted up, and thou hast said, I am a God, I sit in the seat of God, in the midst of the seas; yet thou art a man, and not God, though thou set thine heart as the heart of God:..." (Ezek. 28:2). This very spirit of work in the human heart has aided in producing the major menace to human society which we currently confront and contemplate — Humanism.

Humanism is used a number of ways. Some of them are clearly misleading on the very surface relative to its basic nature. There are even those religious who want to get on the bandwagon of Humanism — "the latest thing, the newest fad...the direction of the times."[1]

The late Pope Paul VI called Roman Catholicism "Christian Humanism." "The claim that Christianity, and in particular Roman Catholicism, is a Humanism is ironic; for free thinkers, atheists, agnostics, and sceptics adopted the name 'Humanism' in opposition to a dogmatic Church. It is a surprise, therefore, for atheistic Humanists to discover that those whom they had most opposed now proclaim the very ideals that the Humanists asserted in opposition!"[2] They are disconcerted at such discoveries.

Among the naive and unsuspecting are those who equate Humanism with benevolence, sympathy and genuine concern for human betterment, happier people and a just and humane society. However, this is **not** the assessment and appraisal Humanist leaders give their movement. Some have suggested that to distinguish their movement from simply an effort to be humane toward others, that the latter be left in the lowercase (humanism) and the former be spelled with a capital H (Humanism).

One does not read much in this field of thought until he comes across Scientific Humanism, Religious Humanism, Ethical Humanism, Marxist Humanism, Renaissance Humanism, Sexual Humanism, etc.

In this short study of Humanism we shall be taking somewhat of a long, lingering look at: (1) its definitions and depictions; (2) its history; (3) the Humanist Manifesto I — 1933; (4) the Humanist Manifesto II — 1973; (5) its fruits; (6) the total incompatibility between the Bible and Humanism; and (7) why Humanism must be exposed and opposed by Christians and by all who are friendly toward the Bible.

Humanism Defined and Depicted

Humanism revolves totally around man. He is the pivot; he is the center of all that is really important. Man is the **measure** of all things. The system is deliberately designed to extol and elevate man into the **chief** or **supreme** measure of everything. As reflected in the Phoenician prince at Tyre in Ezekiel's era man becomes his own god and chooses what will please him and bring him the most in anticipated human happiness and earthly satisfaction. Humanism is of this world. Randall in THE MAKING OF THE MODERN MIND has drawn with graphic distinction the major differences between the religion of this world — Humanism — and the religion of Christ — New Testament Christianity. "You follow infinite objects; I follow the finite; you place your ladder in the heavens, I on earth, that I may not seek so high or fall so low"[3]

In Humanism God is dethroned; man is deified. The Bible is relegated to the antique section of books no longer useful to modern minds. The church is old hat. Salvation from sin is but a relic of a forever passed era. Modern man has by-passed this superstition of a need to recognize sin and be saved from its damnable effects. There is **no** supernatural origin of either the universe or of man. There is no other world for man than this one. Brother J. D. Thomas well argues, "Humanism says, 'This life is all. Live it up.'"[4] In Humanism God is **out;** man is **in;** creation is **out;** evolution is **in;** redemption is **out;** social progress is **in;** heaven and hell are **out;** making the most of this life is **in;** the church is **out;** absolute morals are **out;** free, casual and friendly sex in all forms is **in.** With the latter point it really does not matter whether it is pre-marital or extra-marital; whether it is heterosexual, homosexual or even that of bestiality.

Madalyn O'Hair recently spoke in favor of shutting every church building in the United States and turning each of these buildings into a home for aged people or an outpatient clinic. Does anybody know of homes for the aged or clinics that Mrs. O'Hair has established? If Humanism has its way and sway, neither of these services will be needed. Euthanasia will eliminate the aged; mercy killings will remove the need for caring for the sick, infirm and diseased regardless of age! Mrs. O'Hair spoke in these remarks as a real Humanist. She just did not reveal all the implications of the sinful system when it once gets into full, infamous swing.

Those who delve very deeply into a study of Humanism will confront with frequency three common elements. They are: (1) an adamant rejection of the supernatural plus all religious authority; (2) making the welfare of man in **this life** as the one and only supreme goal; (3) that science has the final say and ultimate answer to all problems faced by man. Consideration of these fundamental factors should convince every intelligent person as to why there can be **no** compatibility between the aims and purposes of Humanism and the fundamentals of the Christian faith.

History of Humanism

Though its dormant principles had been long at work in human hearts, yet as a distinct movement it originated and emerged among the Sophists, Greek philosophers, about 500 B.C. or close to 2,500 years ago. This was roughly the same era of time in which Haggai and Zechariah lived and worked as an aged and young prophet respectively among God's returned people in Jerusalem and Judaea. The foundations of Humanism were already laid when Ezra, Nehemiah, Esther and Malachi lived and functioned representatively as priestly scribe, wall builder, Persian Queen and final Old Testament prophet during the fifth century. Protagoras, 485-415 B.C., taught that man is the measure of all things and that contradictory assertions are true. Modern Humanism still rests squarely upon these two primary foundational rocks. It is far beyond human calculation to sum up just how deeply modern man has been influenced by these two deeply ingrained concepts. Even religious people have been brainwashed in these two realms. The second of the two Humanist concepts goes a long, long way in aiding us to see how the rank and file religionist of our day can listen to five different preachers who contradict each other coming and going and yet he contends that all five are men of God and each is called to preach his particular brand of religion. In its initial stages Humanism laid well the foundation that man is **the** authority, that outside him there is no recognized authority and that there is no such thing as a well defined and definitive body of objective truth to which man owes supreme allegiance.

The second great wave of Humanism came with the 14th century movement known as the Renaissance. This was the self-styled "rebirth of learning" that helped to end a thousand years of Dark Ages that the world had known since about the time of Rome's demise in 476 A.D. This movement called for a vigorous revival of the Greek classics, a restoration of Protagoras' principles and a growing and dominant rejection of so much ecclesiastical emphasis upon man's soul and another world. It called for a deeper emphasis upon man as a creature of this world and this one alone. The Humanists of this period were not nearly as militant in atheism and infidelity as modern Humanists are. Yet they laid the foundation upon which modern Humanists have built their secular system of man's rise and God's demise in human thought.

The third great wave of Humanism has been the latter half of the nineteenth century and nearly all the twentieth century. This has been the time era in which there has been a general acceptance of organic evolution triggered by Darwin's publishing of ORIGIN OF SPECIES in 1859, by the sweeping effects of secularism, the world-wide effects of Marxian Communism which has given a military arm of nuclear power for atheism and the greatly accelerated attacks that have been made against God, Christ, the Bible and New Testament Christianity.

Humanism has done its share of harm and injury to the eternal interests of man's soul in each of these three general eras of time. Surely though no informed student of Humanism will debate or doubt but that the third and latest wave has had its greatest impact upon the world. There are several reasons for this. (1) As a movement it is becoming more and more organized than it was in its earliest emerging origins. (2) It has succeeded in convincing millions that it is the sophisticated **in** for modern man. Brother

Guy N. Woods has called it the sophisticated form of militant atheism for our day. (3) It pleases modern man who wishes to be removed from any and all forms of absolute morality. It allows modern people to be sexually permissive with no fears of hell hanging over their heads while so engaged. Paul said of some in his age, "There is no fear of God before their eyes" (Rom. 3:18). This is eminently true of Humanism in our era. (5) It allows man to become his own god and to chart his own course through life. (6) It removes any allegiance owed a Creator or Maker on high. (7) It enables man to live it up today with no fears for any of his moral and religious transgressions. In view of all this we can with ease observe why Humanism and the Bible have no common affinity at all. The two systems are in a life and death struggle for the minds of men, for the hearts of humanity.

The Humanist Manifesto — I — 1933

This daring document was published and signed forty-eight years ago — 1933. Among those who affixed their signatures to it were educators, philosophers and liberal theologians. Included among the signers was John Dewey, an avowed Socialist and one who has influenced American education more than any modern American. He is frequently called the "father of progressive education." He should be styled the "father of the demise of real education in America." We currently reap the results of many of his educational policies that he pawned off upon the unsuspecting American educational public. Among its adamant affirmations were: (1) the eternality of matter; (2) man's evolution by purely natural means; (3) that all religion has socially evolved; (4) that man only has the here and now (this life) in which to live; (5) that science is our real Saviour; (6) that all religious institutions must be changed; and (7) that man is all there is in helping himself to reach his potential, to fulfill the quest of his dreams and to turn his aspirations into current realities. Its daring denials and blasphemous beliefs stated explicitly and implicitly included: (1) a total rejection of Biblical creation as portrayed by Moses in Genesis 1 and 2; (2) that man possesses no soul but is simply matter in motion; (3) there is no divinely derived religion from God; (4) there is no God, no Christ, no Spirit and no inspired, infallible, all authoritative Bible; (5) that no ultimate good is found in the august and infinite being known as God; (6) there is neither objective good nor objective evil; (7) heaven is not for real; (8) there will be no eternal Gehenna for the unrighteous; (9) worship and prayer are rejected and are classed as just a waste of valuable time that more profitably could be spent in helping man to reach his social potential.

Appearing as it did in the midst of a crippling and world-wide depression and soon to be followed by the holocaust of World War II, it did not make the impact on human thought and human deeds that its dreamy signers had anticipated. But, unfortunately, the document and its poisonous principles did not die. Would God it had the day it was signed by these godless men.

Humanist manifesto — II — 1973

This was simply a militant update and reaffirmation of the document signed forty years before. It was just a new generation of Humanists who were wedded to man's deification and God's demise as their past counterparts had been four decades earlier with the initial document. The signers were different; the sentiments followed basically the same skeptical stance as that which composed document Number One. (1) It declared theism with its faith in Deity and a God who hears prayers as all archaic and outmoded. Modern man no longer needs this religious crutch for his weaknesses if indeed he has weaknesses!! (2) Any and all emphasis upon salvation from sin diverts man from engaging in socially profitable services. Such emphasis is declared to be harmful and injurious to man. It is not just a waste of time but actually is hurting man in the long run to be a Bible reader, a prayer petitioner or a worshipper of God Almighty. (3) Document Two declares quite adamantly and militantly that there is NO God, NO salvation, NO heaven and NO hell. (4) Any religion that touches spiritual interests (the soul or spirit of man) is classed as actually engaged in a disservice to mankind. (5) Faith in heaven and fear of hell are illusory in nature and do signal harm to all who embrace such. (6) They contend that this life is all there is. When man dies, he dies all over. Like Rover the dog, nothing survives his demise. Humanism is as hollow as hollow can be in bringing any real value into the heart of the human personality. (7) Man is matter in motion and will soon return **wholly** to dust. (8) Quite arrogantly and very militantly the second document denies there is any credible evidence of life subsequent to death. This amounts to the calling of our Saviour an outright liar in Luke 20 when he spoke of God as the God of the living and not of the dead and that Abraham, Isaac and Jacob, long dead physically when God spoke to Moses at the Burning Bush incident, yet lived spiritually. This is what Humanism thinks of our Redeemer! (9) With almost an air of infallibility they affirm that science has proved evolution to be so. By such overwhelming proofs they contend that any notion of a "ghost in a machine" or a soul that can leave the body and remain alive is now totally annihilated.

Brother Dan Jenkins has summed up both of these documents rather succinctly by suggesting that Humanism denies: (1) "The Deity of God; (2) The Inspiration of the Bible; (3) The Divinity of Jesus; (4) The existence of the Soul; (5) Life after Death; (6) The Reality of Sin; (7) Salvation and Heaven; (8) Damnation and Hell; (9) Creation." On the other side of the infidelic ledger he states that Humanism believes in: (1) "No distinct roles for male and female; (2) Sexual freedom for all; (3) Premarital sex; (4) Homosexuality; (5) Incest; (6) Abortion; (7) Mercy killings; (8) Evolution." Brother Jenkins offers these summary statements, "The next time you read a magazine, visit a movie, watch television, listen to a talk show remember the chart above. Humanist philosophy is simply an attitude of life that centers on human interests and values, and advocates that human dignity comes from self-realization of one's own worth. It stands diametrically opposite to the Divine teaching that man's values and advancements come from following our holy God."[5]

Humanism and New Testament Christianity are poles apart. Like the proverbial east and west — never shall the twain meet except in a militant confrontation, in a life and death struggle for the minds of men, for the hearts of humanity. If Humanism wins the battle or the warfare, which is really a better term, the world is headed fast for another spiritual period of "Dark Ages" that could well dwarf what the world knew from the fifth century to the fourteenth century of this A.D. era. Let us pray and pray fervently and persistently that blind eyes and deaf ears of our ignorant world may yet be awakened and unstopped to the dangers that lie within Humanism.

The Fruits of Humanism

Movements can be appraised much more accurately if we look at the fruits they inevitably produce. The tree of Humanism has a number of branches. The political branch of Humanism produces Marxists or Communists. The biological branch of Humanism that attempts to deal with origins produces the fruit of organic evolution. The religious branch of Humanism produces modernism, theological liberalism and ultimately atheism. The sexual limb of Humanism produces free love, reckless and irresponsible sex including premarital sex, adultery or extramartial sex, homosexuality, incest, bestiality, obscenity, pornography, etc. The ethical limb of Humanism produces abortion on demand and euthanasia (so-called mercy killings). The historical branch of Humanism produced the ancient Greek emphasis upon man as the major measure of all things and later produced the Renaissance. The scientific limb of Humanism produces Science as man's Saviour, as humanity's god. The ultimate fruit produced by all these Humanist limbs will populate hell with a vast number of patrons and practitioners.

The Total Incompatibility Between Humanism and the Bible

In **no** sense can it be the Bible **and** Humanism. In every sense it must be the Bible **Versus** Humanism. Humanism denies creation. Genesis 1:1 declares that in the beginning God created heaven and earth. Genesis 1:26, 27 affirms that man is made in God's image and after Jehovah's likeness. Genesis 2 details the creation of man and woman. God made man upright (Eccles. 7:29). God made man; man did not make himself (Psalm 100:3). Man is wonderfully and fearfully made (Psalm 139:14). Jesus said man was created or made at the beginning of creation (Matt. 19:4, 5; Mark 10:6). We are Jehovah's offspring (Acts 17:28, 29).

Humanism denies man a soul. Solomon affirms man's possession of a spirit (Eccles. 12:7). Jesus stressed its transcendent value (Matt. 16:26). Jesus based an argument with skeptical Sadducees upon the fact that Abraham, Isaac and Jacob yet lived in their spirits when God spoke to Moses at the Burning Bush (Luke 20; Ex. 3). Physical death results when spirit and body separate (James 2:26).

Humanism contends that man is the measure of all things. The Bible teaches that God is far superior to man (Isa. 55:8, 9). Jehovah — not man — is the high, holy and lofty one who majestically inhabits eternity (Isa. 57:15). Man pales into deep inferiority when he seeks to compare himself with Paul's marvelous portrait of Jesus in Philippians 2:5-11 or the picture drawn to perfection in Colossians 1:13-29. God — not man — is the giver of all perfect gifts; he is the Father of lights; he is the unchanging one — not finite, fickle man (James 1:17).

Humanism teaches that man can chart well his own course and determine prudently his own direction. Jeremiah 10:23 denies this most adamantly. Man's way which seems right at first lands him ultimately in death (Prov. 14:12; 16:25). Judges 17:6 and 21:25 speak of man when he did what was right in his own eyes. In between these identical texts are portrayed some of the most calloused crimes of the countless centuries.

Humanism denies man needs redemption. The Bible says Jesus came to save (Matt. 1:21; Luke 19:10). The blood of Calvary is essential for our redemption (Col. 1:20). Paul was sent to preach redemption in Christ (I Cor. 1:17ff).

Humanism denies absolute morality. Galatians 5:19-23 and Revelation 21:8 affirm absolute morality.

Humanism finds its best blessings in glorified humanity. The Bible places the greatest of blessings in Christ (Eph. 1:3; James 1:17).

Humanism denies the Bible Doctrine of Final Things. Acts 1:9-11 establishes the second coming. John 5:28, 29 establishes the general resurrection of all the dead. Final judgment is set forth as a future reality in Hebrews 9:27. Acts 17:31 does the same. Eternal heaven and hell are portrayed in the final pronouncement of Matthew 25:46.

Why Humanism Must Be Exposed

(1) It is anti-God. (2) It is anti-Christ. (3) It is anti-Spirit. (4) It is anti-Bible. (5) It is anti-Christian. (6) It is anti-gospel. (7) It is anti-moral. (8) It is anti-ethical. (9) It is anti-spiritual. (10) It is anti-heaven. (11) It is anti-hell. (12) It is anti-human when man is considered as a being of both body and soul or spirit.

Conclusion

Christians must **never** call themselves Humanists. We must know its errors and expose relentlessly each of them.

Footnotes

1. P. D. Wilmeth, *The New Manifesto II, Voice of Freedom,* Vol. XXVI, No. 7-8, July-August, 1978, p. 99.
2. Rita Rhodes Ward, *Contemporary Humanism, Ibid.,* 101.
3. *Ibid.,* 102.
4. J. D. Thomas, "Humanism," *Gospel Advocate,* Vol. CXXIII, No. 2, January 22, 1981, pp. 46, 51.
5. Dan Jenkins, *The Glendale Guide,* Vol. 3, No. 7, February 22, 1981.

CHAPTER 37
THE DOCTRINES AND MILITANCY OF ISLAM

Andrew M. Connally

Introduction

The **militancy** of Islam is well known to careful students of Islam. It became the power whereby millions bowed to the sword and embraced the heresies of Mohammed and his followers for generations.

Of late we have seen three classic illustrations of Islam's militancy in our world: the three-day seige in Washington, D.C. by militants in which people were wounded and killed, the fifty-two American hostages taken by Ayatollah Khomeini's thugs and held over a year for ransom and, finally, the shooting of the Roman Catholic Pope by a Muslim terrorist. All such acts are sanctioned by Ayatollah Khomeini in his book *"Sayings of Khomeini"* in which he advocated a "holy war," with all Muslims uniting against the Western governments of the world.

Islam is a force to be reckoned with both **politically** and **religiously** in our world today. Unless Islam is stopped, millions will turn to her and her error. She is militant, aggressive and evil. She cannot be ignored; she will not go away. She is strong and becoming stronger every day. We, as Christians, must meet every error known. Islam is worthy of our best efforts. We must learn her doctrines and meet her advocates. The Bible has the answer and we must stand for the truth and oppose this great error.

A Challenge To Islam

No one can deny the Bible and the Koran exist. They are here. No man can deny they each depict a great religious leader. No one can deny they both claim to be from God. Our problem is to decide which one really is the true, the last prophet of God and which book is God's true and last revelation. They cannot both be from God for they contradict in numerous places as this study will show.

For many years Muslims have felt they could believe in Christ and Mohammed. They believe that both the Bible and the Koran came from God. Seldom has anyone dared say you cannot accept Mohammed and Christ though they do not agree. Seldom has anyone shown that the Bible and the Koran teach conflicting doctrines. Truth is always consistent. It never contradicts itself. If it can be shown that Christ and Mohammed taught conflicting things, if it can be shown the Bible and the Koran disagree, then an honest person must make a choice if he is to remain honest. No longer can we believe both came from God.

You must look to the books themselves for your answer. You must, one day, meet God in judgment and be judged by the decision you have made.

May God help you to make the right choice for you will be responsible for what you do.

The Bible Presents Jesus Christ in Prophecy

1. Man cannot know the future; only God can foretell history. The Bible clearly foretold the coming of Christ. This alone would be enough to prove the Bible is the word of God. Hundreds of years before Christ was born the Old Testament writers wrote concerning Christ's coming. The fact that the Old Testament was complete several hundred years before Christ was born, yet so perfectly points to Him that in **all** points it fulfills the predictions, is proof conclusive that God inspired the ancient writers.

2. Moses himself said, "A prophet shall the Lord God raise up unto you from among your brethren, like unto me; to him shall ye harken in all things whatsoever he shall speak unto you. And it shall be, that every soul that shall not hearken to that prophet, shall be utterly destroyed from among the people" (Deut. 18:15-19). The apostles applied this prophecy to Jesus Christ in Acts 3:18-26. This was never applied to Mohammed and could not so apply. The "prophet" spoken of here was to come "from among your brethren," meaning the Jews; Mohammed was never a Jew! Moses further said the prophet would be "like unto me," meaning like himself. Moses was both the lawgiver and the mediator. Mohammed was never a mediator, yet Christ was both. The New Testament plainly says, "For there is one God, one mediator also between God and men, himself man, Christ Jesus" (I Tim. 2:5). The fulfillment of this prophecy alone would show the necessity of listening to Jesus Christ as God's final prophet for **no other prophet was foretold!** And Moses spoke these words hundreds of years before Christ came.

3. Everything about Jesus' life and character were foretold in prophecy: the place of his birth (Micah 5:2) Bethlehem was fulfilled (Matt. 2:1); to be God's son (Psm. 2:7) and God so declared Christ (Matt. 17:5); a divinely appointed messenger to announce Jesus' coming (Mal. 3:1, 4:5) which John the Baptist fulfilled (Lk. 1:17); to enter Jerusalem in triumph (Zach. 9:9) but should be rejected by the Jewish people (Isa. 53:1-3) which did happen (Jn. 1:11; Matt. 27:22-23); His betrayal and trial were foretold (Zach. 11:12-13; Isa. 53:7), the crucifixion and burial (Isa. 53:8; Psm. 22:15-18) and it happened just this way (Jn. 19:23-24); but He was to rise from the dead (Isa. 53:10-11; Psm. 16:10; Psm. 2:6-7), He was to ascend on High (Psm. 68:18; 24:7), He was to be crowned with power and glory (Dan. 7:13-14), Jesus arose the third day from the dead (Lk. 24:1-6), He ascended into heaven (Acts 1:10-11), He sat down on God's right hand to rule as prophet, priest and king (Heb. 1:1-14). Dear reader, remember all this was prophesied hundreds of years before Christ was born and fulfilled in every detail just as the prophets foretold. Remember the books are here. Witnesses have testified it happened as it is written. The apostles all died for their faith. Not one of them ever denied what they had written. They believed what they wrote. Why don't you?

The Bible Presents Jesus and His Claims

1. Jesus Christ cannot be ignored! His friends love him and His enemies hate him, but all must acknowledge the fact of His existence. The crucial question is, could mere human wisdom have conceived and depicted such a person?

(1) Jesus demands an explanation. He also demands an attitude from us. Every individual develops an attitude toward Him upon which depends the eternal destiny of the soul. As Christ once asked His disciples, "Who say ye that I am?"

(2) A consideration of His character helps to answer the question. He is the world's only universal character. All men, even Mohammed, confessed they are sinners. But Jesus confessed no sin and challenged His adversaries to convict Him of sin (Jn. 8:46). Not even the Koran attributes sin to Jesus, yet it does to all other prophets, including Mohammed!

2. Jesus claimed equality with God. Time and time again Jesus claimed He and the Father were one (Jn. 5:17-18; 19-20; 22-29). He testified He would raise the dead and judge them (Jn. 5:22-29); He declared that to see Him is to see the Father (Jn. 14:7-10); He confessed Himself to be the Christ, "The son of the blessed" (Mk. 14:61-64).

3. Jesus accepted worship: Jesus taught that God only should be worshipped (Matt. 4:10; Jn. 4:23), but, during His ministry He accepted worship from a leper (Matt. 8:2), a ruler of the synagogue (Matt. 9:18) and a blind man He healed (Jn. 9:35-38). After His resurrection, from the disciples He accepted worship (Matt. 28:9) and from Thomas accepted his confession of Lordship and Godhood (Jn. 20:26-29). From this we can conclude Jesus made Himself equal with God for only God was to be worshipped.

4. Jesus claimed sinlessness and challenged His enemies to prove otherwise (Jn. 8:46). Yet, Jesus condemned self-righteousness (Lk. 18:9-14). Therefore, He was the Christ or a self-righteous hypocrite!

5. Jesus claimed to be the only savior of mankind (Jn. 14:6) and stated, "No man comes to the Father except by me." He claimed His blood should seal the covenant between man and God and that His blood would procure the remission of man's sins (Matt. 20:28; 26:28). The apostles proudly proclaimed that salvation was found only in the name of Christ (Acts 4:12).

6. The apostles claimed Christ was the full revelation of God (Col. 1:15; Jn. 14:7-9; Heb. 1:3). This fulfilled Isaiah's prophecy concerning the coming Christ (Isa. 9:6). The apostles claimed Christ reconciled man back to God (Col. 1:20-23). They claimed Christ was the fulness of God Himself (Col. 1:19; 2:9). They said Christ in us is our hope (Col. 1:24). They affirmed that in Christ "all the treasures of wisdom and knowledge" are found (Col. 2:3). If all the treasures of wisdom and knowledge are found in Christ, this leaves none found in Mohammed or anyone else! No one can read these passages and doubt that God affirms Jesus is all any man could ever want or need for salvation. You may reject and refuse to accept it, but you cannot deny the Bible teaches it! The truth is neither Mohammed nor

Islam can improve on or add anything to man that Jesus and the Bible has not already supplied. The fact is both Mohammed and Islam fall far, far short of what the Christ and the Bible expect of the Christian. Why settle for something inferior to the best? Paul affirmed that Jesus was God's final prophet (Heb. 1:1-3). Nowhere does the Bible allow room for another. Jesus was the "son of God" and "if the son sets you free, then shall you be free indeed" (Jn. 8:36).

7. The moral glory of Jesus Christ as set forth in the four gospels cannot be the product of the unaided human intellect; only the Spirit of God is competent to execute this matchless portrait of the Son of God. His relation to sin was sinlessness; His relation to God's law was perfect obedience; His relation to the Kingdom of God was King (spiritual, Jn. 18:36; Matt. 4:17; 6:10; Mk. 1:14, 15; Matt. 7:22; Lk. 23:3); His relation to providence is ruler and sustainer (Heb. 1:3); His relation to the forces of nature was complete controller; His relation to mankind was Savior, Christ, Messiah; His relation to God was complete fellowship, "God in the flesh."

Now consider the application of this argument: Nothing is more obvious than, every effect requires an adequate cause. How did the evangelists solve this mighty problem of humanity with such perfect originality and precision? Only two answers are possible: They had before them the personal and historical Christ....and they wrote by inspiration of the Holy Spirit of God!

The Bible Presents Jesus Christ and Miracles

Miracles are a definite part of Biblical teaching in both Old and New Testaments. They are inextricably interwoven into God's revelation of Himself. As the word of God, the Bible stands or falls at this very point. Either miracles occurred as actual happenings as recorded in the Bible and the Bible is the word of God or they did not occur and it is not the word of God, a special divine revelation. There can be no compromise in the matter. Christianity originates in and with Jesus and Jesus is definitely associated with miracles. Miracles are aids to faith. They come in with decisive effect to convince those tho are impressed by the moral evidence that they are not deceived and that God is in reality speaking through men. According to the New Testament histories, it was in this light that miracles were regarded by Jesus. Where there was no spiritual preparation, no dawning faith, he refused to perform miracles. The purpose of the miracles is stated in the sentence spoken by Jesus when he summoned Lazarus to come forth from the grave, "That they may know thou hast sent me." Jesus' miracles prove He was the "Son of God."

The Bible Presents Jesus and the Resurrection

The resurrection of Jesus Christ is mentioned more than one hundred times in the New Testament and is the very foundation of Christianity. Without the bodily resurrection of Jesus Christ His life and work are meaningless. If the New Testament cannot be believed at this point, how could it be believed at any point? The religion of Christ is a religion of faith, but faith relies upon testimony and testimony must rest on facts. The fundamental fact of Christian faith is the resurrection of Christ! If Christ has not been raised from the dead, then our faith is vain, for there is no fact believed, but only falsehood and if Christ's resurrection is not a fact, then we have no hope He can raise us (I Cor. 15:12-19) and we are yet in our sins. Christ died on the cross for our sins (Matt. 26:28), but He arose to become our High Priest, "After the power of an endless life" (Heb. 7:16); "He ever liveth" (Heb. 7:25); "to make intercession for us." Our hope of the forgiveness of our sins, our hope of the resurrection of our bodies from the grave and death, our hope of God and heaven rests upon the resurrection of Jesus Christ. Reject His resurrection and you are lost, worlds without end!

The Koran Presents the Claims of Mohammed

1. Mohammed claims to be the last and greatest of the prophets. It is said he did not foretell the coming of any other and his law will be in force to the end of the world.

2. Yet, in the Koran Mohammed does not claim to be any more than a man, a prophet, an apostle. On occasions he confessed sin and asked God to forgive him. He is instructed to ask for forgiveness five times. The Koran refers to the sins of all the prophets except Christ. Mohammed did not claim to be a miracle worker; in fact, he said, "God sent me not to work miracles, but to preach." He did not claim to be divine. He did not claim pre-existence. He did not claim to die for men's sins. He did not promise to rise from the dead by the power of God. And nowhere does the Koran make such claims for Mohammed. He is pictured as the prophet and judge.

3. Millions of Muslims believe Mohammed is their perfect example to be obeyed in everything. Thus the example of Mohammed has inflamed Islam and the lives of millions of Muslims. While no doubt some have attained a higher code of conduct than their leader, countless millions fall far short of Mohammed himself. When you realize the moral standards practiced by so many in Islam are so low, we are made to wonder why? The Muslims usually say this is a fault within them and not the fault of Mohammed or the Koran. Yet, when we study the man and his claims and teachings, it is evident that water cannot rise higher than its source; therefore, the source of this weakness is not in them alone but also in their book and in their prophet!

It is evident that Islam started in conscious opposition to Christianity. Yet it has not contributed a single new germinal idea to the religious thought of the world. Surely this is significant.

Consider Islam and the Bible

No doubt Mohammed knew many of the stories of the Old Testament for some of them are repeated in the Koran. Mohammed recognized Christ as a Prophet of Allah. He stated Christ healed the sick, cleansed lepers, and raised the dead. Jesus is called in the Koran the "Spirit of God" and the "Word of God," but Mohammed was bitterly opposed to the term "Son of God" for he probably thought this implied physical sonship. Even today Muslims hate this term and often ask, "Do you think God took a wife and had a son?"

Mohammed misunderstood the teaching of the New Testament on the Trinity (God, Christ and the Holy Spirit). Mohammed thought the Trinity was God, Christ and Christ's mother, Mary. He then condemned Christians for making Jesus and Mary gods along with Allah. The Koran plainly states that Jesus was not crucified. Muslims believe God took Jesus up to heaven and He is alive today in the fourth heaven. They believe that one of Jesus' enemies was crucified by mistake in Christ's place. When Jesus prophesied the coming of the Comforter, the Holy Spirit in John, chapters fourteen, fifteen and sixteen, the Muslims mistakenly apply this to Mohammed. A careful reading of these chapters will show any honest man Jesus was speaking of the Holy Spirit, which God, the Father, would send. When Christians show the contradiction between the Bible and the Koran, and there are multitudes, Muslims deny the Christians have the true gospel, but only a false document which the Christians, themselves, have forged. This is a convenient way to try to deny the Bible, but it is not true, for any man who studies how the Bible came to us, knows it all stands or falls together. You cannot accept a part of it and reject other parts of it. One is forced to realize he must either reject the Bible or the Koran. Both cannot be held together, for it is very evident they contradict each other in many, many places.

Consider Marriage and Divorce

The home is the foundation of all society. Therefore, the laws that regulate marriage, divorce and the home are of the upmost importance. Mohammed was a polygamist. Not only did he practice polygamy, but the Koran encourages it. After the death of Khadijah, his first wife, he married twelve women, one of whom was only seven years old! In the Koran (Sura 4:3) permission is given to Muslims to marry as many as four wives if the husband can act equitably toward them. Polygamy is practiced among many Muslims and often brings dissension and heartache into the family as polygamy always does.

According to Muslim law the man, only, has the right to divorce his wife for any or all causes as he may see fit.

When one considers the low place of women in such a situation, the teachings of Christ become all the more beautiful. Christ granted the right of divorce to either the man or the woman on the grounds of unfaithfulness of their marriage partner (Matt. 5:31-32; 19:1-10). Jesus likewise taught that a man could have only one wife, for if he took a second one or more, he would be guilty of adultery! Jesus' teaching concerning marriage and divorce is infinitely superior to the teaching of Mohammed.

Consider the Holy War

1. It is common knowledge that Mohammed propagated Islam by the sword. His decree was accept Allah or the sword! In Medina, where Mohammed attained prominence as a preacher, ruler and legislator, Mohammed turned against the Jews who refused to accept him as a prophet of God. Finally Mohammed slaughtered thousands of them and banished the rest. Being in need of money, he also attacked the rich caravans of the Meccans as they passed Medina and divided the booty among his followers. This led to bloody wars with the people of Mecca. The Koran (Sura 9:5) authorizes unbelievers to be put to the sword. This was practiced vigorously by Mohammed's followers in Asia and North Africa. Religious warefare is considered a duty for Muslims and many of them long for the day when they will once more be able to conquer non-Muslims and establish Islam as the religion of the world. Muslims believe strongly in the Jehad (Holy War). The Shi'ites say that only the twelfth Iman has authority to proclaim the Holy War (a war in which Muslims unite to fight unbelievers). The Sunnites, who reject the Imans, say their leaders have the authority to proclaim a Jehad. Naturally, all such attempts are doomed to failure because differences of belief and nationality make it impossible for Muslims to act together in such matters. This is an evident failure of Islam.

2. Jesus plainly taught, "My kingdom is not of this world: if my kingdom were of this world, then would my servants fight...but my kingdom is not from hence" (Jn. 18:36). Jesus taught, "Love your enemies, pray for them that persecute you; that ye may be sons of your Father who is in heaven" (Matt. 5:44-45). Isaiah prophesied seven hundred years before Christ was born he would be the "Prince of Peace" (Isa. 9:6). Jesus preached peace; He practiced peace. He taught His followers to "follow after peace with all men, and the sanctification without which no man shall see the Lord" (Heb. 12:14). To any thinking person Christ's life and teaching of peace is infinitely to be preferred over Mohammed's. Mohammed conquered by the sword; Christ conquers with love! Which do you prefer? The real question is, which does God command?

Consider the Resurrection

1. The idea of a future life has great importance in Islam. Most Muslims believe that all will die and then the trumpet will sound and all will be raised to life and then judgment begins. They believe Allah will weigh men in a great pair of balances to determine if their good deeds outweigh their bad deeds. Hence, much emphasis is placed on works of merit in order that they may outweigh the bad deeds at the day of judgment. Also there will be a long, narrow bridge over which all men must pass to reach heaven. The wicked will fall off into Hell. Hell is rightly pictured as a place of fire and torment. Heaven is a place of sensuous delight where there is a pool of wine which does not intoxicate, where beautiful women are found, and beautiful females, called huris, who shall be given to male believers for

their enjoyment. No doubt some Muslims interpret these pictures of future life in a spiritual sense. But to the majority heaven and hell are very material. No doubt this is the reason so little comfort is found in a Muslim home in the hour of death.

2. Only in the resurrection of Christ is the sting of death removed. While Muslims believe in a resurrection, their resurrection is without foundation for they reject the resurrection of Christ. Only Christ rose from the dead to prove He had power over death (Rev. 1:18). To deny this is to deny the cornerstone of Christianity, for everything rests on Christ's resurrection. It is mentioned more than one hundred times in the New Testament. If Christ arose, He can raise us and we have hope. But if Christ did not rise from the dead, we have no hope, our faith is vain and we are yet in our sins, so argues the apostle Paul in I Corinthians the fifteenth chapter, verses twelve through nineteen.

3. Neighbor and friend, you can't have it both ways, either you accept Christ's resurrection and believe and obey Him, or else live and die without hope. Mohammed did not die for you; Christ did! Mohammed was not raised from the dead; Christ was! Christ alone is your only hope of salvation back to the Father (Jn. 14:6).

Consider the Belief in God

1. Islam says, "There is no god but Allah, and Mohammed is his apostle." Muslims place the greatest of emphasis upon monotheism and feel to portray Christ as God is one of the greatest sins. God is pictured as one and absolute. He is transcendent. His will is entirely arbitrary and can be changed at his pleasure in a contrary direction. The Koran says, "Allah leads astray whom he pleases and guides whom he pleases and no one knows the hosts of the Lord save himself. And every man's destiny have we fastened on his neck." Naturally with such a belief men are fatalists believing in Kismet or predestination. This in a very real sense explains the reason for the despair of so many in Muslim lands and contributes to their backward conditions. Such a view destroys initiative and a desire for improvement. For whatever happens, it is "the will of Allah." Naturally, such a view of God makes him an unknown being, for who knows how he will act next?

2. Allah is not pictured as our Father, which is the greatest concept in the New Testament. To the Muslim the Koran rarely mentions the love of God. The most important verse being (3:29), "If ye love God, then follow me: God will love you and forgive your sins, for God is forgiving, merciful...God loveth not the unbelieving." "Verily God misleadeth whom he will, and guideth whom he will" (7:178; 35:8).

3. How different a picture this is of the God of the Bible. From a study of the Bible, Allah is not the God of the Bible! Jesus revealed the Father, God (Jn. 14:9-11). Jesus is the "express image of God's substance" (Heb. 1:3). Jesus and the "Father are One" (Jn. 10:30). To reject Christ is to reject God (Lk. 10:16). The God of the Bible is "One," but there are three personalities, God, the Father, Christ, the Son and the Holy Spirit that

make up this "One God." It is simple to illustrate by an egg. An egg is one, yet it takes three parts to make this oneness. There is the yoke, the white and the shell, yet only one egg. So it is with the "One God." The Bible pictures three beings that make up one deity.

4. The greatest concept of God in the Bible is one of "our heavenly Father." The word Father relating to God, is found more than two hundred and fifty times in the New Testament alone. This Father of the Bible "so loved the world, He gave His only begotten son, that whosoever believeth should not perish" (Jn.3:16). Allah is said to be kind to men, but he does nothing for their salvation that cost him anything. Christians could never have loved God, but that first He loved them (I Jn. 5:7-11). Most Muslims do not love God; they fear Allah and may even try to obey him, but there are no real grounds from which love can spring. Allah is pictured as judge. The great Holiness of God, even as pictured in the Old Testament is foreign to the Koran. The God of the Bible allowed His only Son to die a terrible death in order that we might be saved. Such sacrifice and love begets love in our heart as nothing else could possibly do. The important thing is not the belief that God is one, for Satan and the demons believe God is one and tremble (James 2:19), but the important thing is to understand the nature of God and His love for us, for this produces the same kind of love in our hearts and lives. The Bible plainly says, "Herein was the love of God manifested in us that God hath sent His only begotten Son into the world that we might live through Him. Herein is love, not that we loved God, but that He loved us, and sent His Son to be the propitiation for our sins. Beloved, if God so loved us, we ought to love one another" (I Jn. 5:9-11).

Now Consider the Weakness in Islam

1. Mohammed was arbitrary. Mohammed could be very vindictive. This is easily seen by the thousands slaughtered first at Medina and later in the multitudes of wars which followed. On occasions Mohammed could also be generous and benevolent. He was arbitrary. There are evident contradictory elements in his character. He could revenge himself upon his enemies when he wished and pardon them at other times. He was a domineering and warring autocrat. He often prescribed war and advocated violence toward non-Muslims. Yet, he could remark, "There is no compulsion in religion" and allow the conquered, on occasion, to pay the Jizyah (tribute). Mohammed was arbitrary. The reason for Mohammed's being arbitrary is easily understood in the light of the Koran for it pictures Allah as being arbitrary. The Koran contains a number of passages that affirm the absolute arbitrariness of Allah, "He guides whomsoever He pleases." Equally explicit are statements that Allah misleads certain people. Indeed, numerous passages in the Koran state explicitly and conjointly that Allah both guides and misguides, both punishes and forgives, according to his own inscritible, unquestionable good pleasure (3:124; 5:43; 6:39, 125; 13:27; 14:4; 17:97, etc.). On the whole Allah is represented as a magnificent, opulent, irresistible world-potentate

— an Arab Sheikh glorified and magnified to cosmic proportions.

2. Islam's reliance upon force is a weakness. Perhaps no other religion in the world has used as much force and violence to propagate its faith. At the death of Mohammed his successors, the four Caliphs, had no hesitation in spreading Islam by the sword. Even as Mohammed subjugated Arabia by the sword, so they conquered Syria, Palestine, Mesopotania and Egypt. Ultimately Islam was spread by the sword over Spain, Turkey, India and a part of China. It does no good for a Muslim to deny these facts or say it no longer is being done. Mohammed, their founder, was a man of violence. He preached and practiced war and the Koran still authorizes it today.

3. Islam's belief in fatalism (Kismet) is a weakness. Any observer can tell a tree by its fruits and the nations where Islam holds sway are among the most backward on earth. With the belief that whatever happens it is the will of Allah, it could scarcely be different. Islam offers no real challenge to a man to improve himself or his lot in life. It fatalistically accepts whatever happens as the predestined will of Allah which nothing can change. It is foreordained according to the unchangeable decrees of Allah. This is the fifth article of faith of the Muslim creed. If this were true, which it is not, then Allah would be the author of evil. This, by the way, is a doctrine that most Muslim theologians hold. There are many schools of thought that deny entirely the free will of man. This fatalistic philosophy of life that stems from this doctrine is all too evident in the daily life of individuals over the whole world of Islam. Even the worst calamities are often accepted with no more than stoic shrugs of the shoulders. This, beyond doubt, has much to do with the static condition and lack of progress in Muslim lands.

4. Another weakness of Islam is seen in its excessively sensuous future-Paradise. Paradise, with abundant pleasures for the senses, is pictured awaiting the pious believers in Allah. More than a score of passages, almost without exception, refer to gardens and flowing rivers, luxurious food and ease, and varied sensuous pleasures. Such passages pale into insignificance when compared to the Bible's picture of heaven for spiritual beings. One is earthly, sensual and purely fleshly. The other is spiritual and appeals to the most noble aspects of our spiritual nature.

5. Islam's low estimate of women offers a further weakness. This is a very serious weakness. Mohammed's attitude toward women and the laws of marriage are a constant source of enbarrassment to modern day educated Muslims. Certainly, the sacred scriptures of no other religion intimate that the undesirable wives of the founder might be divorced with the prospect of his obtaining more and better wives through the help of God. The Koran states, "It may be, if he divorced you all that God will give him in exchange consorts better than you, who submit their wills, who believe, who are devout, who turn to God in repentance, who worship in humility, who travel for faith and fact, previously married or virgins" (66:5).

(1) He married Zainah, the divorced wife of an adopted son, Zaird and justified his action by a special dispensation revealed to him by Allah, "that it might not be a crime in the faithful to marry the wives of their adopted

sons, when they have settled the affair concerning them. And the behest of God is to be performed. No blame attacheth to the Prophet where God hath given him a permission" (33:37-38).

(2) Mohammed set four wives at a time as the limit for Muslims, yet, this limit was removed later for him alone by a special dispensation, "Oh Prophet! we have made lawful to thee thy wives to whom thou hast paid their dowers; and these whom thy right hand possesses out the prisoners of war whom God has assigned to thee; and daughters of they paternal uncles and aunts, and daughters of they maternal uncles and aunts, who migrated from Mecca with thee; and any believing woman who dedicated her soul to the Prophet if the Prophet wishes to wed her; this only for thee, and not for the believers at large" (33:50-51).

(3) Concubines are legal wives married for a fixed period of time, be it a day or fifty years, and the marriage tie is dissolved when the time expires. Mohammed absolved himself from his oath to have nothing to do with his concubine, Mary, and was extricated from the trouble thereby caused among some of his wives. Such a use of women is degrading and demeaning to say the very least. One of the things in Christianity which most deeply impresses Muslims is the high standard which Christ has set for marriage, and the love and the harmony which is found in true Christian homes.

6. Islam is weakened by its inconsistent animism, which depicts jinns, devils, the Kaaba stone and repetitious prayers. The Jinn, genii are a group of spirits midway between men and angels; they are considered both good and evil. Some of them have "submitted themselves" and thereby have become Muslims. One of the jinn is the devil. Like the jinns, the Kaaba stone figures greatly in Islam. The chief holy place in Mecca is the Kaaba, a square stone building, twelve yards long, ten yards broad and fifteen yards high. In one corner is the black stone about seven inches in diameter, possibly a meteorite, which attracted pagan pilgrims to Mecca many centuries **before** the shrine was turned into a center of Islamic pilgrimage. Muslims still circle the Kaaba seven times, an ancient rite of the shrine. Mohammed took over both Kaaba and the black stone and centered his new faith upon them, an obvious concession to popular animistic custom. The pilgrimage and the kissing of the stone continues as an Islamic ritual and is linked with further visits to such holy places as the prophet's tomb at Medina.

7. Wherever one goes throughout the Muslim world he will see men saying the five stated prayers prescribed by their religion. Each adult is required to pray at least three times daily, and in most places five times a day. The prayers consist mainly of passages or expressions taken from the Koran, and the same words may be repeated as many as ten times in one day's worship. Since it is not lawful to recite the prayers in any language except Arabic, the great majority of Muslims in lands where Arabic is not spoken understand virtually nothing of what they say. But according to Islamic teaching, it is not necessary for the worshippers to understand what they say. This may account for teaching the children their prayers by

rote memory long before they understand the Arabic words. For most Muslims this is a mechanical act with almost no moral or spiritual value to the worshipper. They are taught that to repeat the words correctly is sufficient, and saying the prayers is a very valuable work of merit which will atone for many sins. Sometimes at the close of the formal Arabic prayer the worshipper makes a brief request of God in his own language for something he needs. But prayer such as a Christian knows, that is, free and joyous expression between a child of God and his heavenly Father, is almost unknown in Islam. This may account for many in the educated classes who seldom perform the duty of worship.

8. Perhaps the greatest weakness in Islam is the pathetic weaknesses in Mohammed the founder's moral character. Mohammed's conduct is held up for minute imitation. Mohammed is considered the perfect man. He is to be imitated and his example followed in everything — in eating, in the use of the toothpick, in dress, in the manner of caring for the hair and beard, in marriage and the treatment of wives, in the treatment of friends and enemies, in worship, and in government and in war. Already in this study we have seen he is arbitrary, vindictive and advocated and practiced violence toward non-Muslims. Any man who would marry twelve women among whom was a seven year old child, is sensual. (It may well be true Mohammed did not consummate this marriage until two or three years later, still it is a disgrace!) His descriptions of Paradise for the faithful further proves this sensual trait. His decided prejudice for man in marriage shows a genuine lack of consideration for women. His repeated revelations which always approved his conduct even though denying the same rights to other Muslims shows a selfishness that is undeniable. Marriage is a classic example. To any one who will take the trouble to compare the lives of Christ and Mohammed, he is bound to exclaim: Mohammed was a sinful man; Christ is the sinless God!

Now Consider the Strength of Christianity

The strength of Christianity is its perfect example, Jesus Christ. No real blame could ever attach itself to Him. No man could ever equal His life. No man could ever improve upon His teaching. No man can overthrow His miracles. No man can disprove His resurrection. No man could ever die for a more noble cause. No revelation could ever give us a greater concept of God, righteousness, justice and holiness. No prophet could ever more carefully obey the law of God. No being could ever more clearly reveal the Father. No person could ever challenge the world with a greater moral concept than the rebirth of the human soul. No religion reaches as deep into the human heart. No concept ever soars higher than the Paradise revealed. Nothing is lacking for this life or immortality in the teachings of Christ. Nothing could be more explicit than the coming judgment and the retribution of a just God. And nothing is more plain than the salvation of every man depending on his obedience to Christ and the rejection of all others.

Jesus said, "Except you believe I am He, you will die in your sins" (Jn. 8:24). Jesus said, "Except you repent, you shall perish" (Lk. 13:3-5). Jesus also said, "Except you are born of the water and the spirit you cannot enter into the Kingdom of heaven" (Jn. 3:1-5).

"These are written that ye may believe that Jesus is the Christ, the Son of God, and that believing ye may have life in His name" (Jn. 20:31).

Conclusion

Jesus has unsheathed the sword of the spirit against all error (Matt. 25; Jude 3; I Pet. 3:15); therefore, we need to challenge this ancient and evil error to protect our world from its wrath and the ultimate wrath of God against all error. May God help us.

CHAPTER 38
THE THREAT OF HINDUISM TO THE SPREAD OF THE GOSPEL OF CHRIST

Ira Y. Rice, Jr.

To those of us brought up in the churches of Christ in the United States, where we always have been taught to worship the one true and living God, who is Lord of heaven and earth and the Creator of all things, the concepts of Hinduism are strange almost beyond all comprehension. There being an estimated thirty-three million deities that the various types of Hindus worship as gods, at first instance there seems to be no way to come to any orderly understanding of what appears just a religious hodge-podge. Surely Hinduism must be the extreme limit to the religious lengths to which mankind will go, when "suffered...to walk in their own ways," as mentioned by the apostle Paul to those at Lystra, in Acts 14:16.

Strangest of all, perhaps, is the fact that Hinduism does not appear to have had any single originator or founder. It is a religion that seemingly had its rise in the myths, legends and folk-lore of ancient India, gathered sweep and momentum as it snowballed across the centuries, and finally has come to dominate the lives of some two-thirds of India's more than 600 million people.

When those of Aryan stock left their homeland near the Caspian Sea about 1,500 B.C., traversing the passes of the Hindu Kush and began populating the great sub-continent now known as India, as they wandered their new domain, they mingled their own native beliefs and started worshipping the sun which gave them fire and light, the air that they breathed, the blue depths of space overhead, the earth beneath their feet as well as the very water that they drank.

As time passed by, they began to record this supposedly sacred lore in writings known as **Vedas,** extolling the gifts of nature as Gods. And yet, from among all these multitudinous deities, there gradually emerged the central idea of Hinduism, the concept of Brahman, the Supreme Being, the God above all gods, as the source of universal life. And although Hindu worshippers might seek some special favor from any of enormous multitudes of deities, yet each god worshipped was deemed to be but another aspect of all-embracing "thousand-headed" Brahman.

Although preserved orally for centuries, the Vedas gradually were commited to writing along with ritual texts, commentaries, and philosophical discourses called the **Upanishads,** which today form the sacred scriptures of Hinduism. From a study of these scriptures as well as the thinking of later writers, Hindus are led to believe in an evolutionary process of reincarnation, the ultimate objective of which is to re-unite the Hindu soul, or **atman,** with the Supreme God of all gods, called Brahman.

In order to achieve this, through each successive rebirth, they have to ascend a scale of merit, which finally liberates them from earthly existence into union with Brahman. Whether they are reincarnated as a human being is in no way assured. The path toward spiritual ascent is called **dharma.** To live righteously they must live according to their station in life, or caste, and they must be faithful to their own inner self. The caste into which a Hindu is borne fixes for his entire lifetime what all this involves.

In reading, studying and meditating upon the Upanishads, the Hindu learns that a normal, harmonious life consists of four stages. In his youth, he is initiated into full religious duties, when given what is known as the "sacred thread." That he may learn what all this requires, he serves and studies in an **ashram** under the direction of a **guru,** as his spiritual trainer. The next stage is many years of marriage devoted to duties to his family and his own local community. Thirdly, in later years, after detaching himself from family and materialistic obligations, he concentrates on concerns of humanity at large. Then, finally, he prepares himself for the great unknown beyond this life.

The result of the **dharma** that the Hindu thus has lived depends upon **karma,** which is the chain which binds action to its fruits. For instance, a foolish man may be reborn as a monkey, a cunning one as a jackal, a greedy one as a crow. One Hindu myth tells of a jealous woman being reborn as a chili plant. On the other hand, an animal that has done all the right deeds to be expected of its animalship, may be reborn in human status. It all depends how well the previous life has been lived as to the status of the reincarnated life to follow.

In the Hindu pantheon of gods, first comes Brahman, as creator; Vishnu, as preserver; and Shiva, as destroyer. Whereas no human rites ever are celebrated to Brahman, observances to Vishnu and Shiva are celebrated in literally hundreds of ways, largely dependent upon the will of the worshipper. Vishnu, for instance, has ten chief **avatars,** or forms, in which he descends to the world. The Hindu usually chooses one aspect of such deity, which he keeps in his home represented by an image of some kind.

Many visitors to India are astonished at the public display of literally thousands of stylized male sexual organs or phalluses, called **lingams.** It is not that Hindus thus are being vulgar or crude. In their concept, their god of destruction, **Shiva,** also is the restorer of life and lord of creation. As the creation principle, he is widely worshipped in the form of **lingam;** and these stone, phallus-shaped pillars are profusely worshipped with fresh flowers, sacred water, fruit and rice being poured on them.

Though conceived as their god of destruction, Shiva also can be loving. And because he is thought to drink the full cup of man's sins in order to save him, his throat is painted blue. His most persistent aspect is the towering Himalayan mountain range in northern India, which are thought of as Shiva's hair. When some of this frozen locks melt in the spring, this frees the goddess Ganges River to begin her long descent to the Bay of Bengal with her purifying waters, which are also worshipped. Besides which there is Shiva's consort, **Shakti,** who commands a large sect of worshippers in her own right. Every fall, in the province of West Bengal, Shakti is honored in a great festival as **Durga,** the divine mother who brings cool breezes and flowers, reunites families, and destroys evil. Shakti also is worshipped in Bengal as the goddess **Kali,** who delights in animal sacrifice. However, this practice is almost non-existent in most other parts of India today.

Although the system of caste continues to be a vexing problem in India and is a part of modern Hinduism, yet it developed without any basis whatever in Hindu scripture and in face of ancient ideals of freedom and openness. Evidently it got started with the invasion of the Aryan type people from the north and west, who invaded India from the Caspian Sea area, conquered the darker-skinned Dravidian people whom they dominated, thus leading to a type of hierarchical system of society, based on vocation. The priests and scholars, thus, became known as **Brahmins;** the rulers and soldiers, as **Kshatriyas;** the merchants and farmers, as **Vaishyas;** the peasants and serfs as **Sudras.** The inequalities inherent in this oppressive caste system have stirred reformers from Buddha to Gandhi. But even though certain aspects of it have been outlawed politically, yet religiously caste continues to dominate the life of the Hindu people. Whereas we here in America are free to pick and choose at will what work we will follow, whom we shall marry and the like, the Hindu's choice of occupation, marriage partner, dress, eating habits, religious practice and even his freedom to move about is immutably fixed by caste at birth. those in a caste below him are viewed by one of superior caste as ritually impure. Even so, at least in some matters, those of lower caste have more freedom, as, for example, Sudras may eat meat and their widows may remarry, whereas those of orthodox Brahmin caste are forbidden to do so.

You can just imagine the consternation of her parents when the daughter of a Brahmin family married the son of an "untouchable" family in Malaysia. Both are now members of the church of our Lord in Kuala Lumpur, Malaysia. In India, however thirsty a Brahmin might be, should a Sudra offer him a drink of water he cannot accept it! Until the child has grown old enough and has been invested with the sacred thread, a Brahmin cannot even eat with his own son. Why? Not as yet bound by caste rules, should the boy contact ritual impurity, this thus would taint his father! In the southern part of India, where the caste system remains the strongest among Hindus, even the proximity of those of lower caste is considered defiling. Thus, a **Tiyan,** a caste that taps toddy, are allowed no closer than 36 paces to a Brahmin; while **Pulayan** peasants may approach no closer than 96 paces.

However unjust the caste system of Hinduism may seem to the Christian, the entrapment of the lowest of all — the untouchables — has filled many with revulsion across the centuries. It continues to be their lot to serve as the scavengers, the cleaners of latrines, and to handle animal carcasses in the making of leather. Looked upon as polluted, they always were forbidden to drink from the same wells, to walk the same paths, or even to frequent the schools and temples of caste Hindus. It was partly in protest against such exploitation that led to the founding of what is known as the Jains, a monastic religion, as well as of Buddhism with its offer of enlightenment to those of whatever rank or caste. These two influences had a profound effect in changing some of the more drastic taboos of Hinduism; and the later teachings of various minority religions such as Islam, Sikhism and at least nominal Christianity have continued to loosen the otherwise iron grip of caste on the Hindu people.

As late as the 18th and 19th centuries — especially seeing that the widow of anyone above the rank of the Sudra caste could not remarry — the practice of suttee was widespread. This meant that when her husband's body was being cremated, according to Hindu practice, his widow would immolate herself by throwing herself on his funeral pyre. However, Hindu reformers of the past 200 years by now have almost put an end to this ghoulish rite.

In more modern times, influential Hindus, such as the world-renowned poet Rabindranath Tagore, winner of a Nobel prize in 1913, as well as the founder of modern India, Mahatma Gandhi, transformed the ancient ideal of **ahimsa** (non-violence to living beings) into a political and social force. Especially when Gandhi recited their sacred texts and denounced many of their religious practices as unethical, Hindus by the thousands embraced his message. To him, instead of any human beings being automatically outcasts by birth, they were "children of God." And it was thanks primarily to his seemingly endless fasts, vigils, marches and boycotts that India's constitution finally banned untouchability. Thus it was that jobs formerly closed to India's lowest class suddenly came open, along with college grants and even seats in parliament. And with modern education further eroding the myth of caste, Hinduism's grip on the people seems to be slowly slipping away. In fact, this probably accounts, at least in part, for the enormous numbers of baptisms we have had in India, since J. C. Baily and others began going there as missionaries especially since 1963.

But religion dies hard. And even though many a village Brahmin may defer to the economic power of a merchant or a farmer, yet many such still strive to maintain the ritual purity prescribed by custom. This is more especially true in the countryside rather than in the cities.

Before he worships in the morning, first the orthodox Hindu must touch purifying waters, so he goes to a stream. Facing east, he sits and sprinkles water on his head. To make himself a "holy seat," after bathing, he sprinkles more water on the ground — then offers food, flowers and sandalwood paste to the sun god. While sitting there, he celebrates the glory of the deity he is worshipping with a holy text, called a **mantra,** which was imparted to him during the sacred thread ceremony when he was initiated into Hinduism. It goes —

Om. bhur bhuvah svah
tat savitur varenyam bhargo
devasya dhimahi
dhiyo yo nah prachodayat. Om.

The syllable **om,** meaning peace, signifies the rounded wholeness of Brahman. Called **Gayatri** (The Savior of the Singer), this Hindu Vedic prayer, from the time one first begins in Hinduism is chanted by the worshipper many times a day. (Just imagine my considerable astonishment, when I got back from the Far East a few years ago, and read the newspaper account of brother Don Finto — supposedly a Christian — leading a large number of the Belmont congregation, in Nashville, Tennessee, in chanting "Om...Om." Here I had been in Asia trying to convert Hindus **away** from such Hinduism — and now Finto was leading Christians **into** it!)

After purifying himself with his morning ablutions, the Brahmin Hindu returns home to make his morning **puja,** or act of worship, to his favorite deity. It could be one god or another, depending on his own whim. However, if, for instance, he worships Vishnu, he will offer no living creature as a sacrifice, but after "awakening" the bronze or stone image, as the case may be, he will wash and dress it, offering it flowers and non-animal food. The family must first sanctify the food before every meal by thus performing **puja.** Should the family be devotees of the god Shiva, of course, details of the ritual will vary accordingly.

A typical Brahmin before his midday puja will concern himself with his sons' course of study with their guru. Then late in the day, he may visit a temple either meditating by himself or worshiping with others. Before departing, walking backward so as not to offend the temple's reigning deity, he may place some offering on an altar and touch his forehead to the floor as a sign of respect.

Of the multitudinous holy objects of Hindu devotion, probably none surpasses the mighty Ganges River. Taking its rise from snow-melt just above the city of Gangatori, it sweeps along for 1,560 miles finally emptying into the Bay of Bengal. Those who bathe in the Ganges River come away feeling that their sins have been washed away.

At various points along the river are bathing steps known as **ghat.** If one goes to Gangatori to bathe, not only is the water glacier-cold, but so swift that a bather has to grasp hold of heavy chains at the ghat to keep from being swept away. So icy is the water there that one soon loses all feeling. When he comes out of the river, an old religious teacher, called a **pandit,** will step forward to smear a red **tilak** on the bather's forehead. Not only is this mark supposed to bring good luck, but also signifies that one has participated in a Hindu ceremony.

While bathing in the Ganges, pilgrims pray not only to that river, but to other sacred streams as well, as gods. They also cast rose petals, sweetmeats and rice upon the water, as worship, then fill brass pots with Ganges water to take home with them. The fact that the filth of the towns and cities along the river flow into it seemingly makes no difference to them; they still think of "Mother Ganges" as holy, beautiful and lovely. Since long before the birth of Christ, Hindus have been coming to that river to worship it, to bathe and drink its waters, and to cast into it the ashes of their dead. Just a few drops on one's tongue at the moment of death they deeply believe will cleanse one's soul of sin. If any one thing is the heart of India and of Hinduism, it almost has to be the Ganges River.

Because Hinduism is so multi-faceted, no single Hindu can ever learn it all. This makes it hard to pin-point and define its doctrines, many of them being so various and seemingly contradictory. However, it all seems to boil down to one thing: will worship. The key to eternal bliss, they seem to think, is the control of one's desires and the imposition of self-discipline.

Just as Moslems making a pilgrimage to Mecca, even so devout Hindus yearn to visit the holy city of Banaras, on the Ganges River, at least once in their lifetime. Vast numbers of them believe if they die there, they will immediately be transported to be with god Shiva in his paradise in the Himalaya mountains. Whether in this way, or in a multiplicity of other ways, the goal of Hinduism is ultimately to escape the cycle of life and death and rebirth so they may enjoy eternal communion with the supreme divinity Brahman that encompasses all the manifestations of the Hindu gods.

Although the nation of India proudly vaunts its constitution guaranteeing freedom of religion, anyone at all familiar with the land is conscious how Hinduism seems to dominate all others. I first visited India in the late '50s, at which time I preached to the one single congregation of Christ that then existed in a little village known as Mawlai Phudmawri, just outside of the city of Shillong, in Assam, in the northeast corner of the country. At least in that part of India, the pervasive influence of Hinduism was not so much in evidence.

However, in 1961, my family and I drove across India, from Europe and southern Asia, traveling all the way from Amritsar to New Delhi to Banaras and on over and down to Calcutta. While in New Delhi, I went personally to visit the head of the religious department of the government there to discover, if possible, what we should have to do in order to get missionaries from the churches of Christ into India.

The head of the religious department I soon learned was a Hindu. He wanted to know just what it was that we wanted to bring into India. I told him we wanted to bring the Christian religion. Is that all, he wanted to know? When I said, yes, he replied that if religion was all we wanted to bring into India that as long as he sat behind that desk we'd **never** receive permission to enter as missionaries. When I asked him why, he said that religion was the one single commodity India had plenty of. "We have religion to **export,**" he almost shouted, "and here you are trying to **import** more!" When I argued, "But we are trying to bring in gospel **truth,**" he parried, "That is what they **all** say!" As I left, I was made to realize fully that we were going to receive no encouragement from such Hindu officials in bringing the truth of the gospel into India. He did say, however, that if we could supply those who could **really** help his country in a **practical** way, such as doctors, nurses, teachers and agriculturists, he might reconsider. Here it is more than 20 years later, and although we have been able to get missionaries into India from Canada and possibly other parts of the British Commonwealth of Nations, at least those of us from the United States have been limited to "tourist" visas, almost all of which expire within three months.

It was during an effort to get the gospel into Afghanistan, in 1962, as I recall, that brother George Gurganus, then head of the Missions Department of Harding Graduate School of Religion, of Memphis, Tennessee, wrote asking me to join him and brother Dale Larsen, then President of York College, of York, Nebraska, on such and such a day in Kabul, Afghanistan, to figure out how to evangelize that country. I was on my way there by air, when I came down with influenza and had to stop short in Calcutta, India.

Boarding an old, ramshackled bus into the city, I encountered two old-fashioned missionary ladies from Canada. One of these ladies was extremely angry. She was born in Canada but since had become naturalized as a citizen of the United States. "I just can't **stand** this old India government!" she exclaimed. Her Canadian sister asked, "Why? What's wrong with the India government?" She explained that she had applied for a **missionary** visa but instead had been given a **tourist** visa and had to leave within 30 days. Her sister said, "That's what you get for becoming an **American!** If you had stayed **Canadian,** like I did, you wouldn't even have to **have** a visa. I came in on my **Canadian passport** and I can stay as long as I want to!" It was in that instant that I knew the way into India, as a missionary, was through Canada or some other Commonwealth country.

The story now is well known how I got in touch with my longtime good friend brother J. C. Bailey and prevailed upon him to give up Canada and move to India to preach the gospel both to the Hindus and to any others who would listen. He first arrived in India in 1963. By now the gospel has been preached in India on an ever-increasing scale for some 18 years. More than a quarter-of-a-million Indian people have been baptized since that time — large numbers of them Hindus.

It just goes to prove that even among the greatest idol-worshipping people of them all — the Hindus of modern India — the gospel of Christ also is quick and powerful. God speed the day when every single one of those thus blinded by the myths, legends and folk-lore of the Hindu religion from ancient times may come to know the truth of the gospel of Christ, who died for all mankind that all, including converted Hindus, might be saved!